5/98 MIDWEST 19.23

TWENTIETH CENTURY'S FOX

TWENTIETH
CENTURY'S
FOX

COVARRUBIAS

Darryl F. Zanuck
and the Culture of Hollywood

GEORGE F. CUSTEN

BasicBooks
A Subsidiary of Perseus Books, L.L.C.

Copyright © 1997 by BasicBooks,
A Subsidiary of Perseus Books, L.L.C.

Designed by Elliott Beard

Library of Congress Cataloging-in-Publication Data

Custen, George Frederick.
    Twentieth Century's fox : Darryl F. Zanuck and the culture of
Hollywood / George F. Custen.—1st ed.
        p.   cm.
    Includes index.
    ISBN 0-465-07619-X
    1. Zanuck, Darryl Francis, 1902–   . 2. Motion picture producers
and directors—United States—Biography.
PN1998.3.Z36C87   1997
791.43′0232′092—dc21
    [B]   97-23961
                                                                               CIP

97 98 99 00 ❖/RRD 9 8 7 6 5 4 3 2 1

This book is dedicated:

To my father, Allen M. Custen

"Everything I ever learnt as a small boy came from my father, and I never found anything he ever told me to be wrong or worthless."
—HUW, *HOW GREEN WAS MY VALLEY*

And in memory of my mother, Lenore Frantz Custen

"There is no fence, nor hedge around time that is gone. You can go back and have what you like of it—if you can remember." —HUW, *HOW GREEN WAS MY VALLEY*

They taught me to love the movies. I remember.

=Contents=

═══PART III═══ THE AGE OF ZANUCK

=Acknowledgments=

HOW DO YOU TALK about writing a book? Making a movie? In both media many people contribute individual bits of work to the final product, and their relations to one another through this labor are complex and multifaceted. Had Karl Marx lived to see Hollywood, the way moviemaking works (its constitutive parts made by many people working both in concert and separately), he would have seen its mode of production as both "serial" and "social." (One fact no one would contest: all workers toiled in an environment in which everyone was aware of who sat atop their corporate and social pyramid.) But it is Margaret Mead, and not Karl Marx, whose observations prove more useful to me in framing the myriad debts I owe to a large number of people (and even to a few institutions) for *Twentieth Century's Fox: Darryl F. Zanuck and the Culture of Hollywood.*

In *The Study of Culture at a Distance,* Mead observed that because Hollywood movies result from an organized group endeavor, films might represent the patterns of our culture more than high art, or communication forms less obviously social than the world and culture of commercial filmmaking. (More recent theorists like Howard Becker—in *Art Worlds*—would find these other worlds outside Hollywood every bit as social as Mead's Hollywood.) Nevertheless, as social as moviemaking might be, I do not think it is any more so than the act of creating a book. If there is rarely unanimity among readers as to what an author is saying, all writers and all books prove one point: whatever else we might be, because we receive so much assistance in preparing the final product, all authors are very social scientists. Thus, with thanks to Dr. Mead, here are the "data"—my patterns of indebtedness and gratitude—for *Twentieth Century's Fox: Darryl F. Zanuck and the Culture of Hollywood*.

The financial support I received from a Fellowship awarded by the John Simon Guggenheim Foundation, as well as the funds granted by the PSC-CUNY Research Grants, made my extended stays in Los Angeles (and thus the research for this book) possible.

Throughout the four years it took to write this book, Charles and Mirella Affron were both sources of critical wisdom and (as always) marvelously supportive friends. I am lucky in that I had a whole legion of friends—Larry Gross, Jeff Hoover, Andrew London, Carolyn Marvin, Leslie Mitchner, David Nasaw, Dana Polan, Len Quart, David Rakoff, Ella Shohat, Janet Staiger, Robert Stam, and Virginia Wright Wexman—whose patience and wise council were greatly appreciated.

At the City University of New York, both in the Department of Performing and Creative Arts at The College of Staten Island and at the Ph.D. Program in Theater at the City University Graduate Center, my colleagues and students assisted in numerous ways. My seminar students at the CUNY Graduate Center were the first audience for some of my ideas: they were also some of the best critics. Thanks also to Jan Heissinger, Caren Kaplan, Eric Smoodin, Joe Shiroky, Carlin Gasteyer, and Craig Manister for their many kindnesses and assistance in preparing the book. At UCLA's School of Film and TV, my colleagues and students in the Critical Studies Program provided useful advice and guidance. I am grateful to Bob Rosen, Peter Wollen, Vivian Sobchack, Nick Browne, Steve Mamber, and Janet Bergstrom for allowing me, when I was twice a Visiting Professor, to feel as if in UCLA I have a kind of second home outside CUNY.

Thanks also to Elizabeth Stankunas for facilitating many of my requests for support services at UCLA. I wish to thank three of my students at UCLA—Victoria Duckett, David Gerstner, and Matthew Solomon—for serving as fine dialectic listeners and even better respondents. In particular, Matthew Solomon's research, which he did efficiently and with a wonderfully generous spirit, was much-valued.

A good deal of the material cited in *Twentieth Century's Fox* comes from archives and special collections. Every writer who has written about Hollywood knows how much we owe to these wonderful people who organize, run, and work in these repositories. At the Saunders County Museum in Zanuck's hometown of Wahoo, Nebraska, Mrs. Ruth Lindquist showed me many of the interesting artifacts in the Zanuck collection. At the Howard Hanson House in Wahoo, everyone was marvelously accommodating. At UCLA's University Research Library, the indefatigable Brigitte J. Kueppers, librarian in the Arts-Special Collections area, was always helpful. Her ability to fulfill many last-minute requests will always be remembered. Thanks also to the people in UCLA's Special Collections area, particularly for the useful material in the Kenneth Macgowan Collection. At the UCLA Film and Television Archive, director Bob Rosen, research coordinator Laura Kaiser, and the wonderfully informed Bob Gitt pointed out many useful leads, particularly in the Vitaphone materials. At the University of Southern California's Doheny Library, Ned Comstock was always available and always an amazing source of information. I am also grateful to Stuart Ng for his guidance in use of the Warner Brothers materials. At the American Film Institute's Louis B. Mayer Library, librarian Alan Braun deserves thanks for his efforts with materials on Zanuck's early years. At the Margaret Herrick Library of the Academy of Motion Picture Arts and Sciences, I owe a huge debt to Sandra Archer (Head of Reference Services) and to Sam Gill, Howard Prouty, and Scott Curtis. At the Twentieth Century-Fox Research Library, Lisa Fredesi was amazingly cooperative. At the Museum of Modern Art Stills Department, special thanks goes to Mary Corliss and Terry Geesken for their assistance and supply of elegant white gloves.

I learned much from interviewing people who had worked closely with Darryl Zanuck: all generously shared what they remembered. Thanks to David Brown, George Davis, Celeste Holm, Edward Leggewie, Gregory Peck, William Reynolds, Peter Viertel, and Robert Wise.

A special thank-you goes to Kathie Berlin for putting me in touch with Richard Zanuck. Mr. Zanuck proved to be everything a writer could hope for: cooperative, razor-sharp, and open to discussion on any topic in his father's—and his own—life. A very busy producer, he always found time for my interviews and my questions. There were innumerable instances where, on his own, Richard Zanuck made efforts on my behalf. I am very grateful. Without his cooperation and insights, this book would have been very different, indeed. At The Zanuck Company, Brenda Beresford was always helpful beyond the call of duty (even with a broken leg!).

At Basic Books, I owe a debt to Steve Fraser, the acquiring editor who left midway through the project. I was truly fortunate, then, to have the skills of Susan Rabiner, Linda Carbone, Tim Duggan, and Michael Wilde. In particular, Linda helped me streamline some of my prose. (This was not always an easy thing to do.) My agent, Virginia Barber, and her great staff at the Virginia Barber Agency were always there when I needed them. Ginger's faith in me, and the book, is a private debt I would like to make public.

Last, my entire family, three generations—my father, Allen M. Custen; Kate and Si Diamond; Miriam and Judy Glassman; my sister, Barbara Custen Feinberg; my brother, Martin Custen, and their families—were always supportive and helpful. My friend Jim Woods died before this book was completed, but he was always an inspiration in so many ways, never more so than during his last years. My companion, Phillip Kautz, had the hardest task, one akin to Margo Channing: living with a Zanuck-obsessed creature. He did it gracefully and effortlessly. Once again, thanks, Phil.

THE MARK
OF ZANUCK

AMONG THE OUTTAKES in the film archives at UCLA is an unused fragment from the 1940 film *The Mark of Zorro*. Tyrone Power, as Don Diego/Zorro, accosts a wealthy couple about to flee with an ill-gotten cask of jewels. Holding up the nefarious pair at sword's point, Zorro snatches the gems and, with his sword, slashes his trademark, the letter "Z," in the upholstery of their carriage. But if you look closer you will see that this Zorro has been improvising: it is not just a "Z" that he has etched into the carriage, but the letters "DZ." "Zanuck!" cries the astonished pair of contract players dressed as Spanish grandees. Imitating his boss's colorful speech pattern, Tyrone Power replies, "Let that be a lesson to you, goddamit!" All the actors, employees of Zanuck (and Fox), break up with laughter.

This joke played on Zanuck suggests the simultaneous fear and respect of the people who populated the world he shaped and who, like the plots he controlled, were literally his property (or at least his studio's). Just as these Fox actors were "marked" with his brand, the films he made inevitably bore his authority. And, as his policy shaped the studio in which they were gainfully employed, it can be said that Zanuck also produced these people, afforded them—or at least approved—their identities, modes of dress, and personalities that publicly distinguished them to their fans.

Though he was one of the few moguls who was both native-born (Nebraska) and Christian, and, moreover, had spent a considerable part of his childhood in the Los Angeles area, in his films he took an outsider's view. Zanuck seemed to thrive when he was tackling subjects—racism, anti-Semitism, crime, mental illness—that American movies were supposed to approach with discretion or gentility, if at all. A handful—*The Public Enemy, I Am a Fugitive from a Chain Gang, 42nd Street, The Grapes of Wrath, How Green Was My Valley, All About Eve*—are among the most brilliant products to emerge from the studio system.

The range of his achievements as a producer is astonishing and unparalleled. He supervised the innovation of sound film and produced the landmark sound feature *The Jazz Singer.* He reinvented the gangster film with *Doorway to Hell,* and then took it and Hollywood in a new direction with its sequels, *The Public Enemy* and *Little Caesar.* While others thought their highest achievements would be attained by making cinematic equivalents of the canon, Zanuck combed the newspapers, magazines, and other media for gutsier materials and for topical subject matter more connected to the lives ordinary people led. He reinvigorated the musical, giving us the world of the backstager in *42nd Street.* He experimented with color when most producers saw little reason to do so. In films like *Young Mr. Lincoln, The Story of Alexander Graham Bell, Stanley and Livingstone,* and *I'll Cry Tomorrow,* he set the standard by which Hollywood's ideas about biography were formed. In making *The House on 92nd Street* and *Call Northside 777,* he was among the first studio heads after World War II to take his crews on location. Because of his own experience with documentary production in the army, he knew how to use locations to capture gritty reality. Zanuck's mixture of realism and documentary techniques made these films the forerunner of today's docudramas. Working out of a studio with few stars, he made the script the center of attention. He innovated CinemaScope.

He molded the star images of Shirley Temple, Tyrone Power, Alice Faye, Betty Grable, Sonja Henie, Richard Widmark, Susan Hayward, Marilyn Monroe, and Rin Tin Tin.

For almost forty years Darryl Francis Zanuck produced in his films (first at Warner Brothers, then at Twentieth Century-Fox, the studio he founded) a distinctive version of American culture. From the late 1920s up until 1971, his last year in power, he managed to be a key opinion leader by gauging what the public would be interested in before they knew it themselves. Then, fashioning a template read from their desire, he would present us with *The Jazz Singer, The Public Enemy, 42nd Street, The Grapes of Wrath, How Green Was My Valley, Gentleman's Agreement, The Snake Pit, The Day the Earth Stood Still, Pickup on South Street, Gentlemen Prefer Blondes, The Robe, The Sound of Music*—pictures that defined their respective decades with the power of selective illumination. In the age before television wrested this territory away from Hollywood, film constituted America's most powerful means of constructing a shared sense of history and culture. Zanuck understood this power. In fact, of all the movie moguls he possessed the clearest vision of how film operated in public culture.

He also was the first producer to grasp a difficult, sensitive, but ultimately transformative fact: the producer does not always attain his highest creative success with his audience by emulating gentility. To Zanuck street life, the daily stuff of urban activity, was itself a form of art. He saw that the novelty and bluntness and fierce economy with which the tabloids were crafted grabbed the public's attention, and the films that arose from this vision significantly reshaped how the American cinema figured in the public sphere. Just as his contemporary and sometimes friend and colleague Walter Winchell was the first newspaperman to see that the reappropriation of journalese through slang was a form of empowerment (both for the man who wielded the pen and for his readership), Zanuck was the first producer in the sound era to realize that by making films culled from daily tabloid headlines, you could speak to the public in stylized versions of its own speech.

Because Zanuck accomplished all this while making a good deal of money for his studio, I consider him, along with Irving Thalberg, the most important and most influential producer in the history of the American cinema. If one of the definitions of this century is that popular culture and the popular mind replaced genteel culture and the refined intellect as the dominant forces in American life, then Zanuck was one of the foremost architects of the twentieth-century edifice.

—

While this book will ask what may seem to be an obvious question—"What does a producer produce?"—my answer may be neither familiar nor at first glance very direct. A movie, in addition to being a physical commodity and business process, is also part of a complex chain of cultural meanings whose motions have shaped, as Zanuck-watcher Vincent Canby noted, "the imaginations of millions of Americans."[1] But whatever Zanuck accomplished, we must see that he operated within a system of production whose organization gave rise to a specific corporate culture, one I call "the culture of Hollywood." Searching for ways to explain what a producer does involves trying to understand what Zanuck thought was possible within the studio system. If we grasp some of this tricky dynamic—between individual and organization, between the division of the professional self as it fits into the compartmentalization of the studio bureaucracy—we begin to understand why, in a pre-television age, Zanuck's mastery of the rules of this world, of this culture of Hollywood, made him the greatest and most influential producer in the history of Hollywood and, by extension, one of the most powerful men in the United States.

Every producer operates within a particular context, and the specific context for most films between 1920 and 1960 was the studio. The studio was the work site that gave shape to the fantasies of writers, actors, set designers, and directors. The studios, before they imploded or collapsed in the late 1950s, were not just corporations. They were extensions of their founders and of the production heads who oversaw their programs. From very early on, Zanuck felt that the only way he could work was as a virtual one-man show, as the energetic impresario manipulating the large cast at his disposal. In addition to the sheer amount of work he was capable of juggling simultaneously—writer, talent scout, head of production—Zanuck's pace could be overwhelming. One Warner's screenwriter recalls what it was like to work with Zanuck under these conditions:

> I remember when I came to Warner Brothers, Zanuck would read a story on Friday, think about it over the weekend, get it set in his head and call the writers into his office on Monday morning. He'd say, "Okay boys, here's the story, it'll have Jimmy Cagney in it. We'll start shooting four weeks from this morning and we'll open at Warner's downtown eight weeks from today."[2]

The title of *Time*'s 1950 homage to Zanuck, "One-Man Studio," suggested that, "for better or for worse," every film on the lot was informed "by the taste of Cinemogul Zanuck."[3] By insuring his life for the highest premium it could get in 1950 ($900,000), the company was admitting what everyone else in Hollywood already knew: Zanuck *was* Twentieth Century-Fox. While MGM was formed out of a struggle of wills between Louis B. Mayer and Marcus Loew, Mayer and Nick Schenck, Mayer and Irving Thalberg (and an earlier battle among Samuel Goldwyn, Marcus Loew, Nicholas Schenck, and Louis B. Mayer) and RKO had so many corporate figures that its identity was constantly in flux, no one in Hollywood had to ask whose ideals were imprinted on the films of Fox.

The true power of a producer as a cultural force lies not in the number of Oscars he has won or in the critical acclaim that accrues to him, but rather in how, out of his *imagination,* he fashions a system of production that can make a shared thing out of something that has been bent to his will. Zanuck was a power in Hollywood because, for over forty years, his talents were given rein to shape public culture.

In what ways did Darryl F. Zanuck shape public culture? Could not the statement "He altered America" be made of any producer in Hollywood or of Hollywood as a whole? Was this ability to shape culture unique to Zanuck, or was it a quality shared by all moviemakers, of whom Zanuck is only the most interesting—or deviant—figure? Indeed, within the culture of Hollywood, what did make Zanuck run?

One of the few observers who tried to gauge Hollywood's significance by studying it as a culture is the anthropologist Hortense Pow-dermaker, who concluded (as did a handful of other writers) that the social structure of Hollywood determined "to a considerable degree the kind of movies we see." Though she knew its industrial base meant that Hollywood engaged in a unique way of doing its forms of storytelling, Powdermaker also insisted that like the situation she found to be true elsewhere, even under Hollywood's *"mass produc-tion more than one kind of social system is possible."*[4] This observation posed a direct threat to the cosmology of moguls like Zanuck. Unlike Powdermaker, they saw the system as monarchs saw the divine right of kings: as theirs, as right, and, therefore, as "natural." They did this for an obvious reason: as it stood, the system gave them the power and authority to do things the way they saw fit. It was at once the "best" and the most "natural" way to make films. As Zanuck once told actor Edward G. Robinson, it was "the perfect system."

Perfect or riddled with flaws, Powdermaker was shrewd enough to see one additional thing about the system: that "although movies are made by many people in the setting of a big industry, certain indi-viduals have power to strongly influence them, while others are rela-tively powerless."[5] Zanuck, of course, was of the former type. The early parts of this book apply and test the truths of these observa-tions. To walk through Zanuck's fascinating career is to look at the evolution of authority and authorship as they evolved within the cul-ture of Hollywood. To see his tough times in entering this privileged world is to know how it operationalized and defined qualities Zanuck needed to learn how to get inside, such as "what constituted 'good movies,' or 'good writing' " or more tellingly, "What did Hollywood mean by 'prestige.' " To chart how Zanuck, a boy from a small town in Nebraska with an eighth-grade education, managed in less than five years to move from being a little-known, powerless figure with al-most no knowledge of this culture to occupying a very public posi-tion reigning at the highest levels it circumscribed is to see the interactions between the solidity of Hollywood's edifices and the flu-idity of its culture.

Only after examining how the corporate culture of Hollywood shaped America's public culture, and how Zanuck was positioned within Hollywood's corporate culture, can I begin to estimate the cultural significance of what he produced. Zanuck's America was seen from the map of Beverly Hills and Palm Springs; its sense of empire was contained by the walls that separated Fox from its neighboring competitors. The Fox empire, only a short distance from rival MGM, was demarcated with an almost medieval sense of territory. Here, you lived and labored, sheltered by the illusion of a self-contained world, surrounded by odd juxtapositionings of sets and fabulations of dissonant eras somehow blended into the daily context of work. But these enclosures also had the effect of cutting a producer off from the rest of the country, giving credence to Bertrand Russell's observation that Los Angeles represents the ultimate segregation of the unfit.[6] And, beyond these privileged studio enclaves—in towns with names like City of Commerce, Glendale, and Covina—lived the people who bought tickets to the films Hollywood produced. This separation of the communities that created the movies from the groups that viewed them would give rise to a key conundrum: in the days before market research blurred the lines between democracy and demography, the fiction of the average viewer was constructed out of what a small group of men who ran the film corporations considered to be the tastes and opinions of a tiny sample of moviegoers who lived almost exclusively in Southern California.

Zanuck knew he was part of a large system. Yet, like a few others, he felt he could both work the system *and* dominate it. Even after he had his own studio, at the age of thirty-one, he would not give up the belief that although filmmaking was a collaborative enterprise, ultimately he and he alone possessed the judgment to successfully run the machinery of storytelling and to regulate the enterprise surrounding it. It was virtually unheard of to have a studio run by someone involved in the day-to-day creativity of moviemaking. His definition of collaboration meant that, should a stalemate arise, his judgment, and not that of the director or writer, would be the one that prevailed. He thus had to be as calculating as the most canny capitalist, yet sly as a fox, to pull off this balancing act in which art and commerce met in what he saw as the culture of Hollywood.

Zanuck the man was as complicated and multifaceted as the studio program he supervised. He was an ardent patriot and political conservative. He was a member of the American Legion. Yet he opposed the Hollywood blacklist. He did more than most producers to shield those accused of Communist ties, but he ultimately refused to confront figures he knew were pursuing red herrings more than reds.

He had no formal training as a writer, yet he was able to fix a script faster than the legion of highly paid professional authors whom he harangued with his perceptive but brutal memos. The model of the producer as predator, he could also be a sentimental family man; he carried about with him until he died the crushed remains of a flower his daughter had given him when she was a child. He was married to one woman, Virginia Fox Zanuck, for fifty-five years. Yet he abandoned her publicly in his later years, cutting all ties to home and living openly in France and New York with a series of female companions. Some described him as a ruthless tyrant who brooked no disagreement; others found him willing to listen to almost anyone's opinions, even those of people whose politics he hated or whom he personally detested.[7]

Unlike other moguls whose duplicitous maneuvers have generated a cottage industry of horror stories, Zanuck was honest and straightforward. At his funeral, his worldly and cynical friend Orson Welles (who in films like *Citizen Kane* and *Touch of Evil* created master analyses of worlds of greed) saw his friend Darryl in a different light: as a man who "was totally devoid of malice," who above all valued loyalty.[8] Yet his son Richard feels that he was a man with no real close friends, a man "who was kind of tough to really get close to."[9] As director William Wellman fondly recalled, "if he shook hands on a deal, it was a deal, period."[10] Zanuck always took responsibility for any decision, right or wrong. His close associate and friend Edward Leggewie recalls that "what he hated most" were people who tried to avoid responsibility. And he was known to haul people onto the carpet. Zanuck could be intense, even abusive, in these sessions. One man who survived a bout with a choleric Zanuck told Leggewie: "I would rather be fired than bawled out like that."[11] But once Zanuck had exploded, all was forgiven. He could even joke about the incident—years later.

He was obsessed with refining his visions so they took the precise forms on screen that he pictured in his mind. Yet this man who knew every subtle nuance of the medium could be overbearing and coarse when not thinking about movies. He was partial to cruel practical jokes. Once he knowingly gave Leggewie, an inexperienced rider, a wild horse. When Leggewie was thrown and severely injured, a contrite Zanuck upgraded his friend's position at the studio—it was a way of apologizing without actually having to speak the words, "I'm sorry."[12]

People were wildly divided about "DFZ," as Zanuck was called by his friends, his associates, and even at times his children. Actress Celeste Holm held him in low estimation for his policy of authorship crafted by the authority that comes with fear. She claimed she had been hired by the Machiavellian producer as a threat to Betty Grable, just as Zanuck had hired Betty Grable as a threat to Alice Faye: "Zanuck always ran a studio by having actors afraid of somebody else." Holm admitted she "never knew him [socially] at all. But what I knew I didn't like." From her perspective, this was due to Zanuck's insecurity around educated people, women in particular: "He didn't know what to do with them. It scared him. He felt threatened by it, which was so stupid. That's what I said: he was a stupid man."[13] (She is one of a legion of people who find it impossible to conceive of the fact that creativity and intelligence can take surprising forms, or arise outside the conventions of certain genteel institutions.) Disparaging remarks had been made about Zanuck, including one by a reporter for *The New Yorker* that it was dangerous that a man with an eighth-grade education was making the films by which the country received so many of its ideas. With less intensity, this view is seconded by writer W. R. Burnett, author of the novel *Little Caesar* and co-author of the screenplay for *Scarface*. Though he never doubted Zanuck's intelligence, to him, "Zanuck's fault was, he wasn't interested in women. He was interested in women, personally, God knows, but not artistically, let's put it that way. He did much better with men's pictures."[14]

Gregory Peck, who worked with Holm in *Gentleman's Agreement*, knew a different Zanuck, "a regular volcano of energy, enthusiasm, and know-how." Peck says, "it never occurred to me that he was not smart, that he was not highly intelligent, education or no education." Zanuck, he remembers, had "total recall of every picture that he had ever made."[15] Similarly, one of Hollywood's most respected writers, Nunnally Johnson, had such enormous respect for Zanuck's gifts that he claimed he'd jump off a bridge if Zanuck asked him.[16] When Johnson left Fox in 1943 to form International Productions, Zanuck tried to keep him on by offering him a salary—$5,000 a week—almost as large as his own. But Johnson, who had always worked for someone else, wanted to try independent productions, for financial as well as creative reasons. In 1948, after International merged with Universal, Johnson decided to look around for another home. He was wooed by MGM's Louis B. Mayer, but turned down a very lucrative contract from the legendary mogul. He was going back to Fox. A puzzled Mayer asked what Fox had that he couldn't match. Johnson's reply: "They got Zanuck."[17]

Zanuck won an unprecedented three Irving Thalberg Awards and three Oscars for Best Picture. In the years he ran Fox, the studio won more Best Picture awards than any of his rivals. But these achievements have often been overshadowed by his behavior and his personal style. The irrepressible Zanuck "had a reputation for . . . outrageous and strange behavior."[18] With his cigar chomping and boundless energy, his fearlessness and penchant toward malapropisms, he made good copy. On his first trip to the Louvre, Zanuck told the cab driver: "We gotta be outa this joint in 20 minutes."[19] Twenty minutes might have been just the right amount of time for Zanuck: the treasures contained within the museum's walls offered little he might include in his kind of cinema. Unlike the angelic Thalberg or the driven Selznick, Zanuck hardly looked or acted the part. Zanuck was largely unself-conscious—though not unaware—that because of his behavior, others took him as a rube or an eccentric.

Then there was his appearance. Zanuck was diminutive (five foot six), with piercing pale blue eyes and somewhat curly hair. "With his out of control mustache and his missing teeth," rival David Selznick thought he looked like "an ear of corn only a maniac would eat." Mrs. Selznick (daughter of L. B. Mayer, herself knowledgeable in reading the semiotics of prestige in Hollywood), was in accord with her husband, noting of this odd genius, "Thank God he's gentile, otherwise he'd give Jews a bad name."[20]

He had virtually no formal education but an astonishing level of energy and a penchant—in hunting, in polo, in croquet, in negotiations—for the aggressive and predatory, or at the least the highly competitive. He played polo until, after a serious accident, he was forbidden to do so by the Fox Board. He hunted on safaris in Africa. He turned his Palm Springs retreat into one of the best, and most bizarrely populated, lawn croquet courses in the country. A weekend visitor might find Zanuck and Clifton Webb screaming at Moss Hart, while Merle Oberon and Howard Hughes watched, amused, from the sidelines.

Zanuck's routine was legendary in a town filled with compulsive workers. He awoke late, swam or exercised with his trainer, played sports with the children or a friend. A little before 11 A.M. he drove to the studio in his green ("Zanuck green") Cadillac accompanied by his French tutor, Edward Leggewie, who taught him this language on the fly. Zanuck then worked at the studio until 3:00 or 4:00 A.M. His regimen included a daily shave from his friend and confidant Sam Silver, his personal barber. He often ate dinner at the studio, in the company of his friend Nick Janios, who ran the Fox commissary. This left little time for his family, though he did play sports with the children, tell them bedtime stories, and write them memolike notes that resonated with the rhythms and syntax of his terse studio missives, but are not found anywhere in Lord Chesterfield's catalogue. In a way, it was a perfect marriage of its kind: "Virginia was involved with Zanuck, and Zanuck was involved with himself."[21] The children loved their mother and father, and the Zanucks were loving parents. But while the "adults" lived alone in the main house at Santa Monica, the children lived with their governess in separate, adjoining quarters connected to the main structure by a breezeway. Strange as such a domestic setup might appear to the average American, it was not an unusual circumstance if you dwelt in Hollywood's stratosphere. How things look—as opposed to how things are—is very important in a town whose main business and very survival is based on a moving, yet static, image.

The Zanucks tried to maintain a private life amidst the most public of industries. Less concerned with his professional image than most moguls, the workings of producer Zanuck are occasionally revealed to us when he presents a producer on film. In a memo to the producer (George Jessel) and screenwriter (Mary McCall, Jr.) of the 1949 musical *Dancing in the Dark,* Zanuck, at the peak of his power and critical esteem as the vice president in charge of production at Twentieth Century-Fox, seemed concerned that the proper image of the studio head—of him—be maintained:

> Everything about Hollywood should be done very honestly and very reasonably. The big boss should be a guy with a sense of humor. He should not be the obvious movie mogul, or the eccentric idiot. If you give him a sense of humor and he is able to laugh at his own tough luck or bad judgment, it will do a great deal toward making the picture honest as well as add a bit of dignity to our industry.[22]

For the character's name, Zanuck approved the use of one of his long-abandoned pseudonyms, Melville Crossman. The final script contained this description of the production chief in his office: "MEL CROSSMAN is a man in his middle forties who is so electric you could plug him into and light up a small city. He's never still; his eyes are sharp and alert. He wastes few words."[23] Of course Crossman *is* Zanuck, down to the familiar mustache of the actor, Adolphe Menjou, who was portraying him.

But because so much of what has been written about moguls portrays them as ruthless, almost atavistic, creatures with one goal—power—we end up seeing producer Zanuck as a series of shifting nouns attached to one adjective, *simple:* simple power, simple vulgarity, simple instinct. How he operated as a producer and what, in fact, his work meant outside of Hollywood are, however, far from simple.

What do we owe to Darryl Zanuck, other than fragments called up from the Fox vault: Bette Davis as Margo Channing, fastening her seatbelt for a bumpy night; Technicolor memories of Betty Grable; the shocking power of the screen's first race riot in *No Way Out;* the mournful, lone accordion heard playing "Red River Valley" in *The Grapes of Wrath;* the poignant voiceover narration stirring our memories in *How Green Was My Valley; Pickup on South Street,* in which Thelma Ritter meets her death rather than rat to a Communist agent; Marilyn Monroe bringing a new brand of sexuality to the screen in the "Heat Wave" number in *There's No Business Like Show Business;* Ty Power as a geek in *Nightmare Alley;* Carmen Miranda, in her tutti-frutti hat, setting multiculturalism back fifty years? We owe to Zanuck and his imagination the Fox, and ultimately the Hollywood, code of much of American public culture. While it existed before him and would survive his retirement, Zanuck changed the way Hollywood thought about its organizing principles—of genre, of history, and about films' role as a cultural force.

To begin with, he virtually invented, in the sound era, the biographical film, or biopic. In these movies, many of which were prestigious for his studio, others of which were pure hokum, he made certain that a specific definition of greatness prevailed and that whatever the actual, known facts of the life, the portrayal of family and love, or selfless service to humanity, would be uppermost.[24] A sanitized, edited version of "the great life" came to form the blueprint for this important genre, and Zanuck's films—biographies of Disraeli, Rothschild, Alexander Graham Bell, Jesse James, Robert Clive, as well as the large number of biopics of entertainers—were the foundations upon which other studios based their narratives.

In the gangster film, almost singlehandedly conceived by this nonurbanite, he supervised and scripted the sublimated violence of both James Cagney (in *The Public Enemy* as well as the earlier *Doorway to Hell*) and Edward G. Robinson (*Little Caesar*) at the start of the gangster cycle's short life. From 1934 on, once the Production Code Administration had effectively changed the representation of sex in the movies, it had to go somewhere, and making violence one kind of substitute for sex (dance was the other) became a hallmark not just of Zanuck's films but, following his lead, of the American cinema as a whole. For many, these glamorous, percussive violations of social decorum defined an era.

Zanuck was also the first producer to systematically use newspaper headlines as inspiration. He did this because he intuitively felt it would be in sync with public tastes; because in the 1930s the tabloids were a phenomenon virtually unknown outside cities (and therefore would appeal to Warner's client base, which was located largely in urban centers and the East); because it was congruent with his unsentimental view of the world; because the stories were in the public domain, and formed a link with the universe of what audiences knew; because it positioned his studio far differently with the public audience than the fare of his rivals.

As for musicals, while other studios had stars dancing in gossamer outfits on fantastic, rotating sets, Zanuck had Fox stars like Alice Faye and Betty Grable and Dan Dailey touring small towns, complete with cows and colorfully attired rural citizens. Judged on the basis of their performance at the box office, the audience was starved for such entertainment.

Considering that Fox's real audiences were seated in flagship theaters located in the Los Angeles area, the decision to focus on the small town and the rural was inspired. Fox extolled rural virtues more than did its rivals. The studio's biggest star of the thirties, Shirley Temple, made a specialty in films like *Rebecca of Sunnybrook Farm* and *Show People* of reconciling life on the farm with big city entertainment, suggesting that the *values* of rural America were really congruent with the norms of popular entertainment. But Zanuck also gauged this program based on his personal knowledge that Los Angeles' demographics in the years before World War II showed it to be a city in which nearly four out of ten residents had migrated from the Midwest. The picture of musical America played to the former "old time" values of these transplanted Americans, not to their actual living conditions, pacifying and speaking in nostalgic terms to the uncertainties of the new Southern California life faced by this urban horde in an era of profound social transformation. Zanuck played upon a selective, and conservative, nostalgia for a world left behind, in the same way that *American Graffiti* or *The Godfather* years later would create mythical suburban and urban landscapes culled from the audience's imagined childhoods and neighborhoods more than from any actual place or past.

From the gritty, cost-conscious urban sets he oversaw for Warner's, to the much-used New York street, to the redressed sets of *How Green Was My Valley* (used again as a Norwegian fishing village in *The Moon Is Down*), Fox films redefined moviegoers' conceptions of cities, villages, and castles. Soon after the movie industry was an established fact of life in the region, its films could be seen to have a material impact on people's lives as Southern Californians were having their houses built, designed, and decorated by some of the very people who were creating styles for the movies. If you thumb through home plans in popular magazines of the era (like *Better Homes and Gardens*), you will see the impact of this hybrid cinematic style on American's concepts of home architecture.

Although he might flirt with the idea of using film as a soapbox, in most cases Zanuck avoided anything that might smack of social criticism unless he could dress it up as a love story. He just did not think the cinema could function any other way and still make money. In films like *Letter to Three Wives, Pickup on South Street, No Way Out, Pinky,* and *Gentleman's Agreement,* or even in *How Green Was My Valley,* criticism of postwar adjustment and feminism, or ideology, or racism, anti-Semitism, or labor exploitation was softened and personalized. American viewers came to see all problems as amenable to some centrist, individual solution rendered in these films. Time has shown us they weren't.

He would alternate between "big ideas" and human stories. Finally, in the 1950s, coming full circle he emerged as the champion of what had first drawn him to the movies: the pleasures of spectacle. After 1953, Zanuck painted only on the largest canvases in films like *The Robe, Gentlemen Prefer Blondes, The Sound of Music,* and *The Longest Day.*

At any given time, producers like Goldwyn and Selznick lavished attention on a single, large project—*Gone with the Wind, The Best*

Years of Our Lives—so that these films became tributes to the taste of their producers. Zanuck's genius was of another kind. Unlike these colorful independent producers, Zanuck had to juggle a large number of films at once; he knew the *system* of production so he understood how a single component fit into the big picture.

How well did he know the system? Ida Lupino, herself a child of theater people who had seen all modes of making entertainment, was awed by his range: "That man could, *had,* read every script on the lot; he watched every wardrobe test of every male star, every female star; he could remember—with all the people under contract!—that he didn't like a spotted tie on a man in test number three, or he didn't like the cut of a skirt on me in test number four."[25] No detail was too trivial to escape his sharp observations, and he never ceased trying to figure out what made Hollywood run. Director Jean Negelescu recalls:

> After a day's work, after dinner, he'd look at the pictures of the small studios, like Republic, to compare them to what we were making. He'd ask one of us, one of his boys, to see it with him. Why? He'd say, "It's making money. Let's find out what people like." There was no greater studio head than Darryl. . . . Twentieth was a family of workers. There was dignity working there.[26]

Zanuck watched every test made by starlets under contract at Fox's on-site Drama School, hoping to see something in these rushes to encourage development of a new personality; like a baseball scout, he was ever vigilant to the possibility of talent nurtured on the sidelines. All the while he kept up a pace that would today be unthinkable. In 1939, the year Selznick was the focus of much attention for his filming of a single film, *Gone with the Wind,* Zanuck moved seamlessly from the antics of the Ritz Brothers in *The Gorilla,* to the balletic movements of the Zorina-George Balanchine collaboration *I Was an Adventuress,* to the plodding steps of *Chicken Wagon Family* (watched over by "B" supervisor Sol Wurtzel), to the extraordinary rhythms of *Young Mr. Lincoln* and *Drums Along the Mohawk,* then shifted gears to supervise biopics of Alexander Graham Bell and Stanley and Livingstone and the epic sequences of the Tyrone Power vehicle, *The Rains Came,* while turning out one Sherlock Holmes film and three Mr. Moto films, as well as overseeing Shirley Temple's first Technicolor film, *The Little Princess!* Long after all the other studios had abandoned the system that located ultimate authority for all films under one figure, Zanuck continued to work this way.

The legends that accrued about Zanuck painted him as a kind of cinematic handyman, the fellow who would take a film made by others and, through all-night editing sessions, turn it into a hit. Bobbie McLean, with whom it was said Zanuck spent more evenings than with his wife, was Zanuck's personal film cutter. McLean was acknowledged as one of the leading editors of her time, one of the few women in this high position. She recalled Zanuck's working regimen:

> With Zanuck, when you'd run pictures in the projection room, nobody made a sound. Even if you had a cigarette packet with that cellophane on it, you'd take it off before. His powers of concentration were terrific. The editor sat next to him and when he didn't like something, he'd just touch you on the arm. I'd write it in the dark. . . . You almost are reading his mind, you almost could tell what he would want done. It was amazing, because look how many pictures he was working on. It was not only one picture, but he had to divorce himself from one to the other. He could. He could remember.[27]

Zanuck's input went far beyond editing. He prepared films so thoroughly before the director even arrived—from the script to the casting—that "most so-called directorial touches, at least on Twentieth Century-Fox productions, had been written into the script long before the director was assigned to the picture."[28]

But as befitting his status as a local deity, Zanuck was famous for both giving *and* taking away. His associate, Kenneth Macgowan, Eugene O'Neill's former producer, worked with Zanuck as an associate producer for a decade. He urged Zanuck to consider a movie about the Nazi death camps, or, alternately, a biopic about the Denver jurist, Judge Lindsay, who founded the country's first juvenile court.[29]

Zanuck told Macgowan that as much as the labor and death camps "appalled" him, he could not picture a "subject less inviting to an audience." Instead, Zanuck urged him to "show me how I can make a good story out of the life of Ernest R. Ball, and the great Irish songs he wrote."[30] These gaps also shaped the hidden screen of American culture, the part of the master Hollywood narrative Darryl Zanuck did not deem fit for entertainment.

While his private life was seldom as wild as many writers have imagined, it was indeed colorful. But here I do not wish to replicate the obsessions with this kind of biographical trivia at the expense of illuminating Zanuck's place in Hollywood and American culture. I delve into his personal life only to the extent that it helps to understand his professional activities or directly impinges on the films he made or policies he set.

Even if one were able to understand and have access to the facts and all of the gossip and rumors about Zanuck's life, he or she still could not explain how Zanuck was able to do certain things and why he could see so far ahead where others failed. A catalogue that focuses largely on the (often inaccurate) sensational stories guarantees only that we would see his films and their cultural resonances through the particular bent provided by this set of lenses, as has so often been done. Most important, such an approach obscures the significant role played by another set of equally powerful forces and institutions: those that make up the culture of Hollywood. As much as his life away from work shaped his films, the rules and conventions of this organizational culture informed Zanuck the person with a set of values, a changing set of identities, and a powerful menu of social roles. Since we know much less about how this last variable affects the lives of most of Hollywood's creative personnel, since we are only just beginning to look into Hollywood as a cultural enterprise, in this book I hope to establish, or to reassert, a sense of equilibrium and proportion by focusing on this culture and Zanuck's place in it.

Twentieth Century's Fox will document Zanuck's attempts to play by the rules when he had to, and reveal his attempts to change them when he thought he could. What differentiates this from other "mogul" books is its emphasis on the studio as context of production and on the understanding that Hollywood was, itself, a culture. Although I argue that Zanuck consciously created a version of American culture in his films, he made the films he did in large part because he worked within a particular set of institutions that formed the town's culture of production.

Darryl Zanuck supervised over a thousand films, and it would be impossible for me to discuss them all. I have chosen to talk about those that illuminate my central concern: in the "central producer" system under which Zanuck worked, all authority led to him and all power radiated from him; using this system, he shaped and in some cases reshifted our agenda and cultural priorities. In a similar light, I have concentrated on certain performers not because I feel they are necessarily the most talented but because each shows a particular facet of how Zanuck figured the actor or the star persona into the whole picture of studio-era filmmaking he carried around in his head.

In Part I, "Foundations," I look at Zanuck's early life and his entry into the movies as a screenwriter in the silent era. In particular, I have uncovered new information on Zanuck's earliest years, his work at F.B.O. studios and in his first unpublished movie scripts, fresh insight into the elements of what would constitute a Zanuck cinema. This material suggests that he had internalized the basic structure of film narrative *before* he went to work at Warner Brothers in 1924, the point at which most serious discussions of his work begin. This earliest work is critical to understanding part of the foundation for what one critic called "the best nickelodeon mind" in the business.[31] In Part II, "Innovations," I will look at two segments of the culture of Hollywood, the worlds of Warner Brothers and the studio Zanuck founded, Twentieth Century-Fox. At Warner's, he will play key roles in two critical moments: the transition from the silent cinema to one with sound, and the radical innovations he created with the gangster film and the biopic as part of his response to the cultural transformation of Hollywood and the rest of the country during the Depression. Part III, "The Age of Zanuck," commences in 1935, and in these chapters I will show how, after his abrupt departure from Warner Brothers, Zanuck's total control over Fox's program enabled him to shape a particular version of culture with virtually no one to block his creative decisions. For the next thirty-six years, from shifting vantage points within the Hollywood system, he produced both predictable fare (with Shirley Temple) and more daring works in *The Grapes of Wrath* and *How Green Was My Valley*. But it is his virtuosic manipulation and mastery of the entire cinematic apparatus that enabled him to become, after the death of MGM's Irving Thalberg, the most important figure and pacesetter in the film industry. After World War II, in films like *No Way Out*, *Pinky*, and *Gentleman's Agreement*, he will be more daring still. But because of enormous changes—in American politics, business practices, and lifestyles—Zanuck was forced to confront a radically altered film industry, one whose hold on the American public was diminishing yearly. In an attempt to survive, he will innovate CinemaScope and try to assert in battles with Marilyn Monroe and other stars what in his opinion made this decision work: his sense of the producer's power.

My analysis of Zanuck and his culture ends with his departure from Hollywood in 1956. The epilogue deals with a number of topics in the period 1956 to 1979: his time in Europe; his stunning comeback with *The Longest Day*; his return to head the corporation; his tempestuous relations with his family; his fall from power; and his sad final years. In this era and after, he unhappily witnessed the sale and breakup of the lot he founded—with its jungles, lakes, castles, Western and New York streets—into office buildings, shopping centers, and the agglomeration of places and businesses that is part of Los Angeles' urban sprawl. Today, though it is vastly reduced in size from its nearly 300-acre reach when Zanuck ruled, there is still a Fox lot. But its largest business is in television, not film. As much as anything, this change shows why with Zanuck's departure from power, with the passing of the way he made films (as well as the virtual disappearance of his cinematic signature in today's product), an age in American public culture departed with him. In a sense, beyond what is called up in our memory when seeing a Zanuck film, the Century in Century City is all that is left of that part of Zanuck's empire. This material is not covered in as much detail as the earlier years because it is decidedly not the Hollywood he entered and in which he was a dominant figure. It is an era and a set of human relationships that deserve to be fully treated in some other book.

Roland Barthes (whose musing would have, I'm sure, elicited profound indifference from Zanuck) has suggested that Hollywood was the psychological center of an epoch, the ideological background against which all our thoughts and desires are enacted. If Hollywood occupies as profound a place in our culture and consciousness as Barthes suggests, then Zanuck was its most powerful, perhaps even its most beautiful, dreamer.

Part 1

FOUNDATIONS

Chapter One

EXCAVATING ZANUCK

Every artist makes himself born. It is
very much harder than the other time,
and longer.

—WILLA CATHER,
THE SONG OF THE LARK

WAHOO, NEBRASKA, the birthplace of Darryl Zanuck, is
over 1,500 miles from Los Angeles, California. Separated
by a mountain range and two time zones, the two places
could not appear to be more different. Yet the rise of Hollywood as
the linchpin of Southern California's—indeed, the whole of America's culture—would be brought about in large part by transplanted
Midwesterners. A number of them, such as Edgar Rice Burroughs
and Zane Grey, were writers who would merge a romantic vision of
the region they adopted with a portrait of life straight out of their
Midwest upbringing. Some of them would run the movie business itself or develop the real-estate dream that, as much as the movies
themselves, would give rise to the culture of Hollywood. One of them
was Zanuck himself, a brash young man who, unlike any other movie

executive or production head in the silent-film era, had lived the small-town life that was about to be immortalized on screen. Among many ironies people could point out about the movies, one of the greatest is that although they are probably the one institution people cede as having the power to define and shape the character of Southern California, the men who produced them were for the most part transplanted Easterners whose ethnic and religious backgrounds (mostly Jewish) were at odds with the Christian, wasp elements crucial to the foundations of turn-of-the-century Los Angeles. The lone exception to this profile was Darryl Francis Zanuck. Darryl Zanuck was the only studio head who spent a considerable part of his premovie life actually growing up in California. But as both a Californian and a transplanted Midwesterner, Zanuck was the exemplar of the new target audience of Hollywood's after they moved from their former centers to Hollywood: the middle-class local with roots in the Midwest. This shift meant more than the centralization of production in one geographic area: it suggested that the California viewer (the audience members most often used for Hollywood previews) suddenly became a synechdoche for *all* American moviegoers.

Thus, in order to win their patronage and approval, Hollywood invented the average, or typical (white) middle-class movie patron. This amounted to a kind of censorship that mainstreamed one set of values to the exclusion of others, and pretended that the selected population was a representative choice. Compared to what they faced in New York's diverse neighborhoods, filmmakers seeking to tap into Southern California's community tastes met a population with a powerfully different set of potentials. Thus, the way film producers and executives viewed the unique demography of Southern California— its new permutation of age, sex, and regional taste—all combined to construct a mass audience with values different from those producers had used as their gauge prior to Hollywood.

Southern California audiences became a kind of laboratory out of which emerged the experimental forms for all America's movie tastes. Through the accident of birth, and through the chance resting points of his youthful migration, Darryl Zanuck was ideally positioned to take advantage of and understand the composition and significance of this Los Angeles audience. Zanuck's roots in this audience go a long way toward explaining his lifelong ability to translate public taste into hit movies. Beyond this, however, from the very beginning of his contact with film he had the ability to "code switch." All his professional life, he would journey with ease back and forth between the excitement and danger of the contemporary urban milieu and the traditional values of small-town American life. For each he enjoyed a different kind of insider's vantage point.

Zanuck broke into the movie business as a writer, but, beyond his early movie scripts, his yearly opinion pieces or letters to the editor in trade papers like *The Hollywood Reporter,* his one novel, and his book of wartime recollections, he never wrote much that was published. It is odd that so few of Zanuck's letters survive, given the position he occupied and the number of eminent people who were his friends and associates. Unlike David O. Selznick, with his uncontrolled desire to write—letters, memoranda, and world-class telegrams—Zanuck's preferred modes of communication were to use the telephone, to use the abbreviated form of the telegram, to respond (in red ink) on a memo sent to him, or else to dictate his thoughts to a secretary or scenario coordinator like the invaluable Dorothy Hechtlinger or Molly Mandeville, women whose ability to read his diverse signals bordered on the telepathic. Those who worked with Zanuck, like his Warner Brothers secretary (and later writer and producer) Milton Sperling, grew accustomed to his way of working out his ideas. They were able to translate his asides, outbursts, and musings (both in and out of story conferences) into instructions about definitive scripts, into letters, or into memoranda. Understanding that they were meant to be taken as utterances from on high, Sperling called Zanuck's précis on a film in production "The Sermon of the Day."[1] These sermons, and of course his films, give us insight into what Zanuck tried to accomplish. But what do we know of his early years?

In his biographical films, or *biopics* (a genre he did more to shape than any producer in Hollywood), Zanuck made certain that the meaning of a famous person's life came through in a single, critical incident, or in the special qualities of an unusual home environment or a unique life circumstance. Thus, *The Story of Alexander Graham Bell* explains the motivation behind the telephone as Alexander Graham Bell's drive to alleviate the social isolation experienced by his beloved wife, who was deaf. In *Cardinal Richelieu,* another well-known Zanuck biopic, a young boy, after witnessing the humiliating defeat of his nation, vows then and there to use the avenue of the church as a medium of vengeance. As the adult Richelieu, he is able to make good on his promise. Zanuck referred to such clear, early establishment of character motivation as a film's "rooting interest." Without it, a great life (or, more accurately, the film of a great life) could not be interpreted.

But Zanuck gave either scant information or contradictory hints about the rooting interest that would explain his own life. In some versions, Zanuck's first contact with movies was as an eight-year-old playing the part of an Indian maid in a western.[2] Zanuck told Mel Gussow, who wrote a biography of him in 1971, that his first experience in film was as a seven-year-old in the prestudio Hollywood of 1909, when (once again playing an Indian maid) he was hired as an extra. As Zanuck recalled it, "I remember once I asked the Kalem [company] cameraman how the cameras worked. I was curious about how it got so big on the screen. I guess the seed was planted along about that time."[3] Other sources and interviews suggest that he was almost twenty before the idea of working in Hollywood seriously occurred to him. The way he reclaimed, and perhaps restructured, his own memory parallels one of his favorite film themes: the critical moment when an unknown young man comes face to face with the destiny that will bring him renown.[4]

Of his ancestry, there is less ambiguity. Zanuck was the second child of Louise Torpin, a homemaker, and Frank Zanuck, manager of Wahoo's Grand Hotel, owned by Louise's father. A brother, Donald, born nine years before Darryl, was tragically kicked to death by a horse four months after Darryl's birth. The Zanucks never had another child. Zanuck's forebears were British on his mother's side (Torpin, a derivative of Turpin) and Swiss on his father's. The Torpins came to Nebraska via Pennsylvania and Illinois. Like many Americans in a time when the population was still predominantly rural, Darryl Zanuck was born, on September 5, 1902, in a small town in a hotel. He was named, with the appropriate gendered spelling change, after the heroine of *Darrel of the Blessed Isles,* a best-seller his mother was reading at the time of his birth.[5] Wahoo, Nebraska, was then a place of some 2,500 inhabitants. Zanuck's birthplace was part of a largely flat, rural region noted for its extreme weather and lush farmland. He was not the only celebrated citizen of this town. For some time a sign has stood at the city outskirts proudly boasting four other famous favorite sons: baseball slugger "Wahoo" Sam Crawford, Pulitzer Prize–winning composer Howard Hanson, Nobel laureate (in genetics) George Beadle, and artist Clarence Anderson. But, befitting a Hollywood figure, Zanuck received top billing.

Darryl recalled terrible fights between his parents. Perhaps their source were his father's gambling and drinking; perhaps, for an already unstable couple trying to recover from the death of a child, it was too difficult to live under the dominant shadow of Louise's father, Henry Torpin, a figure whose fortune and enterprises supported the family. Whatever the reason, in 1909 his parents divorced. He rarely saw his father afterward, and it is difficult even to determine the date of his death or the most general facts of Frank Zanuck's life after the divorce. Zanuck loved his father. But like most children, he also "wanted to admire and look up to him, too."[6] Since Frank made the most tenuous of livings working in a sinecure job as a clerk in the hotel owned by his father-in-law, Zanuck judged that "my father was a failure." What was worse, Frank didn't seem to care. He would later sum up Frank's life by saying "anyone who puts down his occupation as 'hotel night clerk' is admitting that he has no ambition for a start." It was almost "like admitting you're a mouse." Nevertheless, Zanuck recalls that the mouse "had a fiery temper."[7] A poignant scenario set in Los Angeles has the mostly absent father (who worked, like some character in a Nathanael West novel, as a manager of a residential hotel) sneaking away with his son to attend movie matinees.[8] It is a touching but unsubstantiated image. His tubercular mother, preoccupied with her health and her Bible-thumping second husband, seemed not to take much interest in Darryl. The boy grew up in an environment atypical of either the Midwest or the middle class at that time: although they all lived in the same city, he almost never saw his father, and, largely because his mother seemed to wish it, he had little contact with her, either.[9]

Zanuck, however, told his biographer: "I had a very happy child-hood, especially when I was hunting—out in the open—and being free."[10] His main source of security was his maternal grandparents, particularly his Grandfather Henry Torpin, who doted on the boy, teaching him to hunt and fish. Grandfather Torpin, an engineer and surveyor who had helped build the railroad, was a colorful figure who had moved from the farm his British family had worked in Ohio, to the civilized environs of Philadelphia, to the wilds of Nebraska Territory not long after it had been admitted to statehood in 1867. By the turn of the century, he had settled in the small town of Oakdale, Nebraska (100 miles north of Wahoo), and, with his chain of grain el-evators spread throughout fifteen locations, became the local rich man who owned everything, a character out of Willa Cather.[11] Torpin may have been the source of Zanuck's fascination with the purity and essentialism of turn-of-the-century small-town life that was to become the superstructure of so many Fox films. In Grandfather Torpin's ownership of Oakdale, we may have Zanuck's inherited sense of ab-solute authority that came with possession of a small universe. Oak-dale was a rehearsal in miniature for Fox.

FROM OAKDALE TO GLENDALE, AND BACK

A significant part of Darryl's youth was spent outside Nebraska, in California. In the early years of this century, many Midwesterners, tired of that region's flat terrain and brutal winters or just ready to re-tire after a life's hard labor, were lured to California for various rea-sons. Some came for purification, hoping to find in this hospitable last frontier the places advertised variously as the Mediterranean of the West or the El Dorado of the West, the sites for miraculous new beginnings for failed lives, tired lives, discarded lives. Many came for improvement of their financial station, hoping to cash in, variously, on booms in real estate, oil, and gold, spiritual transformation, beauty and youth, movies. Some came to reclaim their health amid the region's temperate climate and pure air.

Louise Zanuck was one of them. After leaving Nebraska, she settled in the Los Angeles suburb of Glendale, future home of James M. Cain's troubled middle-class striver Mildred Pierce. In its climate, she was seeking several things: the environment to improve her tuberculosis; a new site for a life without Darryl's father; and perhaps a retreat from the reach of her powerful father. Initially young Darryl stayed behind with his Torpin grandparents. But soon after his mother divorced Frank, Darryl was sent along to her. For six years, starting at the age of seven, Darryl spent fall, winter, and spring in Glendale, California, with his mother and stepfather, and summers in Nebraska with his grandfather. On the long, solitary train rides between these homes, his mind was stirred by the passing scenery, and his letters to his grandfather describe the vistas in the same economic prose he would use to set up a film scenario ("All we see now is desert with sagebrush every few inches . . . "). The letters are also full of the stuff a young boy might imagine, pastiches culled from popular fiction in which Zanuck located himself as the center of a universe created out of his own observation. His grandfather, impressed with the young author's energy, saw to it that the letters were published in the local newspaper, the Oakdale *Sentinel*.[12] They are Zanuck's first published writing.

The diminutive boy from a broken home might have used such writing as a means of drawing attention to himself. His Nebraska schoolmates recall him as a teller of tall tales, who had a sure sense of the importance of his own interests. One of his classmates remembers him as "the type of a boy that had a very vivid imagination. He would talk whether it pertained to the subject that the teacher asked the question on it or not," a quality those who were to sit in on his script conferences might find eerily familiar.[13] Most people who knew him well recall that he had a streak of hyperbole. Many found it appealing; it struck a few as ridiculous—energy without balance or proportion. His son, Richard, affectionately recalls: "He always had a passion for storytelling. And in his everyday life he would exaggerate a lot. . . . You had to bring everything down twenty or thirty percent."[14] A cousin, Keith Torpin, similarly remembers a fondness for tall tales, and also recollects Darryl sketching the animals he loved to hunt.[15] In both these traits—narrative exaggeration and visual play of the captive creature—we will see the fundamental strengths of the future filmmaker: a man who loves action and who exaggerates in order to make others see what he sees.

While his summers in Nebraska may have been recollected as edenic, the rest of the year in California decidedly was not. This only child with the febrile imagination did not get along with his stepfather, Joseph Norton. Like Frank Zanuck, Norton was an alcoholic. But where Frank was more like the character James Dunne would play, memorably, in Zanuck's *A Tree Grows in Brooklyn*—largely a sweet-natured, emotional, and romantic figure prone to flights of fancy and disappearances when on a drinking spree—Norton was a figure from a very different movie. The son of a clergyman, he was a Bible thumper like the preacher played by Robert Mitchum in *The Night of the Hunter*, an embittered fanatic filled with rage toward women and children. Perhaps the surest sign that, despite his warm recollections, all was not well was the stutter Darryl developed. Years later, Zanuck would recall the unpleasant scenes taking place in the unhappy household. In cinematic terms (perhaps to distance himself), he recalled that both mother and son feared Norton's drunken rages: "I remember lying in my cot. My mother in her bed. Waiting for him to come home. I would be shivering, almost . . . as I heard footsteps coming up to the door. Reeling drunk! Falling down! And with the Bible, always with the Bible. A big black Bible under his arm."[16]

Because of regular fights with his stepfather, Zanuck was placed in a Los Angeles military academy. Unhappy, looking for the home he knew was his, he frequently ran away. Finally Louise shipped Darryl back, at thirteen, to Nebraska and the care of his indulgent grandfather.

Zanuck's life at the Nortons was awful. He put it simply: "they didn't want me around." Zanuck was shipped back to the care of his mother's father, Henry Torpin. It was this colorful figure—a strapping six-foot-tall former Indian fighter, land surveyor, and pioneer—who instilled certain values into his small, worshipful grandson. Though he loved his own daughter, Louise, he told Darryl that like his father, his mother, too, was a failure for different reasons. While inferior in his eyes by virtue of being a woman, Louise had exacerbated this sin over which she had no control by marrying a man who let her have the upper hand. With few other sources of guidance, these were the lessons Zanuck was taught. Zanuck, spurred on by his grandfather's contempt for such creatures, made certain that *he* would not emulate his father or his mother.

Zanuck was never close to his mother. It has been suggested that Louise's seeming indifference to Darryl's welfare instilled in him a feeling of abandonment, one that "color[ed] Darryl's opinion of women the rest of his life."[17] But from what we can see from the available material, in Louise's defense it might be said that with a father who held such a low opinion of women, the fact that she replicated in her marriages the only world she knew is not surprising. As much a victim of abandonment and abuse as her son, she unconsciously passed the syndrome on to him, a scenario not uncommon in families with their pattern. Photos of Louise reveal what Zanuck told interviewers: that his mother was tall, "very attractive" with "prematurely white, absolutely white" hair.[18] Though at the time of his accession to power she lived in Hollywood, she was an infrequent visitor to the Zanuck house. Richard Zanuck recalls meeting her on only a handful of occasions. (There is a photo, taken sometime in the 1930s of Louise with her granddaughter Darrylin watching Darryl play polo at Riviera Polo Field.)

In Oakdale, floated by his grandfather's generous allowance, Darryl assumed a position of leadership. With his Torpin cousins and other local boys, he founded that most American of small-town institutions, an exclusive fraternal organization, the Oakdale Boys Camp. Its rules (written "By = Darryl") specified that there would be "NO fighting, roughhousing, nor talking after 10 P.M." Darryl was elected (or named himself) both captain and treasurer.[19] In addition to the activities of the Oakdale Boys Camp, which demonstrate Zanuck's early desire to lead, during this period he also felt the first stirrings of a theatrical drive. The Torpin barn was the site of Zanuck's first show, a child's version of the old railroad drama *The Black Diamond Express*.[20] While outdoor life and the play he organized were activities he took to with great enthusiasm, in the classroom Darryl was not an exceptional student. In fact, he was recalled by many in the town as somewhat of an indulged hellion, a small, wildly energetic figure known to some as "that Zanuck boy." He made it through the eighth grade before something more interesting than school drew his attention.

In 1917, with his pioneer grandfather's approval (and perhaps even his influence), Zanuck—a diminutive adolescent who barely made the weight requirement—lied about his age (he wasn't quite fifteen) and enlisted in the Omaha National Guard. He was initially billeted on the Texas/New Mexico border at the time of Pancho Villa's raids, but saw none of this action. Instead, he recalled, "all we did was cut sagebrush and live in the open while building the camp." When America entered World War I, Zanuck's division was made part of the U.S. Army's 34th Division. Bored with camp life, Zanuck claimed, he took off one day and rode a horse into town. But this was not the Oakdale Boys Camp, and for this breach of army rules he recalled being punished with kitchen patrol, "thirty days in the officers' mess."[21] The military record, which Zanuck saved, tells a different story. For "disrespect to a non-commissioned officer" on March 5, 1918, Zanuck was punished with "one month in quarters."[22]

After six months of training, Zanuck was shipped to Fort Dix, New Jersey, for two months of special instruction in the principles of trench warfare. Finally the 34th Division sailed for France on the SS *Baltic*. After landing in Brest, Zanuck saw a hospital train packed with wounded Americans. To Zanuck, this was "[m]y first real shock." Seeing the staring men with their "arms gone" and with "holes in their chest," he understood: "This was war where they were killing people."[23] Because of his slight build and great energy, Zanuck served as a runner and messenger. Once, when dodging enemy shells, he had "one shoe blown all the way off and one blown half off."[24]

The excited teenager wrote his observations up for the army newspaper *Stars and Stripes*. And, once again, his grandfather had them published in his hometown paper.[25] For the rest of his life, Zanuck would think of this time as "an adventure," one that he would recall with both wistfulness and nostalgia.[26] He was virtually the only studio head to have had combat experience in World War I, and it would eventually find its way into his films.

AFTER PAREE: TWO COASTS, TWO CULTURES

Zanuck returned to Nebraska in August 1919, but stayed less than a month in Oakdale. "Most of my contemporaries were still in school, and everybody else in the Middle West had long since got bored with the war in Europe. When I spoke of it, they either didn't know what I was talking about or just didn't want to listen. Soon I said to hell with it and kept my mouth shut."[27] Thirty-three years later, we see this anticlimax in *Wait Till the Sun Shines, Nellie,* in which Ben Halper, Jr., receives a bleak postwar homecoming.

To Zanuck, the prospect of settling down as a stable Midwest burgher after his stint overseas may have appeared dull and limiting. There was little opportunity in either Oakdale or Wahoo for the restless young man. Even if he had wanted to stay, he would have had to compete with a number of Torpin cousins to get a foothold in managing his grandfather's miniature empire of landholdings, livestock, and real estate.[28] Outside the hodgepodge skills he had picked up in military service, from his sporadic army newspaper writing, and from the boxing matches he fought during his army days, he did not have any preparation for a conventional career. Bold as always, he claims to have told a cousin, "I want to go into some form of the arts."[29] His cousin told him he was crazy. But Zanuck packed his bags and set out to prove his cousin wrong.

Zanuck identified himself as a writer, but he preferred culture as served up by the tabloids and the movies to the literary New York variety. En route to Nebraska after the army, Zanuck had been stationed in Mineola, Long Island—thirty minutes from Manhattan. He stayed in New York for six months, trying to set himself up as a writer. After a glimpse of this life, he bypassed the literary capital of the country and stopping for the briefest time, like so many of the region's residents, he headed west to California. Choosing the more familiar (and congenial) California over New York was an early indicator that he would develop a sense of popular cultural trends that was very different from that favored by his two biggest rivals, both New Yorkers: David O. Selznick and Irving Thalberg, who, growing up in New York, had been nurtured by the pervasive literary and musical ambiance of the city. But later, unlike another outsider, Minnesota-bred (though Princeton-educated) writer F. Scott Fitzgerald, whose *This Side of Paradise* in 1920 would make him one of the decades' first certifiable "new" or "modern" writer-celebrities, Zanuck would have found New York uncongenial to his style. For one thing, his temperament was not truly that of the urbanite. Additionally, he was not at home in the cultural circles of those artists who felt compelled to be in New York because they saw it as the site of (and dominant force that shaped) their fields. In works like *Doorway to Hell* and *42nd Street,* Zanuck would soon be the chief architect who immortalized the city on film, but he had no great devotion to the trappings or the spirit of the place. Perhaps by leading a peripatetic life from the age of seven—running away from school, going off to war as a fifteen-year-old—he had *already* escaped and thus did not need to flee to New York to accomplish that.

Most important, he did not see himself as the kind of serious writer that Fitzgerald, Zora Neale Hurston, or Thomas Wolfe aspired to be; for the moment, he had no desire to interrogate pressing social issues of the day or overturn forms that gave fiction its shape, nor to bring forth from a source of introspection the dark thoughts for which Freud's writings were providing labels and currency. He was not the urbanite who fit into the world of the *The New Yorker* or *Vanity Fair*, and he would not have been comfortable with the literary avant garde. It was his lack of congruence with a literary culture that made the city a poor match for Darryl Zanuck.

Years later—when the movies had long abandoned their first production sites in New York, establishing almost all their studios in the Los Angeles area—it appeared as if California might adopt tax legislation unfriendly to the movies and Zanuck was asked whether the film industry should move some other place, perhaps back to New York. His answer is revealing: "It would be a terrible thing. Why, we'd all start to thinking like New Yorkers. All our pictures would be like Noel Coward or 'Tobacco Road.'" To Zanuck, movies (and, implicitly, all art) were popular "because they have a half-part Broadway viewpoint, a half-part Hollywood viewpoint and a half-part solid Omaha viewpoint. . . . If picture people came to New York and lived in this atmosphere for a few years, they would automatically start writing for the New York audience which is too sophisticated for the rest of the world."[30]

Although Zanuck's math seems a bit off (his whole contains three halves), his cultural calculus was finely honed.

He arrived in California in September 1919 uncertain what he wanted to do with his life. He tried to complete his war-interrupted education at Los Angeles Manual Arts High School. Later, he recalled how out of place he felt: "I just couldn't get my mind back into it."[31] His classmates (and later, his friends here) were future luminaries Lawrence Tibbett (opera), Goodwin Knight (politics), and James Doolittle (military).[32] After a short stint there, Zanuck dropped out, and he drifted through a variety of jobs. By his own reckoning, he attempted and failed at eighteen occupations, ranging from rivet catcher to poster designer, boxer, and stevedore.

Making the same journey west one year later would be Irving Thalberg, who, along with David O. Selznick and Zanuck, would virtually define how movies operated under the studio system. But in 1919—when Thalberg was starting his climb as Carl Laemmle's right-hand man at Universal; while Selznick had what appeared to be a lifetime of film experience working with his father, Lewis J. Selznick; while Samuel Goldwyn, with his partnerships and feuds, had been in business almost a decade, and Louis Mayer since 1907—Darryl Zanuck's only contact with the movies (aside from his undocumented stint as an extra) was as a patron. He had one qualification, though, that made up for the essential experience he lacked: his enormous energy, recalled by many as greater than that of anyone they had ever known.[33] Further, he understood California and the Californian (which is to say that he understood that this, and not New York, was probably as good a version as any to use for figuring the tastes of the average American), and found himself in Hollywood. And although it was not possible to break totally with the cultural conventions represented by the literary cultures of the east, unlike his peers, he was relatively unburdened by any sense of obligation or inheritance to a creative tradition that did not represent his tastes and that he did not know firsthand. A young man in this young city, he was an unlikely candidate to usher in film's version of the modern.

Chapter Two

ZANUCK
THE WRITER

Human beings cannot live without
stories.

—Ann Douglas,
Terrible Honesty

THE SAME YEAR thirteen-year-old Darryl Zanuck departed
Glendale for Nebraska, Carl Laemmle founded what is considered the first true film studio, Universal. With its capacity
for both indoor and outdoor shooting, an enormous film-processing
plant, and temporary movie sets of towns and castles nestled next to
permanent lakes and real rivers, "Universal City" was not only the
largest but also the most up-to-date filmmaking facility in the country.
It was also the most costly. The arrival of studio-era filmmaking was a
big event in the small, somewhat provincial city of Los Angeles. An
estimated twenty thousand people—nearly 10 percent of the city's
population—turned out for the opening festivities on March 15, 1915.
Laemmle's triumph was only slightly marred when he had to scram-
ble atop the roof of a car to avoid being doused by the rushing flood
waters of a special effects demonstration gone awry.

But Universal's founder had thoughts on his mind other than keeping his feet dry. Laemmle was involved in an internal power struggle with his one remaining corporate rival, Universal's treasurer, Pat Powers. He knew he would soon have to provide positive results to justify the enormous expense of constructing Universal City. Given this pressure, Laemmle's conservative decision on the future direction of the studio was not surprising: Universal's policy would be to release 1915's version of a balanced program consisting of a variety of cheaply and efficiently made shorts. Within a year, Laemmle's judgment would be proved wrong. Though the short film would not disappear, it would be supplanted as the standard by which the industry worked.

In the five years following Universal's opening, the American film industry began its ascent. By 1920, the year Zanuck first tried to find work in Hollywood, the nucleus of what would become the mature studio system was clearly evident: within a few years after Universal's start, Fox, Warner Brothers, First National, F.B.O., Paramount, and the component parts of what would soon form MGM all opened their facilities. The city of Los Angeles—symbiotically linked in so many ways to the culture spawned by this new industry of Hollywood—grew along with the film industry. Film had evolved from one of the many cheap mechanical amusements available in the late nineteenth century into an essential part of the region's economy and culture. By 1926, Hollywood was not only Los Angeles's leading revenue producer; it was in the preeminent position in the state, first among California's thirty-five industries.

The cinematic culture Darryl Zanuck encountered in California was very different from that which had existed a mere five years before. In 1915—the year D. W. Griffith released *The Birth of a Nation* and twelve years before *The Jazz Singer*—a leading trade paper asserted that film was arguably already America's most popular and democratic mass art, "a basic amusement, recreation and instruction for the entire world—for the highbrow and for the fellow whose cowlick grows into his eyebrows."[1] Powerful though Hollywood was, it was still an industry in gestation. Several recent changes in the film industry made the 1920s a decade of enormous growth, and perhaps nowhere was this fluid state more apparent than in the status of Zanuck's chosen profession, the screenwriter.

Beginning in 1912, the film industry gradually changed from a cinema comprised of different kinds of short films to one dominated by longer films, called "features."[2] Rising to the challenge of supply (and demand) that the feature's popularity ushered in, film corporations expanded and restructured all aspects of exhibition, production, and distribution.[3] Amid this wholesale rethinking of how film, as business, could be reordered to meet its growing popularity, specific changes in corporate organization and structure affected how all work—including screenwriting—was conceived and systematically organized at each studio.

While other entertainment media, like the vaudeville circuits and the legitimate theater, offered useful organizational examples to a nascent film industry, it was the American manufacturing industries and the modern retail outfit that provided Hollywood with the principles upon which it would create and sell a refined version of its product. Many of the points adopted by the film industry were enumerated in a book whose publication date virtually coincided with the rise of the feature, Frederick W. Taylor's *The Principles of Scientific Management* (1911). Under the thrall of "scientific management" techniques borrowed from vertically integrated manufacturing and retail business, this new model offered ways for film corporations both to meet heightened consumer demand and yet to increase both worker efficiency and profits. The screenwriter's work was now broken down into a number of distinct and discrete functions, like the tasks of workers on a Model-T assembly line.

Under a "Taylorized" system, large numbers of longer films did get turned out. But—because of time constraints and the persistent demand of meeting large weekly quotas, and because film production had not kept pace with developments in the exhibition or distribution branches of the industry—most were of routine quality. An alternative plan to insure film's popularity suggested that producers could make not just *more* films but *better* films, works that would appeal to desirable middle-class audiences and raise their estimation of cinema's cultural worthiness.[4] This strategy resulted in the production of a small number of well-publicized "quality" features.

These two opposing ways of satisfying audience demands—the rapid turnovers of the "programmer" and the less frequent offerings of "prestige"—gave rise to two distinct writers' cultures. Each can be thought of as defining the screenwriter's world, his or her spot in the evolving system or mode of production, and the scope and the value placed upon writing talent. It might be said that the rise of the feature transformed the larger context of what the studios used to delineate the qualities of a good film, and with it good writing.

THE FIRST SCREENWRITERS

Early audiences made few demands of the first short films: tell a clear story, or show some person, thing, or event, and photograph it clearly.[5] Because many of the first scenarios consisted of a vague outline thought up by the cameraman or director, screenwriters were not necessary. An early "scenarist," Beulah Marie Dix, recalled that prior to the feature, the chore of writing film scenarios was a casual affair: "It was all rather informal in those early days." This memory is shared by the prolific screenwriter Gene Gautier, who recalled that before the feature changed Hollywood, she turned for ideas to whatever happened to be at hand—"[a] poem, a picture, a short story, a scene from a current play, a headline in a newspaper."[6] As late as 1915, many directors were still using an "open form" script, which contained a general breakdown of the narrative but left the type and duration of each shot up to the director, a state of affairs not tenable with the efficient planning required for making longer films.[7] The minimal demands for this early kind of screenwriting meant that amateurs like Zanuck with little or even no professional experience as writers would have been encouraged, sometimes even sought out. Before the studio era, "the free lance scenario market was still quite significant," a place where "producers solicited manuscripts in much the same fashion as literary magazines."[8] After the war, however, film producers started to follow Paramount founding partner Jesse Lasky's hunch that better stories were, with more commodious theaters, one of the most important ways to bring in what producers yearning for respectability coveted: the imprimatur of the middle-class patron.[9]

However, so rapidly did American film audiences grow in the years following World War I that Hollywood could not turn out enough films—originals or adaptations, high- or lowbrow—to satisfy American hunger for their product. It was clear that even with demand outpacing supply, filmmakers who wanted to hire people to write or adapt quality scenarios "could not indefinitely rely on theatrical and literary sources for adaptations."[10] A few perceptive industry figures like Jesse Lasky realized this. A visionary not always accorded the same high place in history as his partners Goldwyn, DeMille, or Zukor, Lasky knew that the programmer was "the very backbone of the industry." Unglamorous as they were, these quickly made films were "the picture[s] that support the million-dollar motion picture palace" and its film versions culled from the literary canon.[11] Nonetheless, even if the programmers were the essential units that made Hollywood a feasible—and profitable—enterprise, Lasky felt that the more costly films made from an original photoplay were the most important, and that eventually Hollywood would have to be able to produce a scenario that was neither an adaptation nor a programmer.

The screenwriter working in the age of the feature found his or her work increasingly subject to the same kind of professionalization and retooling as the rest of the industry. Each studio now had a Scenario Department, and writing assignments went to staff personnel, not outsiders. Suddenly the "profession was fragmented into specialities . . . there were subspecies of gag writers, continuity writers, treatment writers, scenarists, adaptors, titlists, what-have-you."[12] Rather than being the handcrafted product of a sole figure, or a collaboration, "authorship" became a multiheaded corporate creature. There was a reason for this. Despite the large amount of newspaper space accorded stars and other stellar creative figures working at the studios (even, occasionally, a star writer like Frances Marion), over 90 percent of most film corporations' assets were not invested in human chattel, but in real estate.[13] The theaters—not the artistic personnel—were the critical corporate component, and it was for these that the heads of the corporations developed their protective strategies. Their first job was to do whatever was necessary to get people into the movies. Marcus Loew, the founder and head of the company that bears his name (and that controlled the glamorous studio MGM), stated the situation with characteristic bluntness: "We sell tickets to theatres, not movies."[14]

FROM FICTION WRITER TO
YUCCATONE SPOKESMAN

Zanuck appeared on this fast-moving scene as an eighteen-year-old would-be writer. Perhaps the most direct expression of what he was like in those days comes from an unpublished piece of fiction he wrote between 1920 and 1923, *Beyond the Valley of Reason,* described by its author as "a bitter love story of the passionate age." In this work's "Forward" (misspelled in the original), the author/narrator confesses to the reader:

> At occasional periods, I have exaggerated or suppressed the product to a forgiveable degree, but considering the product in its entirety, my incidents, locale, situations, dialogue, dreams and personalities are enlisted from the ranks of life with what uncertain skill I am able to command or borrow. One might honestly criticize (and undoubtedly shall) the crudity of my continuity, the falsity of my phrasing, the earmarks of my confessed inexperience and youth, but I may truthfully recommend that I have written not as an advertisement, but as I have actually seen with my own eyes . . . frankly striving, without malice or sermon, to entertain, amuse or startle those who have the courage to see me through.[15]

He goes on to describe how all the main characters—Gloria (a virgin), her wealthy, vain, but generous husband, Reggie, their friend Charles, "a bromide, a damn fool"—are drawn from the author's experience. In his description of the character of Harold we get to see how Zanuck saw himself, for it matches portrayals of others who knew him at this time:

> And when I say that *Harold* was swayed by a peculiar passion for the emotionally exotic, the sensational, the grotesque, that he loved annoying people; that he had more blood and thunder and romance in his little toe than a dozen average mortals . . . I am again versed in my character. This time I am certain. I confess those failings are my personal detriments.[16]

Other works dating from this period bear similarly recognizable self-portraits. "Say It With Dreams," one of the four stories that make up his 1923 novel, *Habit,* is particularly revealing. The heroine's name is Irene Dare, a choice in accord with the unbridled confidence those who knew Zanuck always attributed to him. When he was told by others that he could not do something (as when his cousin scoffed at his desire for a career in the arts), Zanuck loved nothing better than to take up the challenge and prove them wrong. In the story, Irene opts for show business against the advice of her small-town friends and relatives. Like her creator, Irene bids farewell and leaves her small town—Oakdale, the same name as Zanuck's—"to write her name in bright lights across the theatrical world." Irene refuses to return to Oakdale: "Never, never in all the world would it voluntarily occur."[17] By the end of the story, Zanuck has seen to it that Irene is a big star. He certainly hoped for the same fate.

Zanuck first tried his hand at pulp fiction, combining sensationalist "exposés" that had been popular American low journalistic fare since the 1880s with the plot twists of his idol, O. Henry. (One profile of Zanuck went so far as to claim that "O. Henry is Zanuck's god. For mental nourishment, he reads an O. Henry story every night.")[18] His sense of timing was excellent. People were beginning to notice the funny but compelling way that the Americans talked. With the advent of Walter Winchell and his imitators, the gossipy material that had once been shunned by respectable writers was on the brink of taking center stage in American journalism.[19] Though at first glance the two would seem to have little in common, Zanuck and Winchell had similar ways of approaching popular culture, and each would become, in his chosen medium, a significant architect of the modern.

Born to Jewish immigrant parents in New York City in April 1897, Winchell was a child of vaudeville. The contacts he made traveling the variety circuit, plus his own natural curiosity, led him to journalism. After his song and dance career in vaudeville faded, more for his own curiosity than for professional advancement, Winchell started to experiment with different gossip-column formats as a "stringer." Some of his short columns were published in big-time trade papers like *Variety* and *Billboard.* His big break came when a new trade paper, *The Vaudeville News,* hired him as a columnist.

If Zanuck's world view had been formed by the tabloid and short story, it was vaudeville that forged Winchell's style and persona. Mediating between the highbrow and lowbrow at a time when the nation itself was making the transition from the agrarian roots of the nineteenth century to the polyglot industrial culture of the twentieth, vaudeville, with its mixture of highbrow and lowbrow material, was the ideal laboratory in which to conduct these experiments. For Winchell, these sources would be his schoolroom just as Zanuck would be tutored by the tabloids.

Reappearing in New York the same year Zanuck resurfaced in Los Angeles, newly reborn writer Winchell, five years older than Zanuck, relied on his vaudeville experience to develop his column's unique format and to rethink journalism as a branch of entertainment that might use its material to offer readers the same pleasing mixture found in variety. Like Zanuck the writer, Winchell knew that he was not a great stylist and that what he wrote was not intended for a genteel readership. Rather, in his work he "would try a column run for the masses in their own vernacular."[20] Winchell's rapid rise paralleled Zanuck's, and his methods and attitude toward his audience would not have been lost on the observant, ambitious younger writer.

The kind of language with which Zanuck was most at home—American tabloidese—was suddenly popular, particularly with two audiences Hollywood was intent on wooing, the urban and the young. Once taken as proof that one lacked the gentility to play the American version of the culture game, slang had become "a form of cultural democracy . . . a way for the disenfranchised to reclaim their language from the genteel elites."[21] While *The New Yorker* would characterize Zanuck's writing style as possessing "the unbending grand manner of a half-educated adolescent," even from its admiring (but still very mandarin) vantage point, his rawness and "incorrectness" were recognized more as virtues than deficits.[22]

Although at this time he may not have been able to do so, Zanuck would shortly articulate why his direct approach to screenwriting was characteristic of his era. If Thalberg was a "quality" producer, and Lubitsch and Goldwyn each had an idiosyncratic touch, Zanuck—like his utterly different Soviet contemporary Sergei Eisenstein (who shared with Zanuck and Winchell a love for the primal jolt of entertainment one could find at the circus or in variety)—aimed for a cinema of shock: "What do you mean a Zanuck touch? . . . I don't know that there's a 'touch.' I aim for the smash, the spectacular, the shock, the diaphragm laugh—the audience. I say to myself: 'How am I going to make the audience feel it? What do they want to see here?' "[23] In the age of Winchell, of Krazy Kat, of jazz and mahjong, and of popular songs like "Ain't We Got Fun?," Zanuck would leave his mark.

He had written several first-person reportage pieces during the war, and some of his observations in the form of letters home from the front were published in the soldiers' newspaper *Stars and Stripes*.[24] His early writing demonstrated the powers of observation and the abundant well of energy from which he would draw his frenetic plots, but it was comically apparent that his grasp of syntax and grammar was rudimentary. We see this highly visual (but very undisciplined) approach in the opening paragraph of "Does Love Last?"— a twenty-page short story written by the eighteen-year-old Zanuck:

> As she paused there by the edge of the gushing torrent of angry waters—her pearl gray riding habit the exact shade of the harsh stone banks, the breeze waving the silken folds of her chestnut hair, her sparkling blue eyes as deep in color as the pool itself, her smile as enchanting as the cool nooks in the green, and her worshipping collie pleading at her feet for a single glance—Jervis saw that he had never beheld so gorgeous a creature in all his life.[25]

Those who knew him at the time recall that Zanuck wrote rapidly and regularly—and was turned down by magazines just as rapidly and regularly. In 1920, however, he finally managed to sell his first piece, a short story, to *Argosy* magazine.[26]

But his first substantial financial success would not come in literature, film, or journalism. Instead, Zanuck triumphed in the equally young field of advertising, creating a slogan for Yuccatone, a putative hair restorative made from a plant found in abundance in the West. Yuccatone was the invention of A. F. Foster, an itinerant, optimistic huckster of patent medicines, and a man whose colorful exploits suggest he could have served as the model for the humbug so lovingly brought to life by Frank Morgan in *The Wizard of Oz*. (Foster may have served as the inspiration for Doc "Harold" White, a salesman of patent medicines, the disguise assumed by one of Zanuck's characters in his story "For Men Only.")[27] It was Zanuck's inspiration to come up with the following mantra in an era just beginning to achieve the rhythm of the hyperbolic sales pitch: "You've never seen a bald-headed Indian."

With the confidence provided by the surging sales of Yuccatone (which, being of unstable chemical composition, soon began exploding on store shelves), Zanuck succeeded in selling another story, "Mad Desire," to Bernarr Macfadden's *Physical Culture* magazine.[28] The story's hyperbolic style, its plot of drug addiction and salvation through the love of a woman, fit with the magazine's aggressive peddling of arcane health advice. Spurred on by his modest literary success after so much rejection, he was able to sell several more stories, all of the pulp fiction genre.

"FOR MEN ONLY"

Zanuck had fulfilled his pledge to "go into some form of the arts," for he was now a published author. He had already chosen Southern California over New York, and now he would choose movies over magazine work. One version of how Zanuck got his start is told by his biographer Mel Gussow (who heard the tale from Zanuck himself), and it reads like the script for a B movie. Zanuck claims that in 1919, director Frank Lloyd spotted him on a Los Angeles street. Lloyd was preparing his version of *Oliver Twist* for the recently formed United Artists. At a glance, he was impressed by the screen potential implied by Zanuck's youthful look, and thought the boy might have a future as an actor. He was sixteen at the time this is supposed to have occurred, but Zanuck's youthful appearance and small size make it credible that Lloyd could have asked the young man to do a screen test for the part of the young Oliver.[29] Zanuck didn't get the part, but it was with this contact, he claimed, that, inspired by the possibilities of the movies, his "writing career began in earnest."[30]

The only problem with this story, appealing and dramatic though it might be, is that the dates don't match what we know about *Oliver Twist*'s production history. Lloyd's film was released in 1922. Even if it had been shot in 1921, Zanuck would have already been nineteen years old—hardly right to play the part of a waif. Meanwhile, he was steadily plugging away at his writing.

The earliest movie writing of Zanuck's that has survived is a 1921 story, "For Men Only." On the script's cover, its author described his work as a "comedy-drama adventure." And though "For Men Only" was never produced, it reveals several things about its young author that would remain constant aspects of his professional identity. As he would do later, at Warner Brothers, Zanuck used a pseudonym; in this instance, it takes the form of a ghost co-author, Ralph Dietrich, who may or may not have existed in corporeal form. Zanuck was aware of how important image was in Hollywood, and in this early presentation of his professional self, he tried to give the appearance of having power and substance, or of being associated with people who did. Stamped on the script's cover is the legend, "Submitted by D. F. Zanuck, Authorized West Coast Representative for Curtis Brown, Ltd., London, England." Zanuck was pretending, in the time before agents counted in Hollywood, that one D. F. Zanuck was representing himself, his partner, and the interests of an impressive-sounding foreign operation.

The script is hilariously overwritten. Like Mack Sennett (for whom he would shortly work), Zanuck created a world of people and objects almost constantly in frantic flight, pursuit, and movement. From petty crooks who "get theirs," to the occasional glamorous female "forgeresses," Zanuck's early movie world is an imaginative place populated by the full spectrum of criminal types, all of whom prey on the fabulous (and amply documented) world of the wealthy. In less than ten years, Zanuck would parlay this preoccupation with the excitement of crime and the glamour of the criminal into a major success. At this early date, Zanuck was already demonstrating one of his characteristic writer's traits: using newspaper headlines as source material for his scripts. (He tied "For Men Only" into the novelty of several recent high-speed police chases.) The plot involves a holdup artist named Pacific Crawford, a forger named Kate Jeffries, and Irene Blackwell, a young woman trying to win a bet with her newspaper magnate father by writing a short novel in five days. Before the tale is over, there are automobile chases, near disasters with oncoming trains, double-crosses, and numerous dramatic revelations. But all ends well. Irene has more than enough material for a novel and, in addition to winning her bet, she has also found a fitting husband.

Irene's confidence that she could produce a manuscript within five days is in line with what Zanuck himself demonstrated on this and many other later occasions. As Jack Warner noted, Zanuck "could write ten times faster than any ordinary man."[31] Screenwriter Nunnally Johnson recalled that Zanuck "was such an energetic fellow, with so many ideas . . . he was quite capable of starting at two o'clock in the morning and dictating some sort of outline of a story, roughly, and handing it to a writer or producer the next day."[32] The constant sense of movement and the surprising (and unmotivated) shifts these characters take keep the reader turning the pages of "For Men Only" and disguise the fact that the author is not a very good writer. But he had a knack for conveying a sense of excitement and energy to the reader, and an almost perfect sense of pacing. Unpolished as it might be, his writing incarnated what the *New York Times* observed of the decade: "Philosophy in action, not words, represents the ideal of what is best and most desirable in the drama of these times."[33]

KEEPING MOMENTUM

Zanuck was entering a relatively uncharted, but rapidly developing, territory. With his eighth-grade education and limited knowledge of either journalism or literature, it would seem that he hardly had the training for a career as a Hollywood writer. But the idea that a nineteen-year-old with less than thirty pages of work in print (and no produced movie scripts) could get a writing job with a film studio was not as preposterous in 1921 or 1922 as it might be today. Breaking into silent films as a writer was far easier than breaking into writing for talkies. The biggest obstacles he faced were the barriers of the social codes Hollywood built around its two distinct silent screenwriting cultures: the "prestige" and the "programmer."

Membership in the "prestige" culture was attainable through a number of channels: you had to have previously published a novel, written a play, had a short story appear in a prestige magazine (like the old, established *Saturday Review* or new ones like *Vanity Fair* or *The New Yorker*), or authored a work in a large-circulation magazine like *The Ladies Home Journal* or *Redbook*. The number of prestige writers who did a substantial amount of screenwriting during the silent era was rather small. Instead, less esteemed, but well-known and accessible commercial writers were assiduously courted.

The second writers' culture—the action, or program writer ("programmer")—was where the bulk of the silent-era screenplays were written. Its membership was defined largely by the absence of the qualifications necessary to be placed in the first culture. Since these writers were not deemed figures of prestige, Hollywood was unconcerned with their profile. Thus there was little resistance to women entering this workforce, and many of the early silent screenwriters were women.[34] Not surprisingly, because they were already accustomed to the pressure of deadlines, a number of these early "programmer" screenwriters had also been newspaper reporters. The studio expected them to invent stories or, failing that, to adapt the stories culled from familiar pastiches of tales and types seen on the stage or found in the newspapers. These writers turned out a weekly quota of pages, sometimes covering a bewildering range of assignments. (Before he started writing features, in 1924, Zanuck claimed to have authored over forty short scenarios in less than two years!) Though presumed to lack the creative spark (and the marquee value) of the prestige writer, one of the ironies of this system meant that writers of programmers were frequently called upon to adapt the work of these more eminent authors who were often unable to do this on their own.

As if this work culture did not foster enough pressure, programmer writers were frequently placed in direct competition with one another, assigned to work on the same script.[35] Compared to the autonomy found outside the cinema, the "author" who wrote for the screen during the studio era became a composite creature, a corporate name attached to a stitched-together script. Until 1926, when their names started to appear as part of a film's credits, unlike directors and actors, screenwriters worked with no official recognition that what they were doing *was* writing. To refer to themselves, then, as screenwriters would have elicited puzzled looks, for "the expression per se scarcely existed."[36] Until unions (resisted by all the producers, including Zanuck) strengthened their hand, writers had little job security. While the most sought-after actors and directors were given seven-year option contracts, screenwriters could be signed on for a per-picture, or even a per-diem, rate.[37] It is not surprising that, given the contours of this particular section of film culture, the bulk of the output was efficient but predictable.

Even without this decade's enormous industrywide transformations, screenwriters of this period confronted a conundrum. How could the writer work in a medium where the actual writing could fit on a few title cards? With its sometimes powerful universe that combined visual action with iconic and graphic compositions, with its live musical accompaniment, the silent cinema was not the kind of territory where a writer could shine: it was almost exclusively the preserve of the actor, director, and cameraman. In certain instances, because a silent film's primary identity was the look it created, it was even the handiwork of a strong art director (like MGM's Cedric Gibbons, RKO's Van Nest Polglase, or a freelancer like Mitchell Liesen). Zanuck, with his natural affinity for generating action, could have fit in here. Zanuck's writing was not accorded prestige, but it was full of action. To anthropologist Hortense Powdermaker, even a decade after Zanuck entered the movies, in the culture of Hollywood "a writer's main job is the creation of plots."[38] This was a thing Zanuck could do with ease. In fact, it was his greatest gift. But Hollywood paid far more attention (and a good deal more money) for what Zanuck could *not* create: the conventional, prestigious forms of the written culture—the novel, the play, and the short story.

FUNNY MAN

Zanuck would later recall his feelings of rejection in those days: "I thought the movie crowd had the hardest hearts I'd ever known. I walked about to sell my stories—money was too scarce to include car fare. Then, I was not a big good looking fellow who had a way with him. Believe me, I got my share of rebuffs. But I was still in my 'teens and felt that the world was my oyster—it was only that the opening of the shell was going to be a little tough."[39] By early 1922, he had published some tabloid short stories, and had been a gag writer for Mack Sennett and, briefly, for both Harold Lloyd and Charlie Chaplin.[40] By 1923, he had managed to sell a number of serial scenarios to the movies. "Without being highly original in the comedy vein, Zanuck became one of the most successful writers of funny films."[41]

If Zanuck strove vainly to gain the credentials necessary to enter the realms of prestige authors, Somerset Maugham was a different case. With the exception of Shakespeare or Dickens, Maugham may well have been the prestige writer whose work was most frequently adapted by major film studios. This desire for respectability was manifested by what by now had become a common symptom: a major case of "author envy." One *could* build a successful career by starting out as a writer of programmers and, if your primary identity was not as a writer, use these formulaic assignments to rise to the rank of director or even producer. Those men and women without the desire or the skill to produce who thought of themselves primarily as writers knew that prestige would not come to them through the travails of "B" fare or serials like "The Telephone Girl" and "The Leatherpusher" serials Zanuck would write in the next two years for F.B.O. Power and position as a writer would adhere *only* to those wrapped in the cloaking aura of older forms. This search for a specific body in which to house the legitimate was a permanent part of the rather complicated way perenially insecure Hollywood constantly renegotiated prestige. But the manifestation this took in the early 1920s was different from earlier ties that linked the worlds of film and literature. Unlike earlier phases of such envy, in which the names and works of (mostly dead) writers in the literary canon had been the cinematic cultural coin of exchange,the studio-era moguls did not turn their attention to the familiar and safe shelter afforded by the Western canon. Instead, checkbooks in hand, they pursued living "name" authors.

The conditions for this seemed hospitable: the possibilities of storytelling had been expanded by the increased range offered by the feature, and exhibitors (after reluctance) and audiences had accepted the shift. Buttressing this change were cultural institutions like the importance accorded the latest best-seller, which, along with the new Book of the Month Club (organized in 1923), had become a permanent fixture of the middlebrow culture about the same time as the feature film. Such parallel institutions made these writers and their work logical studio investments. More significant, their accessibility and their targeted market meant that these books were already in the appropriate forms for the kind of prestige that would appeal to Hollywood's desired middle classes. The bulk of the industries' efforts to improve their image looked to living, well-known authors. So desperate were the moguls to acquire the big-name writer that *The New Yorker* (always slyly ambivalent in its attitude toward Hollywood) suggested "Movie magnates were ready to cross the Mojave Desert on their hands and knees in order to be insulted by a Big Name."[42]

The case of W. Somerset Maugham (with whom Zanuck later had a bizarre collaboration) is emblematic of the courtship and maneuvers in which the studios engaged to bring one member from the high end of this prestige spectrum to Hollywood. Despite his professed disgust with what he took to be Hollywood's version of literacy and literary culture (opinions that he shared with a few chosen insiders, like his friend, director George Cukor), the urbane author of *Of Human Bondage* and *The Razor's Edge* enjoyed his visits to Hollywood. A man with a highly developed sense of social decorum, "Willie" Maugham came to Southern California for the parties and entertainment, for the fascination with and access to *monstres sacre* actresses he shared with Cukor as much as for the business of discussing writing screenplays based on his work. The latter point failing, he was not opposed to collecting money and advisor's fees for having others adapt his work for the screen. Over the years and a number of visits, he gladly (and with focused concentration) observed, took Hollywood's money, and happily left after producing only one usable film script. Though Maugham was known to be obsessively preoccupied with the production of his books, he left Hollywood before production began on his only Hollywood-authored film script. The man who owned an estate in South Carolina and a villa in the south of France claimed that the intellectual aversion and horror at what he found at the studios was "mitigated only by the $15,000" he earned for his efforts at Paramount.

The relative positions of Maugham and Zanuck in early 1920s Hollywood show a key dynamic in silent screenwriting and one that operated within the larger culture of Hollywood: prestige versus profit. Zanuck the writer knew what would bring him prestige: he lacked the skill as a writer to pull it off. Conversely, though the critically praised Maugham was frequently asked to write for the screen (and gave it serious attention), try as he might, the man who wrote novels, plays, short stories, and even literary criticism with ease was unable (until late in his career) to master screenwriting. This was the case even when Maugham was trying to adapt his own work.

Rather than (as other writers might) cast the blame for such missed efforts on the coarse intellectual climate of the film studios, the supremely pragmatic Maugham understood what Hollywood needed and, more important, what he lacked: a sense of pure stories written for the screen. This blunt self-assessment showed a perspicacity rare in a prestige writer. In a 1921 article for the *North American Review,* Maugham observed: "I believe that in the long run it will be found futile to adapt stories for the screen from novels or from plays, and that any advance in this form of entertainment which may lead to something artistic lies in stories written directly for projection on the white screen."[43] Darryl Zanuck could do what Maugham could not: he knew how to create a plot that could be projected upon the screen. Soon he was writing a script every two weeks. In July 1923 (a year earlier than most historians date the start of Zanuck's real career), Zanuck hit his stride as a writer of serial, programmer films. His work at F.B.O. on "The Telephone Girl" and "The Leather-pusher" serials demonstrates that, from the first, he had the traits for which he would soon become famous: pace, compression, energy.[44] His handwritten comments in the margins of the "working synopsis" for *When Knighthood Was in Tower* read like his memos from any later decade when he ran Fox: "Entire beginning too long—just get over [the fact that] Boy is broke and Gladys wants to help."[45] But this young man would not receive accolades or prestige for his F.B.O. work. Rather, it accrued to H. C. Witwer, the well-known short story writer whose stories were the source for Zanuck's breakthrough scenarios.

When Zanuck translated Witwer's humor (described by *Cosmopolitan* as being "as American as corn on the cob") to the screen, he endowed his heroine—the young, fun-seeking switchboard operator who works out of the swanky Hotel St. Moe in New York, Telephone Girl Gladys Murgatroyd (Alberta Hunter)—with an energy, spunk, and determination not found on Witwer's printed page.[46] In all two dozen installments (which used punning titles like "King Leary" and "Sherlock's Home"), Zanuck made sure that Gladys was involved in a fast-paced series of improbable adventures and romantic escapades. Zanuck's scenario for "For the Love of Mike" (the February 1924 chapter) took only fifteen minutes (125 shots and 72 intertitles) to tell its story. And while Zanuck refined his filmmaking practices all through his long career, the speed and concision he always insisted were part of any successful film—in fact, these were key components in his overall aesthetic—were formed here, by the serial genre's demands and limitations.

For example, if we look at the opening paragraph of one "chapter" in the "The Telephone Girl" series, *For the Love of Mike,* and then compare it with Zanuck's story conference directives on *Gentlemen Prefer Blondes*, made thirty years later, we would notice few differences in the principles of story construction or in the economical way Zanuck was already using characters' interaction to impart plot information:

> The telephone girls and their pals are back from their brief call on Europe. It is night when the ship bearing Gladys Murgatroyd and her pals . . . lands at the New York dock. . . . Just as the girls are about to step off the gangplank an elbow roughly brushes them apart and it is followed by the reeling body of Kid Ruff, a prize fighter, who steps between the girls.[47]

Here, as later, no gesture is without consequence: Gladys's collision—like Dorothy Brown and Lorelei Lee's in *Gentlemen Prefer Blondes*—leads to romance, intrigue, and even violence. No character, no object or trait remains unconnected with the goals of setting up the story's rooting interest and advancing the central plot. Gladys's chauffeur, Mike (who rushes to the girls' aid after the arrogant boxing champion, "the Kid," pushes them), turns out to be more than their driver. In an O. Henry twist of identity, he is revealed to be a superstitious boxer who, with Gladys's guidance (and love), will win the title back from the unpleasant Kid Ruff. *For the Love of Mike* is not just classic Zanuck. It is of its age, a universe written with a zest for the urban milieu to which Zanuck and his characters were drawn. It is a place of smoke-filled boxing arenas populated with hoods, showgirls, and rubes, all characters who cavort about a safe and exciting New York, a town sprinkled with glamorous nightclubs. It is a New York of the mind, a place whose contours have already been shaped by other authors in different forms, but to which Zanuck's inherent sense of cinematic theatricality would provide new avenues and rejuggled plot twists. Zanuck's earliest films contain the same people, places, and events enshrined by writers like Damon Runyon and newspapermen like Walter Winchell. His immersion in this world at F.B.O. so early in his career foreshadows what he would soon do with the gangster film, the comedy, and the backstage musical.

His work for F.B.O. also demonstrates that Zanuck was not a beginner when he auditioned for the Warner brothers in 1924; he was already a successful screenwriter. But his second incarnation—his metamorphosis from a programmer writer to a prestige writer—would be much harder than his first moves getting started. The upper echelon of power as a writer could be reached only by someone who had written a book.

JOINING THE BOOK CLUB

When Zanuck realized that his output of short stories and scenarios for serials would not be enough to impress a Hollywood culture enthralled with books and plays, he sought advice from a number of older movie people he had come to know through his membership at the Los Angeles Athletic Club. The club's roster was a Who's Who of the movie industry. Entering its rooms, Zanuck might have found milling about star actors Charlie Chaplin or Fatty Arbuckle, director Raoul Walsh, or the man he would one day depose at Fox, Winfield Sheehan.

At first, presuming he was Jewish, the club had blackballed him. As the future producer of Hollywood's first feature films to explore anti-Semitism, *The House of Rothschild* (1934) and *Gentleman's Agreement* (1947), Zanuck was repelled by the club's prejudice. Zanuck's revered grandfather, now relocated to Southern California for his health, was opposed to Darryl's joining an anti-Semitic organization. But his grandson's arguments about the utility of the club for his future job prospects swayed him, and he finally agreed to supply the $500 Zanuck needed as membership money. By aligning himself with a key parallel cultural institution, Zanuck had taken a significant first step in the campaign to redefine his career and identity. He would later recall that the desire to be part of this world was palpable: "Living in the glamour of it, hearing stories about it all day long and not being part of it, hurt."[48] Once he was admitted, his unpolished ambition, his obvious "rube" roots, his diminutive size and distinctive appearance made this very junior member the butt of some practical jokes. One of the tricks played most frequently on the eager

Zanuck was to tell him of some nonexistent film job located on the far side of the city. He would frantically race to the location, only to find out he had been fooled.[49] But Zanuck could take—and give—the ribbing, so he eventually fit in with these aging adolescents.[50]

Among the many industry people he met at the club was the actor William Russell. Russell was part of Fox's impressive array of cowboy stars. Although largely forgotten today, he once loomed large in a studio stable that also included Tom Mix and Dustin Farnum. According to Zanuck, it was Russell's support that enabled him to sell (for $525) his first story to Sol Wurtzel, then head of production at Fox.[51] Zanuck also eagerly sought the advice of the physically prepossessing writer Wilson Mizner, best recalled as the man who coined the phrase "Never give a sucker an even break." Zanuck's son, Richard, later described how his father was "fascinated by Mizner and his storytelling ability. Apparently they used to sit around, like [the Algonquin] Round Table, and Wilson would pontificate these incredible stories. . . . [Zanuck] was soaking it all in."[52]

Many of his respected elders at the club advised him that, instead of writing short stories, he would be better off adapting work from other media or writing a book. Undaunted by this challenge, Zanuck altered his course on the advice of his mentors.

THE STORM

In late 1921, on a trip to New York, Zanuck saw Langdon McCormick's hit play, *Men Without Skirts,* and became convinced that it was the vehicle he needed to be accepted as a serious writer. Like the work of his most admired role model, O. Henry, the play embodied a balance of several qualities Zanuck would turn to for the rest of his career: clearly delineated (even caricatured) characters and heavy emphasis on story and action, rather than character psychology and dialogue, with unexpected plot twists building to a "socko" finish. It also relied on conspicuously spotlighted production values that went into creating a certain kind of spectacle. When it reached the screen *Men Without Skirts* would be renamed *The Storm,* and its mix of romance, spectacle, and action would establish Zanuck's style. In the decades to come, moviegoers would be enthralled by his floods, fist-fights, locust attacks, big musical numbers, fires, mine cave-ins, invasions, typhoons, and shipwrecks.

The story involves a love triangle—soon to become a Zanuck staple—consisting of an earnest woodsman, a man from the city, and a French girl, trapped together in a remote, snowed-in cabin. The tension between the two men for the hand of the girl is upstaged when they are all threatened by a massive forest fire, the spectacular occurrence that is really the centerpiece of the drama. Like "The Johnstown Flood" and "Fighting the Flames," earlier popular exhibits at New York's Coney Island, which drew large crowds with their realistic re-creations of natural disasters, Zanuck knew such pyrotechnics held great fascination for American audiences.

Somehow he was able to convince the playwright's agent to give him a free sixty-five-day option for movie rights. He then approached Lucien Hubbard, the story editor at Universal, and energetically pitched the plot to him. Zanuck gave notoriously mesmerizing pitches. He was wildly energetic and spontaneous as he tried out different ideas. Although we have no descriptions of the techniques he used to pitch *The Storm*, a number of colleagues who worked with him shortly after this time recorded the amazing impression he made at these story conferences. Milton Sperling, applying for a secretary's position at Warner Brothers, recalls his first meeting with Zanuck at a story conference for *The Public Enemy*. Zanuck was by then production head of the entire studio, and Sperling had unwittingly walked in just as Zanuck was trying to show James Cagney how a gangster shoots a rival:

> At the far end [of Zanuck's office] was a desk, and seated against the walls, like in a ballroom, were Jimmy Cagney, producer Hal Wallis, and four other guys I surmised to be writers. They were staring at an empty desk. . . . Suddenly, Darryl Zanuck popped up from behind the desk, aimed a polo mallet at me, and went, "Rat-tat-tat-tat-tat . . . " like the stick was a Tommy gun. I stood there bewildered.
>
> "Fall down, you son-of-a-bitch, you're dead!" Zanuck screamed. . . . The next thing I saw was a pair of polished shoes near

my face and heard Zanuck's voice say, "Good work, kid, you can get up now."[53]

No part was beyond his enthusiasm, and Zanuck even convincingly acted the part of Rin Tin Tin! A reporter for *Time* magazine observed Zanuck in action a quarter of a century later, still acting out all the roles at a story conference:

> [T]he bristle mustache suddenly twitches, and the face looks heavenward in horror. The jaw sags until the huge cigar droops from his lower lip like a wet sheet hanging from a tenement window. He leans back across the grand piano in his office. His voice becomes shrill and frightened. This is Zanuck impersonating a virgin in distress.[54]

But way back when he was making his very first pitch, he needed the approval of the studio's young boss, Irving Thalberg, for the $15,000 price he was demanding for the rights to the play and his rough scenario of it. It is tempting to imagine the first meeting of Zanuck and Thalberg in 1921, the icy boy genius confronting his very different, but equally talented, reflection. It is unclear, however, whether Zanuck and Thalberg actually met face to face during these negotiations. Whether accomplished directly or through intermediaries, Zanuck gave Universal a major film. (The actual scenario was written by J. G. Hawks.)

He felt his sale of *The Storm* would secure his movie-writing career. He was wrong. As Mel Gussow succinctly characterized this period of Zanuck's life, "almost from the beginning Zanuck was interested in Hollywood and Hollywood wasn't interested in him."[55]

HABIT

If adapting a large-scale work was not sufficient for Zanuck to enter the ranks of the prestige writer, he would take the next logical step. He would write a book, an action-packed and eminently entertaining one. He dashed off a trio of stories, reworked an earlier story, and arranged to have them printed. Lacking the money to pay the printing bill for the sample copies, Zanuck approached his old Yuccatone sponsor, A. F. Foster, and proposed an arrangement: If, as part of a larger work, he would write a long story about Yuccatone (the putative hair restorative), would Foster pay for the publication of Zanuck's work? With Foster's backing, in 1923 the literary world was treated to the debut of Darryl F. Zanuck's "novel," *Habit: A Thrilling Yarn That Starts Where Fiction Ends and Life Begins.*

The three original tales were titled "Habit," "The Scarlet Ladder," and "Say It with Dreams" (later sold to Universal). The book's longest section was "The Forgotten City"—the Yuccatone testimonial.[56] All four stories are overwritten, as the opening paragraph of "Habit" shows:

> Ling Foo Gow riveted his jet orbs on the burly figure that advanced on the narrow sidewalk of cracked asphalt, and with an excessive display of facial contortion, brought the aged lines of his poppy-hued countenance to an intensified scowl. His lean bony fingers with their three inch ceremonial nails, clenched fiercely about the handle of the bamboo basket they held, and tiny beads of perspiration glistened beneath the coiled wad of oily black hair that was his queue.[57]

The stories are highly visual, filled with the gestures of cinema—from little close-ups to the segues of a moving camera. All the settings and structures Zanuck would later use in films are found in these stories, and so are the characteristic "types" with which he would cast his films. For example, "Habit" tells us what "rooting interest" motivates protagonist Ling Foo Gow, namely, that force that stabilizes almost all Hollywood film—heterosexual love (here, Ling Foo's for "the gorgeous Mell Wing"). And after a rhapsodic description of Mell's beauty, the reader is told what makes Ling Foo tick: "his passionate respect for her [Mell Wing], which almost rivalled his inbred desire for poppy juice, and his loathing for Bull Lung were the two predominant thoughts of the very few that functioned in his mind. With him they were an obsession. The lofty pinnacle and the dire abyss of his very existence."[58]

Habit was reviewed in the *New York Times,* and the anonymous reader focused on the book's two overwhelming qualities: its energy and the author's fecundity in imagining plots:

> Apparently when Mr. Zanuck sits down to write, he takes all the harness off his imagination and gets off at a gallop without bridle, halter or bit. . . . If he were as skilled in the writing of fiction as he is ingenious in the imagining of it, and as versed in the use of the English language as he is resourceful in fancy, the author could probably look forward to a successful career as a novelist. But, even though they lack some of the essential qualities of good writing, his stories afford much entertainment.[59]

With *Habit,* Zanuck had bridged the gap between Hollywood's two writer communities and positioned himself as a marketable commodity, a novelist. Now his past careers started to pay off, for while touring drugstores and county fairs pitching Yuccatone, Zanuck had learned a thing or two about sales and publicity. Anticipating publicity gestures that would become common in ten years, Zanuck sent the movie studios engraved cards announcing the publication of his novel. This act echoed the genteel custom of leaving calling cards, while at the same time borrowing the vaudevillian's loud clarion call of self-promotion. It got him noticed—and respected. Zanuck, nearly twenty-one, seemed poised to enter a film industry only slightly older than he.

POISED, WITH A DOG

At the time of Zanuck's first, fortuitous encounter with Jack Warner in 1924, he had been knocking about Hollywood for nearly five years. Arriving with no film experience, he served a diverse apprenticeship. First, he succeeded in getting his pulp fiction published. This enabled him to start pretty much at the bottom of the writing hierarchy, as a gag writer for the tightfisted Mack Sennett. In 1922 and 1923 his sales of screenplays to established major companies were sporadic, but soon became regular. Financially secure through his serial work at F.B.O., he made what he read as the next move dictated by the culture of Hollywood: he wrote a book in a town where this was becoming the screenwriter's necessary card of identity.

It seemed possible that Zanuck's developing skill could be molded into writing, producing, or even directing.[60] Because he had yet to demonstrate that he could create "quality" product, it was unlikely that the crucible for Zanuck's development would be one of the industry giants—Paramount, First National, Fox, MGM, or Universal. But, as befitting his brazen attitude, Zanuck wound up at an ambitious, competitive risk-taking operation: Warner Brothers. In an expanding economy, Warner Brothers was a corporation committed to moving forward and had just begun an attempt to catch up to the industry leaders. The studio was badly in need of a film series that could be made cheaply, while turning a huge profit, and a person to manage its facilities and give its films a definable character. There were hints that Harry Warner's strategy to expand the corporation's operations on all fronts was starting to succeed, but the studio lacked the leadership in production to make this transformation complete.

The union of the two—the Warners and Zanuck—was so likely given their natures and the other possibilities open to him that it appears almost fated, teleological. The two case histories—Zanuck's and the Warner's studio—recapitulated many of the significant transformations in the film industry at this moment: changes caused by the rise of the feature; the organization of Scenario Departments and the location of the two writers' cultures; the decline of the director and the star as authors, and the coalescing job and authority of the producer; the producer's and screenwriter's interactions over issues of authorship. Although he could not have known it, the very things that had stalled his rise as a writer—his eighth-grade education and his taste for the tabloid and pulp fiction, rather than the more genteel classics or best-sellers—would be enormous benefits for a producer at a small company looking to differentiate its image by establishing an inexpensively produced, reliable program of modest releases, while tapping into new and unexploited audience tastes. What they needed was what L. B. Mayer had with Irving Thalberg at MGM: an impresario to pull all the parts together.

Zanuck would shortly join other media figures of this era, like David Sarnoff in radio and Walter Winchell in journalism, who seemingly appeared from nowhere and, with little visible training, rose to eminence because they displayed an uncanny sensitivity to what the public liked. The catalyst would be a most unlikely star. Rin Tin Tin, a canine found in the German trenches during World War I. Brought to the United States by his owner-trainer after the war, the owner and his dog had been hanging around the vaudeville circuit, but the talented dog had not made a great impact. As far as animal acts of the day went, it was a good one: Rin Tin Tin (nicknamed "Rinty" by his trainer) could count to ten with his paws and could "pick up a coin with his nose, and deposit it in a cup."[61] The act was remembered, but the performer was not recalled as truly stellar in the way the best-known animal acts, like Fink's Mules, were. Before hooking up with Darryl Zanuck, Rinty had failed to make much of an impression in vaudeville or in his first film, *The Man from Hell's River.*

That a dog would mark the turning point in Zanuck's career with the Warners seemed so unlikely as to be almost surreal. Certainly the Warners' previous experience with animal acts had not been pleasant. Their only film of 1920 had been a fifteen-part serial called *A Dangerous Adventure.* Hoping to save money on actors' salaries, they concocted an animal-centered plot involving lost treasure in Africa. With Jack and Sam Warner directing, they staffed their film with a second-rate traveling circus. But things did not go well: an elephant destroyed several sets and, disregarding Hollywood's pecking order, a rogue chimpanzee attacked Jack Warner.[62] Nevertheless, in 1923, Jack Warner signed the dog up and scored a hit with him in *Where the North Begins.*

Where others saw, at best, an amusing parlor show, Zanuck saw a different set of potentials. Like all great architects or impresarios, he extrapolated beyond a single case, a single unit to envision where something might fit into a larger structure. He saw a chance to test his skills as a writer within the possibilities of the system. Where others had scored some success, by envisioning a new set of permutations, Zanuck would increase this many times over by refracting the image of what "dog" meant through the lens and menu of what he knew, from his constant writing, from what was possible under the system. Zanuck would make the dog a star not by teaching him new tricks (which is what you would do on the live stage), but by creating his meaning through strictly cinematic means, by animating an identity for an almost neutral performer, that is to say, an actor with little personality. Like a scientist attempting to get the highest yield from his experiment, he manipulated Rinty's plots in the laboratory of the studio.[63] The dog's success would thus depend less on what others objectively gauged about the level of the dog's talent, and more on how inventive Zanuck and his experiments could be in mounting a narrative frame to create for the dog a "star personality" that Americans would find appealing.

Zanuck made Rin Tin Tin into a full-fledged star, a figure Jack Warner recalled as "the only leading man in our company history . . . who had no flaws whatsoever, and never gave a bad performance."[64] Soon Rinty's perks on the set included a nightly chateaubriand steak, an orchestra to play mood music, and a gem-encrusted collar. In figuring out the wildly successful formula for what would turn out to be almost twenty films, Zanuck secured both his own career and the financial stability of the overextended studio that had taken a chance on him. Because his films kept so many theater owners out of hock, a grateful Jack Warner claimed his exhibitors referred to the dog as "the mortgage lifter."[65] At Warner Brothers, behind the dour face and sometimes paranoid musings of senior partner Harry and the deceptive badinage and buffoonery of West Coast head Jack, there would be unique opportunities for Zanuck. As his initial foray with Rin Tin Tin demonstrated, the renegade company that many looked down on as crude and small time could provide him opportunities to test his ambitions in ways that the more established and staid concerns, desperate for an imprimatur of cultural respectability, might not offer. At Warner Brothers, confronted with the test of creating an impression out of the tabula rasa of a dog's "personality," he succeeded, and in so doing, finally saw the chrysalis of his own career opening up. With Rin Tin Tin, Warner Brothers had their first real star. With Zanuck, they had a good deal more.

Chapter Three

"THE HARDEST-WORKING LITTLE GUY"

ZANUCK AT WARNER BROTHERS

I was as fond of him as a director can be fond of a producer. I admired him for his guts . . . [and for] generating the speed and enthusiasm all down the line to make a good picture quickly—at that he was a master, and the hardest-working little guy you have ever seen in all your life.

—WILLIAM WELLMAN

I N PREPARING to work for Warner Brothers, Zanuck was about to enter a world of corporate maneuvering and interpersonal melo-drama. The key to understanding the Warners was knowing how hard it had been for them to deal with the enormous financial success and cultural power that suddenly came their way. For generations, the family had lived an existence of minimal expectations as Jews in anti-Semitic prerevolutionary Russia. Its members had learned to fight hard, internalizing an aggressiveness they desperately needed to survive in Russia and then to adapt to life as immigrants in America. Even when they had amassed wealth and influence beyond anything they could have imagined, the Warners still saw themselves as unwanted outsiders who had to struggle for everything, and whose security could be snatched away by hostile forces.

The Warners were a tight-knit family. After settling in Baltimore, then Ontario (where Jack was born), the family moved to the tough industrial city of Youngstown, Ohio. Here, the nine children and two adults lived in four rooms above a store, "jammed," Jack Warner recalled, "like bait worms in a can." The family members all helped to operate a combination general grocery store, shoe repair, and butcher shop. Jack recalled sleeping near a mound of animal hides destined for shoe repair, overwhelmed by the pungent smell of "great slabs of leather piled up in one corner of the room, most of them fresh from the tannery."[1] The brothers rose from nickelodeon owners to moguls over a twenty-year period, from their first acquisition of a storefront theater in Youngstown in 1904, to the incorporation of their organization in 1923. Their hard fight to the top left them with a general mistrust of everyone and the belief that only family could be relied upon. In time, the mistrust would win out, overpowering even their strong family ties.

The four brothers, Harry, Sam, Albert, and Jack—but particularly the eldest, Harry, and the youngest, Jack—seemed habitually engaged in complicated family struggles. (A fifth brother, David, was in poor health and ran a film exchange in Ohio. The women in the family—the sisters, wives, daughters, and daughters-in-law—had nothing to do with the film business. They were viewed by the brothers merely as extensions of their own glory, or as doleful pensioneers who were the responsibility of their dominant male relatives, particularly Harry.) Albert was the company treasurer and ran its important distribution arm. He was described by Milton Sperling (who married Harry's youngest daughter, Betty) as "massive, genial, down-to-earth," a person with "no enemies." Albert, a quiet, unassuming, low-profile figure, ignored the limelight and kept to his accounting books and the racing form. Sam, who played a key role convincing his brothers to invest their future in sound film, was sunny, outgoing, and good-natured, the one brother who got along with all the other brothers—and the three sisters. He was "Jack's comrade in arms . . . the one who held the balance of power in the fractious Warner family by managing to be Jack's ally without being Harry's enemy."[2]

The major policy decisions were made by Harry and Jack. They disagreed on almost everything, from lifestyle (Jack's was grand, Harry's simple) to commitments to their Jewish heritage (Harry was, if not religious, at least observant of many of the Jewish customs, while Jack ignored almost all of them). Jack was an outgoing practical joker and a compulsive storyteller. Some found his manner buffoon-ish. (A frustrated vaudevillian, he had appeared, under the name Leon Zuardo, as a singer on the initial broadcast of the Warner-owned radio station KFWB.) One of Harry's greatest assets was the widespread perception held of him as being moral. Such a stance was made easy when his behavior was compared to Jack's. Jack had com-mitted a long list of ethical breaches, and, with his weird sense of so-cial decorum, had a seemingly endless penchant for outrageous gaffes. At a studio luncheon, Jack told Albert Einstein that he knew little of his theory of relativity but that "I have a theory about rela-tives, too—don't hire them." And he once addressed a banquet of predominantly Asian guests assembled to honor Madame Chiang Kai-shek with this badly misjudged one-liner: "Holy cow. I forgot to pick up my laundry."[3] (Despite his buffoonish ways, Douglas Fair-banks once likened Jack's personality to that of "a sinister clown.") Harry was sober and conservative, while Jack was mustachioed, un-abashedly vulgar, perpetually suntanned, and flamboyant. Harry ac-tively believed his role as the family patriarch, securing this domination through physical intimidation combined with an Old World sense of moral exactitude utterly lacking in his youngest brother, Jack.

Jack spoke to one very basic difference beyond the tensions one might attribute to sibling birth order: Harry was Old World, while Jack resolutely relished the taboos he could breach in the New World. (Harry once chased Jack around the studio with a lead pipe, threatening to kill him: when the opportunity for revenge presented itself, Jack returned the favor by double crossing his brother in a stock transaction.)

But Harry, the eldest son, was the undisputed head of the family and the president of the corporation. He outranked Jack, head of production, two times over.

The brothers would drop their feud when an outsider threatened their dominance or the established power order at the studio. No matter how much Jack admired Zanuck's, or anybody's, gifts, he and his brothers would not cede too much power to anyone outside the family. If other rough-hewn moguls—notably, Columbia's difficult Harry Cohn—could accommodate the Hollywood power structure by giving in to its artistic credos (and then waging other wars privately), the Warners and their films never really lost their paranoid edge, with each other or with outsiders. Their suspicion and mistrust of their "elders" were mirrored in how the rest of Hollywood saw them: as raw, uncouth, even a bit embarrassing. *Anything* might be expected from this crew.

This distinction between the Warners and the rest of the moguls is recalled in a vivid childhood memory by Betty Lasky, daughter of Paramount founder Jesse Lasky. Raised in an environment utterly unlike the Warners' impoverished shtetl, one suffused with Jewish-German *kultur*, Lasky recalls the powerful impression these largely unreconstructed figures made on her: "I remember being struck with them. They were very animalistic types. I wasn't used to types like that—ghetto types. It was their appearance. They were so ugly looking but so ghetto ugly. . . . It was like a child going to the circus and looking at a freak."[4]

RIN TIN TIN

In April 1924 the director Mal St. Clair introduced Zanuck to Jack Warner in a restaurant. Jack was immediately struck by two aspects of his future employee: his abundant energy and his extreme youth. (Looking at the twenty-one-year-old man who claimed to be a

screenwriter, Jack wondered, "What does he write . . . Pablum testi-
monials?")[5] Over dinner Zanuck brashly promised Jack that, with
no preparation, he was certain he could write a script for a Warner's
actor said to be in need of a good property. Four days after the
meeting at the restaurant, the young Nebraskan came to the
Warner's studio to pitch his completed scenario for a Rin Tin Tin
vehicle. Assisted by St. Clair, Zanuck acted out, complete with a nuance of barks, the various parts in the story. In less than a month he
had completed the first draft of "My Buddy: The Story of a Dough
Boy and His Dog."

Like all of Zanuck's stories before being translated into silent film,
the scenario for "My Buddy" is breathlessly overwritten. In retro-
spect, the film eventually made from it contains many of the qualities
associated both with Zanuck the writer and Zanuck the producer.
We have our rooting interests fixed early on, learning immediately of
the sterling character of dog and man. "My Buddy" (the title evokes a
song popular with World War I doughboys) opens in the trenches of
Belgium where Paul Andrews, about to go into battle with his faithful
German shepherd, looks at a photo of the girl he left behind, Caroline. The hungry soldier offers his doughnut to his equally famished
animal companion. When the dog refuses the treat, Paul realizes the
splendid creature will eat the morsel only if they share it equally.

Paul is seriously wounded during the battle. Reaching one last
time for his canteen, he passes out and does not see that an enemy
tank is approaching.

But if the advancing Germans are about to add Paul's lifeless form
to their list of war dead, they had not figured on the presence of
Buddy:

> as the lead-spouting beast draws nearer and nearer out of the mire
> comes a flash of bristly fur—Rin Tin Tin, alert and eager, spots his
> wounded buddy—locking his teeth in Paul's jacket, he claws and
> digs with every ounce of his energy as the tank crushes down almost
> upon them—willing to do or die at his post of duty, the dog forsakes
> all personal danger as he valiantly jerks and pulls and digs to drag his
> comrade from a ghastly death.[6]

Before he is finished, the dog not only rescues Paul from a train wreck but succeeds in reuniting him with Caroline. She declares, "If I can only be as good a wife to you as Rin Tin Tin is a dog, we'll be happy." Like "For Men Only," his first attempt at movie writing, this story closes with a tag line of dialogue Zanuck was certain would serve as a catchy film title. Taking Caroline in his arms, Paul replies, "He's more than a dog to me, darling. He's my buddy."[7] The story ends with the happy couple rowing in a boat, followed by the now mated Rin Tin Tin and his offspring.[8]

The final script, renamed *Find Your Man,* compresses much of Zanuck's overwrought prose into concise economic visuals and a tight, action-packed narrative. As in all of Zanuck's early work, pacing is of supreme importance: this film never stops moving. In addition to scenes that take us from Belgium, to the East Coast of the United States, and then to the American West, the script contains two parallel journeys: Paul's search for Caroline and his attempt to win her back; and Buddy's vigil to protect Paul from a series of villains. After a high-speed train wreck, a murder or two, and pursuit through the woods, *Find Your Man* ends with one of Zanuck's (and Hollywood's) favorite devices, a trial. The villain of the film has framed Paul for a murder he himself has committed. All seems lost until, as in the world created by Zanuck's idol, O. Henry, there is a dramatic twist at the end. Paul's life is saved by the surprising appearance of a star witness: Rin Tin Tin.

Although Rin Tin Tin would be the first in a long line of actors whose reputations Zanuck would build, at this point the dog (or *dogs,* for there were, according to whose account one believes, seven or eighteen different German shepherds portraying the canine hero) was not yet a star. As a point of entry into Hollywood, Zanuck's choice of a talented canine might be viewed as a bit eccentric. But, with a few memorable exceptions, the strength of Zanuck the silent film writer was never his mastery of dialogue. (Rather, writing for silent movies meant mostly that a writer needed the ability to translate a story into concise outlines and highly descriptive summations of plots. Based upon these materials, a producer was able to envision the film.)

Once a story outline or synopsis had been approved, the actual screenwriting was limited to brief descriptions of each shot's action, the setting, and the information, asides, cast assignments, and dialogue contained on intertitle cards. Dialogue, or *intertitles,* was reduced to one-liners. Part of the attraction of writing for Rin Tin Tin might have been that all his films were action adventures that had to be shot largely outdoors, where Zanuck felt utterly at home. In addition, the dog's linguistic limitation may have been a plus for the action-oriented writer. Whatever Zanuck's motivation, his work sold Jack and Harry on the story and its author. As far as Jack Warner was concerned, the proposed film "had a professional polish and a stirring North Woods theme custom-made for Rin Tin Tin." Neither the director nor the writer "realized how good it [the scenario] was."[9] Zanuck and St. Clair needn't have bothered with their hard-sell performance in his office. Under Zanuck's guidance, Rinty was a gold mine. The dog was soon earning at least six times the weekly salary of the film's lead.[10]

CHANGING WARNER'S IMAGE

With the success of Zanuck's first two Rin Tin Tin films, *Find Your Man* and *Lighthouse by the Sea,* Warner Brothers could use the profits to support more expensive and less formulaic, more risky high-profile films. Surveying what other companies were turning out, Harry Warner must have realized that if he wanted to keep pace with the competition, pure profit from unimaginative programmers would not be enough; he would need a few prestige pictures—proof that in addition to business skill and the ability to plug into popular tastes, the Warner studio also took seriously film's charter to uplift public culture. Observing Thalberg's efforts at MGM, and in imitation of similar moves by Goldwyn Studios and Paramount, the Warners decided it was time to test the waters of refinement. Harry announced the studio's intention to compete in this rarefied market, and the result was Warner's Classics of the Screen.

The first two films testing this new policy were David Belasco's production of Avery Hopwood's stage hit, *The Gold Diggers,* and a version of Sinclair Lewis's *Main Street.* The *Los Angeles Times* said of the former: "The effect of Mr. Belasco's allying himself with the silent drama will be profound among producers of motion pictures. The magic of 'David Belasco Presents' flickering in a motion picture title is expected to pave the way to greater and better things in the industry."[11]

In addition to the start of the studio's literary ambitions, Zanuck's first year with Warner Brothers also witnessed Broadway idol John Barrymore's Warner Brothers debut. Barrymore had first gone before the cameras in 1913 and, prior to signing with the Warners, had attained a success in film almost equal to what he had achieved in his celebrated, but rather uneven, stage work. Relying on his reputation as a romantic lead, the Warners typecast him in a costume epic. It was a genre he hated, but one to which he was constantly redirected. His foul-mouthed ad-libs were embarrassingly readable, and moviegoers wrote the studio in protest.[12] Despite the negative opinions of a few skilled lip readers, Barrymore's hugely successful *Beau Brummel* earned its star an outrageous contract, better even than that offered his only studio rivals, Rin Tin Tin and star director Ernst Lubitsch, who had arrived a year before Zanuck. The frugal Warners must have swallowed hard when they agreed to the actor's conditions for a three-picture deal: $76,250 per film (plus additional monies should the shoot go over six weeks); leading-lady approval; and a chauffeur-driven limousine. Barrymore was to have a four-room suite at the posh Ambassador Hotel, and all dinner tabs (including illicit drink) were to be picked up by the studio.

With the luster added by the Classics of the Screen and the acquisition of Barrymore, the Warners cemented their transformation and their carefully charted plan of expansion with another, very different, addition. In addition, in August 1923 they had signed the great German director Ernst Lubitsch, and his first offering, *Three Women,* showcased the sophisticated social commentary for which he was already famous.

THE INDISPENSABLE ZANUCK

By 1925, a year after he had first met Jack Warner, Zanuck was the studio's most prolific writer. That year, Warner Brothers produced thirty films, and Zanuck had a hand in eight of them. Movies made from Zanuck's scripts, stories, and adaptations were filling the Warner's treasury with profits. Jack was amazed at his new employee, marveling at his speed, his imagination, and his productivity. The young writer was exposed to a variety of directors. He worked with George Hill on *The Limited Mail*. He also got to work with his first prestige director by observing the great Ernst Lubitsch in action.

Over the next six years, more than thirty Zanuck plots (including adaptations) were also floated under the shelter of three pseudonyms: Gregory Rogers, Melville Crossman, and Mark Canfield. His real name appeared only with prestige productions. Gregory Rogers (whose specialty was comedy) made his debut in 1925 with *Red Hot Tires*. Rogers's comic persona was balanced by the "high" identity of Melville Crossman, who followed in 1927 (with *Irish Hearts*). The same year, Zanuck hid behind the melodramatic expertise of Mark Canfield (*The Desired Woman*). Sometimes two pseudonyms would share credit on a film: Zanuck's scenarios for *Three Weeks in Paris* and *Hogan's Alley* were both based on stories supplied by the obliging Gregory Rogers.

At first, Zanuck may have used the raft of names because he imagined this was what "real" writers did, but later he needed the pseudonyms because of sheer output. Exhibitors wondered why Jack Warner was spending so much money on stories and screenplays when he seemed to have only one writer. Zanuck even toyed with the idea of using a female pseudonym, and his long, three-part scenario "Beyond the Valley of Reason" is "admiringly dedicated to Geraldine Regardo—which is a *nom de plume* of my own creation that I seriously considered attaching to this narrative—and which this dedication serves as a simple contrivance to pet my vanity."[13] At one point, Zanuck recalled, outside of those in the know on the Warner Brothers lot, Melville Crossman had become one of the most sought-after writers in Hollywood, eagerly courted by MGM and other studios.[14] Remarkably, Zanuck's productivity as a screenwriter soared even as he started to take on more and more supervisory duties. Slowly, screenwriter Zanuck was becoming film executive Zanuck.

FAMILY TIES AND SPLIT IDENTITIES: SEARCHING FOR A CREATIVE SUPERVISOR

Zanuck soon became a familiar figure on the Warner's lot. As his boundless energy found outlets in the growing studio's different departments, he gradually absorbed all facets of moviemaking. Such all-around experience would not be as easy to pick up a decade down the road, when, along with the studios themselves, unions and guilds created formally recognized divisions of production. Because of this organizational fluidity, because in their expansion the brothers needed someone who could do it all, there were few impediments to satisfying Zanuck's wide-ranging curiosity about filmmaking. Although he kept his distance from the director's chair, through observation and participation he functioned at various times as writer, editor, supervisor, and talent scout.

He was particularly intrigued with editing, admitting that he "practically lived in the cutting room."[15] It paid off. While people would always remain divided about his other filmmaking gifts, almost everyone in Hollywood was in accord that Zanuck's editorial abilities were matchless. William Reynolds, the two-time Academy Award–winning editor, recalls Zanuck's skill in the cutting room: "He was really quite phenomenal. He could go through the whole picture . . . [and point out] details of various kinds of structural problems. And he could always do that in great detail . . . just after one screening."[16]

Although he never claimed to be a great writer himself, his editorial abilities with scripts were equal to his skills in the cutting room. Nearly every important writer with whom Zanuck worked, both those whose careers were centered almost entirely about Hollywood and those outside the movies (like John Steinbeck), praised his story sense and his uncanny skill at structuring a successful film continuity—a script that specifically translates a narrative into cinematic terms. (Some felt in his haste to get things going, Zanuck could *only* tell a story in one tempo: *presto*.) Screenwriter Nunnally Johnson talked of his "radar" for bad writing or a weak story, noting that "he was a collaborator on anything I ever did. Every script I wrote was improved by his editing."[17] The skills he concentrated on in these formative years editing and title writing (which could range from simple dialogue to rather complicated, even poetic, commentary) were among the most important in mastering the structural foundation of silent films.

Zanuck was able to climb the ranks in a family-dominated business because he so easily mastered the many parts of studio production. But his rise was also made possible by the increased demands placed upon Jack's time by the full-throttled expansion the Warners were going through during this period. Jack, as the West Coast brother in charge of production, was called upon to be more an administrator than a producer. Although immersed in shaping the studio's program (through contractual negotiations over personnel and properties), Jack was never really a hands-on creative type. In the studio's early years, with its relatively small output, Jack had been assisted in running production by studio managers like writer Raymond Schrock or Al Rocket, both of whom, while fully capable of keeping track of the mechanics of production, were utterly unimaginative when it came to actually thinking about the quality or originality of the films they were supervising. With the expansion Harry undertook from 1923 on (under the guiding genius of financial advisor Waddill Catchings), the Warners were critically short in one area: they badly needed a production expert, for as one writer rather indelicately noted, "the Warners ditched general managers more often than banana republics overturned governments."[18] Jack was searching for a man who would run the production side with both business acumen and a creative mind for story without possessing any of the leverage that came with owning the company. His solution was Zanuck, whose extraordinary drive and ability extended beyond his growing pile of movie scripts so that it now encompassed a broad and expanding range of supervisory duties as well.

Zanuck's rise at Warner's occurred in stages, all built on the foothold he was able to get because of his enormous worth as a writer. It had soon become apparent that he could write original material as well as adapt scenarios from a wide variety of work. But Zanuck's real value lay in a simple, measurable fact: all of his films made money. His track record suggested that he had a kind of writing radar utterly in sync with the audience's tastes, so the Warners started to listen to the opinions of this twenty-five-year-old. Before producers were officially recognized with that title, and to the chagrin of some older directors, the Warners let Zanuck supervise more and more of their films. By 1926, the year of Ernst Lubitsch's departure, they had come to depend on his output to float the studio, and this provided Zanuck with the leverage to be involved in more and more serious decision making. His curiosity was aroused by the challenge of orchestrating *all* the parts of the studio, not just the writing. No one would have predicted it in 1926, but Zanuck had only three or four years left to his career as a screenwriter. No single role would ever again hold his attention as had screenwriting in this period.

Since the title of "producer" did not become common usage until 1932, early film supervisors were not given screen credit, and it is therefore difficult to say definitively who produced what before 1932. Because of this, it is difficult to ascertain when Zanuck was given a certain rank at Warner's, and sources differ as to the dates at which his two elevations—to head of Warner's production, then to head of both Warner's and First National—happened.[19] In 1927, Jack Warner (now a friend and a sort of mentor) surprised him by casually telling him of a change at the studio. The studio manager Raymond Schrock (who, like Zanuck, had started out as a screenwriter) was out as head of production and the twenty-five-year-old Zanuck was in. Zanuck told Gussow he was so excited that he "nearly wet my pants." His average budget per film for his "programmers" would be $65,000, a very low figure even by the standards of the parsimonious Warners.[20] Jack gave Zanuck one bit of advice: "Even if you don't need glasses, get some window panes and grow a mustache. It'll give you a little age."[21]

Officially, his title was executive producer, at a salary alleged to be $1,000 per week.[22] In essence, since they formed the bulk of the studio's output, this meant he was given charge of what brought the studio its largest profits: the programmers. But the boundaries of his duties were, from the first, rather fluid. Further, Zanuck demonstrated that budget alone—typically the gauge used to measure a film's prestige—could not hold him back: some of his most important projects cost less than half of what MGM spent on their *average* feature. Soon he was also involved with expensive and prestigious fare, both writing and overseeing the Sydney Chaplin comedy hit *The Better 'Ole.* Zanuck's production was deemed "a comedy classic" by the *New York Tribune,* and its placement on many ten-best lists was a refreshing experience for the studio. *Moving Picture World* referred to him as "first lieutenant to Jack Warner, studio chieftain."[23]

Beyond the peculiar kind of catechism Zanuck absorbed by working with Harry and Jack, he was able to pick up a diverse education from the odd array of men who occupied the director's chair on the Warner lot. Zanuck learned much in the company of Warner's directors, all older than he. Each of these men would create distinctive profiles at Warner's and other studios, and would go on to long, successful careers in Hollywood. From "Wild Bill" Wellman, he absorbed variations on, and more subtle forms of, what he already knew: the contours of the action film and the essence of melodrama. Their partnership, tested in early fare like *Maybe It's Love* (1930), would coalesce most memorably in *The Public Enemy* (1931).

Europeans Ernst Lubitsch, William Dieterle, and Michael Curtiz each in his own way made Zanuck aware of the world of subtlety and visual nuance in film, valuable additions to Zanuck's previously action-oriented world. Curtiz, a colorful Hungarian with a Goldwynesque penchant for exhibiting creative uses of English, was a pioneer in using the moving camera. His work made Zanuck conscious of how, in addition to action seen on the screen, the sense of movement created by a mobile camera could be used to tell a story and define a character. Dieterle was the most self-consciously literate (though hardly the most original) member of the group of directors with whom Zanuck regularly worked. He helped shape Zanuck's notions of how the prestige picture could elevate a studio's image. In particular, his work with biopics also showed Zanuck the kind of partnership history and Hollywood might have. Both the biopic and the historical drama—genres at which Dieterle excelled—would be important (and prestigious) staples at Warner's and, even more significantly, in Zanuck's later career at Fox.

In addition to the craft of moviemaking, the young Zanuck also learned how to deal with the difficult, even eccentric personalities that comprised the roster of personnel working at a studio. Wellman, a French Foreign Legionnaire and a highly decorated World War I flyer, was a tyrant on the set. His drinking and bad temper led to frequent outbursts, and even, on occasions, fistfights (notably with Spencer Tracy, John Wayne, and Zanuck himself). In contrast, Dieterle was genteel. The German émigré always oversaw his actors while wearing white gloves and uttering pronouncements about the nature of film art. Zanuck worked with established figures like Howard Hawks and Mervyn LeRoy (eventually Warner's most powerful director), as well as with reliable journeymen like Archie Mayo, Lloyd Bacon, and Roy Del Ruth. But at this stage it was Ernst Lubitsch—with three men Zanuck would work with later, John Ford, William Wyler, and Henry King—who was the most gifted of all the directors Zanuck encountered. From Lubitsch, Zanuck learned a very valuable lesson: the difference a great director can make to any script.

Zanuck's tutelage under these figures resulted in a good deal of experience with almost every major film genre. It gave him the advantages of a broad, inclusive education in all facets of film production that was rivaled only by the two men with whom he would most frequently be compared: David O. Selznick and Irving Thalberg.

ERNST AND DARRYL: HIGH AND LOW

What Zanuck learned through the almost ritualized creation of a large body of lower-profile films would stand him in good stead when he came to run his own studio. Unfortunately, the combination of his association with "hokum" (his term) and his refusal to adopt a genteel persona when discussing film made it difficult for people to see him as the serious creative force that he was. Additionally, unlike Zanuck's oversight of his programmers, the high-end pictures were the result of a variety of authors—none of whom had Zanuck's wide-ranging knowledge of the studio or his ability to navigate around Jack's or Harry's attempts to interfere with story ideas—so these films did not display the unity (or, later, the iconoclasm) of Zanuck's work. Routine as most of Zanuck's films were, his overview and shaping of their scripts molded what might have been just a loosely related corpus of programmers into the template that would shortly form Warner's master cinematic narrative.

In an era when stars might change, and sound would shortly shake up Hollywood's sense of what constituted the genre film, like the brand name of a product, a studio's house image—that is, the way a producer like Zanuck shaped the body of work so that its profile constituted a definitive corporate "presentation of self"—was its most valued asset. It was becoming problematic that the man who produced Warner's routine films was, by far, the biggest executive and production talent on the lot. If the Warners wished to compete with the unified vision of MGM or the well-oiled machine operating at Paramount, they needed to take a gamble and place Zanuck at the head of the *whole* operation. At one time Jack had floated the idea of hiring C. B. DeMille as production head, away from his producer-director role at Paramount. Dissatisfied with Adolph Zukor's interference over budgets, the great presence was looking for a new home. He possessed Hollywood's most infallible sense of commercial cinema. And he could bring other assets to Warner Brothers. With his impressive family name and his big reputation (and his even larger sense of self-importance), DeMille was a man with one of Hollywood's most carefully polished public images. He was also one of its most self-important figures. A man of so many qualities, in a contest in which the rivalry would surely have been at a level so high that few scales could provide reliable measure, DeMille was a very serious contender for the title of Hollywood's biggest ego. He would not be an easy man to control. Harry, as frugal as he was suspicious, vetoed the idea. The search continued.

In addition to Zanuck, there was one other in-house candidate:

Ernst Lubitsch. Warner's seemed a very unlikely place for this cultivated European, a figure whose unassailable grand reputation for
artistic excellence was accompanied by the legend that he had an
equally large predilection for artistic stubbornness. But in the first
blush of their ambitious expansion, the Warners had been so eager to
hire him that they made an uncharacteristic move they would soon
come to regret. When they courted Lubitsch in 1923, the studio was a
second- or third-rate operation, an outfit whose owners' dreams of
expansion were leavened by the more mundane preoccupations of
survival. In contrast to the studio's rather modest profile, the director
was already a big name. John Ford (considered by many to be the
greatest of all studio-era directors) recollected: "None of us thought
we were making anything but entertainment for the moment. Only
Ernst Lubitsch knew we were making art."[24] Lubitsch did not want to
be in a situation where someone of inferior artistic intelligence could
overrule his judgment. In order to get Lubitsch to sign, the Warners
acceded to his demand of complete control and approval over all
matters related to any film he might direct—with the exception of the
sacred terrain of a film's budget (Harry would *never* cede that to anyone). His contract was a twenty-page document spelling out every
prerogative the director wanted, including the right to decide what to
censor if the demand arose. In a rare miscalculation, the elder Warner
felt that while DeMille was likely to bring them more trouble than the
worth one could ascribe to his films or the value of his name, "Harry
felt they [the Warners] could 'handle' Lubitsch."[25]

While the five foot, six inch German cut a far less prepossessing
figure than the dramatically attired jodhpur-clad DeMille, he had "an
unerring eye for style, from the surface of clothes and manners down
to the most subtle intonation of an aristocrat's heart." As for his own
style, "he was inclined to reach for the handiest pair of trousers and
coat whether they clashed or not."[26] Lubitsch was a modest man, but
a stubborn one—and he was always meticulously prepared. Like his
equals, Alfred Hitchcock or John Ford, Lubitsch carried around in
his head a complete script—both text and visuals—of the picture he
was shooting. A thorough professional, Lubitsch was generally well
liked by his crew and cast. But he did insist on one practice that was

somewhat alien to the hard-driven Americans he worked with: he liked to take a break around teatime. As part of his contract, the Warners had to supply him and his crew with coffee and cakes ordered from a particular caterer. Soon, what might have seemed cultivated and eccentric, a publicist's perfect example of the director's charming European ways, became an irksome extravagance to the Warners. For, while Lubitsch's much-praised films made money, they never made enough money to please Jack. They certainly did not make as much as Zanuck's less exalted fare. Hoping to reassert the upper hand with Lubitsch, Jack canceled the *kaffeeklatsch*. Lubitsch retaliated by sending everyone home and retired to his office to meditate while playing his cello. (He was a self-taught cellist and pianist.) When Jack demanded to know what was going on, Lubitsch looked up from his cello and replied: "No cakes, no coffee—no scene."[27] The coffee break was restored.

There were more serious issues to consider than snacks. Lubitsch's contest with the Warners foregrounded what was surely one of the film culture's great struggles of the decade, the complicated guerrilla warfare fought between different factions (here, directors and executives) over the right to institutionalize and control the powers of authority and authorship. Harry and Jack tried to use their power and authority to dictate the kinds of films Lubitsch should make, and because Lubitsch was a man who "loved ideas more than anything in the world" this threat to what he saw as his sovereign right to manage his authorship was probably the greatest barrier between them.[28] By 1926, from the Warners' point of view it was clear that Lubitsch was not only the wrong man to run the studio; it was becoming increasingly obvious that the two factions could not peacefully coexist under the same corporate shelter for much longer. Although under the terms of his contract he still owed them four pictures, both sides began serious negotiations to start the next chapter of life at Warner Brothers without Lubitsch. After both sides engaged in skirmishes to see who might gain some advantage, they came to terms. In a highly unusual deal that enabled Lubitsch to work at two studios, he left the sometimes surreal, low-comedy venue that housed the feuding Warners for the world of high-palace intrigue

waged between Mayer and Thalberg at MGM and the relative placidity of Paramount. Ten years later, he would be given the opportunity
to run Paramount. His short, disastrous tenure there was a clear indication that, ironically, the Warners had in part been right, for the eminent director's administrative grasp never equaled his artistic gifts.

THE WORLD TURNED UPSIDE-DOWN

In addition to the five films he made for the studio, Lubitsch did leave
behind two other legacies. First, he showed Zanuck that visual nuance, the famed Lubitsch touch, was an effective way to get a point
across. At his best, no director in Hollywood could come near Lubitsch's visual inventiveness. His tongue-in-cheek wit (typically,
though not exclusively, focused on sexual relations), "his incisive
pictorial detail, his perfect timing, the nuances of gesture and facial
expression that enabled his performers to reveal in a single brief shot
the psychology of the characters they were playing" added a new
level of knowledge to Zanuck's repertoire.[29] The second part of Lubitsch's legacy was the surprising development of Henry Blanke.
When Lubitsch signed with Warner's, he brought the Berlin-born
Blanke along as his personal assistant. The son of a painter, Blanke
grew up in a world where he was accustomed to placing high importance on visual detail and technique. As he had done at his father's
atelier, he now proved adept at absorbing lessons from "the master,"
and after Lubitsch's departure Blanke briefly went back to Germany
to head the Warner Brothers office there before returning to Hollywood to become one of the most successful producers in the studio's
history.

Last, the great director's departure opened up a different kind of
possibility for Zanuck than that available when the two men worked
together. Though one could not have necessarily predicted it would
happen, cutting his education short did not really rob Zanuck of a future source of wisdom. Rather, Lubitsch's flight actually accelerated
Zanuck's progress as a producer. For, without an in-house expert of
Lubitsch's stature to defer to, without another, perhaps competing,

source of ideas to play off against his own, more and more it was Dar-ryl Zanuck's uncontested vision that became the defining force at the studio.

From 1926 on the pattern is clear. As a writer, he had an enormous output; as a supervisor, he moved into prestige projects; as a scout, he discovered (or at least claims to have) and nurtured the careers of many major talents, among them James Cagney, Bette Davis, and Busby Berkeley. Overseeing the studio program and working with Ernst Lubitsch, William Wellman, Michael Curtiz, and William Dieterle, he became a judge of directors. All this experience and ex-posure, coupled with the studio's technological experiments with sound film (which began in 1925), may have placed Zanuck in a privi-leged position, one that would enable him to take advantage of a once-in-history kind of creative critical mass.

In 1926 Zanuck reigned as head of production at Warner Broth-ers. But things now moved almost at the speed of sound, a pace even Zanuck would find daunting. Within two years, the Warners would buy out rival First National studio and install their former head of publicity, Hal Wallis, at its helm in a very definite number-two posi-tion to Zanuck. Though their carefully planned campaign of corpo-rate expansion (of which sound was but one component) would land them by decade's end where they had always wanted to be, at the top, the situation was ripe for trouble. On what kind of films would the studio's money be spent? How much should be allocated for the bud-gets of the films that comprised the two different tiers? Would one person watch over all Warner Brothers fare, or would the two studios run as related, but separate—and possibly competitive—entities? The answers to these questions would lead to unforeseen, dramatic career changes for Zanuck and the Warners.

The catalyst of the Warners' transformation would be sound film. By the mid-1920s, the visual aesthetics of the silent cinema had reached a peak sound film would not achieve for at least a decade. Silent star Mary Pickford spoke for many viewers when, after sound came, she noted, "It would have been more logical if silent pictures had grown out of the talkie instead of the other way round." As Wal-ter Kerr has suggested, the shrewd Pickford's Zen utterance is really

an acknowledgment that silent cinematic art was not made by a Wag-
nerian *Gesamtkunstwerk* ("total artwork") based on an absorption of
all the senses; instead, at its highest moments it was an art form based
on subtraction, on having less, rather than more, of an appropriation
of selective slices of behavior from the real world.[30] What would
sound do to these formulations? It would not be an easy transition,
and whoever could manage to steer the studio through these unpredictable shoals would emerge with enormous power. Zanuck's dominant creative role in supervising *The Jazz Singer,* the picture that
secured the new sound technology, would establish both the studio
and Zanuck as leaders in the industry.

—

While Zanuck's rapid ascent with the Warners was astounding and
even unprecedented, his private life paralleled the arc of his career: it
was never dull. When Zanuck married and had children of his own,
the family existence turned out to be as unconventional as his own
past. In 1923, on a blind date arranged by his friend, director Mal St.
Clair, he met his future wife, Virginia Fox. Virginia's father was a
comfortable West Virginia beer dealer who also owned a coal mine.
When West Virginia became a dry state in 1914, the Foxes moved to
St. Petersburg, Florida, where her father invested his money in an im-
port-export business. A childhood friend recalls that Virginia
dreamed of being a movie star "right from the very start."[31] She was
certainly pretty enough to attain this aspiration. With her mother
supporting this Hollywood dream, in 1920, shortly after her graduation from an exclusive private girl's school, Virginia and the whole
family drove from Florida to California in Virginia's graduation gift, a
new car, to see if she could follow in the footsteps of Mary Pickford.

Though her career in front of the camera would be short, its brief
duration should not mask a critical fact: Virginia understood Darryl's
grand dreams because, in a sense, they were her own. Against all
odds and with virtually no career preparation to suggest that either of
their fantasies of movie lives might actually happen, both Virginia
Fox and Darryl Zanuck uprooted themselves and placed their faith in
the belief that, while most who tried would fail, they could make it in

Hollywood. Throughout their life together, Virginia supported Darryl's frequent risky flights to some new ambitious perch because she and Darryl were drawn to the movies (and each other) by the lure inherent in taking chances. Unlike her husband's early, frustrating attempts to get into the movies, Virginia's first offer came quickly. Mack Sennett (for whom Zanuck would shortly work) offered her the opportunity to be one of his bathing beauties. This was not the script her parents had imagined, but the plucky Virginia accepted. Virginia would later be characterized by the codes of the culture of Hollywood as the typical, perhaps even the exemplary, Hollywood wife, a creature willing to bury her identity within her husband's glory. Celeste Holm's reaction to seeing a picture of Virginia Zanuck on the mogul's desk was typical, strong and immediate: "I said [to Zanuck], 'Is that your wife?' and he said, 'Yes.' The picture looked as if she was saying, 'Don't hit me!' She looked so pathetic. And so, I knew all about him."[32]

But in many ways, Holm was wrong, for Virginia was almost as fearless as her husband. (In fact, it is possible that merely by marrying Zanuck she proved her courage.) She soon graduated to leads opposite Buster Keaton. An outgoing young woman off screen, she made friends with young actresses destined to become the highest-level female stars, including Ruby Keeler, Colleen Moore, Mary Pickford, and Loretta Young.

When Darryl met Virginia, he was smitten at once. Virginia was not. He laid siege to her with flowers, with phone calls, with copies of his recently published novel, *Habit.* Zanuck liked to live well on his small salary, trying to impress her with extravagant gestures like hiring cars. She soon came to the conclusion that many would come to share of this strange, energetic fellow, Darryl F. Zanuck: "There was never a boring moment."[33] After six months of refusing proposals of marriage from Zanuck, Virginia relented. She and Darryl were married on January 24, 1924. Her parents attended. The Zanucks were absent.

The first year of the marriage was rocky. "I was always going back to my mother," Virginia recalled. Darryl was difficult. He insisted his word was final, and he was capricious. One day he came home and with no prior consultation announced that they were moving to a new house, completely furnished. In addition to his willful and unpredictable gift for caprice, he could also be childish and selfish. On a location trip for a Warner Brothers movie in the mid-1920s, Zanuck stayed out with the boys far past the time he had promised to be back. When he came home, Virginia was expecting him to accompany her to a party. He not only refused to go; he forbade Virginia. She went. When she came home later that evening, she found all her clothes had been slashed. She vowed to divorce him. The next day, a conciliatory Zanuck apologized, promising to reform.[34] Yet, for his difficult ways, the couple was in love. Virginia saw what others would shortly know: "I always had such pride in Darryl. I knew he would be a success."[35] Time would shortly prove that her reputation for shrewd character assessment was not colored by the fact that the subject of her augury was also the man to whom she was married.

It was clear from 1926 on, with his increasing involvement in the total studio output, Zanuck was not only Warner's de facto main producer: he was the font of its creativity and the source of its identity. Soon, Zanuck's dominant creative role in supervising *The Jazz Singer*, the picture that ushered in the new sound technology, would establish both the studio and Zanuck in unassailable positions. The company that had been viewed as a second-tier studio, an outfit some in the industry sneered at as a vulgar, cheap throwback to the nickelodeon days, would form a unique bond with the man who had been, until his arrival there, a second-rate writer. After 1927, along with their company's altered status, both Zanuck and the studio would miraculously acquire new industry identities. The former family of outsiders and the young "hick" arriviste, the vulgarians and the rube, would be seen as contenders for leadership in the industry. The biggest surprise was not that Zanuck had risen so quickly by ably fulfilling the particular demands of the silent cinema; rather, what no one could expect was that with the advent of the very different exigencies that would arise with sound, Zanuck was about to start his greatest and most revolutionary work.

Chapter Four

"THE TALKING THING"

THE SAFE ENTERTAINMENT OF
THE JAZZ SINGER

No story was ever written for the
screen as dramatic as the story of the
screen itself.

—WILL HAYS

OUND DID NOT bring an end to Rin Tin Tin's stardom, but it altered his status. While the dog could do many uncanny things, speaking was beyond even his range. More than the O. Henry twist in the careers of a few famous individuals, the new brand of technology offered by the coming of sound would alter the craft of the actor, the skills of the writer and producer, and, critically, audiences' expectations of what film ought to do now that it could talk. After thirty-two years, the American cinema abandoned the silence that had dominated its world, and Darryl Zanuck would play the commanding role in shaping a standard for how Hollywood would use sound in its films.

In the United States, Fox and Warner Brothers vied to be the first to bring sound film to the American public. But, in addition to developing opposite delivery systems—Fox used a sound on film method, while Warners used sixteen-inch records synchronized mechanically to the film's projector—the two companies also had different visions of how sound should operate in Hollywood. Warner Brothers, in conjunction with Western Electric, developed a sound film system called the Vitaphone, which they did not intend to use to showcase the spoken word but to bring the sound of music to the public. The Vitaphone's noise punctuated a world that had enabled—and encouraged—a special kind of fiction engendered by silence, a creative contract that the era's filmmakers and moviegoers had negotiated over time. In so doing, it put the careers of silent-era screenwriters, like Zanuck, up for renegotiation or cancellation. Only months behind the Warners, in October 1926 the Fox Film Corp. started production of their own short films. William Fox soon discovered that trying to catch up to the Warners and their program of what *Variety* would soon call "canned vaudeville" would not work. By bargaining early with the Victor Talking Machine Company, The Metropolitan Opera, and with a number of individual vaudeville luminaries, the Warners already had signed many of the preeminent variety and concert artists to exclusive contracts. Frustrated by the Warners' jump, Fox agreed now to heed Fox Newsreel President Courtland Smith's original advice. Momentarily putting aside live entertainment, Fox looked instead to newsreels as a way of differentiating his studio's fare from that of the rival Warner's.

In addition to altering the corporate culture of Hollywood, film sound made the movies the primary carrier of mass culture. Sound gave a new shape to ideas, imbuing them with a specificity that might be carried in the memory after the image had faded. In newsreels or in fiction, and in musical utopias, sound widened film's repertoire of stories and genres. Critically, as a new, widely disseminated conduit for a kind of unofficial national version of the American spoken language, film sound also altered how stories could be told, adding new emotional possibilities. Thus, it would be an error to measure the impact of sound as a parochial affair whose significance was largely confined to the culture of Hollywood. Rather, like other previous communication innovations, the new rules developed for the control and use of sound were more than the addition of new equipment placed alongside cameras; they were a stage "for negotiating issues crucial to the conduct of social life; among them, who is inside and outside, who may speak, who may not, and who has the authority and may be believed."[1] In the struggle for control of this technology, one means to secure authority was to declare your expertise. Along with the sound engineer and the dialogue coach, the producer became perhaps the most powerful expert at putting all the new pieces of the movie puzzle together.

With sound came a dramatic rise in movie attendance. These box office data also suggested an increase in the movies' authority, a move that upset the delicate cultural calculus that had been calibrated without factoring in one condition: that the previously powerless parvenus now controlled this entertainment monolith. This control of Hollywood thus enabled them to enter circles of power from which they always had been excluded. Those displaced by the new Hollywood power brokers did not accept this putsch as a permanent thing, and the rise of the movies coincided with the proliferation of film-censorship bills at both the national and local levels, and widespread journalistic concern for the social effects of the movies.[2] While the older media still played significant roles in socialization, film—in alliance with other local, interpersonal cultural forms (like pageants and parades)—now took upon itself most of the functions previously reserved for newspapers, literature, and live theater: that of communicating to the American public its definition of mainstream ideas.

Beyond altering the cultural balance of power and the very nature of national popular culture itself, the second change that came with sound was a recognition that the new technology would be the impetus for a major social reorganization of personnel and power in Hollywood. Sound reshaped the very way film production was orchestrated. The coming of sound greatly expanded the payrolls of the studio. Above all, the new order placed added importance on the producer. The uncertainties raised by the changes brought by sound thus threw into sharp relief the centralization of authority that already had been in gestation. As audiences demanded a better product, the moguls had to delegate authority to those (typically to vice presidents in charge of production) who understood the issues of production, and beginning in the late 1920s film corporations began to install supervisor-managers to run the studio. Suddenly, anyone aspiring to power in Hollywood did not dream of writing movies but hoped to *produce* them.

A look at Zanuck's work with Warner Brothers' Vitaphone films, particularly *The Jazz Singer*, provides a case study of an individual and an organization grappling with the consequences of technological innovation and change. But it also draws attention to the real impact of sound: how it altered the American cinema's charter to deal with difficult, even problematic content. While this was an issue with silent film, the turmoil carried by a cinema of words gave rise to evidence that the united country actually housed a host of regional, as well as national, cultural schisms, clashes silence had either sheltered or left muted (if not mute) within the seams of its aesthetic.

THE GENESIS OF *THE JAZZ SINGER*

The Jazz Singer is often held to be the first sound film, but it was in fact the sixth Warner Brothers feature to use sound. In addition to a host of experimental sound films from long-forgotten corporations across the world, *The Jazz Singer* had been preceded by a large number of shorts that contained both speech and music. The previous five features—all produced by Zanuck—were *Don Juan, The Better 'Ole, When a Man Loves, Old San Francisco,* and *The First Auto.* They mixed music, sound effects, and, in *The First Auto* and *Old San Francisco,* some fragments of speech. *The Jazz Singer*'s innovation did not consist of the *amount* of speaking in it. Nor was its claim to notoriety based on the fact that *The Jazz Singer* would be Al Jolson's film debut. In Warner's 1926 short *Al Jolson in a Plantation Act,* he already had appeared in his trademark blackface singing three songs to a brace of chickens wandering aimlessly about what appeared to be a makeshift set consisting of a slave cabin set conveniently adjacent to a cotton field.

Jolson had already used in this short the *exact* lines that would soon be accorded immortal status as the "first" spoken dialogue in a story film. After an upbeat version of "When the Red, Red, Robin" Jolson, seemingly ad-libbing (but actually using the ritualized dialogue he employed before live audiences), turns toward the camera and says, "Wait a minute, wait a minute, folks. You ain't heard nothin' yet, you ain't heard a thing." He then instructs the unseen orchestra leader to follow his song about red birds with one about creatures of the blue-winged variety, "April Showers." He closes the three-song short with a scorcher, "Rockabye Your Baby." But before the expected "wow" finish, Jolson again talks to the audience, launching into a speech defending what he was about to sing:

> It's a little Mammy song. And a very funny thing, people have been making fun of mammy songs, and I don't really think it's right that they should. For, after all, mammy songs are the fundamental songs of our country. And not only that, you take John McCormack, the famous radio singer. He sings "Mother McRae," and that's a mammy song. And folks, he ain't bad. So folks, if you don't mind, I'm gonna sing you my little mammy song, 'Rockabye Your Baby.' Professor, if you please.

By the end of 1926, Warner's evolving view of the sound cinema— and Zanuck's hand in this—seemed to be solidifying. Shorts, like *George Jessel in a Comedy Monologue* (in which the comedian sings "At Peace with the World" and speaks lovingly—if comically—on the phone to his mother) would bring the aural world of popular art to movie audiences. These films, not the five Vitaphone features that preceded *The Jazz Singer,* accomplished the task of gauging audience response to talking pictures. Before *The Jazz Singer* brought spoken dialogue to a feature film, certain of the Vitaphone "flash varieties"—like those featuring Jolson, the Howard Brothers, Jessel, and Bairnsfather—had contained rather extensive dialogue sections, albeit in the context of a vaudeville act, not as part of a film story. Though overlooked, these shorts set up audience expectations that Zanuck would access and try to fulfill by coming up with the correct formula for sound film with *The Jazz Singer.*

The Jazz Singer had first appeared in January 1922 as a short story in *Everybody's Magazine.* Samson Raphaelson's eleven-page effort, "The Day of Atonement," focused on a New York cantor's son torn between his father's desire that, as a cantor—a synagogue official who sings or chants liturgical music—he continue the family's tradition of service to Judaism and his own drive to use his voice in the secular world of show business. Its tale of the struggle between popular entertainment and the older, sacred orders that such new rituals were rapidly supplanting was familiar to many in Hollywood. The story prefigured the moguls' main argument about their industry's role in defining what was American about the nation's developing popular culture: *they* were. Films like *The Jazz Singer* seemed to provide entertainment that, at the same time, might fulfill a social function by asking a serious question: How might a nation of immigrants understand what was characteristically shared, characteristically *American* amidst all of our regional and multicultural differences? The answer provided by the film—that entertainment was the most American of all rituals—was both too simple and too self-serving.

The film that was made from Raphaelson's story marked the first real impact Zanuck had on Hollywood outside his work on Warner Brothers programmers. In addition to its historic function in innovating speech in a feature film, *The Jazz Singer* had several other landmark effects. It was Zanuck's first experience in coming up with a strategy that would make a story with controversial content palatable to a mass public and, consequently, successful at the box office. His evisceration of Raphaelson's original story en route to a box-office bonanza would set the pattern for how he—and the rest of Hollywood—would deal with controversial issues. He triumphed by taming the text. He eliminated the short story's strongest takes on race and ethnicity and replaced them with a more congenial, even a warmer, world where no contradiction was beyond the salvation of a centrist solution. In addition to this significant editorial precedent the film set at the studio, the making of *The Jazz Singer* inadvertently led to two other important consequences. Because he successfully steered the film through its production life, his work altered Zanuck's leverage at the studio. In turn, the complicated maneuverings surrounding the creation and production of this one film might be said to have changed not only Zanuck's career but the direction in which the studio's style would shortly move.

The story had been inspired by Raphaelson's attendance, in 1917, at one of Al Jolson's live shows, a performance of *Robinson Crusoe, Jr.,* in which the entertainer, then at the height of his popularity, played three parts.[3] In one incarnation, he appeared in blackface as Friday. Like most white Americans, Raphaelson could gaze right past the problematic issues of race raised by minstrelsy (that it created a white man's exaggerated and stereotyped repertoire of risible black behavior) and instead be enthralled by the magnetism of the star minstrel performer. Dazed by Jolson's magnetism, when Raphaelson went backstage to meet him, Jolson told him the narrative of his life. Five years later, in 1922 he was allegedly approached by Jolson himself to transform the story into a musical play. But Raphaelson felt that the entertainer wanted just another version of his typical Broadway fare: a weak script, leaving the star free when he saw fit to interpolate a song, ad lib, or joke. Raphaelson had a different agenda, and he felt that the story would be best served as a straight drama in which he could test out how different racial, religious, and cultural traditions were altered by contact with America's great indigenous musical form, jazz. Flattered, he nevertheless declined the offer.[4]

Raphaelson wrote the story up as a play, which opened in New York in September 1925 with George Jessel playing "Jake" Rabinowitz. The Warners were unimpressed with the play—which got mediocre reviews but played to full houses—but Ernst Lubitsch (surprisingly) thought of *The Jazz Singer* as a possible candidate for his next film. Lubitsch had a clause in his contract stating that the Warners *had* to buy any property he desired, so a furious Jack Warner acquired, for the relatively steep price of $50,000, the rights for *The Jazz Singer* for Lubitsch to direct.[5] There was one stipulation: the Warners could not release the film until May 1927, after road companies had finished touring.

Lubitsch and Jack Warner had repeatedly locked horns over how the director, with his "sophisticated" European ways, should make films for a middlebrow American audience. While Zanuck wisely stayed on the sidelines, leaving the great stylist alone, Jack jumped into the fracas. (Usually a situation involving such a primal issue of authority could never stop Jack from getting his way, even if it involved jeopardizing the satisfaction of a highly prized asset like Lubitsch. Jack was fond of ending heated discussions with his employees by directing an opponent's attention to the large, centrally located water tower that dominated the outline of the studio. Gesturing grandly, he would point out exactly *whose* name was emblazoned upon it. The point was not lost upon most employees.)[6]

Few directors were better equipped to deal with music than devoted amateur musician Lubitsch. His work on the landmark musical *Monte Carlo* would shortly prove that he was one of the industry's great innovators in the use of sound. *The Jazz Singer* did not appear to be his kind of material, for Lubitsch had made his reputation first with costume epics and then with sly social comedies spiced by the light touches of his inimitable wry social observation and the deftness of his piquant sexual innuendo. When Lubitsch sought the play out, it is possible that, displaced from his native milieu into a community whose values were often antithetical to his, the cultivated German Jew saw in *The Jazz Singer*'s narrative of identity struggle parallels to his own story. Lubitsch's profound, lifelong love of music might have further enhanced his attraction to the work and its diasporic elements. Although Lubitsch had initially expressed doubts about the artistic possibilities of sound film, he later hailed it as superior to silent film. But the man who had insisted that the Warners make a film out of Raphaelson's play would not be around to direct it. Lubitsch's departure for Paramount and MGM robbed the project of a strong director and opened the door for Zanuck to leave his mark on the film.

In February 1927, trade papers had already announced that the vaudevillian George Jessel was to star in the film.[7] A script found at the American Film Institute (marked "Final Shooting" version) shows that very late in the preproduction process, the film was obviously still a Jessel vehicle.[8] Yet, in a speech delivered at the Harvard Business School on March 30, 1927—two months before Jolson signed his contract—Harry Warner told his audience that the film would not feature Jessel but would star Al Jolson.[9]

Like so much of the murky events surrounding Hollywood's change to sound and the role played by this one film in that process, how the Warners and Zanuck dumped Jessel in favor of Jolson remains unclear.[10] (Scott Eyman's observation—that at a certain point, the evidence of how Jolson replaced Jessel is less "documentary" than "vaguely anecdotal"—aptly summarizes the competing narratives in circulation, now and then.)[11] However it came about, on May 26 Jessel was gone and Jolson officially joined the project. Although no longer at the top of his profession as he had been ten years before, when Raphaelson first encountered the power of his stage persona, Jolson was still an enormously well-known star. After Jolson entered the project, the Warners were willing to up the ante. Jessel might have been a "well-known vaudevillian" but dimmed or not, "Al Jolson was a superstar."[12] At a budget of $500,000, *The Jazz Singer* would be one of the studio's most expensive productions and certainly the biggest gamble the Warners had ever undertaken.

SHAPING TALK

The fact that Zanuck was entrusted with the most coveted assignment in Warner Brothers history, the day-to-day job of producing *The Jazz Singer,* shows the faith the Warners had in his abilities. Known for his brainstorms on the set and in story conference, he was emphatic that he and not Jack Warner, Sam Warner, or Al Jolson, deserved the credit for envisioning that pictures could talk, not just sing. This on-the-spot improvisation was the way he worked then and after:

> I was on the set when they were rehearsing the parts where Jolson sings to his mother. We were all standing around waiting for the music to be played. Suddenly it dawned on me, why don't they have a conversation? The mike was on! I said, "Why doesn't Jolson turn to his mother and say, "Mama, I wanna sing a song for you." Then the guy turned the sound on early. When they played it back, there was Jolson's voice as clear as a bell. That was when the talking thing started.[13]

But the idea for a bold move like "the talking thing"—putting dialogue in a feature film—may have been accelerated by the fact that the Warners were concerned with losing their competitive edge to rival sound systems—like Movietone or Vocalfilm—developed by other studios. In May 1927 the *Moving Picture World* reported that "the arrival of Sam Warner to take charge of the Vitaphone interests of Warner Brothers gave rise to a report that there may be some change in the Vitaphone policy in order to meet the competition of many other talking devices."[14]

Of course, claiming "the talking thing" started that August day in 1927 is also to overlook the nearly two hundred Vitaphone shorts (many of which contained some speech) that had already been produced before Jolson's famous "ad lib" in *The Jazz Singer*. Nevertheless, most written histories agree with Zanuck that, if the narrative of innovation must be scripted so that it contains a single, definable hero, after Jolson, if *The Jazz Singer* owes its shape to anyone, it is to him. Perhaps the most mediocre important film ever made, *The Jazz Singer* was virtually a silent picture with a few musical inserts. (The film contains a scant one and a half pages of spoken dialogue, compared to over 201 titles.)

The film tells the story of a singer in New York's Lower East Side ghetto, Jack Robin, né Jacob Rabinowitz (Al Jolson). Jack's father, Cantor Rabinowitz (Warner Oland) is opposed to his son using his singing voice outside the synagogue: before coming to America, seven generations of his family had served their God as cantors. But Jake is an American boy, and after a meddlesome neighbor, Yudelson (Otto Lederer), tips off his father that he has seen Jakie singing in a saloon, there is a huge fight. Denounced by his father, he runs away from home. In the manner of orthodox Judaism, the cantor proclaims his son is dead.

Some years elapse and Jake, a vaudeville singer, is on the verge of a major breakthrough. He is also in love with a headliner, a (gentile) dancer named Mary Dale (May McAvoy). Mary has faith in Jake's talent and gets him a major part in her upcoming show. Jake returns to New York in triumph, where he is received warmly by his mother.

But his angry father refuses to speak to him, and orders him out of the house. On the eve of Jake's show, his father falls ill, and backstage, his mother and Yudelson plead with a blacked-up Jake to sing in synagogue in his father's place. He is torn between love of family and tradition and his big moment in show business, but decides to go back to the synagogue to sing. His expiring father forgives him, and Jake sings the emotional prayer of atonement, the Kol Nidre. Hearing his son's voice, the old cantor dies. In the last scene a blacked-up Jake triumphs as a jazz singer in Mary's show, singing "My Mammy" as his proud mother beams approval from a front-row seat.

From the opening, "In every living soul, a spirit cries for expression—perhaps this plaintive, wailing song of Jazz is, after all, the misunderstood utterance of a prayer," to the last title card, "Mammy, Mammy," the film is a conventional melodrama very much like those Zanuck was used to writing, editing, and pacing. One thing is certain. Observing his sure editorial hand, Zanuck's years as a pulp writer and the hours passed in the cutting room had paid off.

Zanuck's shorthand notes on the edits and cuts to be made in the film two months before the final release reveal his part in shaping this film. He indicates substantial alterations: changes in title cards; shortening of shots; altering of the rhythm of the picture. A typical Zanuck change was the succinct title he wrote for Sara Rabinowitz when she must carefully choose her words in advising Jakie whether he should sing the Kol Nidre or go on with his show: "Do what is in your heart. If you sing and God is not in your voice, your father will know."[15]

Always a great editor, Zanuck instructed the head of the Editing Department, H. J. McCord, to shorten a shot of the doctor (looking offscreen, out the window of the dying cantor's bedroom toward the sole source of sound he hears, Jake's singing) and to lengthen what should be the audience focus, the star, singing. These shorthand notes, never previously revealed, imply that Sam and Jack Warner and the film's director, Alan Crosland, were all responsible in different ways for shaping this breakthrough film. But they also leave no doubt whose editorial voice spoke to audiences through the finished film. Young Darryl Zanuck was doing for *The Jazz Singer* what a producer often takes on at this stage: fine-tuning, looking for weak sections, and in general orchestrating the means by which the film would achieve its effect.

Beyond the directions indicated in the cutting notes, there are other telltale signatures that mark the film as Zanuck's. Zanuck believed that the audience needed something to be for, or against, as the story unfolded. This "rooting interest" had to be placed early on in the film, preferably by scenes that clearly illustrated it through demonstrable action. So Zanuck made a significant editorial choice: he restored the prologue to *The Jazz Singer* that Raphaelson had removed when he rewrote his short story for the theater. With this change the theme of generational and cultural tension is established minutes into the film, and it is the youthful Jakie (rather than, as in the play, the more mature adult) who confronts his father and asserts his taboo (but very American) love of secular entertainment. Zanuck was setting the Hollywood mold for how one explains a life: through his first actions, the young boy is shown to be the early version of the man.

In one version of the script, Jakie actually tells his father he wants to be an actor in the theater. Zanuck changed this to a more active scene; rather than simply being told that this is the case, the father (and the viewer) "discovers" it after a neighborhood meddler (Yudelson) tells him that his son is singing in a saloon. Initially, before Jolson had signed to play the lead, the script called for Jakie's first on-screen musical performance to be the popular, sentimental ballad "Mighty Lak a Rose." But this moment of great importance—the first time a synchronized song would be used in a feature film—was changed to a more identifiable Jolson specialty to take full advantage of the film's star. After a few bars of "My Gal Sal," we hear one of Jolson's signature tunes, "Waiting for the Robert E. Lee," and "Ragtime Jakie" demonstrates in the way that the movies always signify star quality that he is not merely a run-of-the-mill saloon singer. Like Jolson (who at this age ran away from home to join Rich and Hoppe's Big Company of Fun Makers), Jakie is already a performer with a distinctive style. Like Jolson, he also suffuses the performance with "shufflin'," the same gestures and dance that figure so prominently as a token of white appropriation of black identity in another hit of 1927, *Showboat*'s "Can't Help Loving That Man."

Zanuck was demonstrating here what he would do so often later: tailoring a narrative to conform to the well-known qualities an audience expected to see and hear from a particular star. Bobby Gordon, the young actor impersonating teenaged Jakie, performs the song with all of Jolson's characteristic vocal style and physical gestures. Thus, even though he has yet to appear in the film, the performance of a signature Jolson tune in a recognizable Jolson way reminds us of who the star of the film is. Further, Zanuck knew that the first appearance of the adult Jolson had to be showcased by material that was timely: "The song which is to be Vitaphoned should be one especially written for the occasion as any current number would be out of date long before the picture has played every theatre equipped for Vitaphone by release time."[16]

Along with rooting interests, rapid exposition of the character's motivations, and the importance of the star persona to the narrative, concision was also a Zanuck trait: here, intertitles deemed unnecessary were dropped. Perhaps the most significant change Zanuck made was in the film's ending. The pre-Jolson ending—that is, the ending found in the play—has Jakie seemingly abandoning show business and finally coming home to be the cantor his father always told him was his ordained fate. As he sings the Jewish prayer of atonement, his father's ghost

> appears on the side of the screen very faint and shadowy. The misty form slowly comes to the side of the singer. It pauses. There is a smile on the face of the old cantor, and he slowly raises his hand in a blessing. The shadowy figure becomes fainter and fainter, finally disappearing, leaving Jack standing alone. The music and his figure slowly FADE OUT.[17]

After Zanuck's changes the film no longer ended with the death of the cantor, the one figure whose resistance to change was absolute. How much the strength of Jolson's star persona shaped this change is unknown, but one biographer of Jolson did note that "it had to be like that. No audience could really be expected to see Al Jolson give up show business—even a film."[18]

In Zanuck's Hollywood, unlike in the play and the short story, although it is still possible for one to read the ending as ambiguous, I believe we are meant to think that Jake embraces show business to the *exclusion* of his former life. He has joined his fiancée, Mary, and become one of "them," not a *goy*, but a secular entertainer. This is in line with the ethnic dry cleaning most products underwent as they were transformed into movies. For example, the play and the short story had sprinkled the word *shiksa* (Yiddish for a female Christian) about freely. In the movie, though the word is used in one intertitle, having a girlfriend in show business is agreed to be *schande*—a shame—less dangerous than having her repeatedly profess allegiance to the Christian faith, to account for the angst of a devout Jewish family (and to risk alienating a nation in which a Christian population accounted for 98 percent of all Americans).

Zanuck chose to close the film with a Jolson secular turn, rather than the Kol Nidre. In the last scene, Jolson is given the opportunity to bring down the house with an intense performance not of the *Kol Nidre*, but with his signature song, "Mammy."[19] It is sung to his recently widowed, but remarkably assimilated-looking, mother and her equally reconstituted front-row companion and guest, Yudelson. The latter appears to have abandoned his familiar Lower East Side precinct. Joining the widow Rabinowitz in adoring the power shown by this former "star" of the Lower East Side Jewish *shul* (now the idol of secular entertainment), he is clad incongruously in a tuxedo.

After Zanuck had prepared the final version of the film, Jack Warner made the ultimate executive decisions. But there is no evidence that he overruled his young "supervisor." Jack may have reveled in the ceremonial role as the publicly acknowledged head whose word and signature were needed to make Zanuck's work official, but it was clear that the substantive aspects of the production decisions were Zanuck's.

THE JAZZ IN *THE JAZZ SINGER*

Zanuck conceived, and shaped, *The Jazz Singer* with the values of a national rather than a local audience in mind, and so the film's significance goes far beyond its accorded status as a landmark of technological innovation. He reconfigured Raphaelson's text to make a film that is a classic example of what Richard Maltby calls "harmless entertainment."[20] *The Jazz Singer,* as it passed through the filters of studio-era Hollywood's economic and political considerations, not only missed the opportunity to engage in a serious debate on critical contemporary issues; it actually *reframed* the agenda through which we perceived them. Its enormous financial success for Warner's virtually guaranteed that other similarly formed, potentially controversial or topical films would follow. All of them would be transformed from dissonance to harmony in the same way Zanuck had transformed *The Jazz Singer.*

As Irving Thalberg accurately (if diplomatically) summed it up in 1928, a cinema of dialogue meant that Hollywood could now "delicately" broach topics that "the silent picture was forced to shun."[21] If Zanuck wanted to include many of the potentially censorable or controversial ideas contained in Raphaelson's play, he would have to figure out how to create a Hollywood-approved version and grapple with that challenge for the rest of his professional life. *The Jazz Singer* was the first time anyone had to pay the price for this new cinema. Positioning any film was not easy in an America that was culturally divided. Even though the 1920s are remembered as an era in which there was a great deal of social and cultural experimentation, it was also a time when resistance to "the modern," to the changes found in postwar secular life, was also at its most powerful.[22] Those who sought to control sound faced the same issues confronting any group who held the potential power of a new communications innovation within its grasp: In what ways might the technology change the way people lived? The likelihood that film could now carry the words spawned in the city to small towns meant that culture manufactured in Hollywood would, like other products that were the result of efficient corporate centralization, "threaten the ability of small communities to exercise control over the cultural influences they tolerated."²³ The Vitaphone has been touted as an exemplar of technological progress. Such technology might be innovative in its engineering applications. But in the use to which it was put and the content it carried, although it can be seen as a harbinger of the future and a carrier of progress, a "modern" technology could also demonstrate the opposite: that at the social level, nostalgia was a force capable of tempering any sense of progress.

In its original form—full of Jewish ritual, phonetic yiddishisms, and references to the particularities of urban ghetto life—*The Jazz Singer* certainly appeared to be too parochially Jewish and even, perhaps, too city-based to make any faithful film version a hit outside New York. Zanuck's solution would become the blueprint for Hollywood's response to the problem of how to determine the cinema's place in local and national culture.

As Jews the Warners must have been anxious about presenting a Jewish-themed play written for a New York audience and featuring a Jewish star to an American culture still redolent with anti-Semitism and mistrust of anything from the city, a clamorous place Walter Lippmann had noted most Americans did not wish to acknowledge as "the American ideal." The "wrong" kind of adaptation could arouse trouble and indignation in certain segments of the country, particularly because Warner Brothers intended to present the film with a great deal of ballyhoo. The Warners attempted to make the film less Jewish so it would be safe for its Christian national audience. The souvenir program from opening night describes an ending of religious tolerance we do not see because it was never in the film: "A short while later Mama and Mrs. Jack Robin sat in the front row of a crowded theatre listening to a beloved black face comedian singing 'I'd walk a million miles for one of your smiles, my Mammy.' Sara turned to Mary."²⁴ In truth, Mama's companion is not Mary but Yudelson, and it is nowhere indicated that Jake and Mary have married. In addition to Zanuck's editorial de-fanging of whatever bite there might be in the film, Jack Warner himself claimed that the film was *not* about Judaism, race, and religion. At *The Jazz Singer*'s anticipated opening-night fourth curtain call, Jack planned a speech in which he would have the audience see the film as being of universal appeal: "The spirit of the play we feel is not the glorification of any one religion, creed, race, but has a universal theme. . . . 'HONOR THY FATHER AND THY MOTHER.' "[25]

The Jazz Singer was Zanuck's first important instance of what I call editing for safety, a strategy he invoked to avoid controversy and create a commercially oriented picture. After dictating fifteen pages of recommendations to change the script, Zanuck made a decision that perhaps more than any other sealed the film's fate as "harmless entertainment." He hired (for $750 a week) Alfred A. Cohn, an obscure (but compliant) writer, whose earlier work with safe Jewish-themed material may have convinced the studio that he could do the job.[26] The reframing of the play as a musical would require a good deal of strategic editing and rewriting. Raphaelson, clearly the better writer, proposed to Zanuck an outline in which he intended to push controversial issues. He was dismissed as a possibility. And so the play's searing personal and cultural dramas were transformed into a showcase for a predictable melodramatic story leavened by large doses of vaudeville shtick. Years later Raphaelson could still recollect the shock he felt when, sitting in the audience for the film's New York world premiere, he gazed upon what Hollywood had done to his vision of the Lower East Side.[27] Like most of Zanuck's major works of pure entertainment, it was a huge hit.

In overseeing *The Jazz Singer*, the twenty-five-year-old "associate executive" Zanuck put his faith in the system of production that he and the rest of Hollywood had been slowly developing. Since 1915, the studio mode—in which one centrally organized corporation controlled the production, exhibition, and distribution of film—had gradually shifted more and more of the decisions of film production away from a host of personnel and onto the desk of one figure, the producer. In shaping any single film and the studio's overall program, a producer was counted on to balance the demands of the box office against other issues, like regional tastes or the agendas of groups like lobbyists and pressure groups. With all these forces affecting Zanuck's judgment, and the raft of changes made to Raphaelson's original text, perhaps the biggest missed opportunity was the limited way the film defined jazz (as white). *The Jazz Singer* took a musical form largely indigenous to African-American musicians and, through the performance of a black-faced Jolson, made it more acceptable to white, ticket-buying movie audiences. In controlling what was hot and unexpected, it eliminated the pleasures—and dangers— of jazz. In this respect, the operations surrounding the changes in the making of *The Jazz Singer* came close to realizing Marxist theoretician Gramsci's and Frankfurt sociologists Adorno and Eisler's worst fears about the deleterious effects mass communications and reproduction had on art. They were certain that the studios of Southern California would use this new facet of technology to exercise social control in the guise of entertainment.

Indeed, like the studio's reorganization of the film's more subversive original source material, the music industry reorchestrated jazz in line with what it perceived to be the film industry's needs. Hollywood arrangements toned down jazz's improvisational style to make it fit in with film's (and the culture's) dominant popular musical ethos. Jazz had once been an outsider's music, one whose very form and content was used as a commentary on many of the mainstream culture's musical and nonmusical values, and to the ears of critic Edmund Wilson, Hollywood's stylistic agenda reduced this music's ragged complexity to "an abstract pattern."[28] The reorchestrated versions of jazz were now "happily" married to their counterparts, the glossy visual production values of Hollywood. Together, the two forged a powerful alliance. The tailoring of music to accommodate the imperatives of Hollywood and film went to new extremes when most of the major motion picture corporations (including Warner Brothers and Fox) diversified their corporate holdings and began to buy record labels and music publishing houses.[29] Once they were brought into line with what Hollywood sought to achieve in its film narratives, the music recording and publishing industry as well as radio (which, with its narrower "range" had pockets of resistance nearly impossible in the cinema) were not really rival media. Instead, they were all taken in and, like any ambitious junior partner, housed within full sight of the overlords of Hollywood's—and America's—culture industry.

While the *The Jazz Singer*'s glosses of blacks as both performers and composers is hardly admirable, its definition of jazz as white is hardly unique. Rather, "the film should not be held responsible for using the term in the same way that most whites would have understood it in the 1920s."[30] Lawrence Levine asserts that "the types of jazz that were most easily and widely accepted initially were the filtered and hybridized versions that created less cultural dissonance."[31] Levine's arguments, however, do not really move beyond thinking of jazz as a "live" performance art; he understates, or underestimates, the enormous part that mass-disseminated Hollywoodlike control played in redefining this music.

CENTRISM: BLACKING UP AND WHITING OUT

In writing about jazz, and in his proposed scenario submitted to Zanuck, Raphaelson specifically credited Irving Berlin and Gershwin with the creation of a new national musical language. This geneology made it possible to cast aside the status many Jews in America had formerly assumed, that of an ethnically ambiguous mixed, and racially suspect, "other,"[32] and gain a seat, as it were, in the American orchestra. The cultural economy through which this occurred did one other thing: it made Jews less "other" than jazz's real creators, the people who were still excluded from credit.

Just as the outrageous erasure of blacks from Hollywood's subsequent histories of jazz could be glossed over because, as repeated so often in films like *The King of Jazz*, it became a kind of pentimento, the pain of minstrelsy could also be reframed so that it was received as a key part of the joy of beloved American entertainment. "Blacking up," a vestige of a deeply ingrained racism with antebellum roots, was viewed by the film industry as just another (even one of the most important) part of the American vaudeville repertoire. To take one example, as late as 1953, Zanuck intended a key scene in *There's No Business Like Show Business* to include the marriage of the leads, Ethel Merman and Dan Dailey, as a minstrel wedding. Accompanied by joyfully strutting and singing figures, the happy couple would have marched to the altar beneath a boughed arch of canes and tambourines.[33] Wisely, Zanuck had the scene taken out. Because minstrelsy was framed as a part of our national heritage (with few thoughts about *who* the beneficiaries of such racial masquerade were), it would be unthinkable for a star of Jolson's magnitude to appear in film and not give the audience what it expected.

Minstrelsy flourished in Warner's short films, which would soon include "Harlemania"; the dancing of Bill "Bojangles" Robinson; the singing and playing of Noble Sissle and Eubie Blake; the Utica Jubilee Singers performing "Watermelon Song"; Aunt Jemima, "The Original Fun Flour Maker," doing five "darkie" songs and dances. There was even a short made particularly for "the Colored audience," *Minstrel Days:* "boy, how those colored brethren can dance!" To show how jazz and blackface really could, as Michael Rogin insists, be a kind of interchangeable ethnic cross dressing, viewers of the Warner's shorts could also see and hear the artistry of "Joe Wong, the Chinese Jazz Boy," or more up *The Jazz Singer*'s alley, hear Molly Picon sing "The Yiddeshe Blues."

But if, as in the film, race is coded as Jew and Christian and not black and white, then the real cultural anxieties of black and white marriage—or just plain black and white interchange—can be glossed over. Some of the scenes in *The Jazz Singer* that dealt with race even as masquerade, were toned down from the original script. On the eve of Jake's big debut, Sara Rabinowitz and Yudelson plead with him to sing the Kol Nidre in place of his expiring father. Entering the blacked-up jazz singer's theater dressing room, they both fail to recognize Jake. A title card for Yudelson says, "He talks like Jakie, but he looks like his shadow," a considerably softer statement than Cohn's original "It talks like Jakie, but it looks like a nigger."[34]

Cohn's script went out of its way to avoid even a hint of miscegenation between Jake in blackface and white Mary Dale. A special note tacked on the final shooting script states: "Playing a romantic scene in blackface may be something of an experiment and very likely an unsuccessful one. As an alternative, should it not prove as effective as desired, there could be a scene . . . in Jack's dressing room, showing him enter in blackface and start taking off the makeup."[35] This is what was done. In contrast to the bad case of race nerves Zanuck showed in *The Jazz Singer,* one year later, with *The Singing Fool,* he seems to have relaxed. Ruby Keeler (Jolson's real-life wife) could respond to Al Howard's (Jolson) anxious worry that "If I didn't have this black on, I'd kiss you" with the casual "Don't let a little black stop you"[36] for the simple reason that the audience knew that they were both white *and* married to one another. (By 1930, when he played a black jockey in *Big Boy,* Jolson seemed to have made the transition from white entertainer in blackface to white entertainer playing a black character. But even though the script gave him a child—played by a black actor!—Jolson still wore a minstrel-like, not a naturalistic, black makeup.)

There have been two cinematic remakes of *The Jazz Singer* since 1927 (three, if we count Jerry Lewis's 1959 television version).[37] Jolson also reprised the part on radio in 1936. But we have also come to know the film's leading figure from famous posters by artists Hap Hadley and William Auerbach-Levy: the jazz singer, image keystoned by the cinema's lens, supplicates the audience with gloved, outstretched hands. With its desperate, grabbing hands, blank eyes, and slash of a mouth, it is a kind of *golem,* a creature reaching out, with a sense of urgency, to communicate and maintain contact with the audience. But, unlike the singer in the play, Zanuck's movie jazz singer downplayed his Jewishness, through assimilation and by abandoning it for a career in show business. The compromise—an American Jew who enters show business as a Jew—is actually shown in the film, in the sequences where Jake goes to hear a concert by the famed Cantor Josef Rosenblatt (who actually made several Vitaphone shorts for the Warners). But this would never do. The film's Jake is desperate for the big (read "national") career Jolson had by jettisoning his Jewishness. He is unable either to fully deny or to acknowledge his Jewish culture as one of the firm roots and one of the sources of his talent. At the same time he denies part of his Jewish heritage, his other token of identity, the made-up mask that affirms his musical link to blackness (or a white exaggerated version of blackness), rather than itself being a credible substitute identity, is obviously a disguise that serves only to affirm the very opposite of what he appears to be trying to do: the stylized mask insists that he is not black.[38]

The vitality of Jolson's black-Jewish urban mix, one that formed the heart of Tin Pan Alley's appeal, may have been found on stage, in clubs, on "race records," and on radio, but it "rarely found its way from New York City commercial culture to the Hollywood screen."[39] Instead, like the rest of popular culture dealing with these tensions, if the film affirms any identity, it is neither one of ethnicity nor religion. Rather, born with the sound film, what was carried across the country and held up for all to see was that it was the newly minted white show-business performer and his or her brand of safe entertainment—and not these ethnic stars—who were touted as the triumph of our popular culture, as the real, ultimate Americans. Implicitly, it is *The Jazz Singer*'s operative fiction that, like the allegedly representative mix found in every Hollywood wartime foxhole, show business too is an inclusive community that accommodates Jakie and Mary, the assimilated Warners, and nonpracticing Christian Zanuck (but not the majority of African-Americans) in its folds.[40]

It was surely neither Raphaelson's intent nor Zanuck's job in *The Jazz Singer* to dwell upon these relations as I have, seventy years after and many paradigms beyond the cultures in which they were first articulated and given a cinematic voice and presence. While we can never be absolutely certain what Raphaelson meant by jazz, Zanuck knew it was most definitely the playwright's intention that the film investigate the widest possible significance of this idiom to American life:

> The main point about this play, to me, is that it shows the enormous and colorful traits of American life in terms of jazz. It shows you all that goes into building up the heart of a singer of jazz. It shows you the curious relationship of religion, business and machine-age American city life—contrasts I think that the motion picture can express more effectively than any other medium and that here is a play that offers enormous opportunity for such expression.[41]

It would be an opportunity denied by the imperatives of safe entertainment.

YOU AIN'T HEARD NOTHIN' YET

The high grosses of most of Zanuck's films, including *The Jazz Singer,* were proof of his first injunction: "make 'em entertaining." But, profitable or not, the patterns formed by his body of films were also clearly selling Americans something else: particular versions of how race, ethnicity, and religion met, and were transformed, on the playing field of modern American show business.

If a main goal of the Hollywood studio system was to create the impression that much of its mass-produced standard fare was quite novel, one way to accomplish this was to suggest a film was controversial. But because of the pressures to market each film for the tastes of a national audience, if controversy was desired, it had to be molded to fit the demands of good, safe entertainment. It had to be contained so it could be commodified. The kind of compromise Zanuck made when preparing *The Jazz Singer* would be the stance he—and Hollywood—would take on many other controversial films. Zanuck's version of the Raphaelson play is the first point on a line that runs through a large body of films, from *The Public Enemy* to *The Grapes of Wrath* and, a decade later, on through the problems of black and white America presented in *No Way Out,* and even near the end of his career in *Island in the Sun.* The cultural trigonometry created by the compromises in these scripts—about ethnicity, race, religion, and most of all, about the role American music might play in all this—formed a specific tangent: the "studio line" on how Hollywood rendered hot topics more acceptable.

The Jazz Singer is a classic illustration of what such a compromise produced, the kind of centrist notion through which Hollywood mediated its version of the world. It is a place where all difference is elided, disputes are mediated, and truly problematic things either rewritten or ignored. It is not surprising that Zanuck did not move more boldly to make *The Jazz Singer* the expressive, contemplative narrative its author proclaimed was his goal. In 1927, Zanuck was a very young man with the power to shape the content of a major film only newly acquired. His track record of hits must have convinced him that he could create this "hokum," even in its higher dressings, by delving into the seemingly limitless load of fuel long established as the foundation upon which most of mainstream Hollywood ran. But after *The Jazz Singer* he would soon see other more subversive potentials of sound. Because of the studio's new position of power secured by the profits and the prophylactic power of his work, and because of a radical change in American culture after 1929, the safe approach he showed in *The Jazz Singer* would very shortly change.

The New York opening of *The Jazz Singer* on October 6, 1927, was one of the greatest nights in show business history. The enormous crowd (including nearly every major film mogul) gathered to watch the great American spectacle of a movie premiere. A nervous Jolson entered, and those who could not be inside the theater were entertained by a jazz band provided by the Warners. As if to remind posterity of what was at stake this evening, the Warners filmed a Vitaphone short of the event, combining footage of the opening with a trailer plugging the film. The ovations for the film were enormous. *Variety*'s critic noted that the film's last sequence, "My Mammy," "was a whale, and resulted in a tumultuous ovation. Jolson, personally, has never been more warmly greeted than at this premiere."[42] A weeping Jolson took to the stage at the Warner Theatre to acknowledge the audience's cheers. But none of the Warner brothers were there to savor the film's triumph. Sam Warner—the man who had engineered a significant part of this success with what his brothers had teasingly referred to as his toy phonograph—had, like Cantor Rabinowitz in *The Jazz Singer* on the eve of Yom Kippur, died—of pneumonia—twenty-four hours before the performance.

His death robbed Jack and Harry of the middle brother, the one person who (with brother Albert in New York) could mediate the stubborn fights between the oldest and the youngest siblings, the two family members actually housed at the studio. More than ever, his absence meant that with the company's changed and elevated stature in the industry a new arrangement would have to be worked out between the surviving brothers. With Sam gone and Zanuck poised to take a dominant role in shaping the studio's house style in the era of sound, all concerned would have to come up with a way to integrate the dissonant personalities of the men who ran Warner Brothers.

A flexible working arrangement, one that accommodated Harry's and Zanuck's natural antagonism, would ensure that with *The Jazz Singer*'s triumph Warner Brothers would have a permanent foothold gained through banker Waddil Catching's planning, Sam Warner's faith in the new technology, Harry and Jack Warner's gamble, and Darryl Zanuck's skills as a producer.

Zanuck would be affected by the new tension created by Sam's death. In the power balance between Jack and Harry, he became for each a substitute for the missing brother—an unenviable position for an outsider to occupy. Trying to situate himself in this new order, Zanuck was able to negotiate a working relationship and even forge a friendship with Jack. But eventually the destabilization created by Sam's death would place Zanuck in direct—and dramatic—conflict with Harry. From now on, Zanuck not only dominated the program at Warner's; he moved it and Hollywood in a new direction. This universe was conceivable only within a world that wed the visual to the aural.

Part II

INNOVATIONS

Chapter Five

DREAMING OF THE ACTUAL WORLD

TRANSFORMING WARNER BROTHERS' STYLE

An artist is a dreamer consenting to
dream of the actual world.

—GEORGE SANTAYANA, *THE
ACTUAL WORLD*

*T*HE *JAZZ SINGER* made a three-million-dollar profit.
Overnight, so it seemed, the Warners finally had the edge
they had longed for, and the rest of Hollywood (with the exception of Fox, which was already making its own version of sound
films) scrambled to catch up. The films most studios made after *The
Jazz Singer* indicated that the arrival of sound was accompanied by a
kind of stultifying panic. Uncertain what to do, for the next two years
they copied what seemed to work, notably (largely wooden) musical
revues, film versions of Broadway musical hits, and recycled attempts
at nonmusical stage fare. Mostly, however, sound meant musicals. In

1929 Warner Brothers made eighty-six films: almost half—thirty-seven—were either musicals or contained at least one musical number.

After a brief period of uncertain emulation of the Warners and Fox (who were, in turn, largely copying from the hits of Broadway or vaudeville), each studio confronted the challenge with a different house style that reflected the tastes and talents of its leading personnel and top production management. This situation meant that the producer's role, particularly his newest one as sound expert, would become even more critical than it had been in the silent cinema. For Zanuck, it meant both organizing new personnel (from technical workers to newly signed screenwriters, actors, and directors) and knowing how to orchestrate all of them into a cohesive unit whose work reflected what he wanted the new sound films to say. Sound film, which would bring us the singing heiress, the gangster, and the wisecracking chorus girl, also ushered in the age of the producer.

At MGM sound brought about one of Irving Thalberg's rare displays of misjudgment: "Novelty is always welcome, but talking pictures are just a passing fad."[1] When he saw he had been wrong, after his initial foray into the musical revue (with the leaden but much-praised *The Broadway Melody*), Thalberg led MGM into producing a raft of quality pictures and serious melodramas featuring the studio's female stars Greta Garbo, Joan Crawford, and Norma Shearer (whose brother Douglas headed the studio's sound department). Lillian Gish, the greatest actress of the silent era, left MGM as sound was ushered in.

Fox Film Corporation's ambitious head, William Fox, first clung to his belief that sound meant newsreel. He did score an enormous triumph when he filmed Lindbergh's May 20, 1927, takeoff for Paris. That same night he projected it to the Roxy's packed house of over six thousand patrons, who "stood and cheered for nearly ten minutes."[2] In the wake of the Vitaphone's triumph, Fox moved decisively and had all the corporation's theaters wired for sound. After releasing their prestige offering of Murnau's *Sunrise* (1927) with a synchronized music track, the company decided to do what Warner Brothers had not yet done: thereafter, all of their features would be "Movietoned" (Fox's version of sound).[3]

THE FIRST TALKIES

If the Warners were visionary in sensing that music on film would draw people into movie theaters, they were less so in how they first shaped their nonmusical Vitaphone fare. After *The Jazz Singer* it was logical that many of the studio's features would contain Vitaphone sequences. Nevertheless, the studio proceeded cautiously, in part because, apart from Jolson and the musicals, they *had* no strategy for shaping sound production. They were undecided whether to follow Fox's lead and switch to an all-sound format or to go with a new kind of program made up of "talkies" (like *The Lights of New York*), "part talkies" (like the Zanuck-scripted Fanny Brice vehicle, *My Man*), and silent film. The high cost of the Jolson vehicle meant that the Warners had to find a less expensive way to a winning formula. The studio's Vitaphone shorts (made at a cost of about $15,000 per film, compared to *The Jazz Singer*'s cost of $500,000) were ideally suited to accomplishing this speculative task. These early efforts show that, despite the magnitude of *The Jazz Singer*'s triumph, the form the Vitaphone should take was not yet determined: Hollywood was not at a moment of triumph, but was a cinema in transformation. Two months after Jolson's triumph, the Warners tested the climate of the Vitaphone minus music with a ten-minute talkie, a comedy called *My Wife's Gone Away*. This initial outing was followed by a melodrama, *The Lash,* and then *Non Support,* a controversial film about the tricky issue of divorce, written by and starring Burr McIntosh (of *Way Down East* fame).

Often overlooked in the history of the transition to sound, these efforts had a surprising range. In addition to canned vaudeville, they even included fairly sophisticated parodies of current hits, like the burlesque of Jeanne Eagels's star turn as Sadie Thompson in Somerset Maugham's hit *Rain*. These versatile shorts functioned in a number of ways: as modest tests of the limits of the technology; as a forum for untried performers (like Spencer Tracy), and as a way to see if silent stars with little stage experience would make it in a cinema of dialogue. Because rewiring theaters for sound was an expensive procedure, it was important that the first sound films show theater owners throughout the country that the cost would be worth it. This was particularly true for the smaller theaters, which accounted for 75 percent of all American movie houses. Last, with the issue of the costs of switching to sound balanced against the scanty, inconclusive box office data available from the few theaters wired to show sound films, they were useful as ways of experimenting with possible new directions for the medium. It seemed logical that since many of the shorts became audience favorites, these canned versions of nonmusical vaudeville playlets and skits would be followed by more ambitious attempts. The first longer all-talking Vitaphone was the thirty-minute *Solomon's Children.*

It appeared as if the Warners were using *Solomon's Children* as an antidote to the measure of assimilationism doled out in *The Jazz Singer.* In the wake of the Warners' sudden financial success, the film's unshakable faith in the tenets of Judaism may have been a way of reminding themselves of (part of) what Harry Warner felt should be the foundation of their values. Making two films that showed how unsure assimilated Jews were with their secular success was a clear indication of the larger uncertainty with which the Warners approached their position within the industry. Given the constant fraternal war over money and power that was waged among the siblings, the theme voiced in *Solomon's Children*—a suspicion of, and contempt for, those who lived their lives guided by a shallow value scheme based on wealth—was ironic.

Zanuck immediately became immersed in helping to formulate a policy to deal with the manifold problems of sound, writing stories for four of the studio's thirteen "part-talking" films.[4] Most of the films made under Zanuck's guidance were conventional genre pieces with sound tacked on, or spliced in, to all too familiar narratives. While *The Lights of New York* and *The Singing Fool,* the studio's two biggest hits, were both conventional, in certain respects they also marked Zanuck's first attempts to truly strike out on his own. *The Lights of New York* (which started life as a Vitaphone short) was a sketch for the more famous gangster films Zanuck would shortly produce. It was guided by Bryan Foy (vaudevillian Eddie's son), who graduated to this assignment after serving a kind of apprenticeship supervising the production of the Vitaphone shorts.

But in addition to the fascination the action-packed world of crime held for him, Zanuck was intrigued by the technical issues sound raised, particularly where to place the microphones. As Zanuck recalled:

> Microphones had to be hidden. Every telephone had a microphone in it. We hid them in the chandeliers. We would hang microphones on the wall, [painted] the same color as the wall. . . . The cameramen went out of their minds trying to keep the microphones out of the picture.[5]

Both Jack and Harry Warner were away during the production of *The Lights of New York*. Since the untimely death of the Vitaphone's patron saint, Sam Warner, had removed him from the scene, there was no one to prevent Zanuck from experimenting. He saw this low-profile two-reeler as a way to move one step closer to convincing audiences that pictures should talk, a proposition Harry wanted to approach with caution *only* after audiences demanded it. Zanuck wanted to lead, not follow, public taste. As Zanuck bluntly put it, this little-remembered film "turned the whole goddam tide."[6] Released in July 1928, *The Lights of New York* was advertised as Hollywood's first all-talking picture.

In his eagerness to demonstrate what the Vitaphone could do, Zanuck, one writer observed, had created a self-conscious cacophony of sound that was hardly a creative display of the technology. It seemed "as if a sound man had run amuck."[7] But the novelty of talking pictures was, at this date, still a draw for most moviegoers. The critically panned film grossed two million dollars at the box office, a gratifying return on its $75,000 budget.

Although the film ran less than an hour, its urban Broadway milieu and gangland themes (like a surprising mob murder in a barber shop) were harbingers of what Zanuck would shortly do with *The Public Enemy* and *Little Caesar*. Whatever its deficiencies, *The Lights of New York* demonstrated Zanuck's uncanny ear for gangland argot (the phrase "take him for a ride" originated here). Not for the last time, because it captured the fancy of a public besotted with the real-life exploits of New York nightlife and fascinated by the doings of the nation's crime figures, Zanuck rode ahead of the tide of public taste. His gamble with *The Lights of New York* paid off, and it was a turning point in Zanuck's career. He had trusted his own judgment, and not consulted his bosses until he was done. The film's runaway success convinced him that it was his mission to take risks; "from then on, everything had to be a first something."[8]

THE EXECUTIVE

In 1928, Hollywood made but ten all-talking sound films. They were all produced at Warner Brothers under Zanuck's supervision.[9] In 1929, screenwriter Zanuck's name—or that of one of his pseudonyms—appeared on only three films. He had other work to do. While the rest of the industry was struggling to catch up with them, the Warners consolidated their dominance afforded them by the Vitaphone by fully integrating the three branches of their corporation: production, exhibition, and distribution. They bought out the powerful Stanley Corporation of America with its almost three hundred theaters in seventy-five cities. (Among these was the prestigious Strand Theatre in New York.) Within a month of this move, they purchased the controlling interest in First National Pictures, a powerhouse that had previously made only silent films. In acquiring it, they immediately bought themselves a virtually new production facility over the hill in Burbank. Once wired for sound, the new site would be a state-of-the-art production plant far superior to their current Hollywood lot. The Warners thus moved the bulk of their production from the small, ten-acre Sunset studio they had inhabited since 1923, to their much larger home. One month after that, the Warners purchased the Skouras Brothers' theaters in St. Louis. After all this expansion, they still had enough money left over to pay off all their outstanding loans.[10]

Fully in command, Zanuck started to exercise the producer's traits for which we have come to know him. He was the first to see that color might be a defining characteristic of the musical, and to this end he shot spectacular two-strip Technicolor sequences in four films: *The Show of Shows, Gold Diggers of Broadway, On with the Show,* and *The Desert Song.* While Thalberg and MGM would receive credit as the first to create "original" material for the musical in their production *The Broadway Melody,* Zanuck's musical innovations have been overlooked in most histories of Hollywood. But look at the wooden campiness of Thalberg's effort! Harry Richman's horrible overacting and applause-milking singing style almost make Jolson appear humble. Adding to the guilty pleasure one can derive from enjoying this horrid film are the unexplained mismatched accents of its female "sister" leads, Anita Page (with her adenoidal New Yorkese) and sibling Bessie Love (with her Texas drawl).

Zanuck also displayed great creativity in how he deployed the genre's personnel. In *On with the Show,* he anticipated the industry standard of dubbing the voices of stars with great box office appeal but little musical talent by substituting an uncredited singer for popular star Betty Compson. He even used a double (filmed in long shot) for the dance sequences. Sensing the public was tiring of seeing every studio star showcased in these films (even Rin Tin Tin appeared in *The Show of Shows*), Zanuck looked around for ways to invigorate the genre. In 1929 he came up with a truly novel solution: marrying the musical to the urban crime film. He rehearsed this union in *On with the Show* and *Gold Diggers of Broadway.* Though these are tentative, even failed, efforts, for Zanuck they are the first steps in a process that would eventually lead him to hit upon the correct formula in 1933 with *42nd Street.*

NOAH'S ARK

If musicals, by definition, called upon Zanuck to try skills the silent cinema had never demanded, in nonmusicals like *Old San Francisco,* and particularly in the disastrous *Noah's Ark,* he tried to apply the lessons he learned from his first major film project, *The Storm,* to the world of sound. *Noah's Ark* was almost two years in preparation.

Zanuck turned to Michael Curtiz, whose prior experience with film epics in Germany made him a good choice to direct. Curtiz apparently felt that this lavish, big-budget film was his chance to stand out, perhaps even to become a dominant creative force, as Lubitsch had once been. Knowing that the studio valued a director's ability to work with efficiency and economy, Curtiz tried to endear himself to both Zanuck and Harry Warner. Suggesting ways the studio might economize on this spectacular effort, he wrote Harry: "I am eagerly awaiting your and Mr. Zanuck's answer to my proposition submitted herein, and I hope that you will give me the chance to make in 'Noah's Ark' the biggest box-office and literary success that ever has been done in America, by taking full advantage of the clever organization of the studio and the skillful leadership of the executives."[11] (Though flattery is purported to get you nowhere, in Curtiz's case it seems to have led him straight to the director's chair.)

At 135 minutes, *Noah's Ark* was to be the studio's longest and most ambitious film to date. As Zanuck's notes of July 19, 1928, show, in sixty-three separate items ranging from the length of shots ("Dissolve from dog long shot to insert of the helmet 'to my sonny boy,' then dissolve back to O'Brien's face and FADE OUT for intermission") to the evaluation of a performance ("have O'Brien and Big Boy kick out the window quicker"), like Noah himself supervising the preparations for the ark, Zanuck was on top of every conceivable detail.[12] Zanuck wrote the film's treatment, the short narrative description on which an actual scenario and screenplay would be based. To make certain that the public was aware of the film, Zanuck's treatment was "novelized" by Arline De Haas, a specialist who had performed these chores for three previous Vitaphones, *The Jazz Singer*, *Tenderloin*, and *Glorious Betsy*. Taking no chances that spectacular floods and an unparalleled parade of beasts into Noah's ark might not be enough to attract moviegoers, Zanuck borrowed a page from DeMille and Griffith and interwove the Old Testament narrative with a modern World War I love saga. Capping all this insurance, the necessary sex would be provided by the passion between the beauteous Miriam of Dolores Costello and hunky George O'Brien as Noah's son Japheth. The frontispiece photo of the novelization incarnates Zanuck's strange version of the biblical ethos. It shows the scantily clad pair in a passionate embrace with the caption "Always remember, Miriam. Whatever happens, I love you." So much for the Old Testament.

Despite the fact that *Noah's Ark* would have two of everything (including dual love stories across historical epochs), Zanuck did not count on its thin narrative carrying the picture. Rather, the film would succeed as a piece of spectacular showmanship. He intended to use the novelty of Vitaphone to highlight every physical gesture and movement leading up to the flood, including the moans, shrieks, creaks, roars, gurgles, and crashes as the human and mineral world was swept under by forces of the great deluge. As a big game hunter, he was also delighted to show off the forms and sounds of the film's exotic menagerie, which soon grew to include okapi, sacred Indian oxen, and single striped zebras, among other creatures. In pursuit of pure showmanship, for the film's high point he filled the screen with a spectacular flood that was perhaps a bit too realistic. Cameraman Hal Mohr felt that art director Anton Grot's massive sets were not secure enough to withstand the weight of the water and the enormous number of extras Zanuck intended to deploy. But now fully in the throes of his biggest challenge to date (and sometimes actually directing the film when the stress proved too great for Curtiz to bear), Zanuck overruled Mohr.[13] The sequences were shot as planned, with tragically realistic results: several extras drowned.[14]

For all its ballyhoo, the film was an enormous flop. The New York press seemed delighted that Hollywood and Zanuck could, with sound, serve up a disaster of such colossal proportions. The *New York Times* claimed the film "frequently borders on the ridiculous," while *The New Yorker* called it what it was: "an idiotic super spectacle."[15] According to Marlys Harris, *Noah's Ark* quickly developed a cult reputation—as one of the worst films ever made. When, some time after the film had disappeared from circulation, and Zanuck had gone on to bigger things, he ran into writer Arthur Caeser. "Without ceremony, Caeser gave Zanuck a hard kick in the pants. 'That's for taking a book that was a hit for nineteen hundred years and making a flop out of it.'"[16] *Noah's* failure taught him a valuable lesson: that without a firm story foundation, nothing—not star power, not spectacle, not advertising, not novelty—could save a poorly conceived and executed work. His reputation was not really damaged, though. He was able to ride out what has been estimated as a two-million-dollar loss because in this period of the Vitaphone's novelty, and with the insurance provided by their large theater chain, the rest of the Warner's program he supervised was profitable.

IMPRESARIO

From the violent, sexually motivated murders of *Habit,* to the numerous, manic-paced felonies contained in "For Men Only," Zanuck's earliest writings show his fascination with crime. He was not alone. During the 1920s, crime and its reporting became more than a compelling new set of narratives. It was now a form of public entertainment. These newspaper stories were filled with a cast of unseemly and as often described, unlikely figures (like the "pig woman" in the Halls-Mills murder case). They were real people who, mediated through the new tabloid sensibility, emerged as characters, as leading figures in some new public drama. Before the movies designated which of these "hits" would be selected from a long list of possibilities, for their turn, the newspapers of the 1920s were filled with innumerable "trials of the century": Sacco and Vanzetti, the Halls-Mills murder case, the Scopes Trial. The dramatic reportage rivaled any salacious Jazz Age tale DeMille might concoct. Having tried to write the war out of their collective systems, American authors now seemed eager to turn to other subjects. Crime seemed frequently to be in the forefront.

If Zanuck did not discover the tabloid's "hard-boiled" style, he did something of greater consequence than merely getting there first. He used his knowledge of the studio system in concert with his hunch about what the public wanted to see to reinvent it on the American screen. As an impresario, he imagined that with its different reach, by appropriating to film what others were doing in print or of late, even on the radio, he could transform an entire medium. As a result of this perspicacity, the gangster film joined the long list of novel cultural forms Ann Douglas catalogues as constituting a taxon-omy of the modern: from "athletic bodies and sexual freedom for women" to "skyscrapers, chain stores, and the culture of credit." With very few changes, these forms, including Zanuck's films, have molded and still shape "the modern world as we know it."[17] Zanuck's terse, telegraphic, action-oriented style would fit well with how certain journalists and writers were shaping the Depression era. By expressing themselves in language (and, as the popularity of newspaper cartoons showed, in visuals), their poetic coarseness earned an approving nod from a very different stylist, Virginia Woolf, who heard innovative, true things in this American vernacular, in what she referred to as our "expressive, ugly, vigorous slang."[18] The way he orchestrated these tendencies into a coherent body of work, the way he set up the narratives in the Warner's gangster films, confirms Raymond Chandler's observation that tempo was not about how things are actually recalled, but rather about "how things happen." Even with his limitations as a writer, Zanuck's version of "how things happen" would for a time enable him to break free of certain restraints of the more tame cinema of consensus that he had created in *The Jazz Singer*. With the sometimes uneasy approval of the Warners, he began to forge what was easily "the most distinctive house style in Hollywood."[19]

Moreover, the ethos and style that suffused Zanuck's gangster films became a useful extension of the man himself. Where did Zanuck, whose Midwest and Southern California suburban upbringing was so different from the Warners', a Christian outsider to the studio's controlling family, fit in? How did this young executive impose his vision on an entire studio? The general frame provided by the Warners' feisty, difficult stance toward the rest of the world suited young Darryl Zanuck and his tabloid rhetoric rather well. Arriving at power so young and so fast, and performing its rituals in a highly visible forum, Zanuck needed to adopt a public persona that would make people overlook his youth and his less than prepossessing appearance. Though he quickly took on some of the trappings of the film industry's version of moguldom—such as big game hunting and polo—as much as these activities provided him with props useful to

this new persona, the films he made also functioned as his presentation of self. The hard-boiled manner he created on film spilled over,
verbally, at least, into his public performances.

The slap in the face Cagney administers to "dames" in a number
of Warner crime films carried the same heft as the sawed-off polo mallet Zanuck carried around with him, smacking surfaces to make his
point. The criminal in *The Public Enemy* who breaks the rules as he
rises through the ranks to challenge the older order of established
hoodlums has his parallel in both Zanuck's rise with Warner's and
the studio's rise in Hollywood. And though *The New Yorker* might
poke fun at Zanuck by alleging he greeted one interviewer clad in a
garish, gangsterlike silk robe—"a Napoleon in a vermilion bathrobe
with polo ponies painted on it"—he must have known that such a
costume was the perfect way to disguise his youth, his rural roots,
and his relative lack of sophistication.[20] Like the rest of the moguls,
Zanuck's new power seemed to provide him with a charter to reinvent himself in a land custom-tailored to provide him with the settings and props necessary to pull this off. The films that thrived
under Zanuck became an emblem of his reinvention of a better,
tougher Hollywood self, the only kind of figure who could survive
amid the rough-and-tumble business dealings of Hollywood and the
brawls and intrigues of creatures like the Warners. (Richard Zanuck,
I think, would understand this. And he would later say, "For a little
guy coming out of Wahoo, Nebraska, he did all right in a very tough
town.")[21]

The rural boy, looking for a world to invent and, within it, a place
he might inhabit, discovered a cinema firmly rooted in the city. Its
chroniclers were not the official voices of the genteel; they were the
reporters whose stories ran in the tabloids. As *The New Yorker* admiringly conceded, "Zanuck is primarily a great journalist using the
screen instead of the printing press. . . . Zanuck has this power of getting excited and selling this excitement to the public."[22] His enthusiasm, his sense of timeliness, and his willingness to take a chance
willed the gangster genre into being. A cinema of stark, almost cruel
unsentimentality, it was a radical departure for Hollywood.

Zanuck made us see that dreaming of the world as many average people knew it (or received it from a pungent mediator like Walter Winchell) was as appealing and enthralling as the alternative universe Thalberg offered, where all women comported themselves with the constricted dignity of Norma Shearer, or moved with the balletic, unattainable eroticism of Greta Garbo.

In contrast, Zanuck's world was populated by the likes of James Cagney, Barbara Stanwyck, and Edward G. Robinson. But if his vision was initially inspired by the newspapers or the newsreels, Zanuck knew that story film was a different thing from its ancestors in print, or that which could be glimpsed for a few minutes in a short newsreel. After absorbing from these forms the things that suited his new purpose (and operating in the midst of a culture undergoing baffling changes), he used the powerful chemistry forged by these potentialities to dream about the actual world. In making viewers consent to do the same, he altered the kinds of stories Hollywood could tell.

Chapter Six

A CRIMINAL TALENT

The screen, in acquiring the gift of
speech, had taken on new possibilities.
It was my ambition to make screen
stories live.

—DARRYL F. ZANUCK

THE SUCCESS OF talking pictures ensured that Zanuck's supervisory role would supersede his writer's identity. As a
producer, he "wanted stories that were timely and which
would touch upon subjects vital to the public."¹ A number of these
subjects—American justice, violent crime, urban poverty, prostitu-
tion—were not just contemporary: they were subversive. In taking
the studio program off on a new tangent, Zanuck jettisoned respectability, taking up the noisy cadence of the gangster's machine
gun in place of dialogue spoken in some drawing room. In doing so,
he found that his work fit the Depression's mood.

Zanuck had a gift useful if one wanted to supplant long-estab-
lished ways of doing things: the ability to read social trends very

early. As *The New Yorker* observed, it is not so much the case, in setting trends, that Zanuck possessed clairvoyant powers. Rather, like all great impresarios, he had the ability to marshal the audience's attention and, through a salesman's pitch and a showman's chutzpah, to make moviegoers like what he liked. Zanuck was "the man who says, 'This excites me, and I'll make it excite them.'"[2]

Looking at and listening to many of the earliest sound films, we feel as though Hollywood had lost, rather than gained, something in abandoning silence. Zanuck changed this. People in movies just weren't supposed to talk the way Zanuck had them talk: "dese," "dirty greaseballs," "goil," "ain't."[3] Barbara Stanwyck's series of ungrammatical "dirty tramps" and Cagney's slang-slinging, ruthless gangster Tom Powers (whose final words, "I ain't so tough," are uttered from the gutter) brought a harsh burst of stylized reality to viewers going through their own tough situations.[4] The American cinema had been asleep. Animated by Zanuck's new voice and his spirit of raw originality, it suddenly came to life.

Walter Winchell had invented the modern gossip column, redefining the public's relationship to the culture of the celebrated. In addition to the social leveling power this left in its wake, part of the novelty of Winchell's method (not lost upon Zanuck) was how he mediated the world through a new, distinctive, pungent vocabulary of graphic, tabloid form and urban audacity. These traits had been present in American journalism before, but never in respectable newspapers. Zanuck, like Winchell, made the previously marginalized or segregated lowbrow forms in which they excelled part of their era's mainstream entertainment culture.

The distinctive personalities who became movie stars in the sound era seemed to engage directly with the American public on a scale never before seen. With Zanuck's postwar, utterly American concern for the modern and the controversial (rather than the literary and the genteel), he used his control over Warner Brothers' output to transform the way film was connected to public culture.

MAKING NEWS, AGAIN: *DOORWAY TO HELL*

On the eve of the 1930s, other studios were churning out westerns, melodramas, classics, wholesome comedies, and films based on the new concept of best-sellers. Instead, Zanuck combed the daily newspapers and weekly magazines for inspiration. Sometimes, he did not have far to reach. His former employer and sponsor, A. F. Foster, had become a casualty. Foster had moved on from Yuccatone to bootlegging and got himself murdered.[5] (We would see the repercussions of this as late as 1952, when in *Wait Till the Sun Shines, Nellie,* as a result of his association with a bootlegger, the small-town barber's city-wandering son is gunned down by gangsters.) Stunned by Foster's death, Zanuck suddenly became aware of crime in America. He went about the Warner Brothers lot telling anyone who would listen that "it's war out there!"[6] and "began devouring contemporary Chicago literature and sending for contemporary Chicago historians."[7]

Doorway to Hell was Zanuck's first full-scale incursion into this hard-boiled milieu. Released in November 1930, it signaled a new, more realistic take on organized crime. Its story was based as much on fact as on Zanuck's sense of invention. The Warners felt that *Doorway to Hell*'s world of violence and illegal activities made it a "reckless experiment" that Zanuck should drop.[8] With an "unhappy ending, no hero, no major character that inspired sympathy," the film violated all the rules.[9] This, of course, was precisely what Zanuck wanted. His track record and intense enthusiasm may have convinced the Warners to stand back and let him try things his way. But they feared the project would leave them with substantial losses, and so gave Zanuck a small budget. It didn't matter.

Doorway to Hell would be an enormous hit, in part because of one particular innovation: Zanuck made the gangster a sympathetic figure. He had always insisted that the rooting interest of any film—the unambiguous depiction of what motivated a character—was essential if the audience was to understand the character and then be bound to him or her in sympathy or against them in hatred. Hollywood had almost always portrayed the gangster as an evil figure who in the end gets his comeuppance. But the complicated circumstances in which crime was viewed by Depression-era moviegoers made Zanuck reconsider this formula.

In *Doorway* he made the unusual decision to cast Lew Ayres as gangster Louie Ricarno. Ayres, fresh from his enormous triumph as the hero of *All Quiet on the Western Front,* was seen in the public mind as heroic, poetic, and sensitive. In *Doorway to Hell,* some of this sensitivity would unexpectedly become part of the gangster's psychological makeup. Ayres would play a person who grew up in a slum and saw two of his siblings die—not as a result of gang war but from typhoid contracted from drinking contaminated milk. Louie Ricarno's criminal acts are motivated for reasons that many poor struggling Americans could understand: to give his one surviving brother the good life. Beyond using the profits from crime as a means to obtain material security for his family and himself, Ricarno also attempts to do what many in Hollywood would have found comprehensible: like the moguls sending their children to posh private schools, he tries to use his fortune to buy respectability. Ricarno sends his brother to an exclusive military school to insulate the boy. He then tries to complete his own metamorphosis from gangster into legitimate citizen. After setting up his illegal activities in a structure so businesslike that they no longer require violence to survive, he retires from the racket of crime for good. Like a retired (or deposed) movie mogul, Ricarno has even landed a lucrative contract to write his memoirs.

But—like Michael Corleone in the last installment of Francis Ford Coppola's *Godfather*—Ricarno will come to see that organized crime offers rewards as great as its punishments, and getting out is not as simple as he might think it is. Ensconced in Florida, Louie is trying to enjoy his new life writing about crime rather than committing it. But forces larger than Louie's desires for serenity and respectability keep pulling him back. His girlfriend craves the excitement that comes with the urban gang life. Bored by his sedate new profile and tranquil new venue, she leaves him. Then, his innocent younger brother is kidnaped by unscrupulous rivals, and in the process inadvertently hit by a car and killed. It is these crude, toothpick-chewing creatures who mastermind the kidnaping (and not Ricarno) whom Zanuck shows to be the film's *real* gangsters.

Bereft of the one source of human love that is his connection to "normal" values, Ricarno reverts to type and goes on a vengeful crime spree. But since Zanuck has clearly already established his rooting interest (the crime is done for personal, rather than monetary or psychopathic, reasons), Ricarno's violence does not alienate the viewer. In fact, his decision, at the film's end, to walk to his certain death amid a hail of gunfire only adds to our admiration. It is a kind of heroic existential gesture one is more apt to find in a Camus novel than in a Hollywood screenplay. The movie, full of violence and coded gay references, would normally have run afoul of the censors, but Zanuck felt sure they would "realize that the picture has a strong moral tone, and that is, THE FUTILITY OF CRIME AS BUSINESS OR AS A PROFIT."[10] He was right.

The censors may have been convinced that the film was really a morality lesson, and not a glorification of violence, but the audience never loses sight of the wedding of violence and entertainment that is so central to Zanuck's hard-boiled vision. When Louie claims that he is just like any other businessman, one of the cops responds, "Sure, you sell beer to the workingman with a few murders on the side for entertainment." Just as audiences eagerly anticipated the big production numbers in musical entertainment, in crime films they now waited for the dramatic rubout. (Like the "money shot" in pornography, this is the climax, it is what the audience has paid to see.)[11] In a Hollywood rife with power struggles, labor problems, and government antitrust actions, Zanuck's suggestion that crime's authority is based on business organization more than violence, and his linkage of gang leaders and crime to stars and entertainment are both startling and accurate.

Another innovation of Zanuck's in *Doorway* is the wide use he made of newspaper headlines, an updated epistolary reminder of the honest journalistic work done by these films. The narrative is punctuated by inserts of tabloids whose terse banners tell us the outcome of a battle or scheme. Zanuck also develops and organizes the narrative around the creation of Louie's memoirs. If the former permitted

Zanuck to claim that he was merely telling the facts (and thus should be as free to do so as the press), the memoirs contain Zanuck's editorial opinions on the social meaning of American crime. Louie's completion of his memoirs will signal the end of his life.

There are other parallels, audacious suggestions that entertainment and crime are more closely aligned than most of Hollywood would like to admit. The police chief, like Hollywood's chief censor, envisions a different tale than the one Louie is writing. He warns Louie not to write his history until it includes the final scene at the electric chair. (In a subversive double-edged retort, Louie tells the chief he won't mind this fate if he can have him sitting on his lap.) After learning of his brother's death, Louie tells his inquiring, eager publisher that in light of this new development, his overdue book is "not done yet": he is writing a new ending. The last shot of the film is a closeup of page 214 of Louie's book, accompanied by a full fifteen seconds of machine-gun clatter. Then Zanuck's editorial voice fills the screen, and we read:

> The doorway to Hell is a one-way door. There is no retribution—no pleas for clemency. The little boy walked through it with his head up and a smile on his lips. They gave him a funeral—a swell funeral that stopped traffic—and then they forgot him before the roses had a chance to wilt.
>
> Finis.

That's tough.

Warner Brothers advertised the film as "the picture gangland dared Hollywood to make." A publicity sheet went so far as to allege that during production there were real killers on the set. In the kind of hyperbolic promotion for which Warner's, and the rest of the film industry, were already renowned, they claimed:

> Several ex-gunmen who were the real McCoy in various underworld sections throughout the country contribute to the realistic atmosphere of *Doorway to Hell*. . . . These racketeers, working in the movies under assumed names, are merely known by nicknames or

their first names. Socco, Midge, and Rattler, believe it or not, are three of the names by which these gunmen are known to each other. Their real names, their occupations, and past are known to no one, perhaps, except themselves.[12]

Critics got the point. Headlining his review "Reality Rules Gangland," Edwin Schallert of the *Los Angeles Times* noted that Zanuck had not made "the conventional movie melodrama of the underworld, but a vindictive and accurate depiction of how racketeers war against one another in a world apart from legal enforcement." He cautioned viewers that while undoubtedly "you will be fascinated by the picture . . . you may not really enjoy it."[13]

"BEYOND A MOTION PICTURE": *THE PUBLIC ENEMY*

Zanuck's work gained momentum after *Doorway to Hell,* and he garnered enormous publicity and profit with a succession of follow-up gangster pictures. In moving into sparsely settled terrain, he carefully selected actors with distinctive personalities and speech patterns, trademarks that might engage the viewer in the same way physical action or beauty could, and what had once been abstract (how *did* a gangster or a "bad" woman talk?) became concrete. As James Cagney explained to an interviewer: "The idea was, if you could give them [the audience] something to remember, use it."[14] Zanuck's instinct for selecting actors who could do this was remarkable.

James Cagney was one of his finds. When Zanuck saw Cagney and Joan Blondell on Broadway in *Penny Arcade*, he was impressed with their potential. They were both brought to Hollywood to reprise their parts in a film now called *Sinner's Holiday.* When *The Public Enemy* went into production, Cagney was making $400 a week, far less than the $750 paid to Leslie Fenton, the actor who was playing his gangland mentor, "Nails" Nathan. Cagney was originally slated to play the part of the best friend, Mat, with James Woods playing Tom, and Jean Harlow (on loan from MGM at a weekly $1,000) playing a thrill-seeking society dame who finds Cagney's criminal as alluring as the rest of the country soon would. Playing an inspired hunch, Zanuck decided that Cagney (whom he would claim as "my complete discovery")[15] would make a better gangster than Woods. Cagney, born and raised in New York's tough Hell's Kitchen neighborhood, did not have far to go in search of role models. He often stated that unlike other actors who needed to immerse themselves in research or character study to play such parts, Cagney had a different hook. He *knew* these people: he had grown up with them.

Cagney was a committed professional who took his acting and his craft very seriously. But his most potent link to the spectator lay in what a director once told him: "Everything you are is in your face."[16] Cagney played a tough gangster, but it was not this alone that made him appealing. Starting with Tom Powers, "his gangster showed the dark side of the American dream. He was always a man who too badly wanted to rise above his beginnings, always a man who discovered too late that success at any price was overpriced."[17] He was perfect for the part of Tom Powers, and his uneasy mixture of toughness, psychosis, and vulnerability, combined with an instantly identifiable voice and an inimitable hoofer's way of moving, made him an overnight star.

"I was way ahead in thinking," Zanuck was later to say: "No love story, but loaded with sex and violence."[18] The film chronicles the rise of a policeman's son (James Cagney) and his best friend, Mat (James Woods). Both boys grow up in a rough, poor urban milieu. With little attention from his father, and a naive, overprotective mother, Tom takes to crime early on, though his straight-arrow brother does not. Tom and Mat move from childhood shenanigans to bootlegging to murder. Tom is about to go straight when he is murdered by a rival gang. His body is deposited at his family's doorstep.

The Public Enemy's overpowering last shot—Tom's corpse, wrapped in bandages, toppling wordlessly into his family's doorway—was solely Zanuck's inspiration. At a story conference, Zanuck set the proper creative mood by having a phonograph play Eddie Cantor's "I'm Forever Blowing Bubbles," the song that opens the

picture. In touch with his muses, Zanuck looked toward the rear
door of his office and shouted, "Okay!"

> A voice was heard saying: "Buzz! Buzz!" as if imitating a bell, and
> Zanuck got up and went to the door and opened it. Milton Sperling
> came in. He was covered from head to foot in a sack, which was
> looped around his neck. "Why, Tom!" said Zanuck, in a high-
> pitched voice. Sperling grimaced as he stumbled into the room, and
> looking at Zanuck, said: "Hello, Mom," and then fell flat on his
> face.[19]

Zanuck insisted that despite slapped faces, bullet-ridden bodies,
assassinated equines, and the novel use to which he instructed
Cagney to put a grapefruit (on Mae Clarke's face), *The Public Enemy*
was more a lecture about violence than a film glorifying it. He told a
Hollywood Code administrator that the film still "has a moral."[20]

It needed one. The United States Supreme Court, reviewing the
finding of an earlier federal case (*Mutual Film Corporation v. The Industrial Commission of Ohio*), had stated that film was "a business
pure and simple" and therefore should not be accorded the same
constitutional protection as the other organs of public opinion, particularly the press. To respond to criticism in the court's finding that
film's "dumb show" inevitably sensationalized content (rather than
circulated education and stimulated popular opinion), Zanuck suggested to the MPPDA—the Motion Picture Producers and Distribu-
tors of America, the industry's self-regulatory agency—that his films
used violence as a frightening way to warn and advise.

As long as he had to be wary of the censor, Zanuck never agreed
that his films were a dangerous new genre of fantastic history that
blurred the boundaries between fact and entertainment. In tacking a
warning that crime does not pay onto the last frames of *The Public
Enemy* ("The end of Tom Powers is the end of every hoodlum . . . "),
he was paying lip service to the perspectives of his critics. Zanuck
must have known that after audiences had sat through ninety minutes
of raw, absolutely riveting bad behavior, a thirty-second coda tacked

on at the end would have all the moral and legal force of the warning tag on a mattress.

Milton Sperling recalls of the movie that "Zanuck was determined to make it into a blockbuster. He was all hyped up about it, and kept repeating to [director] Willie Wellman and his crew that they mustn't let a drop of sentimentality seep into the action."[21] Spurred on by Zanuck, Wellman promised he would deliver "the toughest, the most violent, most realistic" gang film ever made.[22]

Zanuck did not see some of the criminals in these films as immoral, but rather as *amoral*. He told Sperling:

> People are going to say the characters are immoral, but they're not because they don't *have* any morals. They steal, they kill, they lie, they hump each other because that's the way they're made, and if you allow a decent human feeling or pang of conscience to come into their makeup, you've lost 'em and changed the kind of movie we're making.[23]

Struggling to overcome the harsh, character-warping lessons of urban poverty, the men who turn to crime as a way out are not barren of human feeling. They usually have room to love one figure: their mother. As Zanuck later recalled, "In *Public Enemy* I gave Cagney one redeeming trait. He was a no-good bastard but he loved his mother and somehow or other you felt a certain affection and rooting interest for him even though he was despicable."[24] These men are not animals. As *The New Yorker* noted, if previous gangsters were "supernatural beings[s] having no legitimate connection to the human race," Zanuck's Tom Powers, a boy from a poor but decent family, the son of a policeman, was "a human being in a human environment, a victim of a corrupt time" as much as an agent deciding in which direction to turn.[25] With a title setting the date at which the film starts (1908), *The Public Enemy*'s documentary-influenced opening attempts to lay out a blueprint of facts explaining *why* Tom took the path he did. Here, as always, Zanuck provided a figure (usually it is a best friend or a brother) who, raised in the same environment as the future criminal, inevitably turns out to be a cop, priest, or some other exemplary figure of moral rectitude. (In *The Public Enemy* it was his brother.)

The film's arsenal of assault contained many memorable shocks. One shows Cagney shooting a rival who had been involved in the death of his mentor, Nails Nathan. While such a vengeance killing is to be expected of the gangster, Zanuck added an unsettling twist: the nemesis Cagney shoots is a racehorse. One of the reasons the film was such a hit was that it enacts events (including the shooting of the horse) that the public had read about in the press. By merging (and then blurring) the boundaries of reportage with those of fiction and popular entertainment, Zanuck moved Hollywood in a different direction in public culture. Other films were connected to the audience through a paternalistic and superior pose: we-shall-teach-you-what-you-couldn't-possibly-know. Zanuck changed the equation. His tabloid-inspired films empowered viewers because he linked them to more exciting versions of "what-you-already-know." Zanuck knew that a vernacular, rather than a high-toned, cinema was more in sync with what Depression audiences were reading in the tabloids or seeing in the streets than the gossamer illusions spun out at other studios. He empowered the audience by speaking to them in their own terms, by treating them almost as equals. Let the newspapers disseminate the facts; Zanuck would provide something more valuable: the meanings and the psychological motivations of this culture.

Many of the reviews noted the power of *The Public Enemy; Variety* crowned it the "roughest, most powerful and best gang film to date."[26] Critics had higher praise still for *Little Caesar,* another Zanuck film, released between *Doorway to Hell* and *The Public Enemy.* The *New York Times* found that in Edward G. Robinson's Rico Bandello Zanuck (and director Mervyn LeRoy) had created "a figure out of Greek epic tragedy."[27] But a large number were uncertain whether this was a good direction in which to lead the American cinema. Even Lewis E. Lawes, the warden of Sing-Sing, attested to the realistic hold Zanuck's films exerted, noting that "many prisoners have told me that crime pictures started them on their course."[28] Zanuck knew he had succeeded when Irving Thalberg, stunned by

The Public Enemy's raw strength, told him, "That's not a motion picture. It's beyond a motion picture."[29]

INCENDIARY MATERIAL:
BABY FACE AND THE CENSORS

If Thalberg felt *The Public Enemy* had somehow passed beyond the emotional preserves of cinema as he imagined it, what must he have made of *Baby Face*, a film so unusual it stands out as one of perhaps a dozen examples of a truly oppositional cinema made by any studio-era major film corporation? When in September 1931, after much public outcry, the studios agreed to produce no more gangster films, these subversive forces had to go somewhere. Zanuck saw that they went to sex. With *Baby Face*, he made what was perhaps his boldest, most complicated move: he extended the outlaw argument previously reserved for men to women. Based on a Zanuck story (one of the last, in fact, for which he received screenwriting credit), *Baby Face* was made in 1933, at the cusp of truly strict enforcement of the Hollywood Code (an act speeded up, no doubt, by Zanuck's contributions to the crime film).

Though Zanuck's story owes much to nineteenth-century literary genres ("fallen woman") and to previous films (like MGM's Harlow vehicle, *Red Headed Woman*), the seedy steel-town milieu of illegal cheap saloons, bleak mills, and sex for barter that Barbara Stanwyck's Lil Powers inhabits in *Baby Face* are, in Zanuck's hands, given a concreteness only he could serve up. The silent cinema from the very first had drawn upon the newspapers for its subject matter (and, like vaudeville, had even featured "criminals" or morally suspect—but alluring—figures like Evelyn Nesbitt, the Girl in the Red Velvet Swing, as headliners on a bill or marquee), but talking films and the actors who inhabited them gave the world of these news stories specific—and widely imitated—ways of sounding, moving, dressing, and, most important, speaking.

Baby Face chronicles the rise and—contrary to Zanuck's wishes, as the MPPDA had its way—the inevitable decline of a woman who uses sex outside of marriage to get what she wants. Writer Howard Smith recalls that both Stanwyck and Zanuck together came up with the sex-for-power exchange at a story conference, as the writer put it, "for amplification and improvement of the story."[30] Lily Powers is born into poverty, and lives and works with her abusive, alcoholic father. Zanuck's innovation in *Baby Face* is that Lil Powers refuses to take the fate ascribed by her name ("little power"). Like any good disciple of Zanuck at Warner's, she refuses to be a victim. She does not accept her fate in order to be a "good" woman—and in violating these laws of "good" society, she has our sympathy. Lil works as a waitress in her father's seedy speakeasy, a joint frequented by working-class clientele. We see family life Zanuck-style: her father pimps her to a local politician in exchange for his protection. Lil resists the politician's advances in classic Stanwyck fashion, pouring scalding coffee on his roving hands. The enraged man storms out and tells Mr. Powers, "No more protection for you!" He will have his joint closed down. Her furious father accuses her of being a tramp. Not flinching, Lily responds: "I'm a tramp and who's to blame? My father! A swell start you gave me. Nothin' but men, dirty rotten men. And you're lower than any of them. I'll hate you as long as I live." (This father and daughter exchange is *not* from a Verdi opera.)

What makes Lil unusual is that her audacious will to power is not just for monetary profit. It's for self-respect, for identity, for survival. When Lil asks, "What chance has a woman got?" Zanuck was really asking men and women in the audience, "What does a woman do during the Depression? How does she get power, and what are the moral implications of getting power?" Rather than feeling outrage, moviegoers might well feel that, given the options open to her by class and gender, Lil's response is normal, motivated, even logical.

Of course Lil was not the first female character Zanuck had imbued with greater abilities than the males with whom she associates. From his first short scenario, "For Men Only," to the resourceful Irene Dare of *Habit*, Zanuck's female characters, outsiders to the world they wished to inhabit, are surrogates for their author's own brash determination to triumph against social prescriptions and the odds of his own success. Lil's goal is unusual for a 1930s Hollywood female: in a world they dominate, she intends to fight for her identity apart from men. She will do this even if she must use men as the vehicle to accomplish her goal, seducing one after the other, each higher up on the economic and social ladder.

Lil initiates her freedom in a grand manner: after a fight with her father, his still (seemingly sparked by Stanwyck's rage) literally explodes, killing him. Everyone around her is horrified, while Lily appears unconcerned. Standing in front of a phalanx of her neighbors who bemoan the "terrible death" suffered by poor Mr. Powers, Lily meets their expressions of sympathy with an enigmatic smile. And why not? With her father gone, she can finally get out of town. Accompanied by a former saloon colleague, Chico (Theresa Harris), a young black woman of even lower status than she, Lil starts her climb to the top with a quid pro quo only Zanuck would try: by seducing a train brakeman for free passage. She will soon move on to higher things.

Already, early in the shooting schedule, Zanuck was running into trouble with the censors. He met with the head of the Studio Relations Committee (to be renamed the Production Code Administration, or PCA), James Wingate, and was forced to make cuts. But the MPPDA was still dissatisfied. Zanuck balked, telling Wingate:

> Although in BABY FACE it cost me a great value in an important situation, I deleted and altered the lines that you objected to—such as "Is it your first," and "I know you have had many lovers before." Elimination of both these lines weakened both situations. I eliminated the locking of the door in the speakeasy [when Lil's father pimps her to the politician]. In the boxcar I stayed with the Negro girl and did not go back to the added cut of the brakeman sitting down with Stanwyck. I shot a new ending to the picture, which gave it a more wholesome and a brighter finish.[31]

Wholesome or not, the very concept of the film—a female who, without guilt, exchanges sex for material gain—was problematic under the Code. Each time Barbara Stanwyck seduces a man, we hear "St. Louis Woman" played on the soundtrack as the camera pans further up a skyscraper that has come to represent, among other things, her Nietzschean aspirations. This repeated single shot, an urban composition accompanied by music appropriated from black culture, activates the film's complex chord of feminism, race, power, and morality all at once. The real problem beyond its raw sex lay in the film's odd superstructure, an embrace of Nietzsche, particularly his ideas of *Übermensch* and what might be thought of as the core idea of all his work, the will to power. While Nietzsche would most certainly go over the heads of most American moviegoers, what Stanwyck was supposed to do with his advice was very readable.

The source of her advice is the film's one genuinely odd character, the old Nietzsche-quoting cobbler Adolf Cragg (Alphonse Ethier). In this awful place, he is someone who might be capable of offering intelligent guidance. Though Cragg drinks in her father's saloon, unlike its other habitués, he refuses to partake of its sexual menu. Lil senses the old man might be interested in her in terms other than those involving his personal exploitation of her body. Immediately after her father's funeral, she visits him in his workshop and is startled to receive a rather modern bit of advice. The original dialogue of the cobbler read as follows:

> A woman, young beautiful like you can get anything she wants in the world. Because you have power over men. But you must use men, not let them use you. You must be a master, not a slave. Look. Here. Nietzsche says: "All life no matter how we idealize it is nothing more or less than exploitation." That's what I'm telling you. Exploit yourself. Go to some big city where you will find opportunities. Use men! Be strong! Defiant! Use men to get the things you want.

But after negotiation with the MPPDA, Cragg's advice was considerably softened to the following pep talk:

> A woman, young beautiful like you could get anything she wants in the world. But there is a right and a wrong way. Remember the price of the wrong way is too great. Go to the big city. There you will find opportunities. Don't let people mislead you. You must be a master, not a slave. Be clean, be strong, be defiant and you will be a success.

You can actually hear the points in the film where sound edits have substituted diluted Nietzsche for the real thing. Nonetheless Lily, mesmerized, murmurs an assenting, "Yeah."

The ultimate challenge Zanuck faced was how to end the film. After Lily has seduced every eligible man she sets her sights on (including a very young, suit-clad John Wayne as an assistant bank manager), the original script had called for her society husband, a bank president she has married but does not love, Courtland Trenholm (George Brent), to commit suicide over Lil's cold indifference to the fact that, though personally innocent, he must take the fall for financial irregularities at his bank. (It *is* the Depression, after all.) But Lil had to be shown paying for her sins. Wingate told Zanuck that there was only one permissible lesson the film could teach:

> in losing Trenholm she [Lily] not only loses the one person whom she now loves, but that her money also will be lost. That is, if Lily is shown at the end to be no better off than she was when she left the steel town you may lessen the chance of drastic censorship action by this strengthening the moral value of the story.[32]

This was one struggle Zanuck would not win. For reasons not connected to this production, he would shortly be off the picture. Without Zanuck to defend his creatures and his world, and with the film's principal actors already engaged in other projects, the protection of their investment was foremost in the minds of the Warner team. They agreed to an ending cooked up by the PCA's Joseph Breen in which after Trenholm's suicide *attempt,* the disgraced and penniless couple have been redeemed. Trenholm writes to the friendly new director of his former bank. In this epistolary solution, the letter tells the avuncular banker that they were taken in by

> a penniless cobbler—who took us into his home and asked no question. We plan to make a new start in life—*from scratch.* I have straightened out all my affairs with the bank and owe nothing to nobody. Of course, we are *cold broke*—but we are happy—both of us—for the first time in our lives. My wife, I regret to tell you, has been compelled to work at night as a waitress in a cheap hotel here but I

have been promised a job in the steel mills and expect to start in on Monday. . . . We plan to go into the business of raising good babies and the first one shall be named after you—providing we have any luck. . . . DISSOLVE into a LS [long shot] of the steel mills.[33]

We learn of Lil's almost miraculous transformation over what is very obviously stock footage of steel mills. With George Brent and Stanwyck already off the film (and with Zanuck off the lot), this was the solution. (It is one that seems to come from the Ed Wood, Jr. school of filmmaking rather than from either Zanuck's or Hal Wallis's world.)

FUGITIVES

Zanuck's hard-boiled films had been cleaning up at the box office since 1929. But with the exception of a few perceptive articles, critics had been less than kind to the impresario and his work. The conservative columnist Joseph Alsop, then a young reporter for the *New York Herald Tribune*, saw Zanuck as a faintly ridiculous figure, a lightweight comic creation straight out of a Hollywood satire like Kaufman and Hart's *Once in a Lifetime*. Zanuck told Alsop that he intended to guide the audience into new, more complex ways to see and use film. But the Harvard-educated reporter could not fathom why he—or anyone else—should listen to the cultural opinions of an eighth-grade dropout. Zanuck's "pretentious" justification of his— and the cinema's—new social agenda struck the reporter as false. To Alsop it was obvious that Zanuck liked crime films for the same reason other old-time showmen found them and similar attractions appealing: controversy, violence, and sex always sold tickets.[34]

When Zanuck convinced the Warners to pay $50,000 for the film rights to Louis Weitzenkorn's hit play *Five Star Final*, he no doubt hoped this exposé of tabloid journalism might be yet another piece of sensational showmanship. In this tale of a muckraking newspaper editor who is transformed to use the paper not for sensation but for social good, Zanuck may have seen a parallel with his own life. Just as he hoped to be recognized for the public good his brand of honesty created, the play dealt with the redemption of a yellow journalist's life, from tabloid sin to public crusader.

As he had done with *The Public Enemy,* Zanuck changed the cast. He replaced fading silent luminary Richard Barthelmess with kinetic Edward G. Robinson. Here was a role the talented and stubborn actor seemed to like. He played the editor of the big-city tabloid *The Evening Gazette* with headlines such as "Ex-Murderess and Husband Suicide" and "Famous Killer's Girl to Wed Society Man." But Zanuck was forgetting (or overlooking) the values of the rural audiences who were the foundation of Hollywood's "typical viewer."

He seemed to take delight in *Five Star Final* in rubbing the audience's faces in the worst excesses of urban cultural life. The outcry against the film was far-flung. Not surprisingly, part of it came from small towns and cities, where the tabloid was still a foreign commodity and where newspapers and their editors had a different image than Robinson's amoral creation.[35] The Ventura (California) *Free Press* noted that "FIVE STAR FINAL has thrown truth, reason and decency to the four winds," and called the film "a monstrous distortion of a great profession."[36] Even moviegoers in big cities seemed offended. Certainly the press was. Newspapers had been hit hard by the Depression, and many felt that Zanuck was committing an outrage in making money at their expense. When the film was accorded that most American of dubious honors—it was banned in Boston— the usually shrewd and diplomatic Jason Joy (whose job it was to help studios shape scripts to avoid this type of outcry) admitted that he had underestimated the outrage the film would raise in the rival media.[37]

After all this (very profitable) furor, what the studio needed was a blockbuster hit that would also provide them with respectability. Zanuck thought he had found just that when he read an exposé of life within the Georgia penal system that had been serialized in *True Detective Mysteries.* En route to New York via train, Zanuck read either the serialized or the book version, and with characteristic speed started negotiations by wire before the train pulled into the station.[38] When he got back, he asked Esme Ward, one of the studio's readers, to write up a report on the book. To Zanuck's surprise, her reply was not encouraging, for she noted that "this book might make a picture if we had no censorship, but all the strong and vivid points in the story are certain to be eliminated by the present censorship board."[39] Undeterred, Zanuck convinced Jack Warner that this property had the potential to be a huge hit. Warner agreed, paying Robert Burns a fairly generous sum—$12,500—for the rights to his story. To signal that this was to be a serious, prestige work, and not just another of Zanuck's hard-boiled shockers, Jack Warner signed for the lead Broadway star Paul Muni, fresh from his triumph in Howard Hawks's *Scarface*. (Trying not to be burned as he had with *Five Star Final*, Zanuck steered clear of anything connected to journalism and print, and changed the hero's occupation from book publisher to construction company owner.) It seemed to the Warners and Zanuck that things were lining up to secure a prestige hit.

Zanuck assigned the project to Roy Del Ruth, then one of Warner's highest-paid directors and a man with whom he had worked frequently for nearly ten years. He must have been astounded when Del Ruth turned down the assignment, explaining in a lengthy memo that in the midst of the Depression, "when the whole public is so depressed . . . that many of them are leaping out of windows," such a "terribly heavy and morbid" film, one in which "there is not one moment of relief anywhere," seemed ill-advised.[40]

Del Ruth was not alone. Many in the industry were anxious about making pessimistic films in the last months of the paralyzed Hoover administration. Days before Franklin Roosevelt took the oath of office as president, Will Hays's "Reaffirmation" of the Production Code was sent to all the major studio executives. Shadowing FDR's inaugural call to action to unite and banish fear, the movie czar told his subjects that "these are times that have shaken the strongest foundations." Hays warned producers against giving in to the temptation to make a quick profit with sensational, even incendiary material. At all costs they must avoid "the tendency towards confused thinking and slackening of standards everywhere."[41] Zanuck's film would be a direct challenge to Hays's authority.

The story was about a miscarriage of American justice. James

Allen (Paul Muni), an unemployed veteran, is wrongly convicted of holding up a lunch wagon. An incompetent judge sentences him to a Georgia prison farm. He escapes and starts a new life, building up a successful construction business. Turned in by his own wife, he is convicted again and sent back to the chain gang. Once again, he escapes.

Having directly and successfully confronted similar tough issues before in the iconoclastic worlds of *Doorway to Hell* and *The Public Enemy*, Zanuck was neither frightened that Burns's tale was somber nor deterred by its downbeat ending. And there *was* at least one other producer who was also excited by the ideas contained in this dark work. Having sat on the sidelines while Zanuck forged an innovative cinema equal to his more refined world at MGM, Irving Thalberg finally decided to enter the fray and bid for Burns's tale. But he was dissuaded by the PCA's Jason Joy, who told him that the very parts that would draw audiences into the theater, the "cruelty" and the "detailed escape methods," simply could not be shown.[42] Thalberg, convinced, dropped out. Zanuck stayed.

Even before Warner's had completed the purchase negotiations, the censors went to work. Several Southern states had learned of Zanuck's plans and began lobbying Warner Brothers to soften the depiction in the film. Jason Joy warned both Thalberg and Zanuck of the dangers of alienating Southern audiences:

> Southerners claim that in a country where there is a large Negro population the chain gang system—and even some of the worse abuses—are necessary. Though to us these methods may seem barbarous relics of the Middle Ages, still from a business standpoint we ought to consider carefully whether we are willing to incur the anger of any large section by turning our medium of entertainment to anything which may be regarded as a wholesale indictment.[43]

Zanuck continued with plans for the film, trying to ignore the fact that the rest of Hollywood was alarmed at the potential liability it would pose to the entire industry. There were renegade instances of a studio or an independent producer (like Howard Hughes) ignoring such rules, but fear of theater boycotts kept the major studios in line.

Zanuck's intransigence threatened to upset the understanding the studios had with the MPPDA. The fact that David O. Selznick was making a chain gang film, *Hell's Highway*, at RKO only stiffened Zanuck's resolve to make what he now insisted was the only authentic chain gang film in town. (Though Zanuck did soften some of the original script's harsher scenes and made sure that no state is identified as the location of the prison, it didn't work.[44] The uproar was considerable.)

His involvement with *I Am a Fugitive from a Chain Gang* went beyond his usual routine of story conferences or running interference with the censors. In a rare act for him, he even paid visits to the sets. Further, in an unusual move that suggested how important this film was to the company's image, Jack Warner allowed Zanuck to preview the film. The screening took place on October 14, 1932, and the favorable audience reaction told Zanuck he had a hit. Nevertheless, deeply involved now, he felt he could still improve the film. He lobbied the Warners for—and was given—something even more unprecedented than the preview screening: permission to reshoot the ending.

But if Zanuck was still running at full throttle, director Mervyn LeRoy was worn down from the breakneck pace forced upon him for this production. He was almost too tired to direct any retakes or to shoot any new scenes. (In fact, he was so exhausted that he passed on the next picture Zanuck assigned to him, a musical based on a little-known novel, *42nd Street*.) With LeRoy of little help, Zanuck drafted an outline for *Chain Gang*'s new finish. Ignoring LeRoy's protests of fatigue, Zanuck rewrote the scene himself, and insisted that the director shoot the now famous ending in which Muni, on the run from the entire world, encounters his ex-girlfriend.[45] Horrified by the scared, hunted animal that unjust persecution has made of her former fiancé, she summons enough sympathy to ask James how he manages to live. Receding into the darkness, skulking along a wall, Muni utters two words that perfectly illustrate both his character and Zanuck's conception of how movies could get a point across in one devastating punch: "I steal."[46]

Zanuck seems to have been utterly inspired when he devised this particular cinema of shock. LeRoy never liked the ending: he thought it too brutal for Depression-era viewers.[47] One expected nothing less from the producer who actually smuggled the real-life fugitive (who used the pseudonym "Mr. Crane") onto the Warner Brothers lot so he could assist the screenwriters, Brown Holmes and Sheridan Gibney (and later, Howard J. Green), in making the film as harrowingly realistic as possible.

In line with *The Public Enemy*'s minimal cost of $150,000, the film was shot for an astonishingly low total of $198,845. Such frugality and the speed with which it was put into production may account for *Chain Gang*'s newsreel-like look. Like other Zanuck works, though the public already knew it as a popular, if controversial, book, the graphic exposé of life on a Georgia chain gang was published when the fugitive was still on the lam, a true tale that was tied directly to a news story. In fact, once a film, it managed to generate news stories on its own. Anchored by an unforgettable performance from Paul Muni, *Chain Gang* showed that Zanuck was not afraid to break new ground. It showed, in defiance of the industry code, that justice is not always impartial: it can be corrupt and cynical. Told he would be pardoned once he surrendered himself to the fairness he (and the audience) believed characterized the American justice system, Muni's James Allen is, instead, incarcerated a second time for a crime he never committed. His outcry of pain—"They're the ones who should be in chains, not me!"—spoke for many in the audience. Though not fugitives like Allen, they were suffering under, baffled by, and prisoners of a system that seemed to punish the average guy while the wealthy or powerful—the bankers, the lawyers, the police—appeared to sail unscathed through the Depression.

In addition to writing the film's last scene, Zanuck thought up another shocking idea that showed just how far the Depression had changed the nation's values, and how far Zanuck was willing to take film along for the ride. James, reduced to near penury, must hock his war medals. He presents a pawnbroker with what, to him, are priceless mementos of a vanished life and value system. Wordlessly, the pawnbroker shows him a case full of similar medals, each one, no doubt, connected to a tale just as wrenching. Zanuck had the courage to note that men who had fought for their country, the figures who would make up the Bonus Army that had recently marched on Washington, would not be protected by their heroism.[48] They could still be victims of the Depression. Their sacrifice bought them the right to suffer as much as the next fellow.

The film broke box office records when it opened at New York's Strand Theatre, and the usually staid National Board of Review called it "one of the best films ever made in this country."[49] Basking in his vindication, Zanuck gloated over the huge box office the film was piling up.[50] Warner's had a masterpiece, and it had been given to them by thirty-year-old Darryl Zanuck. Furthermore, at last Zanuck could justify the claim that these films were civics lessons, for the uproar caused by this bleak film led to reforms in the penal systems of several states.

—

The Warners' refusal to spend large amounts of money on the "production values" so cherished by most of the other majors, and their attempts to save money by operating on a tight shooting schedule created its own serendipitous rewards. Unlike the worlds of Paramount or Metro, except for Zanuck's experiments with Technicolor, the Warner Brothers world was made of minimal sets captured in black-and-white photography, the cinematic equivalent of Walker Evans rather than the glamour of studio photographer George Hurrell.[51] Within the Warners' heavy constraints, Zanuck created what would be best remembered about the studio. In his roles as both producer and writer, there was no doubt that Zanuck was the single most significant force in shaping the studio's identity.

AFTER THE GANGSTER

Hollywood dictated late in 1931 that the studios should produce no more gangster films, but Zanuck managed to sneak a few more in disguised as biographies. Films like *The Match King* (the biopic of swindler Ivar Kreuger) were produced as tantalizing and salacious tales that resonated with the public's fascination (and, through the tabloids, familiarity) with the morally marginal. Zanuck reasoned that what would hook him would do the same for the audience. Like a reporter negotiating with his editors, Zanuck worked out in his story conferences which version of the truth would be acceptable—and engrossing.

Just as contemporary biographer Lytton Strachey differentiated his version of a life's history from that of his fellow historians by telling a life with a characteristic rhetorical style and by seeing it from a unique, often revisionist vantage point, Zanuck constructed his biopics with a particular twist of cinematic human drama. To the public record of the lives of these familiar figures he attached the master plots and Warner star/genre configurations he carried around in his head. Zanuck felt strongly that rather than being served up froth, Depression audiences wanted some films whose content mirrored the time or their current emotional lives: "When times are hard they want dramas, heavy stuff. They don't want anyone up there on the screen being just too gay for words when the factory's closing down next week."[52] He gave them films like *Alexander Hamilton* (1931) and *Voltaire* (1933). His films seemed to echo both Voltaire's and Gibbon's assertions that history is nothing more than a tableau of crimes and misfortunes. Voltaire's sentiment from *Candide*—"*Si nous ne trouvons pas des choses agréables, nous trouverons du moins des choses nouvelles*" ("If we do not find anything pleasant, at least we shall find something new")—might well have been Zanuck's credo in his last years at Warner Brothers.

But no studio could survive with a program made exclusively of serious material in a culture that had, for the most part, long defined popular cultural fare as light. If 1930 marked the beginning of the (short-lived) gangster era, it was very much the tail end of the musical (*No, No Nanette*). In the era's tabloid climate, however, Zanuck felt that even the musical could be rejuvenated and benefit from his hardboiled stance. He had recently experimented with this combination, intermingling crime and entertainment in *Doorway to Hell*. He tested these fusions in other films, like *Show Girl in Hollywood*, a Technicolor effort dealing with the secret backstage intrigues of a Hollywood converting to sound, and *She Couldn't Say No,* which focused on a nightclub singer whose rise to stardom is masterminded by a gangster. And if the film bore an uncommonly close relation to both Ruth Etting's and Ruby Keeler's associations with their helpful "sponsors" (who also happened to be mobsters), Zanuck would not have been displeased. After these small efforts, it should not have come as a surprise that Zanuck conceived of *42nd Street,* the paradigmatic musical backstager, as a headliner, "a musical exposé . . . which dramatically endeavors to lift the curtain and reveal the strenuous, heart-breaking efforts of a well-known Broadway producer."[53]

Zanuck sensed that if it emphasized certain angles of the story, a musical version of the hard-boiled novel by Bradford Ropes could chart a new direction for the genre. Certain he could pull this off, he paid $6,000 for the rights to the book. Bowing to what he knew were censorable plot lines, Zanuck had the character of the British gay producer Julian Marsh twice transformed: into a heterosexual and an American. His kept boyfriend became the male heterosexual juvenile lead.[54]

The new cinematic concoction of musicals from headlines must have seemed like an odd gamble to make in 1933. Yet forty years later, the same principle Zanuck pioneered at Warners'—of creating popular new genres by recombining elements selected from hot news stories—would be resurrected by the TV networks in docudramas, infomercials, and movies of the week. Today's viewers who tune in to television movies of the lives of Amy Fisher or O. J. Simpson are watching its most recent manifestation. Zanuck in the sound era at Warner Brothers was the first producer systematically to perfect the deployment of this headliner practice. Zanuck's films thus set a controversial precedent: in mixing genres, they knowingly forged a powerful connection between the news and entertainment. At times, as in key parts of *Doorway to Hell,* the Warner's gangster cycle even dared to suggest what Walter Lippmann and others knew to be so: that crime *is* a form of entertainment.

The headliner policy had one last, almost serendipitous function. At Warner Brothers, where memos urged employees to shut off lights as they left a room, the policy served a baseline purpose: ideas in the public domain cost nothing.

GENIUS OR MENACE?

As Zanuck had demonstrated in his Rin Tin Tin films, as long as you had a firm handle on the overall sense of cinematic narrative, the content of a film could be negligible. In films like *42nd Street,* where spectacle overtook story, actors could sing in a nonsense dialect, which communicated that no content was needed as long as the film's style intrigued and overwhelmed audiences. When Ginger Rogers and chums sing in Pig Latin to open *42nd Street*'s sequel, *Gold Diggers of 1933,* Zanuck was literally toying with previous cinematic language.

Zanuck's films at Warner Brothers defined the era more than the similar fare being produced at other studios. He turned the Hollywood cinema to the cadence of everyday city speech and pointed us to what might well be an art form, the action of speech and the (American) urban street. Any environment that had James Cagney, Bette Davis, Edward G. Robinson, Joan Blondell, and visitors like Barbara Stanwyck and Ginger Rogers under one roof couldn't help but create, especially to foreign critics, films that were powerful, novel, and compelling. (Thirty years after Zanuck's films had first been released, pacesetters like Jean-Luc Godard were still paying homage to his gangsters and his outlaws, female and male.) It was a dramatic refocusing of the agenda for American film. After gauging the success of his efforts, the rest of the industry had little choice but to join.

By the end of Zanuck's time at Warner Brothers, critics often felt equal parts admiration and condescension toward him. One reporter for the *Saturday Evening Post* observed, "Hollywood is divided into two camps: Those who think he is a genius and those who think he is a menace. There are no neutrals."[55] While the soberly dressed, icily correct Thalberg seemed comfortable wearing the genius mantle, the outré Zanuck (and the corporation for which he worked) made it appear as if Central Casting had sent the wrong actors to read for some very important parts. At what other studio could you find one enraged brother chasing the other around the lot brandishing a lead pipe? Just as Cagney and Robinson and Davis redefined what a leading man and lady could be, their boss Darryl Zanuck altered the image of the mogul. He did this by purposely aiming low in a medium that was in many cases desperately aspiring to be viewed as high. Like Keaton or Chaplin, he was, to use the latter's term, a high lowbrow in a culture ruled by low highbrows.

In humanizing those (like the gangster or the fallen woman) who had been unambiguously coded as outcasts, or the marginal (like the "forgotten men" Joan Blondell urges us to remember in *Gold Diggers of 1933*), Zanuck was riding a wave that films did not innovate but merely (and ruthlessly) appropriated from newspapers, vaudeville, and theater. Zanuck's modern melding of information and showbiz was derived largely from the trendsetting New York–based culture of the 1920s whose writers (arguably) set the tone for much of the rest of the country's output. Even though it did not originate with either him or his Hollywood culture, in Zanuck's hands it became an incredibly powerful agent of socialization and the prime characteristic of Warner Brothers. By decade's end, with almost 25,000 movie theaters in operation, film had replaced these earlier venues—literature, theater, and in particular vaudeville—as the main source of popular culture in the lives of Americans.[56]

If this trend emerged from and was designed by cultural architects who took their inspiration from Gotham, Zanuck would be the savvy West Coast rep who opened up the Hollywood branch of this New York office.

Chapter Seven

1933

STRUGGLES, ARTISTIC AND FISCAL

[The movie business] trade, which is
in dreams at so many dollars a
thousand feet, is managed by business
men pretending to be artists and by
artists pretending to be business men.
In this queer atmosphere, nobody
stays as he was; the artist begins to lose
his art, and the business man becomes
temperamental and unbalanced.

—J. B. PRIESTLEY, *MIDNIGHT ON
THE DESERT*

IN 1933 THE American people decided it was time to say farewell
to twelve years of Republican rule, and along with Franklin Roosevelt's patrician New York accent came the socially activist policies of the New Deal. Fred Astaire teamed up with Ginger Rogers on
the screen, and Mary Pickford split up with Douglas Fairbanks in real
life. The top box office draw that year was sixty-three-year-old Marie
Dressler. Fox, reaching for a different part of the age spectrum,
signed on a young Californian named Shirley Temple.

At the Burbank studio, by this time Zanuck's control over Warner's was a kind of total creative domination that would never be equaled. What he created amid the landscape of the Depression secured the studio a generation of moviegoers. Warner Brothers' greatest asset was not its burgeoning chain of theaters, its first-class production facilities, or even the sophisticated interlocking grid formed by the media conglomerate Harry was slowly assembling. It was Darryl Zanuck's imagination. More and more, he did not shrink in battling with Harry for what he believed was right. He found Harry to be a hypocrite and a misanthrope who hid his greed and sour nature behind a smokescreen of moralistic press releases and hollow utterances about civic good.

While Zanuck struggled to get along with Harry, he had unpredictable and explosive encounters with other Warner personnel. A newspaper article dated September 29, 1931, even tells of a fistfight Zanuck had in Jack Warner's office with publicity director Hubert Voight. Though "Zanuck is of lightweight caliber," the reporter wrote, "he is said to have been able to take care of himself properly." The unfortunate Mr. Voight was not expected to return to work "unless there is a big change of heart."[1] Though it might be frequently tested, even with his fists, his faith in the system seldom wavered. His tenacity can be illustrated in his relationship with Edward G. Robinson, a strong-minded figure who was equally certain that *his* vision was the best way to make movies.

ZANUCK, EDWARD G. ROBINSON, AND THE "IDEAL" SYSTEM

Robinson was one of a score of talents—including James Cagney, Bette Davis, Joan Blondell, and Busby Berkeley—"discovered" by Zanuck on the New York stage and brought to Hollywood. A stage actor since 1915 (after abandoning plans to be a lawyer or rabbi), the Romanian-born Robinson had appeared in silent film as early as 1923 (in *The Bright Shawl*). He then made several forgettable talkies, in one (*Night Ride*) of which he played the role of a gangland leader. Robinson had even made a film for Zanuck (*The Widow from*

Chicago). Finally he scored an overwhelming success with *Little Cae-sar,* in the role of mobster Rico Bandello—a part he had to convince producer Hal Wallis to give him. The performance would forever link his image with toughness.

In joining Zanuck at Warner Brothers, Robinson was entering a studio that already had a diverse array of male stars. Heading the studio roster was Mr. George Arliss, the sixty-five-year-old British elder statesman of Hollywood, whose specialty was recreating his stage versions of great lives. The combination of Arliss's image and Zanuck's notion of history gave Hollywood the modern biopic. Also under contract was the man who had played Professor Moriarty to John Barrymore's Sherlock Holmes, suave, charming William Powell. The Warners were also saddled with fading star Richard Barthelmess. The studio had passed on an actor whom Jack Warner deemed too odd-looking to be a star. That young man was Clark Gable.

Robinson entered film roughly the same time as fellow New Yorker James Cagney. But unlike Cagney, he had not signed one of the infamous long-term contracts that tied an actor to a studio. When *Little Caesar* turned out to be a huge hit in 1930, the actor was in a relatively strong position to dictate some of the terms of his future employment. In early 1931, he signed a two-year deal for $40,000 per film. But the Warners refused to grant Robinson what he really desired, significant control over what they saw as the producer's prerogative: casting, story selection, and script oversight. They accorded Robinson the benefit of consultation about his parts, but this was less than the leverage given two other Warners' stars, George Arliss and Paul Muni.

Still, Robinson had a degree of story approval that was unusual in that era—one that stars like James Cagney and Bette Davis yearned for. (Cagney and Davis both waged fierce battles with Jack Warner over what they felt was indifferent casting in mediocre films. Cagney was so persistent that an exasperated Warner, in a formulation worthy of rival Sam Goldwyn, nicknamed him "the professional againster." Davis even brought a landmark lawsuit against the studio— which she lost.)[2] With the Depression hitting the studio hard, Robinson must have been worried about how two things—Harry's new program of economic stringency and Hollywood's changing cycle of genres—might affect his career. In 1932, the gangster cycle that had brought him overnight fame was essentially over. The Warners and Zanuck were having great difficulty agreeing on a property suitable to Robinson's talents, and the temperamental star turned down nearly every script they proposed. Robinson's stance was a real test of Zanuck's authority.

Trying to soothe Robinson's ego, Zanuck sent him a flattering memo in March 1932, raving about the actor's performance in the powerful film *Two Seconds*. (The title refers to the last moments of a convicted murderer's life as, strapped into an electric chair, he recalls the horrid existence that led him to murder his wife.) This forgotten work, an early analysis of the utter hopelessness that pervaded Americans' lives during the Depression, deserves to be placed alongside director Mervyn LeRoy's and Zanuck's next collaboration, *I Am a Fugitive from a Chain Gang*, for its social critique. Observing Robinson's scenes with Guy Kibbee, Zanuck effused: "To my way of thinking, this is the best scene you have ever done in your life, and one of the greatest climaxes I've ever seen any actor do."[3] The protective halo afforded by such flattery did not last long. Robinson's main complaint was not that his acting was underappreciated. Rather, he was irked that he was not being offered enough interesting projects to demonstrate his talent.

There *were* projects in which Robinson was interested. He had expressed curiosity about playing the part of Pancho Villa. (Just imagine what he might have made of that role.) But, exercising the producer's prerogative (which the actor's requests seemed so intent on diminishing), Zanuck told Robinson, "Personally, I would not produce PANCHO VILLA if you gave me a million dollar bonus as, including THE BAD MAN, a successful Mexican picture has never been made. Every company in the business has had a whack at the subject and rejected it."[4] (Robinson, who would perform memorably in biopics of Dr. Ehrlich and Julius Reuter, later also wanted to do Huey Long's story, but this too the studio refused.)[5] Not only did Robinson hold his ground against Zanuck but he made a new demand to see a completed script of any proposed film *before* he agreed to participate. To Zanuck, the former screenwriter and current orchestrator of writers, Robinson's pose must have demonstrated a lack of faith in his judgment. When Zanuck refused to give in to the ultimatum, Robinson would not commit to any script Zanuck offered. Not bound by the same contract as most other Warner's stars, he called Zanuck's bluff and went to New York for a vacation.

A series of letters and cables then traveled back and forth between Zanuck at the studio and Robinson, ensconced in the Essex House in New York City. Zanuck offered the actor film after film—*The Bowery, Grand Slam, Employees' Entrance, Lawyer Man, Clear All Wires* (all of which would later be made with different stars)—but Robinson refused to commit to any of them without a completed script. Robinson's rejection of *Clear All Wires*, his removal of the "star" part of the equation, led Jack Warner to reduce Warner's offer for what he would pay for the rights to this hit play. It was optioned by MGM as a vehicle for Wallace Beery. Zanuck gloomily forecast that it "was certain to come out as an MGM hit," which it did.[6] Robinson's desire to make a movie out of *Peter Grim* found Zanuck as unenthusiastic as the proposed title. Robinson countered with *Christopher Bean*. But when the play's producers asked an exorbitant amount for the rights, the project was vetoed by Harry Warner.[7]

After almost two months, this cross-country maneuvering seemed to be leading the two debaters toward a stalemate. In a letter to the actor, Zanuck wrote:

> I want to be very frank in this letter to you and also want you to understand that I, personally, believe we are very good friends and whenever difficulties have come up before, I have jumped into the breach and done my utmost to settle them. However, to be honest with you, I see very little hope of our ever mutually agreeing on stories.[8]

By contract, the studio only had to submit three scripts to Robinson before insisting that he accept their choice. Zanuck reminded him of that stipulation, and then zeroed in on what he felt was the true cause of the disagreement:

As I see it, Eddie, the whole fault lies in the fact that you want to be a writer. By this I mean that you want to put your views into whatever subject we purchase rather than accept the views of the men I engage here who are specialists at a high salary in this specific work.[9]

Zanuck's hunch was correct. Robinson was a graduate of City College in New York, and an alumnus of the Academy of Dramatic Arts. An educated, cultivated individual in an industry short on figures possessing these characteristics, he was widely read, was interested in politics, and was a serious art collector. His artistic and political endeavors contributed to the overall way he saw the world: they were the mixture out of which he shaped his career. The actor had even co-authored (with Jo Swerling) a 1929 play, *The Kibitzer*. Zanuck found himself and Robinson in a situation out of Pirandello, or perhaps Pinter: the writer within the actor was advising his client on what roles were best suited for his talent.

Zanuck felt Robinson now had to accede to his demands. (Quite simply, when Thalberg drew this particular tangent in his memorable showdown with actor/director/writer Erich Von Stroheim, he set the creative precedent of how the producer operated within the system.) Robinson should show more faith in Zanuck and "the system":

After all, our record of successes and box-office hits places us as the A-Company in the industry today, recognized thus everywhere. Our system, therefore must be an ideal one. You can't make a lot of hits with a lot of different directors and a lot of different stars and some of them with no stars at all unless the "system" is a perfect one as, in our studio, it isn't just the case of one director or one star continuously making a hit and the other ones flopping. This should be the greatest assurance in the world to you that our judgment is more or less correct, especially on the selection of stories and if I were in your shoes, I would be guided by this "system."[10]

Perhaps egged on by what he took to be Zanuck's authoritarian, even paternalistic, tone, a somewhat alienated Robinson met in New York with Harry Warner. But if he hoped to use whatever leverage he might manage to carry away from this encounter as a means to finesse

Zanuck's opinion, then the meeting was an enormous strategic blunder. It was no secret that Zanuck and Harry hated each other. (Peter Viertel, a writer and the son of well-connected writer Salka Viertel, said "Zanuck thought Harry was evil incarnate.")[11] So while Robinson may have thought he had been playing one against the other in order to get what he wanted, he was making an unstable situation even more volatile. When word of their meeting reached Zanuck, he felt betrayed. Further, it was reported to him that at this meeting, Robinson had made light of what Zanuck felt were his own honest efforts to find a solution to the problem. Since loyalty was a virtue Zanuck cherished above all others, the situation was touchy. On November 30, Zanuck sent a wire to Robinson, telling him that he had "just heard of your visit with Harry Warner and your efforts to belittle me after all the days and weeks of misery I have put in on your stories and pictures." Of the harsh words Robinson had allegedly spoken against him, Zanuck furiously noted that "this is the kind of reward I would expect from an ungrateful person but not from a man."[12]

This was high theater. Robinson's reply was more carefully thought out and better crafted than Zanuck's salvo, for the original pencil version survives on the back of Zanuck's telegram. In Robinson's version of the tale, it was not he but Harry who had suggested the meeting. He went to Harry, he wrote, to clear up misconceptions Harry had about "how difficult and unreasonable to get on with" the actor was. Slyly he mused to Zanuck how numerous tales "from God knows who" had reached Harry and he took the meeting because he wanted to find out what these rumors were. (Perhaps Robinson was implying that Zanuck might have been one of the mysterious sources.) In fact, said Robinson, Zanuck was not even the topic foremost on Robinson's agenda. Then, savoring what he surely felt was a strong exit line, he took the high road, telling Zanuck, "The kind of telegram you sent me is more belittling to the sender than anything you imagine I said."[13]

Their struggle was a paragraph in the story of Hollywood power, and it illustrates the complicated dynamics, the nuances between authorship and authority, that inform the creation of a body of work as well as an individual project. In most cases, Zanuck's will prevailed, but here we might declare a draw. For by early January, Robinson had agreed to do *Tin Gods,* soon to be renamed *Little Giant*—a project that in Robinson's career represented an unusual foray into comedy. A flurry of cordial and enthusiastic wires now passed between the former combatants, with Zanuck praising Robinson's suggestions on script revisions and character development.

The system had prevailed. Robinson was significantly shaping the contours of a script he had personally approved. Zanuck had received from the actor what he was contractually obligated to deliver: commitment to a project *before* the script was completed. In light of the history leading up to its production, *Little Giant* could have referred to the stature of either contestant in this emblematic struggle of wills.

THE TROUBLE WITH HARRY

When the Depression finally caught up with Hollywood, the Warners had a legacy even larger than Zanuck's hard-boiled style: a funded debt of $106 million.[14] Other studios—RKO and Paramount, to name the most notable—solved similarly disastrous problems by going into receivership. But in letting bankers become the dominant force in their corporations, men like Adolph Zukor forever changed the balance of power in the making of movies. Receivership was never an option for the Warners. Instead, uniting the fractious family in a time of crisis to face a common enemy, Harry looked about for ways to economize. After unloading some of their recently acquired theaters (and canceling leases on others), he seized upon Zanuck's former bailiwick, the Story Department, to pare down. Before the Depression, half the Story Department budget had been spent on purchasing the rights to already produced or published fare. Now, its annual budget was not to exceed one-half of 1 percent of the company's gross for the previous year.[15] By linking box office performance to the competence of the department responsible for initiating and evaluating stories, Harry connected its profile and the job security of its members to the overall health of the company. One consequence of this move may have been to try untested, lesser-known sources that could be purchased for a fraction of a big prestige hit. Of course, the change in policy was unnecessary for Zanuck, whose tabloid and pulp fiction sources could be had on the cheap.

Harry was aided in the task of saving money by someone highly placed, the man he had supported for the presidency, Franklin Roosevelt. In early March 1933, shortly after his inauguration, Roosevelt declared a bank holiday. In the spirit of this, businesses used their own ad hoc solutions, and the film studios temporarily cut the salaries of virtually all their employees making over $50 per week. The reasoning was that in shrinking their payroll, enterprises of all sizes could use this temporary relief to increase their liquidity, cut their overhead, and use these monies to help right themselves. Rather than shut down, Hollywood agreed to these guidelines, and all the studios signed on to the program, which called for an eight-week pay cut. After an agreed-upon period, the combined forces of the Motion Picture Academy of Arts and Sciences and the accounting firm of Price and Waterhouse would look at each studio's ledger and then decide whether the fiscal health of the individual studio merited a restoration of full pay. While a portion of industry enthusiasm for this was no doubt motivated by patriotism, in some part the eagerness—and speed—with which some owners complied was spurred on by the idea of getting the same amount of work for half the cost. It is hardly a coincidence that two of the most powerful producers who were nonowners—Thalberg and Zanuck—did not buy into the notion that it was fair to cut a wardrobe mistress's salary while the wealthy mogul's life (and salary) went on largely as before.

On the same day the proposal was to take effect, all the studios called together their personnel to ask them voluntarily to take a pay cut. Over at MGM that great actor, Louis B. Mayer, assembled his impressive cast of employees. Looking like a corpulent version of Jimmy Stewart at the end of his rope trying to ward off a run on the bank in *It's a Wonderful Life*—eyes reddened, face stubbled with days of beard caused by sleepless worry—the emotional Mayer showed his supreme sense of theatricality by making the collected group of actors, technicians, and executives wait twenty minutes past the time of his scheduled arrival. Then, after savoring the impact made by his dramatic entrance, he barely managed to get out two audible words, "My friends . . . " before breaking down. The *verklempt* nearly stricken figure "held out his hands, supplicating, bereft of words."[16]

While the performance had the effect Mayer desired, some read past such Grand Guignol and pointed out that, since MGM's films were doing quite well, a salary cut seemed unnecessary. But the reactionary Lionel Barrymore (a rabid FDR hater) wittily remarked to one of the employees who dared to question Mayer's request that he was "like a man on his way to the guillotine, wanting to stop for a manicure." Egged on and encouraged by the round of applause that greeted Barrymore's superbly delivered riposte, the "cast" responded as if on cue. The full spectrum of stars—from veteran actress May Robson (who had made her stage debut forty-nine years earlier) to child stars—all pledged support for the cuts. Mayer, one of Herbert Hoover's most loyal supporters, was deeply moved and told them, "I, Louis B. Mayer, will work to see that you get back every penny when this terrible emergency is over." They never did. (An outraged Thalberg angrily told Mayer a company could only worsen morale by cutting salaries instead of lowering stock dividends.) Nevertheless, Mayer carried the day. Leaving the emotional meeting, without missing a beat he asked, "How did I do?"[17]

Like part-owner Mayer, it was not surprising that the Warners would rush to support this proposal too. Jack's behavior in trying to do things cheaply proved that he was a true Warner: as *Fortune* magazine noted with approval, he "would not be Harry's brother if he did not look upon the making of movies as like any other kind of factory production, requiring discipline and order, rather than temperament and talent."[18] Without consulting Zanuck, both Harry and Jack eagerly embraced the cost-saving devices.

The Warners had no Mayer to deliver the news, and they were forced to rely on the combination of Jack's dubious charm and, that failing, the coercion afforded by raw power and authority to bring people around. Not all of their employees joined the bandwagon—some, having seen the same performance one too many times, were inured to Jack's charm and Harry's moral preaching. Edward G. Robinson refused to be moved by Jack Warner's telegram of March 9, which, mailed en masse to key employees, claimed that "all stars executives directors writers and free lance players and all branches of mechanics . . . approved" of the eight-week pay cut. Robinson *had* agreed, a month earlier, to allow the studio to alleviate its cash-flow problem by paying his salary for the contested *Little Giant* on a weekly, rather than all at once on a per-picture, basis. Jack had told Robinson, "I want you to know that I deeply appreciate this cooperation on your part and it only impresses me more with the fallacy of the general idea that there is no spirit of cooperation and good between producers and artists."[19]

But now that Robinson refused to go along with Jack's scheme, Jack dropped his charming mask. He threatened the actor, telling him it was obvious that the selfish Robinson did not "fully understand the extent of this calamity that has hit our industry otherwise you could not hesitate under any condition to join your fellow workers throughout industry in coming to the assistance of this business which has paid your livelihood." Because he was the lone exception on a lot full of obstreperous characters, Jack warned him, "please do not compel us to announce your name to the Academy as the only holdout of our company."[20]

Like Robinson, Zanuck was opposed to the cuts. Even though the other Warner executives had not cut their salaries, in a gesture of solidarity Zanuck halved his own.[21] In siding—publicly—with the workers rather than agreeing with the authority of the management and the owners, Zanuck had thrown down a challenge to Harry. When, after the agreed-upon period for lower wages had passed and Harry refused to reinstate salaries at their former level, Zanuck felt that the moral Warner brother had broken his pledge. Escalating his opposition, Zanuck even went before the Academy to argue against Harry's gesture, but to little good. It was clear to both combatants that only one person's version of patriotism and authority could carry the day. Though "he conducted studio business with an air of detachment," a "furious and shaken" Zanuck must have been considering his options as he prepared to make his next move.[22]

There was an additional reason why Harry might have been pre-disposed to overreact if he felt Zanuck were confronting his sense of authority. Harry was in a somewhat precarious mental state in 1932 and early 1933, for he had yet to recover fully from a personal tragedy. Harry had been grooming his only son, Lewis, to take over the busi-ness.[23] To start him on this road, he let the Columbia-educated Lewis take over responsibility for the Warner's music publishing enter-prises. It was a good choice. Temperamentally, the twenty-two-year-old Lewis was as fun-loving and West Coast American as Harry was dour and old country, and unlike his father he was in sync with popu-lar tastes. Hanging about the movie studio, he conceived an infatua-tion for actress Joan Blondell. It was, in part, to cure Lewis of this crush on an employee (and a *shiksa,* to boot) that Harry urged him to take a vacation. Recovering from the aftermath of oral surgery, Lewis did not heed his doctor's advice to remain in New York to rest up and heal. Instead, he took off for Havana.

Once there, he developed an infection that began to spread throughout his system. Harry hired a plane and private train to spirit his son to New York. Less than five years after the death of his brother, Sam, Harry seemed to be witnessing a similar nightmare with his son. Back in New York, Lewis appeared to be responding to treatment.

But quite suddenly, he developed pneumonia. In the age before antibiotics could have saved him, he died. Harry wandered, grief-stricken, about his home. One night, in a scene out of Eugene O'Neill, he woke his daughter Doris, told her to dress, and dragged her to the Warner's offices. There, in a state of high emotion, he re-peated to the confused teenager, "You will learn the business." When he realized what he was doing, he broke down and wept. The idea of the young Zanuck, only eight years older than Lewis, running the business that Harry had intended for his son may have further alien-ated the mogul from his pugnacious lieutenant.

Lewis Warner's unexpected death threw into relief what despite warnings Zanuck had been denying: the impossibility of Harry ever handing the reins of power over to Zanuck. With the spillover from their feud starting to spread across the lot, Zanuck met with next in command, Hal Wallis, at The Brown Derby to discuss the situation and his options. The choice was a strategic one, for Jack Warner owned a one-third interest in the famous restaurant. It would not have come as a surprise to them that a fellow diner that evening might be Harry Warner. When Harry spotted Zanuck, he came over and asked to speak to him in private. What happened next is a matter of conjecture.

All present agree that the two hot-tempered men wound up screaming at each other. Wallis swears that when Zanuck came back to the table, he told him, "I'm leaving Warner's and I'm not coming back. Joe Schenck offered me a job and I'm going to take it."[24] (Schenck, a giant in the industry, was then chairman of United Artists.) But Zanuck denied he had said this, for it would have meant that, in collusion with Schenck, he had planned all along to leave Warner's, rather than being forced out. Zanuck insisted he had resigned "as a matter of principle"—not, as Harry would soon claim, because a more lucrative salary was dangled before him, and he was greedy enough to want (during the Depression!) more than the $5,000 the Warners were paying him.[25] Schenck backed up Zanuck, claiming that at the time of his talk with Zanuck, Schenck was not looking to form a new film business. Rather than planning a new venture with the ex-Warner producer, he was merely talking shop. In fact, Schenck claimed that Harry had told him personally that "Darryl Zanuck did not voluntarily leave Warner's. Warner was anxious to accept his resignation."[26]

For the most part, history has sided with Zanuck. The abruptness of his resignation was a surprise to some within the industry, and the departure of the architect of their program "shook the company to its very foundation."[27] But, given his escalating tensions with Harry and the way similar disputes were resolved within the overall system, it should not have been totally unexpected. Nonetheless, to those accustomed to the subtle art of lying in Hollywood, the fact that he would walk out as a matter of principle over pay cuts when the money at stake was not coming from his own pocket was an attitude "not even [of] planet earth," let alone planet Hollywood.[28]

Jack Warner must have chafed at the knowledge that Zanuck, not he, was of the elect community of truly gifted producers and executives. (He tried to block what amounted to Hollywood's official acknowledgment of Zanuck as the heir to Thalberg—the awarding of the first Thalberg Award to him.)[29] Yet, for all their difficult ways, surely it was the Warners who gave him his start, and Zanuck acknowledged this, recalling his turbulent years with them as "probably the time when I learned most about how to make films."[30] Without their studio, and the things he learned there, Zanuck would not have become the man or the producer he did.

Zanuck's flight was inevitable. Its proximate cause, beyond his trouble with Harry, was a mixture of Zanuck's own huge ambition and the ambivalent relationship he had with his mentor and friend, Jack. For the next year, the trade press would be full of Zanuck and Harry Warner sniping at each other: accusations of theft, of dishonesty and ingratitude, of lack of honor. Zanuck struck first in the war of public relations. The day after his encounter with Harry, he released the following statement to the press:

> On April 10, as Head of Production of Warner Brothers Studios, I announced that the salary cuts decided on March 15 last be restored immediately. This promise has now been repudiated, and since a matter of principle is involved and I obviously no longer enjoy the confidence of my immediate superiors, I have sent my resignation to the Chairman of the Company, Mr. Jack Warner.[31]

Nine years earlier, a fortuitous restaurant encounter with the Warners had started Zanuck on his road to production at the studio. Now, with a symmetry worthy of a well-crafted film scenario, another restaurant encounter had dramatically ended it. At thirty-one years of age, at the height of the Depression, Darryl F. Zanuck was out of a job.

Chapter Eight

TWENTIETH CENTURY—AND AFTER

Success in movies boils down to three
things: story, story, story.

—DARRYL ZANUCK

ZANUCK WAS NOT unemployed for long. Most industry executives held his abilities in high esteem. In particular, he got high marks for his handling of two difficult transitions: the change from silence to sound and his creative stewardship of the Warner program into (and through) the rough terrain of the Depression. Almost immediately after his resignation, he had a number of intriguing offers. One was from Carl Laemmle, the head of Universal, the first studio with which he had been professionally associated.[1] The one he would take was from United Artists' Joseph Schenck.

Schenck was one of the true godfathers of the film industry. Unlike his rather dour younger brother, Nicholas (for whom life was a constant illustration of the survival of the fittest), Joe Schenck was one of Hollywood's most genuinely beloved figures, "a generous and kindly man who couldn't refuse a friend's supplication and whose old girlfriends all wound up on the payroll."[2] Encouraged by film pioneer Marcus Loew, he had left the amusement park business and gone into independent production. By the time of Loew's unexpected death in 1927, Joe (chairman of the board of United Artists since 1924, and president since 1926) and Nick (who would head Loew's organization after his death) were two of the most powerful figures in Hollywood. In an industry rife with Cain and Abel siblings (the Warners, the Cohns, and the Selznicks come to mind as the most famous), the contrasts between Joe and Nick were certainly among Hollywood's most intriguing. Born in Russia and raised together, the two brothers mysteriously spoke with utterly different accents, though both had immigrated to New York's Lower East Side in their early teens. Like the Warner brothers, the Schencks were temperamental opposites; unlike them, the Schencks got along.

Joe Schenck was a womanizer, a gambler, and a bizarre dresser, but in an industry often noted for its pettiness and the amazing range of its duplicity he accepted the frailties of others. He was not a hands-on executive like Thalberg or a Machiavellian manipulator like Mayer, but he had a gift that was described this way by producer David Brown: "Every highly visible person in Hollywood has an invisible partner who is never a threat creatively but makes it happen financially. That was Uncle Joe." He was "a godfather, an elder statesman . . . totally loyal." He was the figure to whom "you could go . . . with a problem and he'd solve it."[3] He also had a deep, abiding love of film. Mired in the interpersonal intrigues of United Artists' star partners (which made that studio far less profitable than it should have been), he was looking for someone to set up an efficient independent film company.

Looking about Hollywood, he considered the possibilities. Joe rejected Selznick (too unreliable) and passed on Goldwyn (too difficult). It was probably at this point, when it was obvious that Mayer and Nick Schenck were looking for a way to diminish Thalberg's power, that Joe Schenck broached to Mayer the idea of hiring Zanuck. He suggested that by giving Zanuck his own production unit on the lot, if the ailing Thalberg did not—or could not—return to the studio, the energetic Zanuck would be "within easy reach as a replacement for Thalberg."[4] Intriguing as it is to think of one studio simultaneously housing four such enormous egos, the discussions with MGM never got very far.

FEARFUL SYMMETRY: ZANUCK'S DREAMS
AND MAYER'S DAUGHTERS

When Zanuck made his defiant move at Warner Brothers, Schenck sensed the time was right for his own gambit. Schenck proposed a meeting at the very venue—The Brown Derby, partly owned by Jack Warner—where Zanuck had severed his connection to Warner Brothers. A mere three days after Zanuck's resignation, the two men met over breakfast. Taking a cue from Franklin Roosevelt's recent exhortation to the nation, Schenck asked Zanuck the right question: "Have you got a lot of confidence in yourself?" It was a query that Zanuck could answer with an unequivocal yes. According to Zanuck, this was enough assurance for Schenck, who told him: "All right. You and I will start a production company."[5] By lunchtime, a deal had been struck. They dispensed with the legion of lawyers typically attendant at such moments; "the original contract between Zanuck and Schenck was drawn up on one sheet of paper without legal advice."[6] To legally bind their forthcoming alliance, Schenck gave Zanuck a check for $100,000, an advance on his weekly salary of nearly $5,000 (higher than Selznick's and equal to Thalberg's, but the same as Zanuck had been getting from Warner Brothers). Schenck would always claim that this breakfast meeting was largely social and the alliance that resulted from it spontaneous. But the signature line of the $100,000 check Schenck passed across the table to Zanuck to seal the deal bore not Schenck's name but that of MGM's Louis B. Mayer.

Why would Mayer, who had two sons-in-law in the business, finance a rival's operation? David O. Selznick, married to Mayer's younger daughter, Irene, was both ambitious and supremely gifted. His other son-in-law, William Goetz, who also had producer's ambitions, was not of Selznick's caliber. It simply would not do to have

Edith married to this plodding *fonctionnaire* while her younger sister was tied to a real powerhouse. In effect, Mayer was trying to protect and enhance the reputation of his oldest daughter by buying his son-in-law an interest in a profitable, prestigious business he was certain would be a good investment: Zanuck's new corporation. Mayer's interest in the new company had other, nonfamilial connections. His boss, Nick Schenck, happened to be the brother of Zanuck's partner. With Mayer's money, Goetz would own a third of the company's stock. Having left one family imbroglio for the potential problems of another, Joe Schenck asked Zanuck if, in hiring Goetz, he had any worries about taking a kind of Mayer family Trojan horse onto his lot in exchange for the mogul's backing. If Zanuck had any misgivings about having a relative of the cunning Mayer in his employ, he dispelled them with a shrewd, but unkind assessment of Goetz's executive worth: he told Schenck that "Goetz wouldn't recognize a good script from a roll of toilet paper. So long as he keeps his father-in-law's money in our company, he can work for me as long as he likes."[7]

In addition to Mayer, the as yet unnamed company had other backers. After their own and Mayer's money, the major source of funding—$3 million—came from risk-taking A. H. Giannini of the Bank of America. Consolidated Film Industries, a processing laboratory, also contributed $750,000. With Mayer's contribution of $1.4 million and their own monies, Zanuck, Schenck, and Goetz were suddenly in the film business together.[8]

It was an odd time for an almost-settled head of a family to risk so much. After seven years of marriage, in 1931 the Zanucks had their first child, a girl they named Darrylin. She was followed in 1933 by Susan and in 1934 by Richard, the son Zanuck longed for. All evidence points to the fact that Zanuck had affairs early in the marriage, and that he continued to do so throughout most of his life. Actress Myrna Loy swears she once walked in on Zanuck in a midafternoon dalliance. But her tale that Virginia once showed up at Zanuck's office wielding a pistol to defend her and the family's honor seems wonderfully invented, as if it came not from an actual encounter, but emerged from a Zanuck script for a Barbara Stanwyck film.[9] Virginia and her husband reached an unspoken accord: as long as he was discreet and maintained a good home life, she would ignore his infidelities. Virginia was certain of one thing: her husband valued her.

She was right. She was better educated and much more refined than he was. She was a gracious hostess, a considerate and loyal friend, and an efficient manager; while Virginia was at ease in almost any social setting, away from work Darryl could be shy, or pull an outrageous prank; he was partial to pushing clothed guests into his swimming pool. People at Fox were often surprised by the high store Zanuck placed in his wife's opinion. It was Virginia who picked out Tyrone Power from a small part in *Girl's Dormitory* and told her husband he could be a big star if he shaved his eyebrows. Elia Kazan observed that the highest tribute Zanuck could give a picture was, "Virginia cried."[10]

Not long after Zanuck's new venture was announced, on April 27, 1933, the new executive took off for Alaska to hunt bear. Though an avid hunter since childhood, this trip turned out to be one of his last such outings. Polo (and, later, croquet) would soon replace hunting as his sport of choice. With Warner Brothers behind him, Zanuck had targets in his sight other than wild prey.

TWENTIETH CENTURY

There are several versions (all equally unverifiable) of how Zanuck's new company got its name. Sam G. Engel, Zanuck's assistant at the new company, claims that he told his boss, "I'll give you a name that's good for 67 years . . . Twentieth Century Pictures."[11] Zanuck's version admits that Engel played a key role but says the inspiration did not occur at the studio, but at another Zanuck venue, the polo field. Zanuck collided with Engel, and erupted: "For God's sake, you play like the game was played in the nineteenth century." It was then that Engel allegedly replied, "Let's call the new company Twentieth Century."[12]

Zanuck would be paid $250,000 annually, and his contract at Twentieth Century Pictures called for him personally to produce twelve films the first year. This large draw would be sweetened by a profit-sharing incentive: Zanuck would be entitled to 10 percent of any profits his films made. Schenck's company, United Artists, would distribute Twentieth Century's films. Despite Schenck's leverage and Zanuck's impressive track record, almost immediately the two had to confront the enormous challenge of running an independent film company in a town where seven large corporations ruled. Five of them—Paramount, Loew's, Warner Brothers, Fox, and RKO—maintained their eminence by combining the functions of film production, distribution, and exhibition. (Universal and United Artists had each for a time owned a small chain of theaters, but focused mainly on distributing films for a number of "independents" sheltered under their logo.) The studio system was structured so that its major players were virtually guaranteed huge profits, while holding potential competitors at bay.

Others (including Walt Disney and David O. Selznick) had dreamed up similar schemes of independence, but what Zanuck wanted to accomplish with Twentieth Century Pictures was the most audacious plan any individual or independent had ever tried. Hollywood had always had independent production companies working in conjunction with major film corporations—in fact, many of the great silent stars operated from this position—but Zanuck would do it on a scale that was unprecedented in studio-era Hollywood. Without an impressive physical production plant, a chain of theaters, a major list of clients under contract, or a distribution organization, Zanuck was still certain he would set himself up as a one-man studio competing with the majors.

For all that was at risk, Twentieth Century started out with huge advantages. Not every company had Schenck's and Mayer's deep connections and access to a complicated network of debts and IOU's based on patronage, power, and blood ties. No one—not even Thalberg—could match Zanuck's track record when it came to sheer profitability. Last, because of the unique structure of its distributor, United Artists, Twentieth Century Pictures could expect to start out as more than just another hopeful newcomer. Rather than generate and shoot films at their own studio, as its major rivals did, United Artists functioned as a kind of distributor and facilitator of other producers' projects. It had no actual "lot." It was thus a kind of chameleon company whose image and shape took the form of whatever producer or organization happened to be the source of most of its films.[13] Between 1927 and 1943, it had the smallest output of any major studio. Because (apart from Goldwyn) they had yet to find an independent who could provide them with a steady source of films, United Artists was a perfect partner for Zanuck. He would still have to answer to the top brass, but in exchange he was made part of an established, prestigious operation whose image he could come to dominate and define.

THE COST OF INDEPENDENCE

But what did the term *independent* mean in the studio era? If we understand how this term was used in Hollywood in 1933, we can see why Zanuck thought his goal was possible. Dissatisfied with how "the system" is set up to limit his cinematic dreams—its reliance on formulae rather than the single unique product, its creativity driven by the imperative of protecting its huge investment in its theaters (rather than by a love of filmmaking)—the independent producer wishes to make his films free of those restrictions. While the Zanuck of Warner Brothers would often extol the genius of such a system—which enabled him to produce, simultaneously, a very large number of interesting films—other producers felt less sanguine about this.

Before he formed Selznick International Pictures in 1935, Selznick had been a major producer who had an impressive list of successes at three different studios: Paramount, RKO, and MGM. Despite this enviable record, Selznick never liked the way the system interfered with his vision. He could articulate precisely what he hated about the system that Zanuck, for the most part, happily accepted. As Selznick recalled,

> When I was at Paramount, we made fifty-two pictures a year and our executive judgments and prejudices and attitudes were stamped on every one of them. You can't make top pictures that way. You can't

make good pictures by a committee system, filtering them through the minds of half a dozen men.[14]

Despite the obstacles in their way, a small number of men like Selznick, Sam Goldwyn, and Walter Wanger seemed able to operate in Hollywood *only* if they worked as independents. This status allowed them to make the films they wanted. But 1930s Hollywood forced them to deal with the limitations of freedom. Specifically, since no one independent figure had the capital or the assets of a studio and its larger parent corporation's distribution and exhibition networks, each had to enter into an arrangement with a company that did. Thus, the companies formed by independents illustrate in specific "ways how the fact of corporate independence" seemed to demonstrate the opposite: that it "provided a producer with little freedom from major studio influence."[15]

Zanuck's first job was to put together a group of creative personnel. To keep overhead down, staff was kept to a minimum. Sam Engel recalls, "At Twentieth I served as a story editor and as an assistant to Zanuck. . . . I could do everything and anything because it was a very, very small group of people. As a matter of fact, I worked as an assistant director, a second assistant—I shot second unit stuff—I did everything."[16] Zanuck also kept costs down by *borrowing* actors and other personnel from other studios, rather than signing them to long-term contracts with escalating raise clauses. As he would do throughout his career, Zanuck insisted on overseeing virtually every aspect of pre- and postproduction himself. It appeared that he could do everything but design sets and costumes, act, and direct.

It was at this point, at the height of the Depression, when a new corporation might have foundered for lack of confidence and security, that the esteem in which Zanuck was held by Hollywood's artistic community paid off. A substantial number of directors who had worked with him at Warner Brothers—Raoul Walsh, Roy Del Ruth, Gregory La Cava, and Rowland Lee—signed six-month contracts with Twentieth Century Pictures. And new directors—like Stanislavsky's pupil at the Moscow Art Theatre, Richard Boleslawski—were recruited. In the critical Scenario Department, screenwriter

Young Zanuck, the late 1920s.
Margaret Herrick Library, courtesy of The Academy of Motion Picture Arts and Sciences

Young man at the top: Zanuck with Al Jolson, late 1920s.
Margaret Herrick Library, courtesy of The Academy of Motion Picture Arts and Sciences

The Public Enemy: Cagney, as Tom Powers, resting between takes.
The Museum of Modern Art Film Stills Archive

Zanuck's right hand: editor Barbara "Bobbie" McLean.
The Museum of Modern Art Film Stills Archive

Virginia and Darryl Zanuck at the premiere of
The Grapes of Wrath.
The Museum of Modern Art Film Stills Archive

The Zanucks and the Goetzes.
Zanuck, Edith Mayer Goetz, William
Goetz (Louis B. Mayer's son-in-law
and Zanuck's partner at Twentieth
Century Pictures), and Virginia
Zanuck. Zanuck described Goetz as
"a born thumbtack" who couldn't
function without Zanuck's thumb.
*The Museum of Modern Art Film
Stills Archive*

Shirley Temple, Zanuck, and his
oldest daughter, Darrylin. Stardom
has its leverage: note that Darrylin has
a Shirley Temple doll, but Shirley
does not have a Darrylin Zanuck doll.
*The Museum of Modern Art Film
Stills Archive*

Zanuck's rural agent: Shirley Temple and Helen Westley (Aunt Miranda) from *Rebecca of Sunnybrook Farm*.

Henry Fonda, Jane Darwell, and Dorris Bowden in *The Grapes of Wrath*.

Not political? Government bureau photo used by the Fox Research Library to create the look of *The Grapes of Wrath*.

Wales via Malibu. Art Director Richard Day's Welsh village set for *How Green Was My Valley*.

Corporal Darryl F. Zanuck, U.S. Army Signal Corps, 1943.
The Museum of Modern Art Film Stills Archive

"Dear Willy" (Somerset Maugham), "the bizarre colonel," and "Dear George" (George Cukor) discuss Maugham's never-used screenplay for *The Razor's Edge* in Zanuck's office. The shrewd Maugham was well paid for his labors.
Courtesy of The Academy of Motion Picture Arts and Sciences

Fighting anti-Semitism. Best Picture Oscar number two. Gregory Peck in *Gentleman's Agreement* being turned away from a resort hotel because they think he is Jewish.

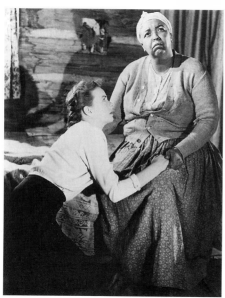

Fighting racism. Pinky (Jeanne Crain) and her grandmother, Dicey (Ethel Waters), in *Pinky,* directed by Elia Kazan.

Dana Andrews and Gene Tierney in *The Iron Curtain.*

Hollywood's first race riot. *No Way Out,* one of director/writer/producer Joseph L. Mankiewicz's collaborations with Zanuck.

The high point: Bette Davis, Gary Merrill, Anne Baxter, and George Sanders in *All About Eve,* Zanuck's third—and last—Best Picture Award.

Looking backward. Jean Peters and David Wayne in director Henry King's overlooked masterpiece, *Wait Till the Sun Shines, Nellie.* Zanuck made sure his thoughts on postwar America found their way into the script.

The new Hollywood. Marilyn Monroe in *There's No Business Like Show Business*. Zanuck urged her to give up the "Svengali" dependence on her drama coach.
The Museum of Modern Art Film Stills Archive

Looking ahead. Jack Warner, Sam Goldwyn, and Zanuck at a 1952 Eisenhower fundraiser. Zanuck's eyes—and thoughts—are already turned to France.
The Museum of Modern Art Film Stills Archive

Old tycoon, young mogul. Darryl F. Zanuck and Richard Zanuck, 1969.
Margaret Herrick Library, courtesy of The Academy of Motion Picture Arts and Sciences

Bess Meredyth, another Warner's alumna, joined Zanuck. He began a number of new associations with newcomers, like screenwriters Nunnally Johnson and John Huston, that would turn into lifelong connections.

One of the least known of this group of new hires (at least to the public) would become the centerpiece of Zanuck's professional world. Barbara ("Bobbie") McLean had worked as an assistant editor (to Raoul Walsh) on Zanuck's first film for Twentieth Century, *The Bowery*. She and Zanuck never actually met during the shooting, but she sat in on his famous night-long cutting sessions. By the time of Twentieth's fifth film, *Gallant Lady,* Zanuck noticed that it was *only* when Bobbie McLean took down his cutting notes that his suggestions were translated as he intended. He made her one of that era's few female editors, and she remained one of his closest, most trusted advisers for almost forty years. The esteem was mutual. McLean felt fortunate to have worked with such hands-on figures as Zanuck and Goldwyn, recalling: "It was like the whole family, so naturally you worked like mad because you loved every bit of it. You loved them, and you wanted the picture to be great, and you didn't mind how hard you worked. And that's the faculty that Zanuck had."[17] (She received seven Academy Award nominations for Editing, winning for *Wilson.*)

Zanuck filled in the screenwriting, editing, and directing staff, and hired one of his most important recruits, musical director Lionel Newman. Then he relied on his silent partner Mayer to deliver what the Warners withheld: stars. Zanuck told Schenck that all they had to do was "watch what players we got on loan from Metro": the bigger the stars, the greater Mayer's commitment.[18] Wallace Beery (No. 5 in the Quigley poll of box office stars) and Clark Gable (No. 7) starred in two of the company's first films. Zanuck did not have to borrow any other stars, since a number of them gladly jumped ship to cast their lot with Hollywood's newest mogul. Warner star George Arliss (who would make three films for Zanuck before returning to England) was soon joined by an eclectic group of colleagues who made two films each for Zanuck, including Loretta Young, Fredric March, Constance Bennett, Jack Oakie, and Ronald Colman. Actors like

Cary Grant, Judith Anderson, and Spencer Tracy made one film each. Yet, for all the wattage cast by these luminaries, at Twentieth the story, not the star, would determine the film's direction.[19] And Zanuck determined the story.

All but four of the films produced at Twentieth Century Pictures were original material, not adaptations.[20] Because he did not have to lay out large sums for pretested hit properties, this strategy of using original stories saved a lot of money for the new operation. Zanuck's decision to operate out of a central producer system after the rest of Hollywood had abandoned this mode of production signaled that Twentieth Century was the fantasy of which Selznick had dreamed: a way of making films whose vision flowed virtually undiluted from a single figure. With no Warner brothers looking over his shoulder to second-guess his judgment or stop him, every script reflected Zanuck's point of view.

THE WARNERS STRIKE BACK

Over in Burbank, the Warner brothers were less than thrilled that their *wunderkind* and several of their former employees had joined forces at Twentieth. Harry Warner would not lose to Zanuck without a fight. When Ernst Lubitsch left the Warners in 1926, Harry had tried to make it appear that he had always felt the great director was more trouble than he was worth. Now Harry suggested that not only was Zanuck ungrateful for repaying him back this way after having been raised by him from nothing to power, but that Zanuck (always known as a man of his word) was morally suspect since he had broken his contract. In June 1933, hoping to convince the MPPDA to censure Zanuck for raiding Warner personnel, Harry wrote to movie czar Will Hays lamenting of Zanuck's "theft" of stars, "directors and writers," and "even stenagrophars [*sic*]." Harry hoped that Hays would see things as he did and call an industry tribunal to lay out a Code to force pirates like Zanuck and Schenck "to abide by a course of fair dealing and business ethics."[21] Hays demurred.

The Warners could—and did—block Zanuck's access to personnel under contract, and they continued to attack Zanuck and Schenck in the press as unethical men. Zanuck and Schenck returned the favors. But there was little else the Warners or Hays could do.

THE ZANUCK TOUCH

All eyes in Hollywood were now turned toward Zanuck to see how he would open his new regime. His initial effort, *The Bowery*, was the story of Chuck Connors, "the mayor of Chinatown," which he had tried to interest Edward G. Robinson in. The characters were based on actual people, but the plot would be largely invented, a mixture of the accurate, the fantastic, and the whimsical.

Set at the turn of the century, *The Bowery* contained that most basic of Zanuck plots: the rivalry of two close friends (here Wallace Beery and George Raft as rival saloonkeepers) over a shared interest. To make him lovable, the gruff Beery has an orphan (Jackie Cooper) in his charge. But when he takes a shine to Fay Wray (perhaps he had just seen Selznick's *King Kong*), he alienates the saloon's resident woman-of-lower-stature-who-happens-to-be-in-love-with-him (the marvelous Pert Kelton). Seeing all this, the disaffected orphan changes sides and goes to live with rival Raft. When Raft wins a bet from Beery by faking a jump from the Brooklyn Bridge, Beery seems ruined. However, sensing fraud, Beery challenges Raft to a fistfight. Proven right, Beery eventually wins everything back, including the boy. In the end, the two men, en route to the army, are reunited.

The Bowery's premiere brought out all Hollywood, including Charlie Chaplin, Joan Crawford, Gloria Swanson, Clark Gable, Loretta Young, and most studio luminaries. But Zanuck could not bask too long in this triumph: he had to turn out a film a month. Less than thirty days after this first very successful effort, Zanuck's follow-up showed another facet of his showmanship. The unlikely star of this production was a former child vaudevillian who was arguably the most powerful journalist in the United States: Walter Winchell. He was as utterly urban in his tastes and style as Zanuck was Californian. (Critic George Jean Nathan once cited Winchell's staccato verbal delivery as a major influence on the acting styles of Cagney and other "tough guys.")[22] With his trademark fedora, tough attitude, and ruthless ambition, he was less a derivative parody of a Damon Runyon character than the vivid personification and inspiration for one. By 1933 his syndicated column in the Hearst chain was the most visible outpost (as well as the main source of power) in Winchell's empire. But he also had a radio show, made record-breaking vaudeville appearances, and enjoyed numerous lucrative advertising tie-ins and endorsements.

Winchell was allegedly in Hollywood for a rest, recovering from the death of his daughter, when he ran into a familiar face: Zanuck's new chief publicist, Harry Brand. (Brand had known Winchell in their New York days.) When Winchell told Brand he had an idea for a story, Brand sent him directly to his boss.

Winchell pitched his idea to a kindred spirit, a man screenwriter Ben Hecht once described as "quick and sharp," a figure who "plotted at the top of his voice, like a man hollering for help."[23] Zanuck liked what he heard. As the amazed Winchell recalled, the whole transaction "probably took a half hour or so."[24] *Broadway Through a Keyhole* contained something for everyone: gangsters, showgirls, and a handsome crooner. It also gave Zanuck what he was really after: the exclusive movie imprimatur of Winchell, the biggest thing on radio and in print. Even though Winchell's part was limited to his voice, this was as potent a weapon as most stars' visual images.

The Winchell vehicle had offscreen drama that nearly eclipsed its on-screen narrative. When word of the project began circulating around Hollywood, one big female star—a Warner Brothers star— was not amused. Ruby Keeler (also known as Mrs. Al Jolson) had good reason to be upset: Winchell's scenario (or Zanuck's treatment of it) was clearly based on Keeler's love triangle with Jolson and mobster Johnny "Irish" Costello.[25] Was Zanuck using this angle to tweak the Warners' noses?

Winchell had appeared in several shorts for Universal, but this was his feature debut. In a fulsome wire Zanuck told Winchell that it was "the best picture I've been associated with in the past two years." This was a mighty statement, given Zanuck's track record. He told the uncrowned monarch of Broadway that his new celluloid kingdom made Zanuck's previous attempts at picturing this milieu (*42nd Street* and the recently released *Gold Diggers of 1933*) "look like a trailer and I mean it sincerely."[26]

For the November 2, 1933, premiere, Zanuck and his publicity people used a number of tricks, and mock tabloid publicity editions trumpeting the film in bold headlines were hurled into the enthusiastic crowd. Zanuck saw to it that the whole festivity was covered with a nationwide radio hookup. The film was populated with Zanuck's and Winchell's cronies (Gregory Ratoff and Texas Guinan). But even the charm of some of its stars—Constance Cummings, Paul Kelly, and crooner Russ Columbo—could not disguise the fact that *Broadway Through a Keyhole* was a Zanuck quickie inflated by Winchell's name. The critics panned it, but the film cleaned up at the box office.

Zanuck's third release, *Blood Money*, starred Judith Anderson as an icy gang leader. The great star of the British theater presided over a cast in which sweet Francis Dee played a kleptomaniac with latent sadomasochistic tendencies. The climax of the picture was Anderson's bold intervention when she saved her boyfriend from an unlikely gangland delivery system: an exploding eight ball. This odd film (which, too, made money) was followed by a series of forgettable but entertaining and profitable programmers.

TAKING STOCK

After a dozen straight hits, Zanuck was secure that his new company would survive and even thrive. His films raked in the profits, but they reinforced his image as a producer whose work was not equal to the more exalted, refined films being made at MGM. In 1934, he prepared to answer the charges that he was incapable of serious filmmaking with a stunning prestige film, *The House of Rothschild*.

The property was owned by Zanuck's main star asset, actor George Arliss (who was also one of Zanuck's biggest boosters). The Hollywood actor who best personified class was unperturbed that he was casting his lot with a man seen by many as a "low-life specialist."

Said Mr. Arliss of his boss: "Mr. Zanuck is an artist."[27] Despite the Warners' best efforts (including the usual litigious threats), Arliss stayed with Zanuck. He had already impersonated three venerable eminences (Disraeli, Alexander Hamilton, and Voltaire), so the saga of the well-known Jewish banking family and its patriarch, Mayer, seemed right up his alley. The film would combine the showmanship possibilities of an action-packed grand historical narrative with a controversial topic the rest of Hollywood refused to touch: anti-Semitism. And it would be made on the cusp of Hitler's takeover in Germany.

There were many elements that made the film a success. Arliss performed a tour de force in the double role of the family patriarch and his son, Nathan. The film was also noteworthy in that it introduced a structure Zanuck would turn to again and again: the "cavalcade" format, in which the history of a single family illustrates the larger tapestry of a nation, a people, and their times. With a large budget and a first-rate backup cast (including Boris Karloff as an evil Prussian minister, and that pillar of the empire, C. Aubrey Smith, as the Duke of Wellington), Zanuck dazzled moviegoers with what would become another of his favorite touches: the film's concluding sequence, Nathan's audience with Queen Victoria, was filmed in the glorious new three-strip Technicolor process. But the most noteworthy contribution to the film's overall success may have been the screenplay contributed by one of Zanuck's new writers, Nunnally Johnson.

Johnson was one of a number of key Zanuck creative personnel who, like their boss, came from small-town upbringings. (Indeed, the fact that so many of his writers and directors hailed from this milieu may have given his future films their legitimate small-town nostalgic feelings of time and place.) Initially a journalist, he was brought out to Hollywood by Herman Mankiewicz when the Depression eliminated many magazine jobs. After he wrote two comedies for Paramount, Zanuck (who liked Johnson's fast-paced, warm, comedic style) invited him to join Twentieth Century Pictures. *Rothschild* was the second screenplay Johnson wrote for Twentieth (*Moulin Rouge* was the first), and it turned out to be a career breakthrough for him, and for

Zanuck. Though Johnson had been known for his comedy work, Zanuck asked him to do the film. Johnson demurred, saying that the film was too serious—he was more likely to deal with "characters [who fell] into flour barrels and things like that."[28] But Zanuck persisted. Johnson's literate, but cinema-savvy script for the *The House of Rothschild* started him on an entirely different career tangent. It was, as they say, the start of a beautiful friendship. Johnson and Zanuck worked together (with Johnson eventually writing, producing, and directing) on dozens of films. He's best recalled for his screenplays of *The Grapes of Wrath, The Gunfighter, The Three Faces of Eve,* and *The Man in the Gray Flannel Suit.*

By the end of Zanuck's first year of operation, Twentieth Century Pictures had spent a total of $4,500,000 turning out Zanuck's quota of a dozen films. This averaged out to $375,000 per film, far above Warner Brothers' budget, and almost equal to those of rivals MGM and Paramount. Receipts from the first four films far exceeded their costs, and he had more than enough funds to finance the rest of his program.[29] With the exception of one censor-plagued project (the truly odd *Born to Be Bad*), all of Twentieth's films made money. Zanuck had triumphed against great odds. But once again, as he had done at Warner Brothers after *The Jazz Singer,* he abruptly changed course.

CHASING PRESTIGE

Zanuck had conquered Hollywood with a formula based on cheaply made, tabloid-inspired "little" films. In late 1934 he signaled that Twentieth Century intended to compete at the same grand level as Thalberg and Selznick, telling the *New York Times* that hereafter his company would "specialize in biographical and classical pictures."[30] The films that followed—*Cardinal Richelieu, The Mighty Barnum, The Affairs of Cellini, The Call of the Wild,* and *Clive of India*—were all grand tapestries of history or cinematic re-creations of works culled from the literary canon.

Why did Zanuck, yet again, change the compass of his career?

Part of the answer lies in his realization that while his output of popular programmers might clean up at the box office, if he and his company were to be taken seriously as a "quality" outfit, he would have to produce a product comparable to that being turned out by the prestige leaders. When Zanuck announced that he intended to tackle the difficulties of Victor Hugo's *Les Misérables,* he was taking on more than the reputations of Hollywood producers already known for excelling at this kind of film: he was also confronting an organized American cultural hierarchy opposed to placing the power to interpret high art in the hands of the vulgarians who ran the movie studios. Even within the film industry itself, the better-educated (but less powerful) screenwriters scoffed at the idea that producers had the erudition and sensitivity to translate the works of the literary canon for the mass audience.

Zanuck had first turned to the tabloids as source material and aesthetic guide because the newspaper's language and view were in sync with America's less restrictive post-Victorian culture. Now he was about to change course because the cultural environment was different. The Depression had undermined the nation's confidence in itself and in what had been almost gospel: the inevitability of progress. Just as World War I had reshaped Americans' frame of reference, the Depression shifted the public's attitudes and desires. Its altering shadow transformed the priorities and uses Americans sought in their entertainment, how we integrated popular entertainment into the new routines of daily living. What kind of movies did Zanuck think Americans wanted to see?

There were copious but contradictory road signs to guide him. While Robin Hood gangsters like Pretty Boy Floyd terrorized the Midwest, in Louisiana Huey Long, with his promise to "share the wealth," gained control through legal means. Red Squads hunted down putative Communists in Los Angeles, while up north in San Francisco a general strike shut down the city. In California in August 1934 Upton Sinclair's scheme to redistribute wealth to "end poverty in California" (EPIC) secured for him the Democratic nomination for governor. While the moguls were terrified of what a Governor Sinclair might do to the film industry, Fox star Will Rogers declared that if this "darn nice fellow . . . could deliver even some of the things he promises," he not only deserved to be elected governor: he should be elected president, as well.[31] Moviegoers were no longer content with taboo-breaking titillation or the distraction of artificial enthusiasm: "[today] it's the theme that counts. That goes beyond the story. It's basic, it's fundamental, it's what people are thinking. *They want interpretive, analytical, educational information on the screen, or any place else.*"[32] Zanuck would rely on his retooled definition of showmanship—a mixture of biography, spectacle, and a new dollop of literary respectability—for the rest of his career. In films like *The Public Enemy*, he had led even Thalberg into new ways of seeing; in films like *Les Misérables*, he now seemed to be imitating Thalberg and Selznick.

But a Zanuck version of a classic could never really resemble those put out by his rivals. Placed in a darkened theater, moviegoers would have little difficulty recognizing his films of the classics: they were so *American*. Critics gave Selznick and Thalberg high marks for their reverential (and Europhile) versions of the classics, whereas Zanuck's characterization of Hugo's novel as " 'I'm a Fugitive from a Chain Gang' in costume" demonstrated "the Hollywood angle of approach to literature."[33] People who felt the movies would always be impoverished versions of books were only too happy to see the frame Zanuck now placed around high culture as yet another demonstration of why, despite such good intentions, Hollywood was more often a parodist's dream of high culture than a successful mediator of it.

When it came to the Hugo book, Zanuck observed that it was enough to grasp the core of the tale and its link with the audience's mood at the time:

> We've known for years that there was a great classic, a monument to literature, a great story. I'm making it now because it is the story of a normal, family-loving man that found himself balked on every hand, a man that was persecuted, a man that was beaten—and a man that would steal a loaf of bread, if he had to, to feed his children. It's the theme of today.[34]

One reporter, after observing Zanuck at a story conference—altering plot lines, acting out the characters' parts, trying alternative ways of doing things—saw this difference between him and other producers: "Zanuck knows instinctively and definitely what he wants." While Zanuck undoubtedly imagined what the average moviegoer might make of things, "it must be admitted that by the time the character gets on the screen the viewpoint he has is Zanuck's."[35]

THE AMERICAN BELL JAR

Unencumbered by the baggage of high culture carried—and internalized—by Thalberg and Selznick, Zanuck made his films as if all narrative forms operated in one basic environment. We might describe it as if his movie sets were timeless American bell jars, tightly sealed worlds in which simple, direct movie-style stories that he knew the average viewer would understand constituted the sole master narrative. In his instructions to the screenwriters and the director of *Les Misérables*, Zanuck must have wondered how familiar contemporary American moviegoers were with Hugo's novel. More important, how would the context of the Depression render this nineteenth-century French work comprehensible to twentieth-century Americans? He instructed director Richard Boleslawski to open the film with a tracking shot into a stale loaf of bread, immediately highlighting the one incident most Americans *could* identify: Jean Valjean's desperate act of theft to avoid starving. Whatever a work's setting or epoch, or the social class of its characters, Zanuck's sense of visual economy and concise characterization meant that every world was translated in such ways. Zanuck's bishop—the compassionate churchman who shelters the fugitive, and from whom Jean Valjean steals silver candlesticks—is not crafted as a figure whose understanding of the human condition emerged from his rather distant world of French politics and religion. Instead, he was conceived in Zanuck's conference notes in terms a Southern Californian might understand: "The Bishop is not a sweet, miracle man type. He's more like an understanding businessman—a charming gentleman. His nearest prototype today would be a psychiatrist."[36]

Zanuck made certain that the film would telegraph shared behavior familiar to an American audience: "Whenever possible in the script keep alive the fact that Valjean is a human being. He smokes, drinks and is indubitably a potent chap with women. We must not have him in the preachy class—not a spiritual type."[37] Matinee idol Fredric March's characterization of Valjean would be similar to the traits found in the new crop of American spiritual figures—like Billy Sunday (who used baseball metaphors to win his flock over to Christ) or Aimee Semple McPherson or Bob Shuler, figures Californians of this time had come to know. Zanuck understood the extent to which a movie-crafted sense of the world might define even spiritual matters, in Los Angeles and elsewhere. After all, Southern California in 1934 was a culture in which one Los Angeles clergyman hoped to increase attendance by inviting Rin Tin Tin to sit at his rostrum as he delivered his sermon.

If his approach to the story was at odds with Hugo's (and flattened out many of its nuances), Zanuck knew that a movie version was not—could not be—the same thing as the book. Thus, when he tackled the editorial problems of doing a screenplay of Hugo's book, the audience hook—a prime editorial guideline on what episodes and characters to include—was that the story's rooting interest always took precedence over any other considerations. What made Zanuck's canon distinctive was the unabashedly American way this dictate of showmanship was put into actual practice so that its specific shapes far outweighed any sense of literary fidelity. Let the Old World, or elite-educated Americans stick to the same old sources of culture they had been following before this country had any white settlers, let alone any movie theaters. No matter. Americans need not feel inferior. We had the movies. This is evident in Zanuck's handling of *Les Misérables*, and we see it even more directly three years later, in the lecture he offered to screenwriters working on another big book, *Drums Along the Mohawk:*

> This script has made the original error of endeavoring to become an epic. The only epics that are successful today are the simple, human epics where the personal story is so vital and emotional that the pic-

ture becomes great because the characters are great. This [as conceived now] is a "broad canvas" type of story and if it is produced in that fashion it will, in my opinion, be old fashioned, ponderous, rambling and unsuccessful. . . . In other words, if we are to see a picture of the Mohawk Valley at this time, we must see it over the shoulders of our two leading characters. It must be the subservient background to our intimate personal story which we must not lose sight of for one second.[38]

Zanuck followed the course he learned from his own considerable past experience with programmers and gleaned from watching how, with an enormous budget, Thalberg did it: "We must forget entirely the line of the book and just take the essence and dramatize it to fit our own needs."[39] For *Les Misérables* Zanuck found this in the key relation between Valjean and Cosette. He took great pains to make certain the audiences got what he intended:

The romance between Jean Valjean and Cosette is the most important human element of the story and should be developed. His feeling for her when he first takes her in is one of attachment. This later develops into devotion and culminates in her being his life blood. By treating it this way, the scene where he finally gives her up will absolutely slaughter the audience. This treatment will strike a human note in the picture and make it something much more important than just a finely conceived melodrama.[40]

In trying to bring Valjean to movie life, Zanuck had been very adamant on his choice of Fredric March. Once this casting had been decided, he specified how audiences should recognize the star actor beneath his makeup, that this part was a continuation of why audiences had thus far followed the actor's career. Since Valjean undergoes a number of amazing physical transformations through the course of the story, Zanuck instructed the director that the actor should sport "a semi-Vandyke beard—something like the one March wore in WE LIVE AGAIN."[41]

Zanuck, refusing to claim high motives for these films, asserted that he was a showman, "not interested in getting a message across, but in making good entertainment. There may be a message in the picture, but that is secondary to the picture's value as entertainment."[42]

In addition to securing the cachet of prestige with these films, Zanuck had another, very pragmatic, reason for his new tack. His new big-budget films may have seemed resolutely American in how they approached their subject matter, but because he no longer had a large chain of theaters at his disposal, Zanuck was forced to craft his films with an eye to the European market: "I am absolutely convinced that there no longer is any money to be made with the ordinary program picture suitable only for this country."[43] The man who would very shortly be named a Chevalier of the French Legion of Honor was wooing the foreign audience by playing a very American version of their own game.

By making his first big prestige films, Zanuck had shown the rest of Hollywood that "his period as an apprentice tycoon were over" and "his era as a producer extraordinaire was about to begin."[44] Alongside Thalberg's and Selznick's, a Zanuck school had opened.

BETRAYAL AND MERGER

One would have thought, with the commercial and critical triumph of *Les Misérables,* that Zanuck's United Artists partners would be pleased with Twentieth Century Pictures. They weren't. He did have an ally in one partner, Douglas Fairbanks, but the enmity between him and another partner, Charlie Chaplin, was long-standing and deep. (Zanuck had been a gag writer for Chaplin.) Zanuck resented that his contract gave him 10 percent of the *net,* and not, as he thought, the company's gross. As he accurately stated, "the pictures I was working on . . . had to carry the whole goddam load."[45] How could this otherwise cagey and shrewd man have made the error of confusing net with gross? He laughingly shrugged off this minor detail, but he and Schenck started to look around for a more favorable host company. They found their gaze returned by Fox Films.

Zanuck was a production genius who lacked two things: his own physical plant and an exhibition organization. Fox Films was an ailing powerhouse with a fading production team tied to a huge chain of theaters, a first-rate distribution arm, and one of the best physical plants in Hollywood. Each party needed something the other had to offer. Would a Fox union with Twentieth Century be a merger or a takeover? On paper, it would appear that even with its diminished status, Fox should have swallowed up Zanuck's operation.[46] But a comparative inspection of the company's respective balance sheets revealed an interesting fact. Though Fox possessed assets valued at $36 million, its 1935 earning power had been $1.8 million. Zanuck's company—meaning Zanuck and his staff—was valued at $4 million. Twentieth Century Pictures had a net earning power of $1.7 million. Zanuck's company turned out a profit equal to that of the larger company.

In early 1935, while Zanuck was off in Alaska hunting seal, Schenck and Fox head Sidney Kent took a trip to Florida together. They claimed they were convening in the Sunshine State to discuss a Florida plan to put up money to lure Hollywood away from high taxes in California to the more corporate-friendly shelter of their state. In reality, they were discussing possible joint filmmaking ventures.

They agreed to a merger. Schenck would resign from United Artists and become chairman of the board, and Sidney Kent president, of what would be called Twentieth Century-Fox. As usual, Zanuck got the top billing. Zanuck would be vice president of Twentieth Century. Joining fellow independent Jesse Lasky (who had been operating out of Fox this way for two years), Zanuck's independent unit in the newly merged company would make twelve of the fifty-five films Schenck claimed the new organization would produce in the first year. Despite the fact that Zanuck, and the entire Twentieth staff, would leave the Goldwyn lot and move to the commodious Movietone City, it was announced that Winfield Sheehan, Fox's production head, would continue to be vice president at Fox. The joint custody between Sheehan and Zanuck over production authority lasted two months. Sheehan could match neither Zanuck's creativity nor his drive. When he resigned, the departure of one of the film industry's longest reigning powers and the arrival of one of its youngest caused "Hollywood's gossip lanes to buzz."[47]

For Zanuck, this was the ascendant moment of a meteoric career. Under the terms of the seven-year contract Schenck offered, he and Zanuck would be the principal stockholders in the new corporation. While Zanuck's yearly salary of $260,000 would be virtually at parity to what he had earned at Warner Brothers and Twentieth, now he was offered 10 percent of the new company's gross profits and generous stock options. In a time when the average American earned several thousand dollars a year, all these remunerations brought Zanuck's annual salary to at least $500,000.[48] Schenck left with no doubt about whose vision would dominate the new enterprise. "Zanuck," he said, "would be in complete charge of all production."[49] His first job would be to assess all films in production or in preparation. He commanded that all current Fox scripts be brought to him. After reading them in four days, he demonstrated the executive certitude for which he would always be remembered, throwing out twelve of Sheehan's projects and stopping six more already in production.[50]

Zanuck brought with him the team that had bonded together at Twentieth. Bill Goetz would stay on (with Mayer's money) as executive assistant, and so would associate producers Ray Griffith and Henry Duffy, casting director Lew Schreiber, and his valued film editor Barbara McLean. Those executives who were let go received generous severance pay. To show how strongly he believed in the new regime, Schenck stated that publicity wiz Harry Brand would shortly resign from United Artists and "will personally take orders from Zanuck."[51]

This was the biggest merger since MGM had been formed eleven years previous, and a great deal of the film industry's attention was riveted on the drama. To show that the new operation was on the march, Schenck announced that Twentieth Century-Fox would spend almost a million dollars upgrading its already formidable studio facilities. Six new sound stages would be built, and an executive office building would be constructed to house the new regime. Most significant, Zanuck immediately set about shoring up and improving the studio's technological infrastructure, which he needed to deliver all the components he would orchestrate into a new house style. He started first by building up the Art Department, hiring gifted figures like Hans Peters, Rudolph Sternand, and Mark-Lee Kirk. Other designers of great quality—notably, Boris Leven, Richard Day, Nathan Juran, and Maurice Ransford—would be hired within the next five years. Zanuck had always placed a premium on the pure power of visual spectacle. He thus made certain that various technical departments were thoroughly revamped. With Ern Westmore in makeup and Fred Sersen in charge of special effects, Zanuck's studio soon set the standards.

By 1935, the producer's place within the studio system had been altered by the trend toward decentralization of his power. Every studio with the exception of Warner Brothers had dispensed with a mode of production organized around a single supreme production authority. But at Twentieth Century-Fox, with Schenck's backing, Zanuck put in practice what Thalberg had briefly attained and what Selznick yearned for: a studio with a virtually autonomous production head. Few could have kept up with its demands. Zanuck would later admit to William Wyler that it was not only the way he liked to work; it was "the only way I know how to produce."[52] Joe Schenck risked almost everything he had in linking the future of Twentieth Century-Fox with that of one figure, Darryl Zanuck. He insisted that the thirty-three-year-old was "the one man in Hollywood who can turn out smash box-office pictures."[53] As the summer of 1935 ended and the era of Thalberg drew to a close, Hollywood was about to witness the first stages in the age of Zanuck.

Part III

THE AGE OF ZANUCK

Chapter Nine

"THE SMILING FACE OF A BABY"

SHIRLEY TEMPLE, MOVIES, AND MEMORY

When the spirit of the people is lower
than at any other time during this
Depression, it is a splendid thing that
for just 15 cents, an American can go to
a movie and look at the smiling face of
a baby and forget his trouble.

—FRANKLIN D. ROOSEVELT

ZANUCK'S WORK AT Warner Brothers had been relentlessly
contemporary, historically minded, urban, fast-paced, and unsentimental. At Twentieth Century-Fox, he would replace
42nd Street with Main Street, the Roaring Twenties with the Gay
90s, Ruby Keeler and Barbara Stanwyck with Shirley Temple and
Sonja Henie. Zanuck shifted from the strategy of terrible honesty to
one informed by nostalgia. It was said (though not within Zanuck's
hearing) that the man credited with creating the cinematic hard-
boiled style at Warner Brothers now headed a studio that should be
renamed Nineteenth Century-Fox.

Indeed, almost a quarter of the movies made during Zanuck's tenure there were set between 1865 and 1920; a third were musicals.[1] And, even though set in contemporary times, an equally large number of Fox films—like *Chad Hanna* (which follows the fortunes of a small circus in upstate New York) and *Scudda-Hoo! Scudda-Hay!* (a film about mules set in one of Zanuck's favorite states, Indiana)—took refuge in a nostalgia of place. Zanuck's direction of the studio's program—both rural and nostalgic—disregarded the advice in *Variety*'s now-famous headline about rural viewers not wanting to see country life: "Sticks Nix Hix Pix." He knew if it were packaged properly, they—and the rest of America—would.

No other studio gave the musical a decidedly rural twist. Even backstage, when his vaudevillians were not country- or village-bound, they lived in a nostalgic soft-focus urban "Gay Nineties" environment of Sunday concerts in the park and twilight barber-shop quartet serenades.

And, before other studios were making wide use of it, Zanuck decided that the nostalgic world of musicals meant our memories would be recorded in Technicolor. Between the years of three-strip Technicolor's perfection (1936) and the widespread industry shift away from black and white (1954), almost two out of every three color films made in Hollywood were done at Twentieth Century-Fox.[2] Was any sky ever so blue as in Fox films? Rather than merely recording an image of the American past, Zanuck's visual look rekeyed our national iconography. Along with his very strong Music Department, headed by the great Newman Brothers, Lionel and Alfred (the latter was the composer of the Twentieth Century-Fox fanfare that opened most of the studio's films), Zanuck's upgraded Art Department translated his ideas into a distinct harmonious version of Americana.

Like Norman Rockwell's popular art, Zanuck's films at Twentieth Century-Fox set a significant social agenda. This visually transformed version of the American past, these film images of a life recently passed away, resurrected the world in a visually perfect but highly modified form.[3] Whether or not they were historically accurate, these images became the stuff of which audiences formed their beliefs.

Why did Zanuck, who had championed the modern, urban, tough world virtually devoid of sentimentality, so abruptly reverse his course when he had his own studio? The answer illustrates Zanuck's absolute mastery, his virtuosic manipulation of key parts of the studio system. Zanuck knew his new company needed a safety net in order to pull off the risky films he intended to make. He found it in Shirley Temple and in similar films of rural and musical nostalgia. Her aura of purity and preternatural goodness would pervade a program of rural, old-time films that positioned the studio's house style at variance with the rest of Hollywood.

The resilient ingenuity with which Temple dealt with the servile positions in which she found herself temporarily demoted prepared Americans to accept the downturns in their own economic situations. In Temple's America, moviegoers frequently heard a favorite Shirley maxim: money could not buy happiness. The plots of her films played out platitudes and taught lessons helpful to both a government and a film industry concerned with stability and even survival: if we waited, better times would surely come. Yet, while Temple and her disciples undoubtedly provided a bromide of optimism in the midst of the Depression, the escapism of these films did something else: they taught us not to question the inequalities raised by our economic system and our class structure.

TURBULENT NOSTALGIA

The nostalgic era in which a large portion of Zanuck's musical films took place was actually among the most turbulent in American history. Framed by two major wars, these decades overflowed with labor and political unrest, disputes with our Native American populations, and migration and immigration upheavals. Yet Zanuck presented them as a time of peaceful rural innocence. Suffused with Technicolor, this was shown as the last era of a "pure" America before mass immigration altered the national population, and the forces of electric modernity replaced the gentle glow of gaslight.

Zanuck used the musical cavalcade to recapitulate an entire career, fusing personal memory with cultural history. Whether located back home in Indiana or in the New York of Lillian Russell or the Dolly Sisters, these cinematic recollections serve the same purpose: they used memory to ascribe a particular meaning to the past. And when it came to what memory could evoke, Zanuck was a virtual genius. And that—memory—is what Zanuck was doing in creating a distinctive image and time for Fox when he sited the musicals in small towns around 1900. The world in the nostalgic musical film was intended to invoke the remembrance of a time and place when certain forums of America's public discourse valued the country more than the city, even as the latter was eclipsing the former as the characteristic mode of American living.

Shirley is so important because Zanuck uses her to show how amid these dualities and dissonances (that hint at darker schisms in American culture) and that some suggest are the musical's most prominent characteristics, *balance* can be achieved with seemingly unfit partners. Most Fox musical entertainment was a struggle to reconcile what Shirley's narratives almost always united: the values associated with urban, ethnic vaudeville and modernity and those extolled in a pre–Tin Pan Alley, all-white Protestant musical universe found most often in the rural small town. The union of these two was both proof of, and displayed the roots of, her appeal: Shirley was able to unite people at a time when Hollywood itself was battling various pressure groups and censors, and as a nation we were divided by the chaos of the Depression.

Zanuck saw great incentives in straying to the past. Each time he embarked on a journey with a contemporary, often controversial topic, he came up against unexpected controversy:

> The history of Hollywood's ventures into the field of contemporary affairs had not been a particularly happy one. . . . We had learned from bitter experience, that any attempt to deal realistically with the problems of the day was bound to bring down on us a flood of vituperation and criticism from special groups. It did not seem to matter how worthy or well-intentioned such attempts might be. We were vulnerable in the sense that the screen did not seem to enjoy the same privileges of expression accorded the press or the radio.[4]

Looked at from this vantage point, the architect of Fox's rural nostalgia policy was not merely being regressive. Nostalgia was a move in a game in which Zanuck distracted audiences with the past, so he could deal selectively in films like *The Grapes of Wrath* with serious present-day issues.

In providing moviegoers with popular, accessible entertainment structured around a selected swath of familiar hit songs, Zanuck also crafted a distinctive world informed by a particular ideology. Zanuck's America was one poised at the moment before the arrival and dominance of Tin Pan Alley, an institution whose songs gave voice to new populations oddly absent in these films. The songs of this era largely displayed a set of homogeneous traits Zanuck was pitching in his plots: a longing for nature over city; for pure love over passion; for pre-electric technology, and for melodic lyricism over syncopation. They were, in fact, in opposition to the tunes of Tin Pan Alley.

The films of musical nostalgia tried to turn back the clock of social fact. Both the films and the period music used in them pictured a home front that was rapidly vanishing as cities swelled with immigrants and as once-clear streams and skies were darkened by polluting industrial smoke. In their love of an idealized past, these songs and the films they inspired spoke to a deep, even reactionary strain that a significant number of Americans must have found appealing. They seemed to suggest that Americans never truly accommodated ourselves to an urban tradition. Because of the relative youth of our cities compared to Europe and Asia, and the remarkable spontaneity of their growth, it mattered little that though most of its citizens no longer lived in the country: "the United States is urban but not urbane."[5] The world of the Fox musical, where Zanuck harvested both actual and traditional vaudeville "corn," confirmed this judgment.

Most critics have written these films off as lightweight escapist confections whose plots and players had no connection to moviegoers' lives. But if you look closely you see that Zanuck's nostalgia was more complicated, for it drew one ideal by erasing another. The aspirations of Fox's small-town people and wasp vaudevillians ignored the populations—particularly Jews and African-Americans—who, drawn to America's big cities, created the ragtime and jazz that were redefining popular culture. These films systematically left out or rewrote much of this period's history. In effect, the Fox musical was able to manufacture a shared sense of our past as harmonious consensus only if Zanuck made certain that other more dissonant voices and parts were denied representation. If his films had included *Winesburg, Ohio,* counternarratives that declared small-town life stultifying, and if they drew attention to the fact that more and more people were fleeing Main Street for America's big city lights, Zanuck would not have been able to placate the values he felt were held by Fox's largely West Coast audiences. More dangerous yet, in films that interrogated nostalgia, he would have had to contradict the myths Hollywood perpetuated about the representativeness, inclusiveness, and egalitarianism of both popular entertainment and America's small towns. To do so would have been to question Hollywood's first principle: that its power came from the fact that it was the voice of democracy par excellence.

Zanuck's films—musicals and nonmusicals alike—took refuge in a certain "approved" version of the past. For example, in *Buffalo Bill* (1943), the screenwriters wanted to dedicate the film to "the valor and devotion of those Indian warriors who are now in the armed forces of our nation." Zanuck vetoed the idea because it drew attention to a situation that he knew was best not discussed, our treatment of Native Americans. And Irving Berlin's treatment for Zanuck's 1938 film *Alexander's Ragtime Band* pointedly denied that African-Americans had made any contribution in shaping this music.[6]

Asserting one kind of history, these films denied other realities.

Understanding one of the true powers of these pieces of "harmless entertainment" is to comprehend that these films make Hollywood's big arguments: that its depiction of history is fair and inclusive, and that as its historical narratives show, the best entertainment too operates under similar laws. Films like *Buffalo Bill* or *Alexander's* showed that acts of cultural transgressions (like appropriation and commodification) are functional and desirable if this outcome emerges as the result of some democratic process. Thus, at the final concerts that close *Alexander's* and *Oh, You Beautiful Doll,* the audience rapturously prefers the middle-ground pop versions of the composer's mu-

sic which had started out life in a more "radical," or elite, form because they have heard both sides and judged, fairly, that it is better
music. It is the people's acceptance of a particular modified taste culture—and the industrial machinery that made it possible—that seals
Alexander's and, in *Beautiful Doll,* Fred Fisher's—and popular culture's—fates.

Zanuck's memos (including those for *Buffalo Bill*) show that he
knew the forces shaping American culture were more complicated
than what he thought he should—or chose to—show. This is also evident in his lengthy correspondence with collaborators like screenwriter Philip Dunne and directors William Wyler and Elia Kazan.[7]
Even so, Zanuck was adamant that just as a film should *never* function
as a public lecture, neither should it be only a mere diversion.

A popular culture based on the myth of the box office equaling
democracy and free choice, of inclusiveness and the melting pot, appealed to Zanuck for other reasons: its operations doubled the
movie's representation of its own world. The musical's myth of consensus was preferable to what Zanuck simply could not show: that
popular entertainment was sometimes formed out of manipulation,
theft, and misappropriation.

THE OKLAHOMA KID AND A SMILING BABY

Will Rogers and Shirley Temple were virtually the only major stars
Zanuck inherited when Twentieth Century merged with Fox. In fare
like *Judge Priest* (1934) and *Steamboat Round the Bend* (1935),
Rogers, part Native American, easily carried the banner of rural entertainment with a populist twist. A workhorse—he made five films
the year he died—Rogers was an enormous moneymaker, and
Zanuck was counting on his droll humor to float his newly merged,
but star-poor, corporation in the competitive waters of Hollywood.

His untimely death in a plane crash shortly after the merger was a
terrible blow to Zanuck's plans. After a suitable interval had elapsed,
he released Rogers's most recent films with great fanfare to a public
who knew these were the popular figure's last works. This proved to

be a financially inspired gamble (the films outgrossed all of Rogers's previous work), but then Zanuck had to figure out what to do without Rogers. The solution was Shirley Temple.

Temple could not speak to audiences as Rogers had, so Zanuck let historical era, setting, and plot stand in for Rogers's homespun speechifying. Shirley was up to the task. At three, an age when most of her contemporaries were happy to be gliding through Piaget's developmental stages, the amazingly talented Shirley was already appearing on film sound stages and in vaudeville. Zanuck's strategy was to mask her kiddie talent school training with its tinge of urban vaudeville and present her as a young, pure creature of the country.

Before Zanuck had a hand in her films, her performances in a series of short films were "a mixture of very sophisticated satire with a little tinge of sex."[8] As Morelegs Sweettrick, for example, she did a wise send-up of Marlene Dietrich in *The Blue Angel.* Temple's biographer commented that these "very strange" baby shorts "played a lot in . . . matinee theatres, and there were a lot of out of work men at that time. And their great appeal had to do with men across the country."[9] Later, watching the star Shirley in *Curly Top,* one of America's most ardent followers of popular culture, Gilbert Seldes, noted one of the (unspoken) sources of her appeal: "At her good moments," observed the author of *The 7 Lively Arts,* "something like a growl of satisfaction rises from the men in the audience."[10]

Her first audition at Fox had been set up by Jay Gorney, the composer of the music for the Depression anthem "Brother, Can You Spare a Dime?" Familiar with Temple's previous short films, Gorney knew Fox was looking for a child to fill out the bill of the Will Rogers film *Stand Up and Cheer,* and he recommended Shirley. She sang "Lazy Bones" to Gorney and the film's associate producer, veteran Harry Joe Brown. Her incredible precocity caused the pair to see her as "a revolting little monster."[11] Nevertheless, sensing her potential, they offered her mother, Gertrude, the Fox minimum contract, and on December 7, 1933, the five-year-old Shirley became an employee of the studio. She would be paid $150 a week and would have to provide her own shoes and socks. Shirley signed the contract with a child's inverted "S." (Mrs. Temple was offered $25 a week for taking care of Fox's investment.) One month later, after altering the date on her birth certificate, studio head Winfield Sheehan announced that the *four*-year-old had been given a long-term contract.

After signing with Fox, Shirley was loaned out (for $1,000 a week) to Paramount for their version of Damon Runyon's *Little Miss Marker* (1934). Wise-cracking and casually tossing about slangy phrases like an experienced Runyonite, the young actress so unnerved experienced co-star Adolphe Menjou that he was heard muttering that she was "making a stooge out of me. She's an Ethel Barrymore at six!"[12] The film nearly returned its costs in the first three weeks of release. But it was in *Baby Take a Bow,* back on her home lot at Fox, in which Shirley, sporting the trademark fifty-six unvarying pincurls, really became a major star. Very shortly, she was noticed by people other than critics and her growing legion of fans. While the Nazis banned her work, upon seeing *Baby Take a Bow,* President Franklin Roosevelt observed: "When the spirit of the people is lower than at any time during this Depression, it is a splendid thing that for just 15 cents, an American can go to a movie and look at the smiling face of a baby and forget his troubles."[13]

At first, needing the money Temple could bring in, the studio made two to three innocuous Temple musicals per year. The budgets on these films were not very large—they averaged $200,000 to $300,00—but their return was enormous. A Shirley Temple film almost always grossed between $1 million and $1.5 million in its first run. In subsequent runs, they performed even better.[14] As he had for Rin Tin Tin, Zanuck set up a special Writing Unit, with almost two dozen rotating screenwriters. At her peak, Temple earned $350,000 a year. In deference to her earning power (but to Zanuck's intense irritation), workers at the studio referred to the administration building as the Temple Building. She had her own bodyguard and ate in her own dining room at the studio commissary. By 1936, the income from a line of Shirley Temple dolls alone would have enabled her to live happily ever after.

Some critics questioned Zanuck's strategy of invariably repeating what worked so well. *New York Times* critic Frank Nugent wondered why "they bother with titles, or with plots either."[15] When her mother and mentor, Gertrude (now paid $1,000 a week to be Shirley's "coach"), requested more demanding and varied parts for her daughter, Zanuck at first cheerfully told her, "Now she's lovable. The less she changes, the longer she lasts."[16] Sonja Henie, Rin Tin Tin, and, to an extent, even Alice Faye and Tyrone Power were stars Zanuck created out of his instinct. He knew they had something that, with the proper genre films, could be packaged and sold to moviegoers. But (unlike his later failure to see any star potential in Marilyn Monroe) from the start Zanuck realized that Shirley had been discovered by the public. "Once you have a fad," he observed, "leave it alone."[17]

THE LIFE OF A CHILD STAR

Shirley's four-year reign under Zanuck as Hollywood's number-one box office draw started with *Poor Little Rich Girl*. (*Captain January* and *The Littlest Rebel* would be released first, but *Poor Little Rich Girl* had been in production earlier.) Zanuck had been attracted to the project because it had proven a 1917 hit for America's previous country sweetheart, Mary Pickford. Rose Franken, the screenwriter assigned to the project, had a view of Shirley that was at odds with Zanuck's strategy. She told Zanuck that transferring the original plot to the screen "presents many difficulties both as a source of modern entertainment and a suitable starring vehicle for Shirley Temple." For one thing, she felt that the title (which dealt with "the unhappiness and frustration of the Rich") could not be pulled off "too convincingly in this day of depression and privation."[18]

But Zanuck did not intend to follow Pickford's plot line. Zanuck told his old colleague and the film's musical director Buddy Da Sylva that since few would remember the particulars of an old play, he had no qualms about dismantling the original structure and merely trading on its name recognition: "I think we could take any liberties we wanted and write an entirely new story—something that is light, bubbling musical comedy with plenty of opportunities for Shirley to sing and dance and do clever pieces of business."[19]

The script put Shirley in the role of the lonely, neglected child of a rich father. En route to a posh private school, she wanders off from her governess at a train station and is taken in by a warmhearted (but poor) Italian organ grinder who thinks she is an orphan. The pampered child soon becomes a member of his large, rambunctious family. She accompanies the organ grinder on his daily excursions, which gives her an excuse to perform. Here her natural and precocious musicality eclipses even the charm of the previous big draw, the trained monkey. Seeing her dance on the street, a lovable vaudeville couple takes a shine to her and "adopts" her until she is happily reunited with her father.

Because his biggest star was a minor, Zanuck wisely got to know the Temple family and learned how to negotiate with the force behind Shirley's career, her mother. At one point Shirley's father, George, approached Zanuck for advice. He had been receiving propositions from women who wanted him to father a fabulous child like Shirley. Zanuck asked him, "Can you guarantee you'll give them a girl?" When Shirley's father said he could not make such a promise, Zanuck advised him, "Then don't be unfaithful to your wife."[20] Shirley's frustrated, ambitious mother had trained her from the age of two for a career in show business. Shirley's stardom surpassed her mother's wildest dreams. But the girl had fantasies of her own: she yearned for a normal life. Zanuck transformed this dynamic he observed from his time with the family into one of movie Shirley's secrets of success. Despite her almost freakish excess of talent, she played characters who pined to be normal. If rich, she yearned for the human warmth money could not buy; an orphan, she pined for a family. Zanuck knew something else: that movie Shirley must have a relentlessly *social* nature. She was a creature whose adaptive innocence and goodness added the missing ingredient into *whatever* household—Lower East Side New York, posh Victorian London—she was dropped.

Yet Shirley was a lot more than sweetness and light. Mary Pickford was an adult who had attained stardom by playing a child. Shirley's innate goodness inverted this: she was a child who was wise beyond her years. Further, she had another, very American trait she could not mask. We can see it in her "all-time favorite photo," a publicity still taken for *Little Miss Marker*.[21] She is standing with hands akimbo, her ripped waif's smock and trademark curls unable to hide the determined set of her little jaw or the gleam in her eyes. It is clear that *nothing* could prevent her from getting what she wanted. She had the same quality that made several other Depression-era actresses—notably, Ginger Rogers and Jean Arthur—great performers utterly in sync with their era: determination. What was intriguing about the Temple persona was not just the sunny optimism she threw off with such little effort. She had spunk. Critic Gilbert Seldes observed, "she is interesting because of something rude and rowdy" in her makeup.[22] This trait, combined with her innocence, allowed her to ask blunt questions, particularly of adults. As Zanuck observed, "Shirley is most effective when she asks the kind of questions to which there are no answers one can give a child, like 'Why is the Depression?' "[23]

Poor Little Rich Girl was a big hit. Zanuck then came up with an inspired bit of casting. In *The Littlest Rebel* he teamed her with one of America's premier dancers, Bill "Bojangles" Robinson. Temple had first danced with Robinson in *The Little Colonel* (1934). Though they were separated by fifty years, a close friendship quickly sprang up between the two performers. Shirley called him Uncle Bill, and he addressed her simply as "darlin'." Robinson's versatility accelerated Shirley's dance education, and she would recall that her "fondest memories of dancing with Uncle Billy came not from our camera takes but from rehearsals."[24] The infectious mutual admiration is visible in the four films they made together. In a historic breakthrough Zanuck had paired up the screen's first interracial dance couple. Poignantly, though the pair roamed the Fox lot hand-in-hand, their appearances on film were a different matter. Even in Shirley Temple musicals, Hollywood's brand of utopian togetherness only stretched so far; "to avoid social offense and assure wide distribution," Shirley claimed that in certain venues, the studio cut out any shots that showed the two touching.[25]

If Zanuck wanted to prove that Shirley mediated all differences, in *The Littlest Rebel* Zanuck started at the top, with the two sides in the

Civil War and, to an extent, the uneasy dynamic between whites and African-Americans. Next, in *Captain January*, Zanuck teamed Shirley, this time playing a real orphan, with Guy Kibbee, who played a gruff lighthouse keeper warmed by her ways. His fisherman/assistant (Buddy Ebsen) was partnered with her in the memorable song and dance number "At the Codfish Ball." She soon caught the eye of MGM's Louis Mayer, and in 1937 Mayer asked Zanuck to lend her out to star in *The Wizard of Oz*. When Zanuck countered that he would buy the rights from Mayer and make the film at Fox, the shrewd Mayer sweetened the deal with the promise of a loan-out of both Clark Gable and Jean Harlow. Zanuck—who wanted the pair for the epic *In Old Chicago*—was intrigued, but never got the chance. Harlow died while filming *Saratoga Trunk*. *In Old Chicago* stars Alice Faye and Tyrone Power instead, and we never got to see Clark Gable and Shirley Temple together.

Most child stars have rather short careers. Temple herself knew that someday she would "see my star decline, not keep rising or hang there." She couldn't know when or how this would happen, but she never doubted who would be overseeing and controlling it: "Zanuck," she observed, "was supreme."[26] Zanuck knew that, particularly with a big star, there was a limit to how far you could carry repetition. He also knew that if Shirley could be pushed beyond mere precocity into real dramatic territory, her professional life could be extended. He continued to star her in boilerplate musical films while waiting for the right moment to test her dramatic range. By the end of 1936, one and a half years and four films since Zanuck had begun working with her, Fox's in-house magazine sent to its exhibitors, *Action*, referred to her forthcoming projects as "Shirley Temples." No names. No plots. Shirley was the only performer accorded this tribute. She had become her own genre. While most Americans fell for Zanuck's versions of Shirley's rural purity, not everyone felt Temple was a paragon of childhood innocence. Graham Greene, in an October 28, 1937, review in the British magazine *Night and Day* thought he saw through the kabuki-like mask Zanuck had placed over Shirley's face. He suggested there was something a bit too . . . professional about her talent:

In *Captain January* she wore trousers with the mature suggestive-
ness of Dietrich: her neat and well-developed rump twisted with the
tap dance . . . in *Wee Willie Winkie* . . . she measures a man with ag-
ile studio eyes, with dimpled depravity. . . . Her admirers, middle-
aged men and clergymen, respond to her dubious coquetry, to the
sight of her well-shaped and desirable little body, packed with enormous vitality, only because the safety curtain of story and dialogue
drops between their intelligence and their desire.

Greene's observation on Temple's allure was not far off target. Before
she signed with Fox, Temple's principal output had been the eight
short films (called "Baby Burlesks") she made for Educational Films
Corporation. In *War Babies,* at age three, "dressed," as she put it, "in
an off-the-shoulder blouse and trademark diaper, a giant rose
perched over one ear," Temple played a hard-boiled French bar girl.
In *Polly Tix in Washington* she was "a strumpet on the payroll of the
Nipple Trust and the Anti-Castor Oil Lobby" whose task was to se-
duce a Jefferson Smith-like bumpkin senator.[27] Looking at these odd
masquerades, it is clear that their appeal was not so different from the
adult versions upon which these juvenile miniatures were modeled.
Zanuck was well aware that Temple's image had to be defended
against such outrageous kiddie porn accusations. Shirley's value
could be lessened by letting criticisms like Greene's go by unan-
swered. Fox sued *Night and Day* in a British court. The magazine
(which soon found itself out of business) was found guilty of libel.
Greene himself, at the studio's vengeful insistence, was forced to pay
a fine of $1,500. (In addition, Victorian *pater familias* Zanuck in-
sisted the caddish writer personally apologize to Shirley.) Although
Greene publicly joked about the incident, privately, in a letter to his
colleague on the magazine, Elizabeth Bowen, he may have enjoyed
the unique distinction of being the only living human who referred to
the diminutive star as "that little bitch Shirley Temple."[28]

Shortly, though, Zanuck would match her with the odd duo of actor Victor McLaglen and director John Ford in a gender-altered
adaptation of Rudyard Kipling's *Wee Willie Winkie.* Ford was then
known mostly for his westerns and male-oriented action films
(though he had won the Oscar for Best Director of 1934 for *The In-*

former). When Zanuck informed Ford that his next project would be a Shirley Temple film, the director's "face fell to the floor."[29] A million-dollar budget helped mollify the director, and so did Zanuck's explanation: "I feel the only way to make this story is to disregard the formula of all the previous pictures Shirley Temple has appeared in to date." Ford was instructed not to see *Wee Willie Winkie* as a Shirley Temple picture: "We don't want to depend on any of her tricks. She should not be doing things because she is Shirley Temple, but because the situations—sound and believable—call for them."[30]

From 1935 until 1940 Temple appeared in fourteen films. Despite departures such as *Wee Willie Winkie,* most of them were still made to conform to her old image. All but one (*The Blue Bird,* an interesting failure) were enormously profitable. In Temple's films Zanuck oversaw a world of country simulation, one in which mixed architectural styles blended with flora and fauna from Fox's greenhouses and Central Casting. The simplicity, honesty, and charm of Shirley and rural friends and neighbors straight out of her small towns, farms, and nineteenth-century European dwellings was part of a plan to define both nature and culture in line with the studio's studied pose needed to shield the rest of Zanuck's more ambitious films from criticism. Shirley's rural outposts were meant to be held up as contrasts to the falseness and insincerity one would encounter in cities, in general, and in the artifice of the urban theater, in particular. But, of course, by first passing through the lens of a Hollywood Art Department and then refracted through the lens of a Zanuck story conference, Shirley's simple country life was, itself, already a stage.[31]

REBECCA

As Zanuck's formula and her precocious but Protean talents kept her atop exhibitor's polls as the industry's top draw, there seemed to be no obstacle Shirley could not surmount, save one: time. The six-year-old who had captivated the nation waltzing up the aisle of an airplane singing "On the Good Ship Lollipop" was growing older, and as the decade drew to a close, the studio was running out of ideas.

Zanuck offered $25,000 to anyone who could come up with an acceptable story line. The studio files still contain some of these odd proposals, including one from a New Orleans cab driver who owned "a common ordinary Inglish Sparrow of the streets but the bird expert of the Conservation Department says I have never seen or heard anything like him he is a wonderful bird." The cab driver's proposal, "Sherly and the Match Makeing Sparrow," contained a juicy role for himself:

> I myself would be the gardner in a rich man's house in the yard there would be a tree with a bird's nest in it a little bird would fall out of the nest the Gardner which would be myself and Sherly would pick the little bird up and Sherly would feed the bird with egg putting the egg in his throat with a tooth pick. Sherly and the gardener train the bird, as he grows up. He then has the bird fly over to a neighbor's estate. Shirley's brother chases after it and meets a beautiful, rich young lady . . . and that meeting makes the match—that makes the title THE MATCH MAKING SPARROW.[32]

Like millions of Americans, this cabbie had obviously seen a Shirley Temple film.

George Bernard Shaw cabled from London asking Temple if she would consider assuming the female lead in his stage version of *Caesar and Cleopatra*. (It turned out that Shaw did not know that she was only nine years old. In fact, he had never actually *seen* Temple; he had only heard she was a remarkable young actress.) And Helen Hays offered to play the Nurse to Shirley's lead in *Romeo and Juliet*.[33] These possibilities were no more peculiar than Zanuck's announcement that he was going to pair Shirley with Fox's most unique stars, the Dionne quintuplets. None of these projects got off the ground—and nobody got the $25,000.

In 1938, turning for career guidance to Mary Pickford one more time, Zanuck turned Kate Douglas Wiggin's famous 1903 novel, *Rebecca of Sunnybrook Farm*, into an updated musical for Shirley Temple. More than any other Temple film, *Rebecca* shows the function Shirley performed for the studio. Its production history illustrates Zanuck's mastery of studio politics and a sure sense of where in the system his little star fit. It also demonstrates his certitude that he—and he alone—knew how to sustain the value of his property. *Rebecca* suggests that, at Fox, family life need not be antithetical to the values of urban entertainment. Bold as ever, Zanuck goes so far as to insist that family solidarity can, in fact, after a suitable struggle, be cemented *through* popular entertainment, at least the kind he was able to supply. Zanuck intended the musical remake of the film to be a rumination on the country and the city. This can be traced through the way he developed and sustained these motifs in different drafts of the script, and also can be seen in his insistence that the message-laden songs commissioned for the film be written with Temple's rural persona specifically in mind. The 1932 Fox version adhered to the original story line far more than the Temple vehicle. Zanuck's decision to make *Rebecca* a musical for Shirley altered the script. (Unlike his predecessor, Winfield Sheehan, Zanuck would never conceive of a Temple script without at least one big musical number.) In this first draft, Sunnybrook Farm is populated with hillbillies (musical ones, of course). Zanuck did not like the angle and switched writing teams. Since Shirley was almost always an orphan, Rebecca would be, too, even though in the novel, Rebecca is one of seven children of a widowed mother. Here, the first writing team assigned to the film made a dreadful blunder. Rather than voicing a suspicion of big-city entertainment one would expect from an old-fashioned country matron, the first draft had Rebecca's guardian, Aunt Miranda, actually rather excited about putting Rebecca into show business. Zanuck changed this, for he knew that by placing a figure in the film whose life seems motivated by the goal of preventing Shirley from entertaining, the scales would be tipped in favor of Shirley and popular entertainment.

In Zanuck's opinion, it was not the issue of whether or not Miranda's country way would squelch Rebecca's vaudeville instincts. Rather, since this was a Shirley Temple vehicle, it was only a question of when and *how* the show business–hating aunt would be convinced of the wholesomeness of Temple's talents.

Zanuck was dissatisfied with the early drafts. The second team, William Conselman and Ben Markson misunderstood Temple's function in the genre. In their version, actual money, rather than spiritual happiness, figures as the heart of the tale. Krackly Kornflakes, the sponsor of a radio program, is offering $100,000 to any of its listeners who can match the broadcast songs with the puzzle picture on the cereal box.[34] (The authors would have derived this plot line from the real-life schemes and giveaways movies were using to lure Depression-era customers into the theaters.)

Rebecca's family is obsessed with winning the money. It was a very believable Depression-era fantasy to hit the jackpot on the radio and save one's home. In this draft, the villains Shirley faced were not the usual host of cruel orphanage officials or sour, child-hating millionaire curmudgeons. As in the real world outside Hollywood, evil here would be the banks, which were slowly foreclosing on the financially overextended holdings of small farmers. This danger lurks close to Sunnybrook Farm's door, for their greedy neighbor, Landford, is buying up the properties of beleaguered Indiana farmers so he can create polo fields and golf courses for his wealthy friends. (Ironically, Landford's scheme recreated the sort of conspicuous consumption favored by the Hollywood elite. The script mirrors what was happening in Southern California, as farms gave way to housing enclaves, and rural pastures formerly the turf of cows began to house country clubs, getaway homes and ranches, and race tracks.) To show how badly these authors misjudged what a Shirley Temple musical was, observe the entrance of the film's romantic lead. Like a figure stranded from an RKO musical, Landford makes his initial appearance in an airplane surrounded by five blonde chorus girls. But Landford is no mere speculator: he actually owns a farm. It is an exemplar of modernity, full of scientifically raised, healthy cows fed by state-of-the-art machinery, well-financed by a city-based fortune that gives him an enormous advantage over his fellow agrarians. Sunnybrook Farm, by comparison, looks as if it came from the late nineteenth century: set in the midst of Indiana (the Midwest home of the Ku Klux Klan) with its chickens and oil lamp–illuminated clapboard house full of homey furniture, it is a mythic enterprise overseen by black servants in overalls. Thus the same year John Steinbeck's *The Grapes of Wrath* brought the farmer's plight to readers' attention, a version of the script had a rural Shirley doing what people might do in real life: scrapping for money against an insensitive capitalist bent on destroying them.

Zanuck knew that Shirley could not be in pursuit of money. In fact, she was portrayed as an orphan so often precisely to emphasize that her search was for wealth of a different order, for human happiness and family. While the movie Shirley only had good will and cheer to take to the bank, in real life, Shirley was earning more money than the president of the United States. Fox, however, made certain that publicity stressed the fact that Shirley was an unspoiled child. Photographed in the healthful natural California outdoors playing with neighborhood children, or shown entertaining those less fortunate than herself at a party, she was a special kind of star, one brimming with love, good will, and talent. For their failure to realize this, Zanuck dropped the second team of writers, and switched back to the original one.

To disguise her age, the "aging" ten-year-old's curls would be shorn for this film (though she sports them at the end, when she does a nostalgic medley of her greatest hits). The film opens against a background of gingham. Aunt Miranda Wilkins (a childless spinster) personifies Fox's country values. Mistrustful of urban entertainment, peering suspiciously at the world through pince-nez, her energetic body contained by an old-fashioned *bustier,* she is outspoken in resisting radio, modernity, and anything urban.

She relates the tale of how her sister ran off with an itinerant opera singer. This nameless figure, Rebecca's father, inconveniently died, leaving both his wife and child penniless. Rebecca's mother dies, too, but not before marrying a fourth-rate theatrical manager named Harry Kipper. The film implies that were it not for her unhealthy devotion to urban entertainment and its types, Rebecca's mother might be living still.

A wonderfully urban figure of meager talents, Kipper wears an Al Smith derby and has an adenoidal Brooklyn twang. Urged on by his new wife—a heartless, vulgar, and blowsy golddigger—he sees Rebecca's talent as their meal ticket. As played by old vaudevillian William Demarest, Kipper is a scheming, inept comic figure, rather than the orphanage official we are accustomed to seeing as Shirley's adversary. His main function is to serve as a foil to Aunt Miranda and the country. Harry had been counting on going to the bank with Rebecca's talent, but through a mistaken identity Rebecca fails her audition. Kipper's paternal feelings disappear proportionately with the diminution of Rebecca's career. He decides to ditch the kid in the country with her mother's sister, the rigid Aunt Miranda. Shirley/Rebecca may be left in the country with her show business–hating aunt, but no obstacle placed in her path—not even banishment to the sticks—could stop a determined Temple. Who should turn up as their neighbor but beleaguered radio producer Tony Kent, the very person for whom Rebecca had auditioned.

Kent owns a country property adjacent to Sunnybrook Farm. In the midst of bucolic repose, he is preoccupied: he must find a child star to anchor his variety show, or he will lose his sponsoring account, Crackly Grain Flakes. Shirley, of course, saves the day.

Rather than pollute Rebecca by taking her back to the broadcasting centers of the city, Tony decides to broadcast directly from his country home. But they can pull this off only by keeping Miranda in the dark. Thus, while Aunt Miranda is hosting the local clergyman and his wife to tea, Rebecca is spirited out of the house. Though Miranda hates modern entertainment, she accedes to her visitor's requests to hear their favorite radio show, which is, of course, Tony Kent's.

The song the surprised Miranda hears Rebecca sing, "Come and Get Your Happiness," was composed for this film, and Zanuck intended it to carry the message he believed Shirley's films must. Unlike the first scripts (in which she and her family are in hot pursuit of money), Shirley's song is a palliative to the real money the radio and movie audiences could not have had, and which a contest would seem, cruelly, to dangle as unattainable bait. Temple sells the audience's poverty as a state of divine grace, and in her fashion, notes that grownups' obsession with (absent) money is the root of all unhappiness. Thus, as "On the Banks of the Wabash" had done forty years before, in "Come and Get Your Happiness" nature and poverty are linked to spiritual goods: healthful sunshine on the farm is better than material success. The song suggests an almost servile acceptance of a humble state ("All God's chillun got success").

It is, Rebecca tells us, "money" that makes people act like "crazy loons." Why not turn to nature, to "gold sunbeams," and "to heaven" to find happiness? (She advises us there is no "income tax" on these riches.)

In tandem with the song's rural message, Rebecca also gets the point across in one of two obligatory duets with contented farmhand Aloysius (Bill "Bojangles" Robinson). Despite Robinson's enormous warmth and charm, Aloysius's cheerful servility is but one uncomfortable step from the happy plantation darkie Robinson played opposite Temple in *The Little Colonel.* Added very late in the production, their other duet, "An Old Straw Hat" became the hit of the film. In many ways, it was the paradigm for their numbers together.

While Temple's roles usually called for her to dispense advice to adults desperately in need of a child's clarity and optimism, here the tables are turned. The veteran dancer, while depicted as Shirley's social inferior, nevertheless has lessons to teach his young charge. Aloysius teaches city girl Rebecca how to pick peas and how to sing and dance. In wise asides, he explains the ways of the world to his eager protégé. The lessons in tap and voice are Zanuck's moral catechisms, and beyond the signposts contained in her musical numbers, it is what we, watching her films, are meant to absorb.

In "Old Straw Hat" she sings and dances a song that extols rural attire, and values, not flashy urban clothes—and all that go with them. She prefers

> *An old straw hat, a suit of overalls;*
> *And a worn out pair of shoes.*

(Worn out, no doubt, from all that joyous dancing.)

As always, in *Rebecca* Shirley provides the spiritually valuable gifts of her unwavering love and good cheer. Her special practice is to dispense solid country values to anyone in need of succor. Often it is to an unhappy (often wealthy) creature who, though strongly denying it, is badly in need of such care. The target of her persistent social work here is the crusty Miranda, who inevitably succumbs. Finally, Rebecca serves as matchmaker for Tony Kent and even for Aunt Miranda.

The film was a huge hit. Zanuck was relieved: "I'm knocked dead . . . it's beyond the case of being a freak. I always thought when we dropped the curls, this is the end, the gold mine has gone dry. Now, she's good for years."[35]

And, for that duration Zanuck kept Shirley perpetually stuck at about age eight. He did this by strictly enforcing a set of instructions: "keep her skirts high," "have co-stars lift her up whenever possible." These were geared, in Temple's words, to accomplish one goal: "preserve babyhood." Beyond age ten, Zanuck was unable to find the same formula for the adolescent that had clicked with the child. With the onset of puberty, Temple's physique was changing. The father of two young girls very nearly Shirley's age, Zanuck knew there was a limit to what illusion could do in hiding Shirley's maturity. Nevertheless, he tried. Looking at costume photos, he noted, "You've got her looking like Mae West. Give her a streamline. Minimize her, back there." The changing contours of her frame caused Zanuck to wonder if they fed his biggest property on a diet of Hershey bars.[36]

From here on in, uncertain what to do with an in-between star, it was pure repetition. In *Little Miss Broadway*, Shirley scored a hit playing her usual orphan. Despite a cast filled with George Murphy, several troupes of midgets, Jimmy Durante, Edna Mae Oliver, and trained penguins (who, along with a lascivious midget, almost manage to do the impossible—upstage Oliver), Temple considered the film "unfailingly bland." She scored again in her penultimate orphan fantasy (and her first Technicolor film) *The Little Princess*. But after these, trying to figure out how to handle an aging Temple became a real issue, and it took the studio two troubled years to come up with a working script for *Susannah of the Mounties*.[37] It was only a modest hit. *Heidi* was the best-reviewed of any Shirley Temple film, but it also performed modestly. By the culture's gauge of the box office, the Temple story was drawing to a close.

SAYING GOODBYE

The Blue Bird (1940), Zanuck's response to MGM's *The Wizard of Oz,* was the first Temple film to lose money. In former times, the studio had rushed her from film to film. Now it stalled. Taking advantage of such a novel hiatus (she had previously only had three to four weeks between films), Temple enrolled in Los Angeles's exclusive Westlake School. It was the first time in her twelve-year life that she had ever attended a conventional educational institution. As the priorities of her life and her career shifted, so did Zanuck's. The end of her career coincided with the beginning of Zanuck's rise as Hollywood's most honored producer of serious pictures. In the meantime, in the midst of the Temple crisis, the studio had its worst box office profile in 1940 than at any time since Zanuck had taken over the studio. Serious consideration had to be given to what was best for Twentieth Century-Fox: a retooled or a released Shirley Temple.

Zanuck came up with an idea he was certain could provide one last hit for Temple. The film, first called *The Come-Back* and then renamed *Young People,* would be a valedictory effort that displayed his love of vaudeville, small towns, and variety performers. (He even considered luring W. C. Fields over to Fox to play Shirley's father.) He would use footage from Temple's previous films "to show that the little girl, who is to become Shirley Temple, is reared in backstage dressing-rooms of cheap vaudeville houses."[38] Since Shirley was too old to play a four-year-old, a little double with her back to the camera would run into her parents' arms at the end of the show.

To the master writer of all of Fox's scripts and the overseer of all of the player's lives, this film had one meaning: it provided Zanuck with a solution to his problem in the form that "gives us the marvelous situation of a girl who has been a star in the theatre finding herself, at ten, in a position of having to practically start all over again and beg for opportunities." But even while he looked at all the angles for a successful story, as he supervised, one last time, the trajectory of Shirley's celluloid life, Zanuck did not take the attitude of the little trouper herself into account. To Shirley Temple, the film meant something quite different.

Zanuck knew that in most real-life narratives, not every star returns from retirement to attain new heights of career popularity. Yet, in the *Young People,* even as he prepared to cut her loose from the studio she had saved, Zanuck pretended that he had every faith that, like her movie character, the real Shirley would come back bigger than ever: "At the end, of course, she will make a sensational comeback in some way—on the radio, in a musical show, or in the movies."[39] When the film was completed, the end of the Zanuck-Temple relationship was not as neat, nor as rosy, as the conclusion of *Young People.* In the last scene, Shirley and her family announce their retirement from the stage of a theater in the small town that has come to accept these odd actors as their own. When the pit orchestra strikes up "Auld Lang Syne," everyone (in the film and in real movie theaters) basks in the emotion and memories of the pact Zanuck is about to rupture: the powerful, shared bond between star and audience. (Temple later admitted she knew it was a "shattering" piece of symbolism.)

In real life, Zanuck decided to sever Temple's connection to Fox. Her parents (who had seen this moment coming) hired Frank Orsatti, a former gangster, to negotiate the contract, probably not realizing that doing so breached a clause in her agreement that barred hiring an outside agent. After much maneuvering, on May 12, 1940, Joe Schenck announced "with regret" that, for $250,000, the studio was allowing Temple to buy out the thirteen months remaining on her contract. He told the public that Twentieth Century-Fox was "proud" to have shared Shirley with the world. Schenck, unfortunately, added an unnecessary—and inaccurate—dig. "I look forward," said the man with the sunny nature, "to Shirley someday winning as great popularity as an actress as she has as a child star."[40]

Temple had served the studio better than any performer in its history. Her farewell on the eve of war provided symmetry to a career begun when another struggle, the Depression, was foremost on our minds. Though Shirley Temple would intermittently venture into film and then television over the next twenty years, it was her fourteen films for Zanuck between 1935 and 1940 for which she would be remembered. To a nation fighting fear and poverty, the smiling, talented little girl's brave optimism inexplicably had given Americans momentary courage. Where others had tried and failed, along with the indomitable spirit of its wheelchair bound president, Shirley offered something beyond the usual Hollywood commodity. She gave hope to a dispirited people.

AFTER SHIRLEY

Zanuck had a penchant for remakes and repetition. For a while, Shirley's torch was taken up by Alice Faye—a good girl who only *looked* as though she were bad. (Oddly, with her peroxided hair, she looked startlingly like Zanuck's mother.) He would do the same thing a generation later with Betty Grable. Zanuck had discovered Grable after seeing her picture in the newspaper. Edward Leggewie was with him, and watched as "he called [studio manager] Lew Schreiber and told him to 'get hold of this girl.' "[41] While we tend, today, to think of Grable as the ultimate World War II pinup, Zanuck also sold her as a star of nostalgia. In *Sweet Rosie O'Grady, The Dolly Sisters, The Shocking Miss Pilgrim, The Lady in Ermine,* and *Mother Wore Tights,* Zanuck presented her in turn-of-the-century roles.

If some saw vaudeville as a way of dealing "with the new culture that clashed with Victorianism," the Fox musical was an experiment of a different sort.[42] It was a regressive compromise that froze the past in a way that rewrote history: it reconciled Victorianism with its successor culture. Although World War II and its aftermath refocused much of the American cinema's agenda, the issues raised by Zanuck's films of musical and rural nostalgia diminished in importance but did not disappear. After 1940, in films like *Remember the Day* (1941) and *Good Morning Miss Dove* (1955), Zanuck was still celebrating the union of memory and the rural in major musicals, as well as in nonmusical films. But this vision became more clouded and difficult to sustain after World War II.

Zanuck's rural orientation had a strategic root beyond its role as a shield held up to deflect the accusation that Hollywood was out of touch with the desires and tastes of the average American. It had its basis in the demography of theater location, of who comprised these West Coast audiences. While the New York market added up to less than 1 percent of its total, California and the far west accounted for 90 percent of Fox's theaters. The bulk of the studio's test screenings were conducted in and around Los Angeles. Any changes calibrated to audiences' responses were thus based on this particular group's preferences. It therefore could be said that, in part, the culture made by Hollywood was determined by the very people who had abandoned the small towns in the Midwest Zanuck was enshrining in his films. Having come from the same background as many of them, Zanuck saw what other producers did not: that although they might have relocated to Southern California, they still nurtured a nostalgia for a small-town, midwestern home left behind. Fox's films thus functioned as a strategic link mediating between the old values of the studio-era California audience (themselves, largely and disproportionately from the Midwest) and the world confronting them in their new Southern California culture.[43] Like the nativist picnics so beloved of transplanted Midwesterners (which functioned as *memento mori* of their own pasts), it was Zanuck's shrewd perception that part of the audience would forever long for the world left behind. However life in their new state might transform the transplants from Nebraska, Iowa, and Indiana, try as it might, Southern California could "never fully meet the hungers of the Mid-Western heart."[44] Zanuck had heard and rejected the small town's siren song in his own life. Nevertheless, it was a melody he knew from the inside of personal experience, and which he could reproduce—with significant fine-tuning and remodulation.

Beyond what he placed on the stage before us, behind the curtain, in what we can read in his memos and see in his story conference notes, we know that beyond the profits he expected from making entertainment, they forced him to ask the important question of precisely what shape the value of the past should take when placed on film. Zanuck's nostalgic recollection transformed contested issues into placid memories. The American moviegoer would pay a price to play Pollyanna's "glad game" rather than engage in serious debates on issues glossed over, elided, or happily danced away by this "harmless entertainment," nostalgia. If Shirley Temple proved that the smile of a baby was the right image to infuse us with the spirit and the courage needed to overlook the pains of the Depression, and this nostalgia covered up the uglier seams of one kind of raiment used to dress history, in the next decade, starting with *The Grapes of Wrath,* Darryl Zanuck showed that the American cinema had other options.

Chapter Ten

"THE ONLY WAY I KNOW HOW TO PRODUCE"

Let Zanuck make a mess of it.

—SAM GOLDWYN TURNING DOWN
LILLIAN HELLMAN'S REQUEST TO
ADAPT *THE GRAPES OF WRATH*

THE 1940S BELONGED to Darryl Zanuck. In this decade he would transform himself from a purveyor of colorful but basically escapist entertainment into the industry's preeminent serious producer. After missing the Best Picture Oscar with *The Grapes of Wrath* (1940), he would win the coveted award three times: in 1941 for *How Green Was My Valley*, in 1947 for *Gentleman's Agreement*, and in 1950 for *All About Eve*. He became the undisputed trendsetter who took the commercial Hollywood cinema to new heights. In 1950 alone he produced *All About Eve*; he oversaw Hollywood's first race riot in *No Way Out*; and he took film noir to a dizzying height with Jules Dassin's *Night and the City*. It was a record most producers would have been satisfied to offer up for an entire career.

The Grapes of Wrath, released in 1940, was as much a turning point in Zanuck's career as *The Jazz Singer, The Public Enemy, Les Misérables,* and his partnership with Shirley Temple. In bringing Steinbeck's novel to life, Zanuck addressed serious social issues. He had done this in the past—in *The Prisoner of Shark Island* (the biopic of Dr. Samuel Mudd, the physician unjustly imprisoned for treating John Wilkes Booth), *Young Mr. Lincoln, Les Misérables*—but never in a film set in our own era and our own country, and did not rely on those previous Zanuck hooks he perfected at Warner Brothers, sex and violence. Zanuck's version of *The Grapes of Wrath* was as gutsy a use of the commercial cinema as anyone had ever made. He was willing to risk his reputation and his money to see that it did what he thought it must. And he managed to create a commercially successful film that also functioned as a serious and powerful social critique.

Heretofore, people who have written appreciatively of *The Grapes of Wrath* and another classic, *How Green Was My Valley,* have seen them as sterling entries in the canon of John Ford. Zanuck? He was only the producer. He was the fellow with whom, in the Faustian pact between art and commerce struck in Hollywood, creative people like Ford were forced to deal. Typical of this stance is a comment on an earlier Zanuck-Ford collaboration, *Drums Along the Mohawk.* The writer refuses to attribute any weaknesses in the film to Ford (whom the author sees as "the cinematic poet of American history"). Rather, if this is banal stuff, it is due to the sad fact that in the studio era, the vision of people like Ford was clouded because he "had to deal with anyone like Zanuck."[1]

That writer would have been surprised to learn that Ford considered this "anyone," this Zanuck, a "genius," "head and shoulders above all other producers." In Ford's estimation, only one man—Irving Thalberg—was Zanuck's equal.[2] If one traces the work each man did on their many joint projects one must conclude that Zanuck was as dominant a creative force as Ford. With all the forces at work in the culture of Hollywood militating *against* accomplishing anything of value, it was this "anyone" who kept these entities from spinning out of control. He acquired the rights to the books, he fought to get them made into movies, he cast the roles, he staffed the film's production team, he supervised the music, the sets, and the scripts. It was he, and not Ford, who edited the film. Taking nothing away from the other creative people upon whom these films depend for their collective lives, on the whole it was Zanuck who afforded the world of each film its definitive contours.

In making *The Grapes of Wrath* and *How Green Was My Valley,* despite compromises and alterations, Zanuck created something of profound value in a cinematic public culture never rich in these commodities. And he did it when no one else was even willing to try.

THE GRAPES OF WRATH: "A HARSHER THING THAN THE BOOK, BY FAR"

Zanuck recalled that when in 1939 he announced he was going to make a film of John Steinbeck's controversial best-seller, he knew he was taking a gamble. He was told people "wanted to see the brighter side of life on the screen, particularly in a period of economic gloom."[3] Specifically, he was warned that the chairman of Chase National Bank (which at the time held the largest block of stock in the Fox corporation) "would probably raise hell with me because I was attempting a controversial subject that did not hold capital in too high a light."[4] But, as he had with the Warners, Zanuck held to his position: bleak and difficult as it might be, like his earlier controversial projects, *The Grapes of Wrath* was the film he wanted moviegoers to see. While few, if any, producers were tempted to take up the challenge of turning Steinbeck's novel into a PCA-approved film, others in the Hollywood community saw the possibilities that Zanuck did. Lillian Hellman, finding Steinbeck's novel both powerful and the kind of material at which she felt she excelled, urged Sam Goldwyn to acquire the property. But Goldwyn was scared away for the same reasons almost everyone else in town was. He was alienated by the "gloom and the sordidness of the background and the people," not to mention the novel's "pro-Communist indication." Goldwyn's verdict: "Let Zanuck make a mess of it."[5]

If Goldwyn, one of the shrewdest and most successful independent producers in town felt this way, why did Zanuck think he could pull it off? Zanuck simply said he wanted to make the film because he found the book "a stirring indictment of conditions which I think are a disgrace and ought to be remedied."[6] But he also knew his will to get it done was inevitably stronger than the power of those who opposed him. Shortly after he announced his intention, while in New York he encountered the alleged ogre who would block the film, Chase's chairman, Winthrop Aldrich. The banker surprised Zanuck. He told him that on his wife's advice, he had read Steinbeck's book. Aldrich told Zanuck, "It should make a wonderful movie."[7]

Zanuck purchased the rights directly from Steinbeck for $100,000, a large (though not outrageous) sum in 1939. (One year later, he would pay twice that amount for the rights to Erskine Caldwell's hit theatrical adaptation of his own 1932 novel, *Tobacco Road*.) Steinbeck's outright sale meant the author had abdicated any rights over the screenplay. Nevertheless, Zanuck wanted the writer—whom he gauged to be suspicious of the movie's ability to do justice to his work—on his side. Steinbeck was already somewhat familiar with the way things were done in Hollywood: a year earlier, Hal Roach had produced a film adaptation of his play *Of Mice and Men*. He was now being advised by those wise to the ways of Hollywood that Zanuck was undertaking "the whole scheme . . . for the purpose of taking the social significance out of the story." Appalled, the once-burned Steinbeck told Zanuck that "if he realized this company was actually controlled by big banking interests," he would never have sold him the rights.[8] Zanuck reassured him he was misinformed, and invited him to his office for a discussion.

Right off, he told the writer that he "intend[ed] to follow the exact book."[9] (What Zanuck did not tell him was that due to time constraints, most of the film would be drawn from the first third of Steinbeck's work.) Zanuck explained to him that the PCA would censor certain sections, such as the part where Roseasharn, the Joads' eldest daughter, breastfeeds a dying old man with milk intended for her stillborn child. (Even Steinbeck's book editor had tried to dissuade him from including this scene.) Thinking of what a movie audience conditioned by Hollywood's conventions of harmless entertainment, as opposed to a book reader, expected to see, Zanuck told Steinbeck that with the flight of the fugitive Tom Joad to organize labor and with the future of Ma and Pa Joad very much up in the air, he found it disturbing that the novel ended on what he saw as an unsatisfying, inconclusive note.

At the moment when the discussion seemed headed for difficulty, Zanuck was saved by a kind of *deus ex machina* found only in Hollywood, none other than Shirley Temple! It seems that Temple had broken a tooth—a front tooth—and Zanuck was wanted on the set by her frantic director. Listening to the telephone exchange, Steinbeck said to him, "Don't bother about me. *The Grapes of Wrath* is unimportant compared to Shirley Temple's tooth."[10] The tension broken, the two resumed discussion. In the end, as Zanuck had promised, Steinbeck was granted a rare privilege: he viewed the completed film before it opened. He told his agent: "Zanuck has more than kept his word. He has a hard, straight picture in which the actors are submerged so completely that it looks and feels like a documentary film and certainly it has a hard, truthful ring. No punches are pulled."[11] Steinbeck felt so strongly about what Zanuck had done that, had his sentiments been made public, they would have silenced many of Zanuck's critics, who felt that once again, Hollywood had eviscerated and trivialized a great work of literature. But Steinbeck insisted that without the novelist's prose, Zanuck's film was "a harsher thing than the book, by far. It seems unbelievable but it is true."[12]

Because of its hot subject matter, Zanuck was bound to receive a good deal of flak from various critics, both right- and left-wing. To downplay the controversy, all those concerned with the film cooperated in the useful fiction that what they were doing was not political. Director John Ford insisted, "I'm apolitical and so is Darryl. Darryl just said 'I think there's a good story in it.'"[13]

But the archives at the studio's own research library show that it was precisely the political angle, as covered in newspapers, on which Zanuck was accumulating material. Actual ads for fruitpickers (like those that lured the trusting Joads to think of California as a land of milk and honey) were clipped from Oklahoma newspapers. Accumulated, too, were actual handbills almost identical to the one the Joads carry about in the film. The Research Department's material (from the New York press and from California's Hearst and Chandler chains) makes it clear that unsympathetic newspaper coverage had created an ill-informed climate of prejudice against people like the Joads. Unlike Steinbeck's attempt to document and explain how all this tragedy—both natural and economic—had come about, Zanuck and his team saw that many journalists turned their xenophobia in only one direction, inward at the unfortunate, desperate victims of the dust bowl and away from the powerful institutions whose policies first exploited, then cruelly mistreated, these people from whom they had profited. Headlines like "Hoboes by Scores Flee East Facing Blockade at Border" (from the *Los Angeles Examiner*, February 8, 1936) and a searingly horrid photo from *New York News* of February 13, 1936, showing unemployed American men being deported from Los Angeles, record the shocking persecution of Americans by other Americans.

The caption for the *New York News* photo "And Don't Come Back!" noted that "Facing an influx of thousands of undesirables, Los Angeles police are taking drastic action. Here the 'unwanted' are being deported by train. Courts are questioning the rights of police to bar them." The feeling one gets looking at these poignant images of young men, barely out of their teens, driven from border to border as if they were not in their own country, suffuses the film. It is clear that these Research Department materials contributed to the film's final shape—from its visual look to the screenplay—and that, whatever his public stance, Zanuck felt sympathy for these people. Where journalism had failed, the cinema would succeed.

Amazingly, given the honor it brought him, John Ford was not Zanuck's first choice to direct the film. On the cover of the first story synopsis, in pencil, Zanuck scribbled two other possibilities: Clarence Brown and John Cromwell. Nor were the actors who became esteemed for their performances necessarily Zanuck's first pick: both Zanuck and Ford preferred Beulah Bondi for Ma Joad, over Jane Darwell (who won the Best Supporting Actress Oscar for her portrayal); and Zanuck thought about casting Walter Brennan, Warren Hull, or James Barton (of *Tobacco Road* fame) in the part of Pa

Joad, the role eventually given to Russell Simpson. He even toyed with casting Jimmy Stewart in the part of Al, Tom's gawky younger brother. But one casting decision was never questioned: Henry Fonda was always Zanuck's choice to play Tom. And he wanted Nunnally Johnson to write the script.

Zanuck sensed he would be closely scrutinized, and he told Nunnally Johnson: "I want complete secrecy in reference to *The Grapes of Wrath* script. . . . I want you to make only three copies—one for yourself and two for me. A number of more or less unfriendly newspapermen are waiting to grab our first script to actually find out what we have done with this great book."[14] Zanuck was anticipating the general complaints that were to be lodged against all his serious pictures: that by focusing on the personal human relations, he had softened the larger social and political angles.

Zanuck was happy with Johnson's first draft, and made few changes. Yet there were decisions made *before* the script was written that altered the book and, some say, weakened it. Where Steinbeck's novel clearly stood for organizing the oppressed against powerful institutions like banks and agribusiness, Zanuck (who opposed most Hollywood unionization of "creative" personnel) was content to suggest something as vague as that the American spirit would overcome the Depression. There were reasons why Zanuck, antiunion or not, softened parts of the novel. He believed that people did not go to the movies to hear a lecture (which is what long sections of Steinbeck's novel are). They could get a lecture at church. At the movies they wanted entertainment. He could address the same issues as Steinbeck's novel had, but he was certain that if a film of the book was to find favor with the vast majority of American moviegoers, these issues had to be presented in terms that people would want to hear.

Zanuck was also fearful that an accurate depiction of the labor situation in California could bring lawsuits, so he avoided pinning the blame on specific institutions. In the novel, there is a scene in which the area's big growers try to break a strike by flooding the market with handbills advertising high-paying jobs they have no intention of delivering. When there are more workers than jobs, they can lower the minimum wage, knowing that desperate people like the Joads would do anything to feed themselves and their families. Here Steinbeck was showing how one powerful institution, agribusiness, was just like the enemy banks denounced earlier in the film: they both care more for profits than for treating people humanely. On the advice of the Publicity Department's Jason Joy (formerly of the PCA), Zanuck told Johnson: "we must express doubts where the handbills came from—so we don't give the definite impression that the big growers did it. Get in the idea that they might have come from the fly-by-night labor contractors." Softening the blow against agribusiness interests was a way of warding off an attack on himself and the parallel institution of the movie business, whose own labor practices and attitudes toward unions were far from admirable. In another characterization, Zanuck instructed Johnson to show the government only in a positive light, so as not to run afoul of the Roosevelt administration. He should "be sure to characterize the Caretaker of the Government Camp as being a particularly fine, good man."[15] This was done to such an extent that the actor cast as the caretaker actually *looks* like FDR, down to his glasses and leonine, oversized head.

Yet Zanuck's hand is evident in more than what he took away, or in the caution he displayed in catering to powerful interests. For example, in a story conference of July 19, Zanuck told Nunnally Johnson that he was sure the film needed "a new scene in town." Johnson wondered what Zanuck meant. Here we see Zanuck at his inspirational best. He felt Johnson had not been harsh enough in showing moviegoers the dehumanizing, dispiriting conditions endured by people robbed of their homes. The Joads have crossed the desert and are finally in California. Zanuck wanted Johnson to set the scene better:

> Their money practically gone—gas low—and the terrible realization that what they were told [about there being no jobs] is true. . . .
> We come in on them driving into town and asking somebody where they should go about finding work—maybe showing the fellow the handbill. The man just looks at them and laughs. Someone else comes along and they ask him. We see the fellow look at the car and down on the license plate. "Oh—Oklahoma. There's a camp on the edge of town—maybe somebody there will tell you—"
> Their hopefulness and terrible disillusionment. They drive into

the Hooverville camp and their hearts drop at the terrible sights. The futility of what has occurred. They just look at each other as the stark truth dawns on them. "Don't seem very encouragin', does it?" . . . Ma snaps them out of it—they'd better pitch the tent, etc.[16]

In looking at the sequence as it appears in the film, we see that director John Ford had not just followed the general tenor of Zanuck's suggestions: the sequence as shot is a virtual transcription of the memo, down to the lines of dialogue. With Ford using a very slowly moving camera and filming through the front windshield of the Joads' truck, we see, as Zanuck intended us to do, with their eyes. Before them in this promised land passes a tightly choreographed, carefully selected parade of dispirited, defeated grotesques. Their stooped shoulders, worn clothing, and suspicious glares into the camera are unnerving and accusatory. They are an index of life in this and all Hoovervilles. It is one of the most shattering scenes in the film. In contrast, a subsequent scene of the orderly, well-lit, government-run "Farm Workers' Wheat Patch Camp" seems like heaven. If we do not know whom to blame for Hooverville, here at Wheat Patch the camera tracks in on a sign that says "Department of Agriculture." Zanuck and Ford (with a reminder from Jason Joy) have made certain we are aware to whom credit is due.

By the time he made *The Grapes of Wrath,* Zanuck had grappled with the issues raised by literary adaptations for almost twenty years. He had operationalized and internalized the rules of the culture of Hollywood as they applied to adaptations. Zanuck thus believed that a book and a film based on a book were *always* going to have major points of departure. In a culture whose courts would not afford film the same First Amendment protection as the printed word, this is inevitable. Yet, with the barely disguised baleful glee of prosecutors drawing up an indictment against a defendant who all believe to be guilty, people have compiled an extensive catalog of changes or compromises orchestrated under Zanuck's instructions, a bill of particulars "proving" Zanuck's *mens rea,* his guilty Hollywood motives in altering the narrative to fit the demands of the medium. Yet, Steinbeck himself told his agent that long parts of the book—the growth of revolutionary consciences among the dispossessed, why the government was dumping food surpluses when people were starving, how California's farming developed into a large-scale industry—were "descriptive material." Since Zanuck felt such scenes inevitably slowed down his narrative, they were almost always omitted. Further, what was included was often altered or simplified—rather than dropped. For example, in the novel, the neurotic character of Uncle John is either holding forth about his guilty obsession with sin or is on a bender acquiring useful sinful material to talk about. Zanuck told Johnson: "We are going to drop the element of Uncle John's sin. This issue is in the past and bears no relationship to our main issue. Also, it is neither clear nor interesting."[17]

Zanuck also reversed the order of two of Steinbeck's scenes so the film would have a more optimistic slant. In the novel, the exploitative peach picking at the Keene Ranch comes *after* (not as the film has it, *before*) the Joad's arrival and warm welcome at the government's camp. Steinbeck's sequence gave the Joads a false sense of optimism about their future in California. The horrid conditions at the migrant camp subsequently saw this illusion shattered. On the contrary, Zanuck's insistence that the camp and its Roosevelt-lookalike head be shown in a positive light gave the Joads—and moviegoers—a sense of hope that *something* was being done.

But *The Grapes of Wrath* was not all compromise. There were scenes harshly critical of established American institutions that film could render more powerfully than any book. Zanuck did not hesitate to show unmotivated police brutality against a people already so downtrodden as to be virtually without power and stripped of the ability to defend themselves. The attempt to arrest the Hooverville agitator who tries to explain to workers their contractual rights, the shooting of an innocent female bystander in the ensuing melee, and the savage murder of Casey once he had refound his calling as a labor organizer, instead of a preacher, were radical by Hollywood standards. When Zanuck was advised to take out any reference to Communist influences in the American labor movement or, worse still, to demonize organized labor as pawns of the wily reds, Zanuck insisted that Tom Joad's sympathetic question be retained. Tom has heard labor organizers berated by the police and the minions of the big ranch and farm owners as troublemakers, agitators, and, most puzzlingly, "reds." Yet he has seen the "reds" fight for the rights of decent people, while the forces of authority resort to lies, brutality, and starvation to get what they want. Observing all this with the innocent intensity only Henry Fonda could muster, Tom asks what many Americans wanted to know: "What is these reds, anyway? Every time you turn around somebody's calling someone else a red. What is these reds, anyway?" In reply, a sympathetic farmer answers, "Oh, I ain't talkin' about that one way or another." Tom, and American moviegoers, have here been given a rare chance they would be denied after World War II. On this matter, Zanuck is suggesting it is best for Tom and for us to make up our own minds about "these reds."

Perhaps the major difference between the book and the film (duly noted by many critics) was the ending. This was purely Zanuck's invention. From his first conference with Steinbeck, Zanuck had expressed dissatisfaction with the book's ending and felt sure viewers would feel the same. Cannily, while he voiced his uneasiness, clever as a fox, he did nothing about it during the shooting of the film. Ford, thinking his work was done, was off to Honolulu. As Zanuck was cutting the film, he took an earlier episode in the book (Ma Joad's speech in which she proclaims, "We ain't gonna die out. People is goin' on—changin' a little, maybe, but goin' right on") and rewrote it so it became not just the ending he was looking for, but a scene that served as a valedictory for the entire film.

Zanuck's speech has Ma, seated in the front of their truck, proclaiming to a dispirited Pa that after what she had been through,

> I ain't never gonna be scared no more. I was though. For a while it looked like we was beat. Good and beat. Looked like we didn't have nobody in the whole wide world but enemies. . . . It made me feel kind of bad, and scared, too. Like we was lost and nobody cared.

Ma philosophizes that while men's lives proceed in spurts, women's are like a stream—they just keep flowing in an unstoppable, continuous movement whose slow but certain momentum means that they can take everything in stride. (This is how Ma alleviates Pa's admission that he is no longer capable of leading the family.) Pa tells her:

"Well, maybe. But we've sure taken a beatin'." But she explains that this barely perceptible tenacity, almost as natural as the movement of the waters, is precisely what makes the poor strong:

> Rich fellas come up and they die. And their kids ain't no good and they die out. But we keep a comin'. We're the people that live. They can't wipe us out, they can't lick us. We'll go on forever, Pa, 'cause we're the people.

The sheer force of Ma's beliefs lifts Pa's hopes, and the Joads drive off into the California sunset with the strains of "Red River Valley" swelling around them. Zanuck hoped that with these final images and words, Ma would carry the audience with her, too. Here, Zanuck speaks through his character. He was an eternal optimist, a small-town boy of little formal education whose own success proved the truth, the eternal viability, of the American dream. He was very proud of the speech. His biographer Mel Gussow wrote: "to his way of thinking, it should have been in the book in the first place."[18]

Like most films Ford directed, once the script was "locked," the rest went quickly. Though most of the film was shot at the studio, to obtain authentic backgrounds a second unit also filmed in parts of California, Oklahoma, and Texas. While the film had changed parts of the novel, even its author acknowledged that *The Grapes of Wrath* reached the screen with his novel's spirit, mood, and feeling intact. The studio offered up something even Steinbeck could never deliver: the look and the sound of the Joads' world. John Ford's supreme visual sense was given life by cinematographer Gregg Toland's magnificent black-and-white cinematography. The film's score was made up largely of sparingly used American folk songs, most memorably "Red River Valley." Accompanying the stark simplicity of a film in which Zanuck saw to it that the major actors wore no makeup, Alfred Newman wisely set all music with the simplest arrangements.

The film justified, once more, John Ford's admiration for Zanuck. "One of his greatest assets," noted Ford, "was to supply the proper music—and sound effects." Unlike other producers—for example, David O. Selznick's overwhelming use of Max Steiner's score for *Gone With the Wind*—Zanuck "held music down to a minimum."

Moreover, Ford noted, *The Grapes of Wrath* demonstrated Zanuck's unique ability to shape mood with the smallest change in detail:

> He'd put things in I'd never dream of. In *Grapes of Wrath* there was a scene with an itinerant preacher [John Carradine] and a swamp under a bridge, and Darryl put in the sound of crickets, and you *knew* you were in a swamp. Later, there was this English picture [*The Third Man*] with one instrument, a zither playing all the way through it that they talked a lot about, but it was not the first time that was done. In *Grapes* Darryl used a single, lightly played accordion—not a big orchestra—and it was very American, and very right for the picture.[19]

The Grapes of Wrath premiered on January 24, 1940. Not only was the film an enormous critical triumph but confounding its many negative prognosticators, this "unfilmable" story would be the studio's biggest moneymaker that year. Even former Zanuck-basher Frank Nugent, the *New York Times* film critic (later related by marriage to John Ford) couldn't restrain himself: "In the vast library where celluloid literature of the screen is stored, there is one small, uncrowded shelf devoted to the cinema's masterpieces. To that shelf of screen classics, 20th Century-Fox yesterday added *The Grapes of Wrath*."[20]

HOW GREEN WAS MY VALLEY: "THE VOICE"

Undoubtedly his triumph with *The Grapes of Wrath* emboldened Zanuck to try another controversial project, Richard Llewellyn's best-seller of life among Welsh coal miners, *How Green Was My Valley*. After his magnificent work on *Grapes*, Zanuck wanted John Ford to direct the film. But Ford was unavailable (he was working with Nunnally Johnson on another Zanuck project, *Tobacco Road*), so Zanuck turned to an artist he had long admired but never worked with, William Wyler. He arranged to borrow him on a twelve-week loan-out from Samuel Goldwyn.

The choice was logical on artistic grounds, but it was also risky and bold. By 1940, Wyler most certainly was one of the most highly regarded directors in Hollywood. He had already been nominated three times for Best Director: in 1936 for *Dodsworth,* in 1939 for *Wuthering Heights,* and in 1940 for *The Letter.* (He would be nominated a record total of twelve times, winning for *Mrs. Minniver, The Best Years of Our Lives,* and *Ben Hur.*) Along with this enviable track record, Wyler was considered very stubborn. He would steadfastly refuse to budge until he got the exact performance, set design, or line of dialogue he wanted. (At the studio most noted for the rapid frugality with which its directors were coerced into shooting pictures on schedule, a Warner's daily report on Wyler's progress with *Jezebel* sent to production head Hal Wallis noted, "I do not believe anyone is aware of just how slow Mr. Wyler is.")[21] It was not uncommon for Wyler to force a stubborn actor to go through so many repeated takes that exhaustion—and Wyler's will—ultimately prevailed. (Bette Davis may have been the one actor whose own sense of artistic rectitude and stubbornness enabled her to occasionally wear down even Wyler himself.) Through this method, he had earned the nickname "Ninety-Take Wyler."

It was no secret that Wyler worked deliberately and carefully. Philip Dunne summed up his qualities:

> [No mogul] could force Willy to hurry up, to skimp, to turn in a shoddy piece of work. . . . His favorite line was "You can do it better"—and nobody left the sound stage until everyone, including Willy himself, had done his very best. If he was tough on others, he was twice as tough on himself.[22]

He had the reputation—and the ability—of being a capable script doctor. Unlike Ford, he liked to collaborate with screenwriters.[23] In the age of increasing rationalization of the director's work, whatever its drawbacks Wyler's approach obviously got results. (Unfortunately, from the producer's point of view, they were achieved at his expense.) Most recently, his obsessive perfectionism brought *Wuthering Heights* in thirteen days over schedule and $100,000 over budget, causing frustrated producer Sam Goldwyn to declaim "that Goddamed Wyler is trying to kill me."[24] The collaboration between these two giants (who knew "the book" on one another) undoubtedly would prove as interesting a test of the system as Zanuck's confrontation with Edward G. Robinson during the previous decade.

Because Zanuck had already paid a very high sum ($300,000) for Llewellyn's novel, Wyler's reputation for extravagance would be a factor in getting New York to approve him. But with or without him, Zanuck seemed determined to make *How Green Was My Valley* a blockbuster. In part, this obsession with scale was due to Zanuck's rivalry with producer David O. Selznick, whose *Gone With the Wind* had, at nearly four hours running time, set new Hollywood standards of showmanship and profit in 1939. The next year, Selznick upped the competitive ante further when *his* adaptation of *Rebecca* edged out Zanuck's *The Grapes of Wrath* for Best Picture. Zanuck thus conceived of *How Green Was My Valley* as his response to *Gone With the Wind*. Thus, like Selznick's Civil War opus, it would be shot in Technicolor, run four hours, and be full of stars. Among those Zanuck contemplated: Laurence Olivier (as Gruffyd), Katharine Hepburn (as Angharad!), and Greer Garson (as Bronwen). Zanuck planned to use the studio's top male star, Tyrone Power, for the film's lead, Huw Morgan. To add to the authentic atmosphere and increase the film's showmanship value, Zanuck intended to one-up his rival in a key area: bypassing the artificiality he feared might result if Fox tried to recreate Llewellyn's beloved Wales on a movie soundstage or on the Fox back lots, Zanuck was going to bypass Southern California entirely to shoot the film on location, in Wales.[25]

Wyler had his own ideas about casting: for Bronwen, he saw either Greer Garson or Geraldine Fitzgerald; for Angharad, his list was even more intruiging than Zanuck's: Vivien Leigh, Katharine Hepburn (again), Ida Lupino, and Merle Oberon. Oddly, for the mine owner Old Evans, Wyler was considering casting Donald Crisp, who went on to portray not a capitalist but Gwilym Morgan, the coal miner father who heads the Morgan family.[26] These colossal plans, plus Wyler's profligate reputation, gave the Board of Twentieth Century-Fox pause. In fact, many board members questioned whether they should be embarking on this venture at all, given that 1940 was unfolding as a relatively poor year for corporate profits, that parts of the story were bleak, and that the production could get expensive.

Further, with Europe at war, revenues there—particularly in France, Spain, and Germany—were lost. All these factors led Zanuck to modify his initial grand conception. The first thing to be dropped was the Welsh location shooting—the coal-rich area was now a prime bombing target—and, with it, Zanuck's dreams of a Technicolor valley. At Zanuck's request, Philip Dunne checked out Malibu as a possible substitute. He regretfully told Zanuck it would not do for Wales, but it did under the supervision of the art director, Richard Day, and using the visuals and data contained in the many books collected in the studio's research library, a set for an authentic Welsh village was built amidst the hills of Malibu.

In addition to these problems, there was the nature of the story itself. One of its main elements concerned the coal miners' attempts to unionize. This was *not* a topic beloved of producers, most of whom saw unions as a threat to their sovereignty. So rabidly were producers opposed to unions that at the urging of L. B. Mayer, in 1927 they formed the Academy of Motion Picture Arts and Sciences "to delay any serious labor organizing in Hollywood for over five years."[27] It worked. As late as 1933, Hollywood was yet an "open-shop" town. The only recognized union in town, the IATSE, covered electricians, engineers, grips, and musicians. In 1940 labor's right to organize was *still* a hotly contested political issue, all over the United States. Unions hadn't even received the right to such basic protections as collective bargaining until 1935, with the National Labor Relations Act. Hollywood directors (who first organized into a guild in 1936) had attained recognition for their union in 1939, but in 1940 screenwriters were still fighting for this right.

The right of screenwriters to organize, like the right of Llewellyn's coal miners, was an issue that divided families and organizations alike. The original writer assigned to the screenplay was Ernest Pascal, president of the Screen Writers Guild—an organization to which screenwriter-turned-producer Zanuck had always been strongly opposed. (Unlike Harry Warner, Zanuck was willing to discuss the issues the picture raised about unions.)[28] This antagonism is more than a footnote to the film's history. Despite the fact that he had used hardball tactics (like providing them with resignation forms) to dissuade Fox writers from joining the SWG, his sense of fairness and professionalism meant that a person's politics had nothing to do with his or her ability to get the job done. Anti-union man Zanuck had hired a union activist to mediate his vision of how to depict the vicious, unprincipled means the mine owners used to block unionization.

How Green Was My Valley was not the first occasion Pascal and Zanuck would debate the union issue. In 1936 the two had engaged in a lively exchange on these issues in *Variety*. Zanuck insisted he opposed unions not because he wished to impede writers' conditions. Shouldn't he, a former writer, know the progress that screenwriters had made? But recalling his own tenuous and financially unstable start, and meteoric rise, he felt progress could be made without recourse to modifying a system he felt provided ample opportunities— under *his* authority. Could not Pascal see in Zanuck's career that screenwriters had already come so far? They were well paid. They had representation on the Academy. Why rock the boat? (Writer Dorothy Parker, taking in Zanuck's logic on the protection afforded writers by the producer-dominated Academy, wittily observed that "Looking to the Academy for representation was like trying to get laid in your mother's house. Somebody was always in the parlor, watching.")

When it came time to assess the script, Zanuck's judgment was not based on any disagreement with Pascal's political views, however. Rather, he was dissatisfied "mainly because it has turned into a labor story and a sociological problem story, instead of being a great human, warm story about real living people."[29] Approaching the problem from different niches within the culture of Hollywood, the producer and the screenwriter had failed to find what common ground there might have been in the system. Moreover, Zanuck found Pascal's script too critical of the English mine owners: "In view of what is happening today, we certainly don't want to attack the English manner of things, right or wrong."[30]

Zanuck turned to Philip Dunne. Staunchly pro-union, Dunne felt uncomfortable about critiquing a colleague's work, particularly since Pascal was a fellow SWG officer. But Pascal told him he should "say exactly what [he] thought"; after all his arguments with Zanuck, "he was sick of the whole project."[31] Dunne began working on the screenplay in July 1940, still operating under Zanuck's assumption that they were going to make a four-hour film. By late August, he had completed his first, lengthy draft and was surprised to receive a phone call from Zanuck the next day. His boss had read the script overnight, and now knew they would have to cut it in half. It was to be a two-hour, black-and-white film. Dunne knew he was in for a long haul.

The rest of the film's long production history shows two things. First, when Zanuck was determined to make a film, he made it. It also demonstrates how obsessively involved he was with every aspect of production. He would consider virtually *anything* that he thought would help ensure a good script. For example, eager to gauge what audiences would like to see in a film version of a beloved book, he took to heart a letter he received from a book reviewer for ladies' clubs.[32] In an age before Hollywood turned to extensive market research and focus groups, maybe this woman's data was just what he needed. Her opinions were also attractive because they were congruent with Zanuck's: "without exception," she told him, "every audience reacted similarly to those situations that showed man's spirit unbeaten and unconquerable, that portrayed a poor, devastated Wales rich in heroes." This was precisely the kind of depoliticized, uplifting human angle Zanuck was endeavoring to use for the film. A day after he received the letter, he passed it to Wyler, telling him: "I thought you would like to see this. This woman is very brilliant. She talks to groups of club women and reviews books for them."[33] A cooperative Wyler asked Mrs. Denitz to make an appointment to see him.

While Zanuck and the director had never been close, Wyler and Dunne had been friends since the early 1930s and shared a common political perspective. Script doctor Wyler was somehow able to convince Zanuck that he and Dunne should work on the script together, away from the studio. Such an unorthodox arrangement would mean that Zanuck would have little control over the script, the very part of preproduction at which he excelled. Nevertheless, out of respect for their talent, he let them retire to the mountain resort of Arrowhead Springs with the proviso that they telephone him daily. Restive at being so far away from the action, Zanuck would call each man sepa-rately—sometimes very late at night, when he was up screening rushes and editing—hoping to catch either of the two alone, away from the influence of the other.

Thus far, the Wyler-Zanuck collaboration was off to a civil start. In Wyler's collaborations with Sam Goldwyn, notably on *Dead End,* these two strong-willed figures commonly mediated their disagree-ments by engaging in long screaming matches conducted in colorful and sometimes imprecise English. But, as editor Danny Mandell rec-ollects: "The big difference between [Wyler and Goldwyn] was that Goldwyn could never admit he was wrong."[34] While Zanuck usually felt he was right, he could—and frequently did—admit he was wrong. A legendary story (told to Philip Dunne by Zanuck's favorite writer, Lamar Trotti) illustrates this.

Zanuck was at a story conference in his long, green-painted office. As usual, he was pacing restlessly, carrying his sawed-off polo mallet, throwing off a spray of ideas. Sometimes these were "the most outra-geous clichés" and his writers knew not to take them literally. They were meant to be a starting point that would later translate into a workable scene. Stymied at a particular point of story development, Zanuck was seized by an inspiration:

> "And now," Zanuck asserts, "and *now* her love turns to hate." A pause. He stops, stares at the writers, and repeats, "Her love turns to hate."
>
> Another pause. Then [writer] Kitty Scola says, "Why, Mr. Zanuck? Why does her love turn to hate?"
>
> Zanuck glares at Kitty for a moment, then strides into the dress-ing room behind his office and on into the bathroom which ad-joins it.

> All present were familiar with Zanuck in action. Sitting in anticipa-tory, but bemused silence, they wondered: "How would Zanuck get out of this one?"

> They hear the sound of the toilet flushing and Zanuck reappears, paces the length of the office, and turns dramatically, pointing the

polo mallet at Kitty Scola. "All right," he says, "her love *doesn't* turn to hate."

If wrong, Zanuck admitted it, albeit in his own inimitable, sometimes roundabout manner. The people who worked with him had to reinterpret his statements into a kind of Zanuck code of advice. As Dunne recalls, Zanuck once told him, "And now, we get into a tender love scene: he rams his tongue down her throat." Dunne's years of experience working with Zanuck translated this to mean that the scene "could be tender, but not boring."[35]

Now, Dunne was caught between two stubborn perfectionists, men who would go to great lengths to get on film what they felt was right. Once ensconced at Arrowhead, he discovered his friend Wyler's reputation was well earned. Wyler refused any suggestions made by either Dunne or Zanuck. After ten weeks spent in relative isolation, the two returned with a completed screenplay—tighter, but no shorter. They still had a very long script, and "not even Zanuck seemed to know what to do about it."[36]

Though this set a precedent, Zanuck nevertheless began discussions with Wyler about casting before the script had been finished. For the part of Bronwen, the wife of the eldest Morgan boy, Ivor, Zanuck toyed with either Geraldine Fitzgerald or a longer shot, Gene Tierney. Tierney would be a major star by mid-decade, but in 1940 was still at the outset of her career. To Zanuck's surprise, "although she practically had nothing to do in the film," Tierney had scored big with audiences in *The Return of Frank James*. She was too young for the part of Bronwen, but Zanuck assured Wyler that "strangely enough, she does not look young on the screen."[37] To make sure she had the optimum conditions, Zanuck asked Wyler to do something very unusual for a director of his stature: direct a test with Tierney. He also wanted him to direct tests for the best prospects selected from a raft of young English boys rounded up to play the young Huw. Wyler agreed. Thus far, the stubborn men were happily coexisting.

For the part of Mr. Gruffyd, the minister in love with Huw's sister, Angharad, Zanuck suggested Wyler's colleague from *Wuthering*

Heights, Laurence Olivier. With England at war this seemed unlikely. Zanuck concluded "that if we cannot get Laurence Olivier, and it doesn't look like we can get him," and if another choice—Walter Pidgeon—could not be borrowed from Metro-Goldwyn-Mayer, they would have to proceed with extreme caution. Of another possibility, Zanuck felt that although he would come at a lower price they should not be seduced by economics, for "we would still be making a mistake to take Brian Aherne." Beyond the obvious rationale of marquee value, Zanuck's reasons for Olivier or Pidgeon were clear and pragmatic. The Gruffyd-Angharad love angle was "the only halfway happy love story that we have in our entire film." The balance would be placed in jeopardy "if we cast a man in this role who lacks personal charm . . . what is absolutely essential is that we get someone who HAS AN APPEAL FOR WOMEN. I cannot emphasize how vital this is."[38] For that reason Zanuck wanted to cast Walter Pidgeon, and he did.

Their main problem—the unwieldy length of the script—remained to be solved. Taking up an idea Zanuck had first broached to Pascal, Zanuck, Wyler, and Dunne came up with a way to shorten the script: rather than have the film follow the main character between the ages of ten and sixty, they agreed that the boy, Huw, would remain young throughout the story. The film would be presented as the *recollection* of his childhood. This solution altered the film's structure. Both Zanuck and Dunne, independent of one another, then came up with one of the devices that give the film its distinctive quality and tone: using the adult Huw as the narrator. Zanuck had used the voiceover extensively in *Stanley and Livingstone,* another project on which he and his writers had a tough time staying focused. Here, unlike Spencer Tracy's voice of Stanley narrating his trek for Livingstone *simultaneously* with its unfolding on the screen, the voiceover of an adult Huw would be heard from the vantage point of a man of sixty, looking fondly back at the verdant memories of youth. The film would be narrated by, but not shown from the perspective of, the older man. Thus the past would come across as a deeply personal memory rather than a flashback narration:

This is a very unusual book and we must tell it in an equally unusual way. We want to put the BOOK on the screen and not do, as has been done, put the book into our standard technique. There is no question that this would give us an opportunity to get into the picture the essence and guts of it, possibly even greater than GRAPES OF WRATH. It can be something startlingly new in screen technique.[39]

True to his overenthusiastic nature, Zanuck overstated the novelty of this type of voiceover. The device of the voiceover recollection, as opposed to voiceover narration, was not absolutely new. Hollywood had used it at least once before, in Preston Sturges's *The Power and the Glory* (1933). (It would also be used in a film that would open six months before *How Green Was My Valley*, Orson Welles's *Citizen Kane*.) But it was still unfamiliar to moviegoers, and therefore somewhat risky. In his conference notes, Zanuck referred to this narration simply as "the VOICE." It was an unseen character he would use in innumerable films, ranging from *All About Eve* to *Mother Wore Tights*. Its all-knowing quality, the warm authority with which it spoke, perhaps represented Zanuck himself: the overseer of the world of Twentieth Century-Fox.

With the decision to have a young actor play Huw throughout the film, things started to fall into place. Rather than being unhappy about being dropped from the project, Tyrone Power told Dunne he was actually relieved not to have to star in *half* a movie. The young actor cast as Huw would have to anchor the film.

Here, luck intervened. A twelve-year-old British actor answered a call put out by MGM for the lead in *The Yearling*. He wasn't right for the part, but the casting people at MGM suggested he try Twentieth Century-Fox. Looking at tests shot to find a suitable Huw, Zanuck, Wyler, and Dunne had been watching a parade of English schoolboys with pink cheeks and Mayfair diction pass unconvincingly before them. Suddenly, with young Roddy McDowall, they saw "a big-knuckled, big-footed, awkward-looking kid with enormous black eyes and an even more enormous talent for acting."[40] While the casting director didn't think him conventionally pretty enough for a major film, all agreed that they had at last found their Huw. After all the problems he had encountered on this project, with the discovery of McDowall Dunne was so excited that he and his wife went out on the town with the Wylers to celebrate. Less sanguine, Zanuck was still thinking about his too-long script; he was still looking over his shoulder at the long shadow cast by Selznick's Civil War opus. He was concerned about pace, regardless of whether he made a two- or four-hour version: "If it dealt with the Civil War, in Technicolor, and had Clark Gable and everybody else in the business—perhaps we could have a seventeen-reel picture, but to deliberately try to start out to make one is suicide."[41]

Though Dunne and Wyler had worked very hard, they had made little progress in cutting the script. As they approached the scheduled starting date, Zanuck started to take on the kind of authoritarian mien Wyler found difficult. He was tired of waiting for Wyler and Dunne and began cutting the script himself.

"The valley, the labor troubles, and all of this should be in the background," his memos to Wyler explained. They must place priority on what the *audience* would want to know: "what happened to little Huw, his mother, his father, his brothers, Mr. Gruffyd and Angharad." Zanuck was trying to teach two very adept—but stubborn—pupils his principles of dramatic compression. For example, Dunne had written a scene in which Huw, the youngest of six sons, gets his first "trews," that is, his first suit with long pants. In addition to denoting the passage of time, the scene shows Huw's coming of age. As Dunne wrote it, it contained several ribald comments between Huw's father and the tailor concerning the mysteries of sex. An exasperated Zanuck lectured the pair on why this scene, though nicely written, wasted seven and a half pages of script:

> The tailor business is amusing but good heavens, we are in the middle of a story and we cannot stop for vaudeville acts. . . . Let's take the bull by the horns and get it over with one short silent scene with the Voice over it. . . . What good is there in showing this? It is only background to our real people.[42]

In this case, the two persuaded Zanuck to retain the scene. But, as he warned them he would, he cut it later. As Dunne recalled fifty years after the events, "Darryl had merely done what he always did: cut to the bone of the story line."[43] Zanuck cut the script so dramatically that the part of Bronwen was changed from a lead to a supporting role. Aware of this, Zanuck candidly noted that "I don't blame a first rate actress for not wanting to play this part as it is really only the fifth or sixth role in the whole story and is, of course, overshadowed by almost everyone else."[44]

He also cut long debates on the merits of labor unions. He gets the main points across in one scene in which the preacher, Mr. Gruffyd, mediates the dispute among the divided family by coming down firmly in favor of the union. He tells the assembled, "Well, then, here is what I think. First, have your union. You need it. Alone you are weak. Together you are strong." Then, Zanuck couldn't resist playing devil's advocate: "But remember that with strength goes responsibility—to others and to yourselves. For you cannot conquer injustice with more injustice—only with justice and with the help of God."

Dunne later recalled that when they finally had an acceptable script, Zanuck was reported to be going about the lot loudly complaining for all to hear that the screenwriter had talked him "into making a goddam pro-labor picture." As Dunne wryly notes, "This was absolute nonsense; nobody ever talked Darryl Zanuck into making anything he didn't want to make."

It was clear that while Zanuck had been willing to let Wyler and Dunne work with a good deal of autonomy, he was now utterly uncomfortable with where the uncharacteristically uninvolved position he had agreed to take in the preproduction phase had led them. This freedom was in part what had attracted Wyler to Fox, and abandoning it was sure to mean that Zanuck would have to deal with what he had thus far avoided: a direct confrontation with Wyler. With pressure coming from the Fox Board of Directors in New York, and with time on Wyler's loan-out from Goldwyn running out, he decided to intervene. As Dunne observed, "Darryl Zanuck's 20th Century-Fox was no place for an Auteur."[45] In a December 6, 1940, letter (marked "Confidential") to Wyler and Dunne, he spelled out the specific course they hereafter would follow on *How Green Was My Valley*.

Zanuck was sensitive to Wyler's stature, and aware of his combination of stubbornness and insecurity. Admitting "it is very embarrassing for me to write a note like this," he plunged in. "I do not claim," he wrote, "to be a first-class writer." But both men had to recognize that it was Zanuck's *abilities,* not just his authority, that entitled him to take the picture out of their hands: "what success I have had in this business for the past twenty years has come mainly from my 'knack' in [story] construction." Unlike other producers (perhaps he had noncreative executives like Jack Warner or Louis B. Mayer in mind), Zanuck was

> not the type of producer who stands on the side-lines and hires people to express their views for him and takes the screen credit. I expect every picture that I am associated with to equally represent the views of the writer, the director and myself. I have been associated with a great number of successful pictures—and when I say associated I mean that I creatively contributed my proportionate share and I never avoided the responsibility.

Now came his *coup de grâce,* an assertion of authority over Wyler delivered in terms so unequivocal that there could be but one interpretation. Unlike Wyler's battles with Goldwyn, Zanuck made sure there would be no screaming:

> Once you get on the set, Willie, you will find that you will never have any interference from me as I rarely go near a set. I believe that a director is engaged to direct and that he should be allowed full opportunity to express his ability—but I do want to say that the script that he shoots must, before it goes into production, represent the combined viewpoints of the writer, the director, and myself. It has always been this way with me—it is the only way I know how to produce—and it will have to be this way on this assignment. I pride myself on being reasonable and just and not wed only to my own ideas, but, at the same time, I am not, at this stage of the game, going to change my plan of work or sit on the side-line and let someone do the thing for me.[46]

Dunne was under a long-term contract to the studio. He could do little but comply with Zanuck's orders, or go on suspension. Wyler was a different story. He was a freelance director hired for this one project. Confronted with Zanuck's well-reasoned, well-written letter, he did what many people in an asymmetrical power relationship do: he let off steam. The director drafted, but did not mail, a rebuttal to Zanuck's letter, which is published here for the first time. In looking at Wyler's response to Zanuck, we must consider two things: that French and even German, but not English, was Wyler's first language, and that he had to tread a dangerous line between firm diplomacy and bold disagreement with a man far more powerful than he, a figure who was used to getting his own way at what was, after all, his own studio.

> DD [Dear Darryl]
> I don't think you give me sufficient credit for fully realizing your problems in the production of our picture and of general considerations as they are. I can only assure you that you will find me more than cooperative in this direction, but I must ask you that in matters of taste you limit your interference. I am frightened of your attack on this script since of course you have the last word. I'm not trying to infringe on your authority, but you and I have entirely different styles in the telling of a story and I honestly think that for this one mine is better. Before I started to work for you I was greatly encouraged by your apparent eagerness to get for this picture all that I could possibly give it. I am not a good director in the strictest sense that I could direct well a number of scenes as instructed. If you want to tell a straight line story of Angharad and Gruffyd I'm afraid I can't be very interested. If however you want to tell the story of *How Green Was My Valley* and be faithful to the spirit of the book and retain and dramatize the things that made it successful—I'm *very* interested.

Wyler's letter closed with the same call for civility that had ended Zanuck's: "I repeat that you can depend upon me to comply with every reasonable request in an effort that we can have done an economic successful and fine piece of work."[47]

We will never know how this dispute would have been resolved. They would have to wait until spring or summer to film the many outdoor scenes, and Wyler's loan-out time was up. He was due back at Goldwyn's studio to begin work on his next project, *The Little Foxes*. It is possible that beyond the dictates of scheduling, Wyler's departure had been set in motion when the uneasy Fox Board of Directors, closely monitoring the saga of this, their most costly production, took action. They told Zanuck they were withdrawing funds for the film. They hated the script and the absence of big stars, and, with Wyler's reputation for profligacy apparently confirmed, they predicted the worst financial fate for *How Green Was My Valley*. Dunne presumed that after all his hard work, like many a narrow miss in Hollywood, the project was through.

But he had not counted on Zanuck's faith in his own judgment, his commitment to his employees, and his tenacious strength when he believed in something. In stopping the funds for the film, New York was questioning his judgment, period. Though Zanuck had no power to free up the funds, he did something that Dunne said "endeared him to me forever."[48] He wrote a defiant letter to the members of the board telling them that Dunne's effort was the finest screenplay he had ever read. If they would not authorize the money, he proposed a simple solution: he would go to another company and produce the film there as a freelancer. This threat, coming from the man who had quit Warner Brothers on a matter of principle, and had founded the very studio he now threatened to desert, had its effect. Less than a month later, the project was on again. But unlike the previous month's goings-on, this time it would be directed by John Ford on a preset budget and shooting schedule. In the end, John Ford would win the Oscar for Best Director for a film whose look—its sets, costumes, and Dunne's script—had been to a large extent prepared by Wyler and Zanuck.

It is intriguing to imagine the film Wyler would have produced. His cinematographer, Gregg Toland (of *The Grapes of Wrath* and *Citizen Kane* fame), left with him, to be replaced by the equally gifted Arthur Miller. Whereas Wyler loved working on the script with writers, Ford was much more secretive. He was known for having a tightly worked-out plan before he shot, and he wanted little interference from anyone. Ford cut a film "in his head," leaving very little unused footage. Because he composed his frames with master shots that would be ruined by inserting cutaways or closeups, once he started shooting, little could be done afterward in the editing room to tamper with his version of a story. While Wyler's work with Bette Davis and other great actresses showed his understanding of and respect for the complexity of female characters, Dunne felt Ford lacked this insight and so failed to fully realize the scenes Dunne had crafted for the sad love story of Angharad and Gruffyd.

Yet, Ford certainly brought his own unique strengths. It was at his insistence that Barry Fitzgerald was hired to play Cyfartha, a companion of Dai Bando, a former pugilist (now blind). With Ford's suggestions, including actual lines of dialogue, Fitzgerald enriched the film and went on to steal nearly every scene in which he appeared. (This was no small feat in a cast populated by beauteous young Maureen O'Hara and veterans Sara Allgood, Donald Crisp, and Walter Pidgeon.) Ford also accomplished what Wyler never would have been able to pull off: he shot the film under schedule, in eight weeks. Having worked so hard with Wyler and Dunne to get the script in shape, Zanuck's only major suggestions to Ford focused on how he would handle the ending, and a concern whether there was too much of the famous Welsh singing in the film. (When the film was shown in Wales, moviegoers would attend the first show and then sit through successive screenings so they could sing along with the roster of old-time favorites.)

Midway through the shooting, in July 1941, Zanuck told Ford that if things "keep up like it is going it will be the greatest directorial job that you have ever turned in." In this type of drama Zanuck felt "audiences expect to see a thrilling and exciting climax that is fraught with suspense and danger and then winds up with a beautiful scene between father and son."[49] Zanuck got what he asked for. *How Green Was My Valley* ended with a mine cave-in in which Huw, answering the call ("Who here's for Gwilym Morgan?") goes below ground to save his trapped father. In one of the most poignant images in all of Zanuck's works, emerging from the mine's innards Huw reaches the surface cradling his father's lifeless, coal-blackened body in his arms. The narrative closes, "the Voice" tells us that death ends not with the cessation of life, but only with the extinction of memory. Over shots similar to those that opened the film (young Huw walking the beauteous valley with his father), the Voice tells us, "How green was my Valley, then, and the Valley of them that have gone."

How Green Was My Valley opened on October 28, 1941, at New York's Rivoli Theatre. Its ten Academy Award nominations were still three fewer than Selznick's *Gone With the Wind* had received in 1939. Zanuck faced stiff competition from nine other films for Best Picture. (In 1944, the Academy would reduce the number of nominees to five.) It was the year of Bogart's breakthrough in *The Maltese Falcon,* of Gary Cooper's star turn in *Sergeant York,* of Alfred Hitchcock's bit of stylish Grand Guignol for RKO, *Suspicion.* It was the year of *Citizen Kane.* Nevertheless, *How Green Was My Valley,* and not the much-praised *Citizen Kane,* walked off with the prize. Zanuck had his first Best Picture Oscar.

There is a strange symmetry to these Oscars. In 1941, thirty-nine-year-old Darryl Zanuck shared one thing in common with fellow nominee, twenty-five-year-old Orson Welles. In *How Green Was My Valley* and *Citizen Kane,* they had each made films of memory. But where Welles's multiple narrators are uncertain what meanings the past might reveal, Zanuck's narrator was not because of the warmth, directness, and believability Zanuck's vision of this world was able to evoke. If Welles's narrators shatter the past into so many pieces that we can never be sure we can put them back together, then Zanuck's Huw—a narrator we hear as an adult but see as a winsome child—does the opposite: his storytelling fuses the past and the present. This impossible fantasy, this union, provides us with the clear meaning and the harmony we are denied, intentionally, in *Citizen Kane.* In *How Green Was My Valley,* Zanuck has surrounded us with the echoes of song; he has gently called up images of the past, of some miraculously fabricated Welsh countryside created at Malibu. As we gaze up at the silvery gray wisps of cloud that blanket and suffuse its frames, we accord the ultimate testimonial to fabricator Zanuck's skills: we believe *How Green Was My Valley*'s world is real.

Very shortly, the tranquility of its dream world would evaporate before our eyes. President Roosevelt, in accepting his party's nomination for a third term, expressed the feelings of many:

Like most men of my age, I had made plans for myself, plans for a private life of my own choice and for my own satisfaction, a life of that kind to begin in January 1941. These plans, like so many other plans, had been made in a world which now seems as distant as another planet.

Zanuck's Wales now seemed as remote as another planet.

Chapter Eleven

"THE GLITTERING ROBES OF ENTERTAINMENT"

You cannot in the last reel give Joan of
Arc novocaine to ease her pain. She
has to burn at the stake.

—DARRYL ZANUCK ON *PINKY*

SIX WEEKS AFTER *How Green Was My Valley* opened, the United States was at war. Zanuck had been commissioned a Reserve Lieutenant Colonel in the Army Signal Corps in January 1941, nearly a year before Pearl Harbor. When war broke out he was thirty-nine, not too old to enlist in active combat. With his cinematic expertise and executive abilities, he had much to contribute to the war effort. At first, Zanuck used these skills on the home front. After December 1941, entertainment at Twentieth Century-Fox took on a decidedly military cast, and Zanuck turned out a large number of propaganda films: *A Yank in the RAF, Berlin Correspondent, Little Tokyo USA, Manila Calling, The Pied Piper, Secret Agent of Japan,* and *To the Shores of Tripoli* were all made by Zanuck before he entered the army. (Showing his patriotic spirit, for *Thunderbirds* and *China Girl,* Zanuck reactivated his old writing persona, Melville Crossman.) But Zanuck was itching for active duty. When colleagues like William Wyler and John Ford enlisted in the air force and navy, respectively, to make training and combat films, Zanuck decided he had to go to war too. For almost fifteen years he had been used to giving orders. Would he be able to take orders from someone else? Could a man whose work day started at 10 A.M. and lasted until 3:00 or 4:00 in the morning adapt to regimented army living?

He was appointed by the army to their Signal Corps to supervise and produce training and combat films and promoted to colonel in January 1942. (Jack Warner was recruited to make films for the army air force. Jack told his general that since "Darryl Zanuck has been made a Col. in the army," it was only fitting that as Zanuck's senior, he should hold a higher rank: "I wouldn't mind being a general."¹ His bemused senior officer commissioned him as a lieutenant colonel— one rank below Zanuck.)

Beyond his stature in the industry and the obvious executive abilities he had demonstrated at his own studio, Zanuck was a natural choice because he was head of the Research Council of the Academy of Motion Picture Arts and Sciences—an organization that, among other things, served as a liaison between the industry and the armed forces in the production of military training films. This arrangement was terminated by the army in December 1942 under circumstances that embroiled Zanuck in one of the greatest controversies of his career.

At his own request, on April 29, 1942, he was granted a leave of absence from his work with the studio. While he was away, Mayer's son-in-law, Bill Goetz, was in charge of production at Twentieth Century-Fox. Zanuck also asked that his weekly salary of $5,000 be discontinued for the duration of his period in the army. Like his request for a leave, this proposed pay hiatus needed the approval of the Twentieth Century-Fox Board of Directors. Because it did not go into effect until they met and considered it, in August, for nearly four months he continued to draw his salary as vice president in charge of production while on active military duty. Zanuck refused the army's pay, never signing the vouchers he received. Additionally, from August until he was back in civilian life the following June, he never stopped receiving the ample dividends from the 90,000 shares of Twentieth Century-Fox stock he owned. He also retained the chairmanship of the Research Council, as well as his position on the Board of Directors of Twentieth Century-Fox.

Those few months that he continued to draw his full salary while serving in the army, and the fact that he did not put his stock holdings in trust, would come back to haunt Zanuck. Twice he became the subject of investigation as part of domestic surveillance of corruption and unfair profiteering in war-related industries. The first investigation was conducted by the Senate War Investigating Committee headed by Missouri Senator Harry Truman. While he was hardly the sole object of scrutiny, Zanuck (unfairly) received quite a bit of adverse press publicity as a "Hollywood Colonel" whose inflated rank was based more on image and influence than on merit and war-related work. It was not known until very recently that Zanuck was the main subject of a second secret hearing conducted in Los Angeles by the Army Inspector General in January 1943. This tribunal concerned Zanuck's role in alleged financial irregularities in the interaction between his role on the Research Council, his coordinating of the Army Training Film Program, and the possibility that he used his position in both institutions to show favoritism to Twentieth Century-Fox over other studios in the production of these films.

Zanuck was sent to England in April to observe the training film program there. He then was sent to Alaska. Zanuck saw his greatest activity when he spent almost eight weeks accompanying General Mark Clark at the North African front, mostly around Algiers and Tunisia. In North Africa (one of the turning points of the war for the Allies), Zanuck saw quite a bit of action. He was shot at by German airplanes while he and his crew were filming an attack for part of his film *At the Front*. In his book *Tunis Expedition,* he recorded the sensation:

All hell has suddenly broke loose. Antiaircraft guns are blazing away all around us. Our Spitfires rise to the attack. . . . Planes are now coming at us from all directions. . . . A Nazi plane crashes near by.

Another explodes in the air and floats down, a mass of brilliant yellow and scarlet flames. We finally have sense enough to run off the field to a slit trench. . . . One by one the spits come home to roost.[2]

Anticipating the arrival of what by now were commonly called Hollywood Colonels, the permanent army staff thought they would meet an egomaniacal, status-crazed amateur who was only in this to enhance his image. Zanuck arrived with his trademark cigars now augmented by a new prop: a .45 automatic pistol rakishly shoved into his belt.

Robert Gordon Edwards, a staff sergeant, found Zanuck "dynamic, aloof, full of nervous energy, and anxious to get into battle." Zanuck bunked with his men, albeit it in a sleeping bag of stupendous proportion and comfort. Though he found himself "tired and hungry," with the same enthusiasm he mustered at fifteen for the Great War, Zanuck exulted, "I wouldn't miss this show for all the cigars in Havana."[3] The men found Zanuck to be "a good C.O. who looked out for his men and asked no special favors for himself because of his rank." To their considerable surprise, they also saw what many in Hollywood already knew: "Zanuck was a man of considerable personal courage." Edwards shrewdly noted that while it is one thing to be brave at twenty, it is "quite another to be bold at forty. . . . In any number of quite perilous moments I never saw him run, break, hesitate or even show signs of deep concern."[4]

One of the men assigned to assist Zanuck in producing films was his old friend John Ford, then a commander in the navy. Upon his arrival in Algiers, Ford greeted his boss with the insult that in his lingo passed for affection: "Can't I *ever* get away from you? I'll bet a dollar to a doughnut that if I ever go to Heaven, you'll be waiting at the door for me under a sign reading 'Produced by Darryl F. Zanuck.'"[5] By the time Zanuck left the army, he would oversee the production, by all of Hollywood's major studios, of nearly 200 training films. In addition to combat footage for propaganda films, Zanuck's training films taught soldiers about a variety of subjects ranging from weapons care to the use of prophlyaxes. Because their instrumental value undoubtedly saved lives and aided the war effort, some think that they "were

probably the most important films Zanuck had ever helped produce."[6] His experiences on the battlefront also resulted in the forty-
minute film *At the Front* and the book *Tunis Expedition*. During his
active duty, Zanuck had kept a journal and field notes, which he
showed to Clare Booth Luce and Nunnally Johnson when he returned to civilian life. Both urged him to have them published. *Tunis
Expedition* (published in 1943) was one of the first books published
about the North Africa campaign. In the foreword, Damon Runyon
called it "one of the finest pieces of reportorial work that has so far
come out of World War II." At forty, Zanuck was living the high-
flying fantasies denied the fifteen-year-old who had run away to join
the army. As Mel Gussow has observed, he was experiencing his time
in the army in the way most familiar to him: as if it were a Fox war
epic and he had been cast in a key role. Thus, in *Tunis Expedition,*
people look like famous actors (Basil Rathbone) or talk like younger
versions of George Arliss. At one point Zanuck claimed he felt like "a
character in an Edward G. Robinson epic."[7]

ZANUCK vs. TRUMAN

After thirteen months on active status, with three spent at different
fronts, Zanuck's request to be returned to inactive status and civilian
duty was granted on May 31, 1943. By July 25, 1943, the *New York
Times* reported "Colonel Zanuck Back at the Helm."[8]

But it was an uneasy reentry. Throughout the war members of
Congress had been making certain that the taxpayers' money was be-
ing well spent. Missouri's Senator Harry Truman, then Chair of a
Senate War Investigating Committee, had been looking into a number of key defense industries. In September 1942, while Zanuck was
preparing to go to North Africa, the committee turned its focus on
Hollywood's role in the war. A number of Hollywood people, like
James Stewart and Tyrone Power, had served with great distinction
in active combat. Others, like directors Wyler, Huston, Ford, and
Capra, did their soldiering as filmmakers, often close to or in the
midst of dangerous fighting. The committee wondered whether some

of the other men who had received officers' commissions had done anything (beyond the leverage and utility they were accorded because of their celebrity status) to earn these high ranks. While the Committee singled out Frank Capra, Anatole Litvak, Hal Roach, and Arthur Loew, it was Darryl F. Zanuck who earned the brunt of Truman's sarcasm and invective.

The investigation centered on the issue of Zanuck continuing to draw a salary from his studio while serving as the overseer of army-Hollywood efforts. Did his behavior constitute a conflict of interest? It is true that a disproportionate number of the two hundred films turned out under Zanuck's tenure had been produced at Fox, but in his defense (Zanuck was not called to testify) it was pointed out that Zanuck drew no army salary and that his "dual status" had been known to the army throughout his enlistment. Perhaps *if* he had favored Fox, it might have been because he felt things could get done with greater speed at his own studio. Speaking in his behalf, Undersecretary of War Robert P. Patterson admitted that Zanuck's double role might have been "unwise." But rather than being subjected to personal attack, Patterson felt that Zanuck should be thanked "for his courage, energy, patriotism and accomplishment."[9]

Enraged at what he felt was the impugning of his pure motives, Zanuck offered to resign. But the stubborn Truman resisted such theatrics. The man known for giving hell and plain speaking leveled a broadside at Zanuck: "I think he is an officer in the Army and he ought to stay there." Truman then lectured and goaded this Hollywood Colonel: "He knows his business. The Army has spent a lot of money training him. . . . Why don't you send him to school and make a real officer out of him? I cannot understand how an officer would want to quit. . . . I don't believe in these fellows backing out."[10]

Around the time of the hearings and their aftermath in the press, Zanuck, a staunch Republican, was invited to the White House for dinner by his friend Franklin Roosevelt. In full view of nearly his entire Cabinet, a laughing Roosevelt, himself a master at dealing with the press, told Zanuck to "pay no attention to the press. Pay no attention. I know it's annoying but don't dignify them by answering."[11] While Zanuck could ignore the press, Truman was not as easy to shake. Since no wrongdoing had been proven, the affair appeared to have died down. Three weeks after the height of Zanuck's involvement with the Committee, Army Chief of Staff General George Marshall wrote a letter to Truman defending the actions of a man who had become his friend. Marshall had been so concerned with the unfairness of the allegations that he conducted his own inquiry, carried out at his personal orders by General Moses, the assistant chief of staff of the army. Moses could pin nothing on Zanuck. While Zanuck may have breached some army protocol to cut through red tape, Marshall told Truman that this was a "motive I am in full accord [with] as it represents my own state of mind in the present emergency."[12] Shortly after Truman received Marshall's letter, a spokesman for the Committee said its members were "completely satisfied" with Zanuck's role—in fact, they were sorry they had even brought the entire episode up.[13]

There the matter should have ended, but another investigation of the army film training program (kept secret from Truman's committee) was conducted by the army inspector general. Zanuck was called to testify. He had received permission to pace, rather than stay seated. At war or peace, this was the way Zanuck worked best. The questions began. Had he profited personally from the films? Had he shown favoritism to his corporation in the allocation of work? Zanuck became so outraged that, in the words of the court stenographer, his shouts "could easily be heard throughout the building and down on the street." In a powerful voice filled with emotion, he screamed to his superiors that "it is a dirty, lousy outrage to do such a thing to a patriotic American and I'm not going to stand for it. I'm going to the President with this and I want the record to show it."[14] He felt the whole set of accusations had been instigated by an old nemesis. The unseen hands were not in the corridors of the Pentagon, or the halls of Congress. Rather, looking back at one of his oldest grudges, he pointed the finger where he felt the blame lay: Harry Warner. When called to testify, Harry claimed that if Warner Brothers, and not Darryl Zanuck, had been put in charge of producing the films, they would have turned out three to four times what Zanuck's inefficient, corrupt team had managed.

Zanuck responded to accusations of inefficiency and fiscal mismanagement the same way he would have handled such charges at the studio: "[W]ho cares about a few measly pennies or $50,000? What does it matter if you can make a picture that will help someone kill a German, or save his own life?" Zanuck was building up to a climax. Didn't these men understand what it took to make great films? "I have never stopped for any picayune matters or where a penny was involved, but I did make certain that no studio made a dime out of this program, and no studio did. Those things," he swore, "I looked into." Then, as he might at one of his story conferences, he came up with a great tag line that summed up his feeling. A good friend of Wilson Mizner, the man who coined the saying "Never give a sucker an even break," Zanuck reached back to his movie beginnings for his own dialogue:

> I am to blame for being a sucker and trying to help my country. That's what I am to blame for. And now I am investigated. Well, let them get all of the auditors in the world. . . . What have I got out of it? They wanted pictures and I made them. Gen. Marshall says they are great films, useful. I thought that this was the main consideration.

Then, like a raft of figures he had crafted at Warner Brothers and Fox, particularly the hunted James Allen from *I Am a Fugitive from a Chain Gang*, Zanuck defiantly and dramatically concluded his testimony with as strong a curtain line as he ever afforded one of his creations: "They will never catch me, Major, ever doing anything again for anybody."[15]

When all testimony had been heard and the evidence had been thoroughly gone over, the officer conducting the inquiry found that, indeed, because he had not placed his Fox stock in trust for the duration of his time in the army, Zanuck had violated Section 41 of the U.S. Criminal Code. It was a breach of law punishable by two years in prison and a $2,000 fine. In the end, no charges were filed. And since the hearings were secret, when Zanuck resigned from the army it was assumed to be because at age forty-one, he had done his duty. Only a few army personnel, Zanuck, and his family knew how close he had come to being involved in a scandal that would have wrecked

his life and his career. The wounds and humiliation of the accusations would be somewhat salved by the War Department's awarding
him the Legion of Merit in 1944.

But like many soldiers who return home, though safely away from
the war and very busily back at the work he loved, Zanuck was ill at
ease. He wrote to his friend and protector General Marshall, "I cannot begin to tell you how strange it feels to be in civilian clothes after
17 months on active duty." After the last war, Zanuck had never appeared lost, when many in his generation assumed that pose. Now,
he felt otherwise. "I feel," he wrote, "quite lost and out of it all."[16]
Painful and unaccustomed as this feeling was, it would help him understand how others in less exalted situations felt. His postwar films
would clearly reflect this.

ZANUCK AND WILLKIE

After the war, the army hearings, and Harry Truman, dealing with
Bill Goetz seemed simple to Zanuck. Goetz had sworn his fealty to
the liege about to depart for war. Like a scene from Samuel Goldwyn's soon-to-be-made film *The Best Years of Our Lives*, the depart-
ing soldier Zanuck was assured by Goetz that his civilian job would
be waiting for him when he returned. At a farewell dinner for Zanuck,
"Billy Goetz got up and swore, 'You'll find nothing has changed
when you come back.'"[17] But Goetz had always bridled at being under Zanuck's thumb. Right after Zanuck left, Goetz had all of
Zanuck's colorful furnishings—the trophies from big-game hunting,
the white piano, the large George Washington desk—removed.
Worse, he had the characteristic Zanuck green painted over in the office and even in Zanuck's inner sanctum, the executive steam room.

In defense of Goetz, at a time when every studio made wartime
profits, he ran Fox smoothly and profitably, if unimaginatively, during Zanuck's absence. From one of Zanuck's right-hand producers,
Kenneth Macgowan, he asked for weekly story reports keeping him
updated on potential films in development. He negotiated contracts
and left the creative decisions to others. Because Goetz's emphasis

was almost entirely on organizational efficiency rather than creative development, this was the very antithesis of the way Zanuck worked. One of the producers who worked with both Goetz and Zanuck describes how Fox was run while Zanuck was in the army:

> I never had one story conference with Goetz in my life. I never consulted Goetz about one phase of the making of pictures, except as it was his due as head of the studio, and these instances could never come within the definition of producing pictures.[18]

When Zanuck came back, the reports of how he handled Goetz's insurgency vary. One version has him so upset with the quality of Goetz's films that he swore they "would make the public vomit . . . if we make the mistake of showing them."[19] Another has Zanuck sitting behind his imposing desk and dramatically sweeping all the scripts Goetz had in preparation to the floor. Declaring an end to such "crap," he vowed he was going to make pictures "with real significance."[20] The least probable version of the story had the two in a heated showdown before the entire Twentieth Century-Fox Board of Directors. Zanuck allegedly berated the quality of Goetz's productions. Goetz responded "in a blaze of hysterical anger" that he would not be bullied by Zanuck: he was no longer Bill Goetz, doormat. After this display of gumption, Goetz allegedly "rushed out of the room, on the brink of tears."[21] While the stories vary, the end is always the same: Goetz leaves Fox. Certainly Goetz's fate had been decided by May 31, 1943. The *Los Angeles Times* reported on that date that, while Zanuck had been "permitted to revert to inactive status May 31 by order of Secretary of War Stimson, William Goetz, who had been in charge of production operations in Zanuck's absence, recently tendered his resignation and will leave the lot as soon as he completes his current commitment."[22] Aided by Mayer's money once again, Goetz formed International Pictures (with partner Leo Spitz), which would shortly merge with Universal. He was replaced by the shrewd Lew Schreiber. Zanuck had returned.

But was he back? By all reports (including Zanuck's letter to General Marshall), even though he had his studio back, he was dissatisfied. Before the war, Zanuck's typical regimen kept him at the studio until the wee hours of the morning, but now "Zanuck stayed home for days on end" swimming, reading, and doing anything *but* going to the studio.[23] The war had changed him. He had seen things that altered the way he viewed the world, and his producer's role in it. Zanuck had seen young men die, had even "had them die in my arms."[24] He had met and talked with world leaders. Though friendly with Franklin Roosevelt, he was most influenced by the internationalism espoused by his hero, Indiana's Wendell Willkie.

Willkie (a first-rate corporate lawyer) had spent most of his life as a loyal Democrat. But he parted ways with the Democrats because he felt that Roosevelt's government interventionism was hurting business. Head of the huge Commonwealth and Southern Corporation, he nevertheless tried to picture himself as a victim of the New Deal, as "an honest, enterprising businessman overwhelmed by big government."[25] In 1940, when Roosevelt tried for a third term, Willkie seized the Republican nomination from party regulars Taft and Dewey, running under the slogan "Washington wouldn't; Grant couldn't; Roosevelt shouldn't; no third term."

Willkie was an appealing candidate, one whom fellow Hoosier Booth Tarkington found "as American as the courthouse yard in the square of an Indiana county seat."[26] In part, Willkie the homespun icon was a clever pose strategically taken by the man said to have sprung from "the grassroots of every country club" in America. The perceptions of his fellow Hoosiers were not so much incorrect as incomplete. Although raised in Indiana, Willkie had spent most of his adult life in the high-finance world of New York. Beneath the carapace of the Hoosier facade was a shrewd, calculating urbanite.

While Willkie, with his rumpled suits and open face, presented a high contrast to the aristocratic theatricality of Franklin Roosevelt's pince-nez, cigarette holders, and dramatic capes, he was no match for the old Fox. FDR's strategy was to sit out the campaign and look what he was, presidential. But Willkie's unexpected strength forced the century's greatest politician into high gear. Though FDR actively campaigned for only two weeks, it was enough. Reporters observing Roosevelt's magnificent kickoff performance in Philadelphia, where to a wildly enthusiastic crowd he declared that "I am an old campaigner . . . [pause] . . . and I love a good fight," knew from the crowd's frenzied adulation that Willkie was finished. Roosevelt brought his full arsenal of verbal registers and facial expressivity to his performances. Observing FDR in high form, an awed reporter observed: "He's all the Barrymores rolled into one."[27] In an era without Roosevelt, Willkie might well have been the man of the hour. Though Willkie and his running mate Senator Charles McNary polled nearly 45 percent of the popular vote, FDR and Henry Wallace crushed the pair in the electoral vote, 449 to 82.

Willkie was a member of the Fox Board, and on more than one occasion he had been a guest at Zanuck's house. Many of Willkie's ideals seemed to dovetail with Zanuck's views: fiscally conservative, yet socially progressive and increasingly internationalist in outlook. Zanuck was sold on Willkie before the war. As early as 1941, in *Remember the Day*, Zanuck was trying to boost Willkie's chances for another run at the presidency. The project had been acquired from MGM as a vehicle for the popular Claudette Colbert. The original plot centered around a small-town boy who, nurtured by a loving, caring schoolteacher named Nora Trinnel (Colbert), goes on to become a world-famous ship builder. But under the thrall of Willkie, Zanuck had one of his inspirations. The picture, he told writers Tess Slesinger and Frank Davis, "should be full of nostalgic touches and brim with the flavor of the period before the first World War." The master of evoking the past, (and, in particular, this period), Zanuck reminded them to "be sure that you mention sets, clothes, etc. in your descriptions, so that the various departments will know exactly what we are trying to do." Furthermore, he said:

> We need a dramatic bombshell of framework to drop it in, to take it out of its present category where the customers would go out saying: "This is a beautiful story—sentimental, weepy, fine. . . ." This is allright in itself, but it limits its appeal to the kind of ticket buyer that goes for that kind of a show. What we want them to say is that this story is not only that, but it is the story of so-and-so—an outstanding figure of the day. Not that we would ever pin it down specifically to that person, but the audience would go out saying that it MUST be. . . . The person I have in mind—*and this must be kept strictly*

confidential—is Wendell Willkie, who has captured the imagination of millions of Americans.[28]

By the time the final version was completed, the politician, now named Dewey Roberts and, like Willkie, from Indiana, had enough of Willkie's real-life characteristics and views to be recognizable from the last row of the balcony. When in the film's last scene, out of an enormous crowd of well-wishers Dewey finally recognizes Miss Trinnel as his beloved childhood teacher, he insists she be given a prime seat from which she can see and hear him deliver his key political speech. Again, like Willkie, Dewey Roberts's speech bucks the wishes of his party's old guard and comes out in support of a Roosevelt-brand of internationalism. Zanuck reminded the writers that, in part, this was based on a well-known real life episode:

> [E]verybody will readily recall that on the day of Willkie's first broadcast to the nation at Elwood, Indiana, his first visit on his arrival was to his old schoolteacher whom he embraced on the steps of the country school, and who actually sat on the platform when Willkie delivered his talk to the nation.[29]

Two years after his trial balloon with *Remember the Day*, Zanuck tried to make a film of Willkie's paean to internationlism, his best-selling book *One World*, but wound up abandoning the project. In fact, seeing no inconsistency, Zanuck was working on the Willkie film and his biopic of Woodrow Wilson simultaneously. Casting the right actor to portray the leading part in both pictures was turning into a bit of a nightmare. At first, Willkie wanted to play himself, which even Zanuck, a fervent fan, found unfeasible. Zanuck admitted that he did not "expect to be able to find an exact double for Mr. Willkie" but he did have a rather interesting short-list of candidates he thought would do: Gary Cooper, Dean Jagger, Paul Muni. He energetically tried to lure his first choice, Spencer Tracy, into playing Willkie, but Tracy was not interested.[30] Always the showman, he thought that *The Good Earth*'s Louise Rainer could create a memorable cameo by appearing as Madame Chiang Kai-shek! This effort on behalf of the film was fueled by the fact that, as he had been in 1940, Willkie was once again seeking the Republican nomination for presidency to oppose Roosevelt who, incredibly, despite the fact that his health was nearly shattered, was seeking a fourth term.

After being forced to withdraw from the race by the conservatives who once again dominated his party, Willkie suddenly died in October 1944, of a coronary thrombosis. Though his death freed Zanuck to be more fanciful with his plot for a Willkie biopic, the energy seemed to go out of the project. But Zanuck never really gave up on Willkie. In October 1944 writer Lamar Trotti agreed with him that "Willkie is bigger today than he was before he died, and I believe the time is still right to do the picture."[31] In November 1945, two months after the war had ended and a year after his death, Zanuck was still trying to get the Willkie project off the ground. He sent John Ford Lamar Trotti's *One World* script with the wistful hope that "if ever the world needed a picture with the theories of Wendell Willkie it certainly needs it now."[32] Ford passed. The two made *My Darling Clementine* instead of *One World.* He would have to be content to see Willkie's social and political opinions come out in other guises. He thought he had found the perfect figure in the inspirational life of Democratic wartime president Woodrow Wilson, particularly in his losing fight to found the League of Nations. In fact, he was overjoyed when writer Lamar Trotti brought his attention to the March 1944 issue of *Harper's* magazine in which Willkie told how hard he fought for the League of Nations, and proclaimed that he was a "Woodrow Wilson Democrat at heart."[33]

But if the global and national state of affairs had changed, the situation at the studio had also undergone significant shifts. Sydney Kent, president of the entire corporation, died in March 1942. From the very inception of Twentieth Century-Fox, he had total faith in Zanuck's tastes, and when he died some of Zanuck's leverage also departed. Kent was succeeded by Spyros Skouras, head of Fox's theaters. While Zanuck learned to negotiate a working relationship with Skouras (who was headquartered in New York), the two men neither liked nor understood each other.[34] To further complicate matters, Zanuck's other main sponsor, Joe Schenck, had to resign as Chairman of the Board. Investigated by the government for tax evasion and for payoffs he allegedly made to organized crime to avoid labor troubles, he was convicted in 1941 and went to jail. He returned to the studio in 1944 (as an "adviser" and occasionally executive producer) with greatly diminished power.

This was the situation Zanuck faced when he "addressed the troops" at Fox shortly after his return. Though the war still had two years to run, it was apparent in the fall of 1943 that the tide had turned. Zanuck told his assembled writers, directors, actors, and craftspeople that the returning soldiers would not be the same people who had left. "They have learned things in Europe and the Far East. How other people live, for instance. How politics can change lives and start wars." In short, the war "had made Americans think." This was bound to affect their tastes in movies: "they aren't going to be so interested in trivial trashy movies anymore." Then he made his main point, previewing the Zanuck who would become the undisputed leader of Hollywood:

> Oh yes, I recognize that there'll always be a market for Betty Grable and Lana Turner and all that tit stuff. But they're coming back with new thoughts, new ideas, new hungers. It's up to us to satisfy them with our movies. They'll want to know more about our world, and this is where I think we at Fox have got to plan to measure up to their new maturity. We've got to start making movies that entertain but at the same time match the new climate of the times. Vital, thinking men's blockbusters. Big-theme films.[35]

Listening to Zanuck's agenda, an amused Nunnally Johnson notes, "Jesus. Darryl's gonna make the Hundred Years War."[36] Although Zanuck never issued a single credo, he did give a remarkable speech that explicitly spelled out how he intended to fulfill what he thought was film's—and his—new destiny.

"THE GLITTERING ROBES OF ENTERTAINMENT"

In early October 1943, Zanuck was the keynote speaker of the Feature Film seminar of the Writers' Congress. The gathering was sponsored by the Hollywood Writers' Mobilization, an organization committed to advancing the free expression of democratic ideas and to investigating the writer's role in the war. In a grim foreshadowing, for organizing and hosting the conference, both the Hollywood Writers' Mobilization and UCLA (which hosted the seminar) drew angry accusations of abetting a group known for being "notoriously anti-American" and "Communist-inspired" from the ever vigilant Los Angeles County Council of the American Legion.[37] The gathering was attended by a disparate group of writers, composers, and industry people. Luminaries such as Thomas Mann mingled with producer Dore Schary, social scientists Robert Merton and Paul Lazarsfeld, writer and lyricist Oscar Hammerstein II, mogul Y. Frank Freeman (of Paramount), screenwriter Jane Murfin, and actor James Cagney (then president of the Screen Actors Guild). Over a three-day period the 400 conference attendees went to seminars with titles such as "Minority Groups," "Writers in Exile," and "Humor and the War." Zanuck's speech, "The Responsibility of the Industry," later published as "Do Writers Know Hollywood?" showed his changing mode of thought on Hollywood's role in shaping America's public agenda.

"Is it possible to make pictures which have purpose and significance and yet show a proper return at the box office?" he asked, and answered, "I believe it is." Then Zanuck gave a name to his solution: "I believe the answer is entertainment."[38] He illustrated what he meant by the very different cases of two recently released films: Fox's *The Ox-Bow Incident,* a grim film in which three innocent men, unjustly accused of stealing cattle and of murder are lynched by a mob, and Warner Brothers' version of Lillian Hellman's anti-Fascist parable (with a screenplay by Dashiell Hammett) *The Watch on the Rhine.*

Based on Walter Van Tilberg Clark's best-selling novel, the film of *The Ox-Bow Incident* happened only because of the tenacity of director William Wellman, the lure of star Henry Fonda, and the courage of Darryl Zanuck. While the money he could realize if he independently produced the film might have been one incentive, Wellman wanted to make the film because when he bought the rights to the novel from Harold Hurley (a producer recently working at Paramount), he was certain its subject matter was timely, important, and that it would make a great picture. He shopped it all over town but was turned down by every producer. He then turned to Zanuck, with whom he had collaborated on the memorable *The Public Enemy*. As Wellman recalled, "Zanuck was the only one with guts to do an out-of-the-ordinary story for prestige rather than the dough."[39] The two men shook hands on the deal.

Zanuck knew the risk he was taking. As a sign of the importance he ascribed to this project, Zanuck assigned it to his favorite writer, Lamar Trotti. But reading Trotti's chilling draft, he told Story Editor Julian Johnson his anxieties:

> I read the novel before publication, more than two years ago, and even then its material seemed too bitter and sunless to be good box-office. . . . As a prestige picture, yes, definitely, provided it is well cast and well directed. But in my opinion, this is certainly not entertainment for these times.[40]

But Zanuck was always willing to take a risk, providing there were some odds in his favor. While every other producer refused to touch its depressing subject, Zanuck took a chance on *The Ox-Bow Incident* because of the contribution he could make by seriously looking at an issue like mob violence. "Maybe," he told Julian Johnson, "today's psychology calls for stories so shocking that they compel one to forget the current bad news by blotting it out with something worse." If this were the case, "there's a fortune in this. But I doubt it." Although fully committed, Zanuck had already correctly predicted its fate: it would be a prestige picture if done right, not a money maker. Former *New York Times* gadfly-turned-Fox-writer Frank Nugent concurred, telling Zanuck "While I feel it is a gamble, I would never suggest that the studio hedge by compromising. If the story can't be done this way, it shouldn't be done at all."[41]

The film very nearly didn't get made, because Zanuck went off to war and Goetz, with a bookkeeper's brain, promptly canceled it. But director William Wellman had shaken hands with Zanuck on the deal, and after Wellman informed him what was going on, Zanuck told Goetz he had to honor that commitment.[42] With a superb script

by Lamar Trotti and firmly anchored by Henry Fonda's performance, the film won praise from the critics but, as Zanuck predicted,
was a disaster at the box office. Zanuck told the audience at UCLA
that "in these piping box-office times," the financial failure of the film
did not bother him. What was important for the future was that this
"honest, sincere, and adult picture with something to say got only a
lukewarm reception from the audiences." Therefore, however noble
its goals, "any picture is a failure from our standpoint, yours and
mine, unless we can get it before as wide an audience as sees the average good picture which has no purpose but to divert." The secret to
doing this was to make films with serious themes, but wrap them in
showmanship so that even as they were illuminated by their purpose
and significance, people would view them as diverting and entertaining. This is what he meant earlier by the oxymoronic phrase, "thinking men's blockbusters." Zanuck was trying to tell the screenwriters,
in particular, that the goals of intellectual integrity and entertainment
were not antagonistic.

If ever there was a play full of messages to test Zanuck's hypothe-
sis, it was *Watch on the Rhine*. Hammett's adaptation of Hellman's
play retained most of the play's original themes, and, as Zanuck
noted, rather than being softened "the theme is hit hard." But producer Hal Wallis had, as Zanuck put it, succeeded in creating a film
with "supreme" entertainment values by "sugarcoating the pill":
Hellman (and Hammett) "brilliantly designed her story so that" even
while being warned about complacency in the face of fascism, the
audience was so consumed with the fate of the characters that "the
personal elements would appear to predominate." To Zanuck, there
was "a profound lesson to all of us" in Hellman's example. As long as
writers can carry ideas by using the human rooting interest, "we need
never worry about the failure of motion pictures to make a contribution for the betterment of world humanity." On the other hand,
Zanuck "wouldn't give ten cents for the Lillian Hellman play if the
showmanship had been omitted and if the play had concentrated entirely upon the philosophy of its theme."[43] In his opinion, any film using such an approach would have been a failure.

Zanuck closed with a colorful image. He very much wanted to—knew he must—make serious films. But "he wouldn't dream of making [them] if we didn't think they would be outstanding successes financially. There would be no reason to make them otherwise." No films can be successful "if people do not see them in great numbers." Zanuck gave his troops their marching orders: "[W]e must play our part in the solution of the problems that torture the world. We must begin to deal realistically in film with the causes of wars and panics, with social upheavals and depression, with starvation and want and injustice and barbarism under whatever guise."

He ended with a bit of advice aimed at the writers in the audience, couching it in the very kind of rhetoric he wanted them to use to get *their* ideas across: "That is why I call upon you, the writers, to lead the way—if you have something worthwhile to say, dress it in the glittering robes of entertainment." Without these raiments, he warned, "no propaganda film is worth a dime."[44] He started his own personal proof of the efficiency of this formula with a biographical picture about Woodrow Wilson.

WILSON

Wilson would be, after *Gone With the Wind*, the most expensive American film ever made to that date. Zanuck summed up what he was trying to do in mounting what was a virtual crusade in making *Wilson*, against the advice of nearly everyone: "I am gambling $3 million in an effort to prove that audiences are ready to accept something more than straightforward entertainment. I am making one mighty bid to try to open the floodgates of production toward the making of entertaining films that are enlightening as well."[45]

Zanuck's main goal in the film was to argue convincingly for the brand of internationalism espoused by his political idol, Wendell Willkie. It was a lesson he thought Americans needed to be taught. But like one of Billy Sunday's or Aimee Semple McPherson's attempts to woo their flocks through showbiz-suffused sermons, the film had to dazzle and divert as it lectured and converted. *Wilson* would be shot in Technicolor, and as this and other changes were added, its budget soared from an initial estimate of $2 million to a figure more than twice that large. To play Woodrow Wilson, Zanuck chose a little-known Scottish actor named Alexander Knox. This extravagant risk would not have a single star in its cast (save Thomas Mitchell in a supporting role and Sir Cedric Hardwicke as Wilson's archrival, Henry Cabot Lodge). The script's message and its showmanship elements would have to sell the film.

Zanuck was in a frenzy of activity putting the film into production. He assigned the script to his most trusted writer, Lamar Trotti. As director, he chose Henry King. In films like *In Old Chicago* and *Stanley and Livingstone,* King had shown himself adept at orchestrating the grandiose elements of spectacles without losing sight of the human drama. On *Wilson,* Zanuck did an unheard-of thing: he visited the set to make certain everything was going just as he imagined. (A startled Henry King recalled, "It was the *only* time I saw him on the set.")[46] From its sets and props to its script, he micromanaged every aspect of the film. He knew that Wilson, the man, had to be sold as he had pitched his other biopic eminences, as a regular guy. He thus told Trotti to remind viewers that Wilson faced the same problems they did, and to put in "some line such as this, 'His problems as a father were no different than those of any other father.'"[47] Pains were taken to show the president "playing hooky" to attend vaudeville, and Zanuck even dictated the smallest of details to show the great man when he was not being a great man: a rewrite of the script dated January 4, 1944, specifically calls for Wilson to be reading the detective mystery *Murder on the Waterfront.*

Zanuck was very particular that the film evoke the look of the period before the Great War, and through his scenario coordinator, Molly Mandeville, the Art Department was told:

Mr. Zanuck wants to see a sketch of this set [a wartime canteen]. There should be an old-fashioned phonograph on this set, one of those things with a huge horn, and it is this which is giving out with the music of SMILES. Mr. Zanuck wants to make sure that we know the music is coming from that instrument, and is not just part of the scoring.[48]

The research on the film was prodigious. The Fox Research Library has separate entries for "Wilson's automobile while Governor of New Jersey," "Wilson's ring," and details on Ivy League football when "Princeton played Harvard 1911 & 1912."[49] Zanuck spent a small fortune having detailed, virtually replica sets of the White House built, and hiring extras for his reenactment of the 1912 Democratic Convention at which Wilson bested Missouri's Champ Clark for the nomination. Editor Bobbie McLean recalls Zanuck's obsessive quest:

> I can remember *Wilson*. Holy mother. I know more about the White House by working on the picture than by going back to [Washington]. . . . I'll never forget the convention . . . when you had miles and miles of film. And all these bands. You sit down, "Where do I start and what do I do?" You just sit down and figure it all out.[50]

Zanuck always tried to get across the essence of what motivated the great person as soon as the film began. Late in the production of *Wilson*, new scenes were written and shot that Zanuck hoped would accomplish this rooting interest. Wilson is first seen attending a football game as president of Princeton University. This introduces him as a man like many Americans, but it also introduces the film's characteristic themes: Wilson's competitive desire to win hidden behind a haughty reserve, his dry wit, his fairness, his love of family. Almost immediately after the football scene, we learn of Wilson's campaign to democratize the Princeton clubs, a fact that Zanuck uses to carry the germ of the idea for the League of Nations.

Wilson was a very complicated man. He was an intellectual who thrived in the cutthroat arena of action and politics, an aloof, almost aristocratic figure who nevertheless tried to look after the interests of the average American, a wily politician who could also behave like an obstinate fanatic. The real-life Wilson was so intriguing a figure that he was the subject of one of Sigmund Freud's few full-length forays into historical biography, *Thomas Woodrow Wilson: A Psychological*

Study.[51] Completed in 1932 (but not published until 1967, after the death of the second Mrs. Wilson), the book explained Wilson's stubbornness as a playing out of unresolved hostility toward his father, the Reverend Joseph Ruggles Wilson. Freud's Wilson so adored (and feared) his father that he saw him as a god. Identifying with him, "he had to believe that somehow he would emerge from the war as the Saviour of the World."[52] (In place of the Freudian framework, Zanuck hired Wilson's worshipful biographer, Ray Stannard Baker, as the film's technical consultant.) Zanuck tried to present his life in such a way that we might see Wilson as an original, someone perhaps easily misread.

For drama, Zanuck had much to chose from in the real life. Tragedy was supplied by the death of Wilson's beloved first wife. Venal enemies were plenty, but his sense of story construction told Zanuck to choose one. Zanuck focused on the powerful Republican Senator Lodge and his opposition to the League of Nations as the true villain of the film. Zanuck was never fully satisfied with Trotti's work on this part of the script. Late in production, new scenes were written and shot for the key showdown between Wilson (and his internationalism) and Lodge (and his isolationism). After the Senate turns down Wilson's appeal for a League of Nations, Zanuck told Trotti that the audience must know this is a critical moment:

> The entire attitude of Lodge has changed. We must feel that he is ice-cold. He knows he has the President where he wants him and he makes the most of it. He is never rude, but he is sharp, bitter and at times *almost* rude.
>
> While this is not a fight, it should have the semblance of a fight—a bitter clash. This will make the scenes that we have of Wilson trying to control his temper all the more effective. . . . *I am sure it will build as we go along to a real climax.*[53]

Final pathos was provided by Wilson's futile, and ultimately tragic, cross-country train tour to sell the League to the American people after it had been turned down as part of the Senate's rejection of the Treaty of Versailles. At Zanuck's insistence, Trotti's script notes that by the time of this tour, "We definitely feel that the man has reached the breaking point, that this is the beginning of the stroke. . . . The crowd is moved, touched, somehow aware of his condition."[54] The script also contains one of those unintentionally campy moments that seem to flourish in biopics. Trotti has Edith Wilson, concerned about her husband traveling across the country in the summer, tell him, "But oh my dear, if they had only developed the radio, the wireless, so that you could sit here and talk to them without having to go out in all this heat." Of course, this evokes images of FDR and his masterful use of the radio. (She might have done better had she wished for a time machine for Zanuck to travel ahead and see the disappointment that lay in store for him on the picture.) Like most Zanuck biopics, the film ends on an uplifting note, with the final lecture delivering the film's theme. Wilson, no longer president, enfeebled by a stroke, receives a telegram telling him he has received the Nobel Prize for Peace. Vindicated, the final big speech is delivered to his wife and daughters, but it is aimed at the audiences of 1944:

> Yes, I'm not one of those who have the slightest anxiety about the eventual triumph of the things I stood for. The fight's just begun. You and I may never live to see it finished. But that doesn't matter. The ideals of the League aren't dead just because a few obstructive men now in the saddle say they are. The dream of a world united against the awful wastes of war is too deeply embedded in the hearts of men, everywhere. . . . And I'll even make this concession to Providence, my dears—it may come about in a *better* way than we proposed.

For its premiere, Zanuck imported a whole trainload of stars (including Betty Grable, Gene Tierney, and Tyrone Power) to Omaha. He pulled out all the stops to push the film, and Fox's Publicity Department took out ads proclaiming "WILSON—The most important event in fifty years of motion picture entertainment." Despite very favorable reviews and initial high attendance, *Wilson* could not give Zanuck the commercial hit he desperately wanted. That year, 1944, people preferred to see *Meet Me in St. Louis, Double Indemnity, Going My Way, Gaslight,* and Zanuck's own *Thirty Seconds Over Tokyo* or his magnificent mystery cum film noir directed by Otto Preminger, *Laura*. (Preminger's million-dollar film brought in twice that much, while another Fox hit, *A Tree Grows in Brooklyn*, cost nearly $2 million and brought in $3 million.) More profitable than any of these—in fact, the biggest grosser in the studio's history to date—was a project Goetz had initiated, *The Song of Bernadette*. Part of the problem with getting people into the theaters to see this almost three-hour extravaganza was Woodrow Wilson, himself. Despite his admirable achievements and his far-seeing internationalism, he was a cold, judgmental idealist, who had little in his real makeup to endear him to moviegoers weaned on expectations gleaned from Zanuck's previous icons of American virtue, like Lincoln, or the lovable shrewdness of the foreign ones, played by George Arliss.

On a visit to Wahoo to show off the film, he was confronted with the reality of the Wahoo he had remembered all his life, one embedded in his mind in mythic terms. Its diminished scale forced him to revise his sentimental memories of an idyllic boyhood as, gazing upon his birthplace, he realized with some pain that "Early memories can murder you."[55] Adding a further dose of reality, Zanuck's hometown doctor explained what had gone wrong. "Why," he asked Zanuck, "should they pay seventy-five cents to see Wilson on screen when they wouldn't pay ten cents to see him alive?"[56] After telling an enormous hometown crowd that "I am proud to be a Nebraskan," Zanuck arranged for the studio to wire him that he had to deal with an (nonexistent) emergency. He sped back to Hollywood, and would not return to Nebraska until 1957. It would be his last trip home.

For the rest of his life, Zanuck talked about the film in unusually personal terms. "Of all the pictures I have made in my career," he noted, "*Wilson* is nearest to my heart."[57] Its failure stung him deeply. He later admitted that had he read his own memos to screenwriters over the years and followed his frequent story conference advice to come up with a novel and humanly appealing perspective from which to tell a story, it would have made all the difference. If only he had "told the story of *Wilson* through the eyes of his second wife, I would have had an enormous box-office hit."[58]

MR. MAUGHAM, MR. CUKOR, M. MONET, AND
"THE BIZARRE COLONEL": *THE RAZOR'S EDGE*

While still mulling over *Wilson*'s failure, Zanuck tried to capture the audience's attention with another serious film, an adaptation of W. Somerset Maugham's *The Razor's Edge.* The book had appeared in April 1944 and, like most of Maugham's novels, it was a best-seller. Considered Maugham's last major novel, it is the story of Larry Darrell, a hard-working, upwardly mobile Chicagoan whose typical American get-up-and-go approach to life and his desire for material success are subverted by his experiences in World War I. Larry, an aviator, cannot stop asking himself why his good friend Patsy was killed while he had been spared. In place of a life spent acquiring material wealth, he embarks on a series of quests for spiritual identity. He even travels to India to try to get at the secrets of holy men whose brand of serenity cannot be found in Paris, the French Riviera, or Chicago. (With disciples like Christopher Isherwood and even Maugham himself, such mysticism *could* be found in Hollywood.) While Larry does gain his spiritual salvation, he loses his rich, beautiful fiancée, Isabel Bradley, who cannot understand the new Larry. In *The Razor's Edge* (the title comes from one of Hinduism's mystical texts, the *Katha-Upanishad*), Maugham created his usual cast of pointedly defined characters. The most memorable is Elliott Templeton, a rich, snobbish expatriate American who is Isabel's uncle and Larry's spiritual foil.

Zanuck paid his good friend, agent (now independent producer) Charlie Feldman, $53,000 to relinquish his rights to the book. (Maugham, as shrewd a businessman as he was successful an author, received $250,000 against a 20 percent share of the film's net profits.) His Letter of Agreement with Fox (dated June 29, 1944) stipulated that the film's director have an "accepted and legitimate value in the motion picture industry as being a director who commands the sum of at least $100,000 per picture."[59] Maugham's first choice—his good friend George Cukor—certainly fit this description. In fact, so eager was Willie (Maugham's never-used first name was William) to have

"Dear George" direct *The Razor's Edge* that, in a supreme gesture of friendship, his agent forwarded the director a copy of the manuscript in advance of its publication. One night soon after this magnanimous event, Cukor attended a party at Zanuck's house. Amid the usual din of social sound, Cukor overheard an immediately recognizable voice whose owner's snippet of conversation was arrestingly familiar: "I'm not really an educated man," the well-modulated voice intoned, "and I wish I were. I'd love to read the *Odyssey* in the original Greek."[60] Cukor pondered where he might have come across these words. In an instant he realized he was not experiencing *déjà vu;* the words were spoken by the character of Larry in Maugham's novel. The wily Maugham had flooded Hollywood with copies of his manuscript, and Cukor was merely one of the "exclusive" recipients of the prized proofs. A bemused Cukor realized that he was hearing Orson Welles trying out his version of how Larry might appear if Welles directed and starred in the film version.

Though the two men had different temperaments and backgrounds, Zanuck liked Cukor and respected his professionalism. Recently, the two had worked well together on *Winged Victory*. The problem was that Zanuck had hired his old reliable Lamar Trotti to adapt the novel, and Cukor hated Trotti's script. Cukor told Zanuck he would love to work on the project, but that the script needed work—perhaps Maugham himself could be persuaded to take a crack at it? Cukor later recalled that Zanuck agreed this would be wonderful, but said he "was certain that Mr. Maugham was completely inaccessible, and besides, his price would be astronomical."[61] Maugham was recovering from the death of his lover, Gerald Haxton, when Cukor called him with the idea. It might be just the thing to ease him out of mourning. Cukor and Maugham cooked up a scheme whereby Maugham would try writing the screenplay with Cukor serving as a kind of script doctor. The arrangement would be made easier by the fact that Maugham, accustomed to comfort and luxury and, though reserved, highly social as well, would be staying with the well-connected extrovert Cukor at his famous Cordell Drive home.

Maugham told Zanuck he would do it. Further, if Zanuck did not like his script, he did not have to pay him. Unaccustomed to such offers, Zanuck quickly accepted.

At the first meeting of Zanuck, Cukor, and Maugham, Zanuck (whom Cukor described as "a dynamic little man") held forth on his story-oriented, philosophically diluted version of the film. Unfailingly polite, Maugham said he would do his best to see if he could write such a script. If Zanuck did not like his work, he could "chuck the whole thing into the wastepaper basket."[62] Maugham's only comment to Cukor after his first exposure to Zanuck was, "He speaks very loud, doesn't he? I don't like people who shout." Maugham went to work. But according to Philip Dunne, Lamar Trotti said that the problem with the project from the start was that Zanuck never really understood what Maugham's character Larry was searching for.[63] In contrast, sophisticates both, Maugham told fellow enlightened spirit Cukor that "you know the subject by heart" and that "no one can possibly bring the distinction to the picture that you can."[64]

The film was to mark Tyrone Power's return to the screen after his military service, and Zanuck intended it to be an enormous hit. Lining up all the players during wartime was difficult, though. By December 1944, because of a variety of scheduling problems (and while Zanuck was still editing the script), Maugham was told by Zanuck that Cukor would not be the director. Tongue in cheek, Maugham relayed the news to Cukor that Zanuck had "wired me to say that you were not to be had(!)" and that in his place "he had got Edmund Goulding," who apparently could be had.[65] But Cukor was soon back on the project, trying his best to interest his good friend Katharine Hepburn to play the lead role of Isabel. Cukor wrote Willie that "Kate loves the script, is really excited about Isabel," but there were roadblocks: Hepburn had a New York theater commitment. She would do the part if the film could be postponed until the following November. Zanuck refused. Maugham had a clause in his contract stipulating that, should Zanuck fail to begin shooting *The Razor's Edge* before February 2, 1946, either Fox had to pay Maugham an additional $50,000 (with all rights on the novel reverting back to the author) or, if the start date were extended one year (until February

1947), it would cost Fox $100,000 as an advance against Maugham's 20 percent net interest. To legally preclude this possibility, in August 1945 Zanuck dispatched a second unit under the supervision of Art Director Richard Day and veteran B producer Sol Wurtzel to Denver. There they spent nine days shooting the Himalayan sequences.[66]

Zanuck then proposed Bette Davis for the part of Isabel. Twenty years before, Cukor had fired Davis from a summer stock troupe, and in the intervening years his opinion of studio-era Hollywood's greatest actress had not improved. He told Maugham that "I am not a great admirer of Miss D's art, but Zanuck feels she would be interesting in the part and says she is a tremendous 'name.'" Of course Cukor, the ultimate survivor and an inveterate lover of gossip, told his soulmate Maugham that "whether she will take on the whole project—and if the great inter-studio politics can be arranged—is another question."[67]

As was typically the case on any Zanuck film, the real problem was the screenplay. Trotti told Dunne that where Maugham, Cukor, and Trotti knew what motivated these characters, "Darryl can't bring himself to understand that his and Maugham's concepts of life are as far apart as the North and South poles."[68] To Zanuck, *The Razor's Edge* fit in with his new vision of the kind of films postwar Fox should make, for he felt it was a serious investigation of man's spirit amid the world of postwar alienation and changing cultural values. To Maugham and Cukor, the work was meant to be played as a probing social *comedy* whose irony was leavened by its serious moments. We see this in the Maugham-Cukor "Prologue," which contains instructions that were written, but never used:

> Please note that this is, on the whole, a comedy and should be played lightly by every one except in the definitely serious passages. The actors should pick up one another's cues as smartly as possible, and there's no harm if they cut in on another as people do in ordinary life. . . . The director is respectfully reminded that the action should accompany and illustrate the dialogue. Speed, speed, speed.[69]

Holed up at Cukor's Hollywood Hills home for months, Maugham did turn in a script in July 1945 to the man he and Cukor had privately nicknamed "the bizarre colonel."[70] But Zanuck found the script too verbose and not full enough of action. Cukor told Maugham that while Zanuck did have some valid points, "for the most part I do not agree with him." The problem with Zanuck, Cukor sighed, was the same as with the rest of Hollywood:

> They are accustomed to treating books and plays, etc., for pictures with either a matter-of-fact realism, sentimentality, or in a sanctimonious, Sunday-school way. They shy from any elevation of spirit. They are in strange territory with *The Razor's Edge*. Its approach is unfamiliar to them. That's what worries them.[71]

Earlier, the pragmatic Maugham (who had worked in Hollywood before there even was a studio system) told Cukor that in looking over Zanuck's suggested cuts he didn't find any great damage had been done. Maugham even told Zanuck that the changes had his stamp of approval. After all, noted Maugham, "as they were going to do it as it now stands" by telling Zanuck he thought the script "first rate" he was not being hypocritical, merely realistic: "It was better that they should do it with conviction of its excellence rather than with the feeling at the back of their minds that they might very well be proving you and I right."[72]

Meanwhile, beyond the complicated doings of this odd trio, there were other intrigues. By late August, studio manager Ray Klune informed all departments that *The Razor's Edge* had "temporarily been removed from the schedule"—only to be put back within a month. Hedging his bets should Power not be available at the start of principal photography, Zanuck had shown the script to Jimmy Stewart. Cukor was amused that the actor "was frightened off because he thought Larry was a Christer," decidedly *not* the kind of image Stewart wanted for his return to the screen. In a way, Cukor was relieved. Though he thought Stewart a good actor and "a nice boy," nevertheless "his literary opinions do not have a great deal of weight with me." In any event, Cukor found him all wrong for the part. Stewart was far "too homespun," with an alarming inclination "to be cutie-pie."[73]

In the end, as was the case with the script for *How Green Was My Valley*, time ran out. By the time principal photography started in early April 1946, Cukor was no longer available, and the equally worldly (but more pliable) Edmund Goulding directed the film. As for Maugham, though very little of his script was salvaged for Trotti's final version, Zanuck still felt he should be paid something.[74] When asked what he was owed, Maugham showed Zanuck his own code of *noblesse oblige:* "One dollar for a haircut." Zanuck was perturbed. The next day he took Cukor aside and asked him what kind of gift his friend would like in recompense for his hard work. "Would he like," for example, "a beautiful gold cigarette case from Cartier?" How about "some grand cuff links?" Cukor, who understood both men, said he thought Maugham would be delighted to be given a painting. Cukor recalls that "Zanuck was very taken with the idea," and told him, "Mr. Maugham would go and select any painting he liked from any dealer he liked."[75]

Pleased, Zanuck told Maugham of the arrangement. He was surprised that an artist who wrote of mystics with such deep feeling came back with the worldly reply, "You can't buy a picture for nothing."[76] (He would have been less taken aback by Maugham's reply had he known that in chapter 51 in *Of Human Bondage,* Maugham had observed that, "Money is like a sixth sense without which you cannot make a complete use of the other five.") Now on familiar turf of negotiating, Zanuck told him he could spend up to $15,000. ("Clever fellow," thought Cukor.)[77] Maugham soon wrote Cukor from the Plaza Hotel in New York that "I have bought at the expense of 20th Century-Fox a very fine Monet."[78]

And that is the story of how Tyrone Power returned to the screen to star in a film about a generation's quest for spiritual identity in which Cecil Humphreys was paid $1,650 a week to wear a long white beard and sit atop a studio mountain playing a holy man, while W. Somerset Maugham, the multimillionaire writer whose screenplay was not used, still managed to have his soul salved by acquiring (for his spiritual and physical travails) a French Impressionist painting. At the end of *The Razor's Edge* the audience is told: "Goodness is the greatest force in the world, after all." After all.

PORTRAIT OF A LADY: *LAURA*

In *The Razor's Edge,* for the first time in his long career the novelist al-lowed the narrator to carry his own name. In the film, "Maugham" was played by Herbert Marshall. Zanuck liked the film so much, he asked Maugham to do what came naturally to Hollywood producers, but was less common with novelists like Maugham: Would he write a sequel, this time taking Larry up after he comes back to America? Perhaps Zanuck was thinking of a kind of glossy *The Best Years of Our Lives.* But Maugham demurred, telling Zanuck: "The only ex-ample in history of a sequel being as good as the original is *Don Quixote,* and I should be crazy to attempt one in *The Razor's Edge.*"[79] As was the case with *Wilson,* Zanuck thought he had made the year's best film, and was miffed that the rest of the world did not see eye to eye with him. The film brought Anne Baxter an Oscar for Best Sup-porting Actress for her portrayal of Sophie, Larry's Chicago friend who turns into an alcoholic slattern when tragedy shatters her life. Zanuck did not want to cast the rather patrician Baxter (Frank Lloyd Wright's granddaughter) in this role; he felt she lacked the erotic abandon this character needed. But Zanuck's good friend Gregory Ratoff was also friends with the actress, and, improvising, he told Zanuck that he *knew* Baxter could pull the part off: "Please, darling. I have had it. It's marvelous."[80] Based on Ratoff's inspired (but in-vented) testimonial, Baxter got the part.

Though she walked off with the Oscar, the film belonged to Clifton Webb's Elliott Templeton, whose snippy delivery and superb dancer's hauteur etched a memorable portrait of an expatriate who, as much as Larry Darrel (though through radically different means), is seeking to find fulfillment by escaping his country's changed ways. Webb nearly stole the picture with his deathbed speech. With Larry at his side, he dictates a letter of regret, telling an even more snobbish American expatriate (now a princess) that he cannot accept her invi-tation (which he has coveted all along) "owing to a previous engage-ment with his Blessed Lord." Satisfied with his own brand of salvation, he dies. It is the highlight of the film. Though nominated for his performance, Webb lost that year to nonactor Harold Russell, who in *The Best Years of Our Lives* played what he, in part, was—a war veteran who lost both arms below the elbow.

Zanuck's experiences on *Wilson* and *The Razor's Edge* suggest that his transition to the role of "serious producer" was not without its rough edges. Despite his best efforts, his inability to shape certain big projects with the same originality he was able to bring to other films showed there was a point in his own spiritual quest beyond which he was in over his head. But the years 1944 and 1945 were not all civics lectures and journeys into existential angst. Particularly in *Laura*, Zanuck showed he could create stylish entertainment that still—albeit obliquely—dealt with issues of interest to Americans. One of these was the changing role of women. With many men off to war, women took on tasks from which they had been previously barred. Many households were now headed by women, and the war had also showed that women could not only compete with and surpass men in certain professions, they could live full, rich lives *without* men. A number of films noirs dealt with this issue by displacing cultural anxiety about female authority and male utility onto the figure of the treacherous, double-crossing woman. Adjustment to the postwar world was hard, and it was not only women who bore the brunt of straight male anxiety; we see in *Laura* a noir film in which the figure slightly "off" in this canted world is not the woman but the crypto gay male. The career woman Laura Hunt is loyal: it is the waspish gossip columnist Waldo Lydecker (played superbly by Clifton Webb, looking like an epicene Alexander Woollcott) who is the unstable figure here. Waldo is not only threatened by Laura's ability to survive— both professionally and socially—without him, but also he feels emasculated by the meat-and-potatoes demeanor of the man Laura loves, Mark, a rough-edged New York police detective.

Fox paid Vera Caspary a very frugal $30,000 for the rights to two novels and a play (*Ring Twice for Laura*, *Laura*, and *Ring Twice for Lora*). The film was to be produced by Otto Preminger and directed by Rouben Mamoulian. Mamoulian and Zanuck had worked together on *The Mark of Zorro*, an experience that had been artistically uneven and highly volatile. Yet, after his smashing success with the stage version of *Oklahoma!* Mamoulian was again considered hot. The story of a detective who falls for a murdered advertising executive after seeing her portrait fired Zanuck's imagination. But apparently it did not do so for Mamoulian (or, looking at the footage Mamoulian shot, Zanuck thought this was the case). After about a month of shooting, he was replaced by a director Zanuck swore he would never work with—Otto Preminger. The dislike between Preminger and Zanuck stemmed from an episode in 1940 when Preminger, assigned to direct *Kidnapped,* had the audacity to change the dialogue in a Zanuck-approved script (absolutely *verboten*) and then, to compound matters, to argue with Zanuck over it. He was summarily taken off the film and found that in bucking Zanuck, he had placed himself on a kind of "graylist": no studio would hire him. So Preminger, a cultivated Austrian Jew (whose father had risen to the extraordinary position, for a Jew, of Attorney General of Austria), went to New York, where he directed Clare Boothe Luce's play *Margin for Error.* During Zanuck's stint in the army, Bill Goetz acquired the work and agreed to let Preminger appear in it as a Nazi *and* direct it (Preminger waived his director's salary just to direct again). This was how Zanuck's enemy came to be at the studio when Zanuck returned from the war.

But Zanuck was, as Otto Friedrich understatedly observed, "a very remarkable man." Summoning Preminger to his Santa Monica beach house, reading a newspaper and not even bothering to face the man he thought he had forever exiled from his lot, he said: "I see you are working on a few things. I don't think much of them except one, *Laura.* I've read it and it isn't bad. You can produce it but as long as I am at Fox you will never direct." Still reading his paper, Zanuck ended the interview with a terse, "Goodbye." Preminger recalls that he also said "goodbye" (to Zanuck's back) and left, elated.[81] With this strange rapprochement, the two proceeded to fight over casting. Zanuck wanted John Hodiak for the part of the detective, Mark; Preminger wanted (and got) Dana Andrews. Zanuck wanted either Monty Wooley or Laird Cregar for Waldo Lydecker, with Preminger opting for a man who would soon become a close friend of Zanuck's and a mainstay at Fox, but who had not made a film since 1925,

Clifton Webb. (By the time he appeared in *The Razor's Edge,* he had, thanks to *Laura,* firmly established a second career in the movies.)

Webb had already had a major career as a dancer. On Broadway he had introduced with co-star Marilyn Miller Irving Berlin's "Easter Parade" in *As Thousands Cheer* (1933). He was under contract to MGM, but had yet to appear before the camera. Webb was appearing locally, in Los Angeles, in *Blithe Spirit* where, as Fox's casting director told Zanuck of the gay actor's deportment, "He doesn't walk, he flies." Zanuck relented and gave Preminger permission to screen-test him, but Webb proved to be less enthralled than expected. "My dear boy," he said to Preminger, fourteen years his junior, "if your Mr. Zanuck wants to see if I can act let him come to the theatre."[82] Zanuck was enraged. But Preminger figured out a compromise. He filmed Webb on stage. Zanuck liked what he saw, and Webb got the part.

Just as they had fought on *The Mark of Zorro,* Zanuck and director Mamoulian locked horns on *Laura.* When, on the spot (and in full view of a number of Fox employees), Zanuck asked Preminger if he should replace Mamoulian, the ambitious Otto answered, "yes." Preminger was once again a director.

After Preminger became both director and producer, he and Zanuck battled over the script. While Mamoulian was still on the project, Zanuck had told him and Preminger that "the character of Laura herself is flat and uninspired." Zanuck was sure that Laura "should come into the story like a breath of spring, like something out of this world." Since nearly all the other characters were venal and hardboiled, "by contrast Laura should be everything that they are not . . . she is neither bright, nor witty, nor particularly smart."[83] Zanuck gave the two and screenwriters Jay Dratler and Ring Larder good advice: "Laura's charm should be her frankness and honesty. Where the others are Park Avenue cutthroats, she should be as fresh as a child." Waldo, too, needed work. His dialogue should have "the biting flavor of *The Man Who Came to Dinner*"—that is, he should be "likable and charming, so that Mark can tolerate having him around." Of course, should Monty Wooley get the part, the ending violent scuffle with Mark would have to be changed. Zanuck was sure "you cannot have a fistfight at the finish where somebody hits this bearded old man, or the audience will hiss." Hilariously vague as to how the writers should do this, Zanuck merely suggested that they should "find some way of arranging his capture by symbolic suggestion, or something of this sort." As it stood, unless they gave Waldo more charm, "I believe Mark would throw him out the window, and why Shelby doesn't shoot him I'll never know." The part of the feckless kept lover, Shelby, was slated to be played by Zanuck favorite Reginald Gardner. Gardner was a frequent houseguest at the Zanucks' Palm Springs getaway, Ric-su-dar, and his real-life qualities would be put to good use in the film. "As you know," Zanuck told the writers, "he plays and sings delightfully risque songs, and there is a good opportunity for us to understand why he is so acceptable and likable to this set. He should be likable and weak." In fact, Zanuck insisted, "these are the very things that have attracted Laura to him."[84]

Preminger and the writers were able to craft characterizations for Mark, Waldo, and Shelby once these parts had been cast (Vincent Price played Shelby). Zanuck once again provided them with a good guide, pointing them to a hit of three years before:

> All of the people, Mark included, should seem as if they stepped out of THE MALTESE FALCON—everyone has a distinct, different personality. This is what made THE MALTESE FALCON. It wasn't the plot, it was the amazing characters. The only chance this picture has of becoming a big-time success is if these characters emerge as real outstanding personalities. Otherwise it will become nothing more than a blown-up Whodunit.[85]

Like Mark's fascination with Laura's portrait, the character herself still remained a mystery beyond the writer's grasp. To Zanuck, she was "a mess . . . a puppet."[86] Mark had been toned up when Zanuck told the writers that "there ought to be more of Cagney about him." Perhaps by "curing Shelby," as Zanuck put it—"by making him a more physically attractive personality"—he could help solve the problem of Laura. Or, alternately, Waldo could be made somehow more evil or repulsive, despite his charm. Zanuck had a suggestion that he warned all "may shock you." Reaching back to his earliest days as a writer (perhaps thinking of *Habit*'s opium addicts), he suggested that they make Waldo a secret dope fiend! When Waldo receives the stunning news that Laura is in fact alive, he faints. Then "in a hoarse whisper he tells them to get a needle out of his pocket." Mark obliges, and brings out an elegant "little medical kit about the size of a cigarette case." It contains a hypodermic needle, already "loaded with a shot." Mark administers the dope. Zanuck's story conference notes explain: "Now I know the Hays Office will let us get by with this as it will indicate nothing more than a hypodermic shot for a fit of some kind, but this little touch will be very helpful to us later on when we find out that Waldo is actually a maniacal murderer."[87]

But, even though medically motivated, Zanuck was sure this episode would have a strong impact on the audience's conception of Waldo. Thinking that the needle contains "morphine or something of the sort," viewers would be shocked and repulsed—but fascinated. Zanuck told Preminger that "in a strange way that I cannot explain on paper" such a scene "will symbolically suggest that he is some sort of a dope addict who occasionally lapses into such things as a fiendish desire to kill the woman he loves."[88] In the end, Zanuck made do with Waldo fainting and, upon being given mere tablets, telling Laura, "I hope you will forgive my wee touch of epilepsy, my dear. It's an old family custom."

As always, Zanuck was focused on the ending. Caspary's original had the diabolical but well turned-out Waldo dispatch his victims with a gun concealed in his elegant cane. This was to be how he tried to kill Laura a second time. But Zanuck thought the cane gimmick corny and obvious. Two other endings were tried. In one, the weapon of Waldo's downfall is a siphon of carbonated water wielded by Laura herself. When she realizes Waldo has come back to kill her, she "momentarily blinds" him by dousing him, like the heroine in a Mack Sennett two-reeler. "Laura takes advantage of his being off-balance to dash forward and seize the lethal walking stick from his hands."[89] She has used one of the props of sophistication against the man who taught her style. Another ending had Mark hit Waldo in the head with a Cracker Jack–type puzzle, which Waldo had always held up with disdain as proof of Mark's "common" nature. In the film,

Waldo prerecords his usually live radio program, and while it is broadcast he sneaks into Laura's apartment to retrieve the murder weapon, a shotgun he has secreted in a clock he had given her as a gift. But Mark is there to intercept him. In the end, a good old shooting ends Waldo's plans for revenge.

Zanuck did not like Preminger's ending (in which Waldo is shot). Inspired (or so he thought), he dictated a new finish in which the whole search for the killer is revealed to be a dream. The *new* ending would show what really happened.[90] It was old friend Walter Winchell who dissuaded him. The lights came up after a screening of Zanuck's version, and Winchell exclaimed, "Big time! Big time! Congratulations, Darryl. Except for the ending. I didn't get it. Didn't get it."[91] Turning to the man he swore would never be allowed to direct, he asked Preminger, "Would you like to put your old ending back?" When Preminger said he would, Zanuck told all assembled, "If this is a big success, it will be all to Preminger's credit."[92]

Shot for a bit over $1 million, the film grossed twice that amount. Preminger would later characterize Zanuck as "basically one of the fairest men . . . the amazing thing about Zanuck is his flexibility." Zanuck's take on Preminger? "I fired him, hired him, fired him, hired him. A great talent . . . but he has to be controlled."[93]

GENTLEMAN'S AGREEMENT

In 1947, the House Un-American Activities Committee (HUAC) began its public hearings on alleged Communist influences in the film industry. There had been closed-door hearings in Hollywood the year before. But the public nature of the 1947 hearings meant that this investigation of entertainment would undoubtedly be written about and consumed as a chilling public spectacle. Three films Zanuck made in response to this crisis show a divided side of his essentially fair nature. *Gentleman's Agreement* and *Pinky,* for their faults, have been held up as examples of Hollywood civil liberty at its 1940s best. The other film, *The Iron Curtain,* shows that Zanuck was also capable of exhibiting the kind of cold warriorism and anti–civil libertarianism antithetical to views expressed by the man who made *Wilson* and *Gentleman's Agreement.*

The previous chair of HUAC, John Rankin of Mississippi, thought that Hollywood contained "the greatest hotbed of subversive activities in the United States."[94] What convinced Rankin this was so was the prominent position Jews held within the film industry. Rankin was a virulent anti-Semite, who felt free to vent his feeling on the floor of the House of Representatives in a form unimaginable today, except perhaps in the language House members use in speeches against gays and lesbians. Rankin peppered his speech with words like *kike, Jew boy,* and *nigger,* and once referred to Walter Winchell as "a slime-mongering kike."[95] *Time* magazine reported that, despite his inflammatory rhetoric, "in the entire House, no one rose to protest."[96]

Rankin's use of the word *kike* against Winchell and *Time*'s coverage of it gave novelist and sometime screenwriter Laura Z. Hobson the germ of an idea that she turned into the novel *Gentleman's Agreement.*[97] Hobson was Jewish, the daughter of the editor of *The Jewish Daily Forward.* While Hollywood after the war was starting to deal with subject matters previously taboo, it still refused to deal with the Holocaust.

Hollywood in fact would not touch the Holocaust for at least a decade. (The lone exception was Orson Welles's *The Stranger,* which contains an unusual sequence of silent 16-millimeter footage of concentration camps.) But if the grotesque truth of the Holocaust was too much for producers, with much arm-twisting Hollywood could be persuaded to take on a genteel form of anti-Semitism. Gregory Peck recalls that when Zanuck decided to face the issue both Mayer and Goldwyn "called him and advised him not to do it. 'Why rock the boat? . . . Why bring up an unpleasant, controversial subject on the screen?' Darryl told me that." But, Peck laughingly recalls, "He didn't pay any attention to them. He talked about it quite openly that he was utterly confident that it was time for such a picture, and that we were going ahead full blast. Their phone calls didn't give him any pause for thought at all." Looking back on the incident, Peck mused that Zanuck "was not short on ego. He could make a decision and stick by it."[98]

But if Zanuck felt that way, another Hollywood reaction to anti-Semitism was that expressed by Harry Cohn, the congenitally difficult and contrary head of Columbia Pictures. When approached for a donation to a Jewish charity, Cohn, himself Jewish, exploded: "Relief for the Jews? What we need is relief *from* the Jews. All the trouble in the world has been caused by Jews and Irishmen."[99] Rabbi Edgar Magnin, unofficial spiritual leader of Hollywood's Jews, using his own brand of Talmudic logic nevertheless arrived at a similar conclusion, claiming that drawing attention to the suffering of the Jews would only alienate people: "the more you tell gentiles that nobody likes us, the more they say there must be a reason for it."[100] Sam Goldwyn agreed. He told Jack Warner that he thought anti-Semitism after the war "was worse than it has been in years."[101] The contrary Goldwyn wanted to make a film on the subject. He invested a good deal of money (including $100,000 to purchase the rights trying to make a film of *Earth and High Heaven,* a novel with an interreligious love story). Goldwyn imagined Gregory Peck playing the gifted Jewish lawyer. Both Ring Lardner, Jr., and Elmer Rice tried to adapt the novel, but Goldwyn finally gave up.

Zanuck had Peck in mind for a bigger assignment, *Gentleman's Agreement.* The story revolves around a gentile journalist, Phil Green, who decides to expose anti-Semitism in a magazine serial. He will pose as a Jew and write up his account of what it is like to experience, firsthand, anti-Semitism. Beautifully played by sincere Gregory Peck, Green walked America through a rather tame version of what it was like to be the victim of anti-Semitism.

After intense bidding, Zanuck bought the rights to film the novel for $75,000. His involvement in the screenplay was extreme. Gregory Peck recalls that "he was absolutely keen" about this project.[102] Director Elia Kazan observed that Zanuck did his job "with passionate devotion." He recalled that on *Gentleman's Agreement,* "the production was perfectly managed by Zanuck, with an energy that never relaxed and a determination that on every shooting day he'd get the best out of everyone working."[103] Kazan had received Zanuck's tacit agreement that, continuing a trend Fox had pioneered after the war, the film could be shot on location in New York and Connecticut. But when Moss Hart (whose milieu was theater) was hired to write the screenplay, this approach was put aside. Zanuck wanted no one outside of those immediately concerned with the film to know anything about Hart's screenplay. He told executive production manager Ray Klune, "It is *very important* that you do not discuss the dramatic treatment of this story until the final script has been distributed."[104] While Zanuck and Kazan agreed on most aspects of the film, a key scene found the two at odds. Zanuck felt Phil's fiancée's reaction to the news that Phil was Jewish is "too hard." Zanuck wanted it played lightly. To him, the scene was not intended to show that Kathy was a closet anti-Semite but illustrate how even good people unconsciously internalize prejudice:

> I always visualized the scene like this: When Phil says that he is going to tell everyone that he is Jewish, Kathy first has a puzzled smile as she repeats, "Jewish?" Then, suddenly for a brief second she betrays herself when she gives him a startled look and says, "But you're not, are you Phil?" Then she quickly realizes that she has put her foot into it and she tries to get off the hook by saying that it wouldn't matter to her if he was Jewish.[105]

To Zanuck, Kathy's hesitation was the theme of the picture in a nutshell. Kazan, however, thought the key scene came later, when a distraught Kathy goes to Phil's best friend, Dave (John Garfield), to show how unfair Phil's attitude toward her has been. She tells Dave (who is Jewish) that she is not an anti-Semite. Why, just recently at a dinner party in an exclusive, bigoted Connecticut suburb, she was outraged by a story told by a mindless anti-Semitic neighbor. When Dave asks what she did about it, she says she just sat there, feeling sick "all through me." He wonders if she would have felt better if she had "nailed him." It is here, after Dave has pointed out that enraged silence merely enforces the "gentleman's agreement" not to talk about "disagreeable" things, that Kathy finally understands Phil's anger.

Gregory Peck concurs with Kazan, but thinks what are today perceived as limitations in this approach were, in their time, rules that Zanuck daringly broke:

> We were conscious of what we had to say. What we wanted the audience to carry with them when they left the theater *had* to be presented in an entertaining form. You had to avoid polemics, outright blunt statements of social criticism and social comment. . . . [I]t had to be woven into the fabric of the story and come out of the character.[106]

Though the film seems rather dated by today's measure, in its day it was considered almost shockingly daring. One should recall that in *The Life of Emile Zola,* an earlier Warner Brothers biopic about the Dreyfus affair made only ten years before *Gentleman's Agreement,* the word *Jew* is never even spoken! In 1947, anti-Semitism was like other social problems now on the film industry's agenda. Hollywood would deal with them according to the culture's updated codes of harmless entertainment, selectively and tastefully. In addition to *Gentleman's Agreement,* a few key films of the period—*Crossfire, The Best Years of Our Lives, Pinky, The Lost Weekend,* and *The Snake Pit*—did deal with previously taboo subject matter. And in addition a number of genres—the film noir, the horror film—dealt with some of these issues through a kind of code or disguise. But for the most part, as screenwriter Philip Dunne recalls, during the postwar period of adjustment and turbulence, "everyone wanted to go for escape. Nobody wanted to *uplift* after the war."[107]

Producer Dore Schary was one of the few who, like Zanuck, did try to uplift. His *Crossfire* (based on a novel by Peter Brooks, *The Brick Foxhole*) dealt with the murder of a Jew by a sadistic anti-Semite. But all is not as it appears. In the novel, the victim is gay. Suddenly inspiration, Hollywood-style, came to producer Adrian Scott and the character became a heterosexual and a Jew. The daring inclusion of the Jew and the annihilation of the gay character necessary to get the film made suggests that the question about these matters is never, "Is there censorship?" but rather, "What form did each decade's censorship take?"

Zanuck's enlightenment was shaped both by his individual value scheme as well as his secure awareness of what was possible—or finesseable—within the culture's dominant paradigm. His own desires and the ability to mediate these both had their limits. When he heard that Schary was also doing a film on "his" subject matter, however, he became irritated. And competitive. He wrote to Schary to protest. In response, the amused head of RKO told Zanuck that he had "not discovered anti-Semitism." It would take more than their two films to eliminate this menace. Though *Gentleman's Agreement* was completed ahead of schedule, Schary's much lower-budget film was released earlier. As he prepared to open the film, Zanuck and the studio's publicity machine went into high gear. They reminded audiences that Zanuck "had shown courage and foresight in producing such memorable epics as *I Am a Fugitive from a Chain Gang, The Grapes of Wrath, Wilson* and other controversial films" and was now topping his previous efforts with *Gentleman's Agreement*.[108] Zanuck and New York publicity head Charles Schlaifer carefully orchestrated the preview screenings. Zanuck thought word-of-mouth among certain influential people would be as useful as critical reviews. Moss Hart, Laura Hobson, and Elia Kazan were thus asked to invite "certain critics and opinion makers as well as some of your personal friends" to see what Zanuck and Kazan had wrought.[109]

The reviews were all Zanuck could have hoped for. Archer Winston of the *New York Post* claimed that with this film, "American movies gain new honor." Walter Winchell raved in his Sunday broadcast that "it is not only Darryl Zanuck . . . but the Hollywood industry at its very, very best . . . a battle cry for democracy." Writing in *P.M.*, showman Billy Rose went further. Hurling his challenge where he knew it needed to be placed, he said: "I think this movie means more to our way of life than [J. Parnell] Thomas and all his Un-American Activities Committee." If the Thomas Committee "decides to investigate *Gentleman's Agreement*," said Rose, then "it might not be a bad idea to investigate the Thomas Committee."[110] Zanuck was flooded with congratulations from famous American Jews, including Irving Berlin and Bernard Baruch.

At the 1947 Academy Awards (held, of course, in 1948) *Gentleman's Agreement* (nominated in seven categories) was competing against *Crossfire.* Kazan was nominated, and so was Celeste Holm, for Best Supporting Actress. When Fredric March opened the envelope to reveal the Best Picture winner, for the second time in his career Zanuck's name was called. He told the audience what was by now almost his catechism: "I would like to emphasize that *Gentleman's Agreement* was primarily planned for entertainment rather than for any social message. I believe this is the chief reason for the success of the film." But instead of exiting gracefully, he added: "This makes up for a sharp disappointment I suffered some years ago. I'm sure I will be forgiven for mentioning the name of the picture, *Wilson,* of which I am still proud." Afterward, Zanuck celebrated until 4 A.M. at a party he hosted at the Mocambo. *Crossfire* did not win a single award.

Zanuck would win a whole wall full of awards commending him for this film. Perhaps in the flurry of congratulations, few were willing to hear any criticism of what the film had failed to accomplish. It was only a writer himself who, about to be discriminated against by Zanuck's company, had the courage to state that, for all that was right and good and daring about the film, there was something so halfway about how it defined discrimination that one wondered if anything really trenchant could ever make it to the American screen intact. Ring Lardner, soon to be blacklisted and then fired by Zanuck at the insistence of the Fox Board, observed: "the movie's moral is that you should never be mean to a Jew, because he might turn out to be a gentile."[111]

"THE ADVENTURES OF PINKY"

The next film Zanuck made was *Pinky,* which attempts to argue for the same kind of fairness for African-Americans as *Gentleman's Agreement* had for Jews. But in 1949, African-Americans and Jews had different status in the country. Some Hollywood Jews, themselves sensitive to being discriminated against, nevertheless held bigoted attitudes toward African-Americans. Jack Warner, outré in this regard as in so many others, once commanded that footage of a black couple kissing be not only deleted from a film but destroyed. He was alleged to have said, "It's like watching two animals. Terrible."[112] While miscegenation—the sexual relationship between whites and blacks—was precluded under the PCA Code, *Pinky* added a twist: the central figure, played by Jeanne Crain, is a light-complected African-American woman who passes for white. Her grandmother, Dicey (Ethel Waters), does not want to (nor could she) pass. Pinky, a nurse, can. She has been living up North, where she attended nursing school, where no one was aware of her "mixed" ancestry. But heeding the pleas of her grandmother, she comes home to the South to minister to the dying Miss Em (Ethel Barrymore), the old woman for whom Pinky's grandmother has worked for many years. When her fiancé, a white doctor, comes down to visit, Pinky must decide whether to continue to pass as white or to acknowledge that she is African-American. Miss Em dies and leaves Pinky her antebellum house. She decides to stay down South and transform the house into a public clinic run by her as a nurse—an African-American nurse.

The film was based on *Quality,* a novel by Cid Ricketts Sumner. Though Zanuck had picked Dudley Nichols to write the screenplay, Philip Dunne, active in the civil rights movement, desperately wanted the assignment. Dunne told Zanuck that though "there is no question that you will be attacked by the professional leftists as well as by the professional Negrophobes," if he approached the problem of racism head on and did not "pussyfoot in any way," then he had a "rare chance to make a film which combines social importance and entertainment value."[113] When Nichols needed help, Dunne and later Jane White were called in. (Eventually Dunne and Nichols would share a co-writing credit.)

Dunne was Zanuck's liberal conscience, just as Zanuck worked as a conservative devil's advocate for the writer. Here, he suggested to Zanuck that the legal position taken by many Southern states and seemingly upheld by the film—that even one drop of Negro blood made a person Negro—is "far from a universal definition." Why, an anthropologist or a geneticist would not call Pinky a Negro, but say that she is "caucasoid with one Negro strain in her ancestry." While he admitted this was a touchy subject, he feared their approach would leave them open to ridicule because "there is an implication that we think that having Negro blood somehow sets one apart, that it makes one *internally* as well as *externally* different, that the possession of a trace of Negro blood makes one feel a mystic identity with the race." In essence, this was the same argument used in *Showboat.* Had nothing changed in the intervening decades? Dunne asked Zanuck, "If you or I . . . were to discover suddenly that we had a near Negro progenitor, would we feel 'different' inside?" He felt certain that whatever position he took, they might raise trouble by criticizing the current American take on race, but that "the key point is that she doesn't say she *is* a Negro, but that she *chooses* to be one."[114]

Zanuck pondered this, and decided Dunne was right. It was a more risky but also a more enlightened solution. When one of the Fox lawyers tried to dissuade him, he became once again the crusading Zanuck of *The Grapes of Wrath:*

> I do not believe that in this kind of picture you can afford to compromise. I discussed it with [director] Jack Ford again today. You cannot in the last reel give Joan of Arc novocaine to ease her pain. She has to burn at the stake.
>
> It is a sacrifice that Pinky makes in which she loses love but in which she finds herself. . . . I believe the audience will appreciate the ending. . . . Pinky *chooses* to be a Negro. It is her choice and it is made voluntarily, and in doing so I think she rises in the estimation of the audience.[115]

But having arrived at a solution that left him satisfied that he had created both good entertainment and true social critique, Zanuck was having troubles with the director. Ford, who had performed so brilliantly on *The Grapes of Wrath,* could not extend his empathy to racial matters: he simply did not understand the material. He had Ethel Waters and other African-Americans acting as though they were in outtakes from *Gone With the Wind.* To compound matters, because of this Waters and Ford cordially hated each other. Looking at the flatness of the daily rushes, Zanuck made the difficult decision to replace Ford. He brought in Elia Kazan, whom he had originally wanted to direct but who had been unavailable earlier. Zanuck made sure Kazan understood the familiar Zanuck pose on social problem films. Stick to the personal story of Pinky, he told him, for that is what "interest[s] and fascinate[s] me":

> I don't believe you could ever get me to read a book which was strictly about segregation of Negroes in America. Factual as it might be, I simply would not be bothered with it, and I am sure 99% of the American public feel the same way.
>
> I am convinced that if we really want people to see the horrors of grinding poverty as suffered by these people, if we want the audience to see the results of lack of education and proper medical treatment . . . we will have to make it pure entertainment in terms of the adventures of Pinky.[116]

Pinky turned out to be the biggest Fox draw of 1949. And one of Zanuck's last social problem films.

THE IRON CURTAIN

If *Pinky* and *Gentleman's Agreement* showed that Zanuck was what Kazan called "a man of the people," then *The Iron Curtain* showed that while this was usually true, sometimes Zanuck seemed to know the wrong people. The film's title phrase had been first uttered by ex–Prime Minister Winston Churchill in 1946. That year, an October 9 gossip column in *The Hollywood Reporter* issued a prescient warning:

> If you have a membership card in the Communist Party under your mattress, or certain interested parties are sure you have, begin getting nervous and sleeping in your pants, because (and how they do it is a big secret) you've got a big surprise coming.

As one of the industry's most powerful leaders, Zanuck sounded the call for better pictures before the war was even over. But while the sweetest part of his plea called for quality films, Zanuck left open the possibility that "better" might include the kind of strident propaganda he had supervised during the war. Zanuck told Hedda Hopper that, "However silly our pictures may be, they still reflect our way of life."[117] The cold war, exacerbated by the HUAC hearings, made every piece of film a potential piece of propaganda. Zanuck insisted this was the case, even before the end of World War II realigned former allies into Cold Warriors: "If we do not succeed in showing to the world the advantages of the American way of life," Zanuck reasoned, "then somebody else will probably come forth with another way of life that may impress the peoples of all countries more, and then all that we have fought for in this war will have been lost."[118] Hedda Hopper, an uneasy ally, tried to help her good friend Darryl find the appropriate subject matter by sending him the gift of an anti-Communist book, *The Hope of the USA*.[119] She also forwarded to him two letters she had received accusing certain Fox employees of being Communists. Zanuck returned the letters, diplomatically telling Hopper it was "of course the type which I receive many of. Since *Boomerang* [a film dealing with police corruption] everybody wants me to expose somebody else." He gently tried to tell Hopper he was not interested in playing this game: "Usually the so-called exposures are based on petty or personal grievances."[120]

As the cold war heated up, in 1947, Zanuck started production on *The Iron Curtain*. The film was a response to the general political climate, Zanuck's answer to the specific accusations that Hollywood was not doing enough to hold the line against communism. For daring to attack the activities of Soviet spies in North America, Zanuck received hate mail, some of it "violent."[121] Ignoring the controversy, he turned to figuring out how to tell a good cold war story.

Zanuck decided to shoot the film in the quasi-documentary style he had pioneered in such films as *The House on 92nd Street, Call Northside 777*, and Elia Kazan's hit *Boomerang*. Because, like the gangster film a decade before, the drama of the cold war was being played out in the media as well as in the government corridors of power, Zanuck decided he would also resurrect his Warner Brothers headline style. After screenwriter Martin Berkeley's first draft failed to do the job, Zanuck replaced him and hired Milton Krims. In a memo marked CONFIDENTIAL (underlined two times), Zanuck told production personnel that the film "was inspired by J. Edgar Hoover's speech before the Un-American Activities Committee in the House of Representatives dated March 26, 1947."[122] Hoover had claimed that Soviet spies were very active in the United States (*The Iron Curtain* would shift the location to where the events occurred, in Canada).

Hoover *wanted* Zanuck to make this film. Accordingly, Zanuck confided in his team that "We have been given private information to believe that if and when the files of the FBI have been opened to us . . . we will find sufficient current material and established facts to enable us to devise a semi-documentary screenplay," one that would permit Zanuck to deal "both dramatically and factually with the problem." Now on comfortable ground—the factually based bit of sensational entertainment—Zanuck brought out his voiceover, first used in *How Green Was My Valley*. In a four-page memo, he dictated off the top of his head the entire structure of the film. After "the Voice" told viewers, "On February 8, 1946, a diplomatic bombshell exploded in Canada, the repercussions of which are only exceeded by the atom bombs dropped on Japan," Zanuck intended to mix documentary footage with staged reenactments. He told his writers,

> It is our idea to give substance to our theme and story by showing at the start of our picture that these things actually did happen and that not only were Russian secret agents involved but that corrupt Canadians had operated with them and betrayed their Government. I am sure this part of the picture can be made very exciting, factual and dramatic, and in it we may use the reenactment of certain dramatic highlights of the testimony.[123]

The villains would of course be the Soviet spies and the misguided Canadian Communists who helped them. The heroes would be Canadians modeled on (and sometimes assisted by) FBI agents and those Communists heroic enough to heed his pro-American call.

As he had done so often in past films, he warned his writers *not* to deal with the specifics of warring ideologies. *The Iron Curtain* would be a fact-based spy melodrama whose arguments would persuade via entertainment.

Zanuck thought the personal story of the spies should be kept to a minimum. There were certain givens, certain genre and story conventions that always had to be considered: "of course our leading man must be placed in positions of jeopardy" involving "conflicts, and suspense and ever-present danger."[124] The characters of Gouzenko (Dana Andrews) and his wife Anna (Gene Tierney) turn to the cause of democracy because of the warmth of their non-Soviet neighbors (in contrast to the cruel indifference of the spies) and, tellingly, because Anna, expecting a child, is delighted and overwhelmed by the *material* comfort she finds when she sees the apartment the Soviets have rented for her clerk-spy husband. As usual, Zanuck's decor told a story and he wanted the Art Department clear on how important a motivation this would be in winning this struggle of the cold war:

> Make sure that the Art Department understands that this is not an elaborate apartment in any sense of the word. It should be, in fact, very ordinary. It probably rents for less than $50.00 a month, and it is important that it should look like that. Anna's delighted reaction to the place should be all out of proportion to its actual values; it is very ordinary, but to her it is magnificent.[125]

Zanuck knew that in the postwar, consumer-oriented American culture, it was the daily quality of life—the very things Americans take for granted—that must make us realize the genius of our system. The real turning point for Gouzenko is not only the material lure, the physical manifestation of some undefined democratic principle of fairness or goodness. Rather, it is the fact that *Communists have different human values.* They have little regard for what Americans hold dear: the sanctity of a single life. Zanuck concocted a bit of Grand Guignol sure to win over even the most open-minded American to his point of view. One night Gouzenko is called to work late at the embassy. He is concerned about leaving his pregnant wife, whose due date has passed. Anna tells him, like a good American wife, to advance his career: he should go to work and not worry about her. Of course, she has the baby while Gouzenko is working and his evil coworker, Kulin, fails to give him the message: work comes first.

Zanuck plays his hand shrewdly. Kulin, it is soon revealed, is not inherently evil. We will shortly learn that he is as much a victim of the evil Communists as the people he himself persecutes. Both Kulin and

Gouzenko are stealing unspecified atom bomb secrets. When Kulin sees a newsreel of the impact of the bombs dropped on Japan, he becomes unhinged. Told to get more information to steal more secrets, Kulin cracks up and is sent back to the Soviet Union. Gouzenko, observing the callous interchangeability with which the Russian government treats its personnel, now wavers. Anna, already tempted by the blandishments of the West, asks, "What are we going to do?" Zanuck then scripted the following exchange as if it were a silent movie, making sure to telegraph the reasons *why* Gouzenko decides to become a traitor to communism:

> GOUZENKO: We are not going back to Russia.
> ANNA: (aghast) Not going back!
> GOUZENKO: No . . . There must be *some* way, something I can do!
> He looks at the baby. Anna looks at her husband.[126]

The scene dissolves into Gouzenko's first act of theft from the Russian embassy. The tables—and the spy—have turned. Zanuck's rooting interest has done its work. The Iron Curtain has parted. But Zanuck was still not satisfied that the explanation he offers up for the spy's change of heart—of keeping the family intact, the same one he had used for *The Grapes of Wrath*—was clearly telegraphed. After the film had been shot, he decided to add a scene to clarify Gouzenko's motives. Even Kulin (who is revealed to be the son of a military hero) is more human, more victim than perpetrator. Kulin tells Gouzenko about how he was forced to shoot five fellow Russians to get a volunteer for a dangerous mission. He bitterly tells Gouzenko, "As a man I am called a sadist. But what do you call Governments [that do this on a larger scale]?"[127] The seeds of doubt have been planted in Gouzenko's mind. In the added scene, he leaves the embassy and walks down the street, thinking:

> Gouzenko stops suddenly, turns around, and goes to Kulin's quarters, then goes home and has the scene with Anna which ends with his telling her, "We are not going back to Russia."[128]

In places where *The Iron Curtain* opened, pro-Soviet protesters clashed with anti-Communist forces. Protests in Chicago and Milwaukee were peaceful, but in New York the police had to get involved to haul off Catholic war veterans who clashed with pro-Soviet protesters. Even more surprising, four Russian composers whose music was used in the film—Shostakovich, Prokofiev, Khachaturian, and Myaskovski—attacked Fox and Zanuck in order to ingratiate themselves with the Soviet Communist Central Committee. This organization had recently accused them of imitating the bourgeois music of Europe and America. The four wrote a letter to the editor of *Izvestia* denouncing Zanuck and Fox ("the American reactionaries"),[129] and sued Fox to enjoin the studio from using their names and their music in Zanuck's orchestrated propaganda campaign. They lost; it turned out there was no American copyright on their music.

The protests did not stop there. Zanuck claimed he, director William Wellman, and stars Dana Andrews and Gene Tierney "were sent abusive letters," and that "Hollywood Communists and fellow travelers" somehow got his home phone number and "bombarded him with calls, day and night, arguing with him and threatening boycotts and labor troubles."[130] Even *Pravda* got into the act, somehow obtaining a copy of the script before the movie opened and attacking it viciously.

Zanuck was amazed at the whole episode. Baffled by the notion that anyone could support what he saw as an authoritarian regime, one in which each film scenario would have to obtain government approval, he wrote producer Sol Siegel, "Can you imagine our being able to make pictures that were critical of America such as *Grapes of Wrath, The Best Years of Our Lives, Gentleman's Agreement* and hundreds of others?" Thinking back to his days at Warner Brothers, he said that under such a system he would never have been allowed to make "a picture where the policeman or law enforcement officers were in the wrong." Zanuck admitted that such a world "frightened" him.[131]

As the 1940s drew to a close, Zanuck had completed perhaps the most vitally creative decade of his professional life. In addition to the films I have already discussed, though Fox made fewer and fewer pictures each year Zanuck nevertheless managed to turn out serious popular entertainment like *The Snake Pit* and *A Tree Grows in Brooklyn*. He introduced new stars like Richard Widmark in *A Killer's Kiss*. He also let one, Marilyn Monroe, get away. Signed in 1946, she was dropped the following year after appearing for a few frames walking behind little Natalie Wood in *Scudda-Hoo! Scudda-Hay!* He took both serious and comic looks at the rise of the suburb in *A Letter to Three Wives* and in the film that made Clifton Webb the decade's least likely leading man, *Sitting Pretty*.

But nothing seemed able to stem the desertion of moviegoers who once filled America's theaters as if they were taking part in some programmed cultural ritual. As the decade ended, a pugnacious Zanuck admitted to his old friend, director Henry King, that "we are in a 'fight to the finish' in an effort to revive the box office."[132] Wistfully he asked King a variation on Freud's question: "What is there left—what do audiences want?"[133] The answer was to be found in the changing industry patterns of the next decade and in the new culture of Hollywood, which was not to Zanuck's liking.

Chapter Twelve

SEEING RED AND GETTING RELIGION . . . IN CINEMASCOPE

For good or for bad, this is the age of entertainment. Audiences are sick of lectures, even though they are good ones.

—DARRYL ZANUCK, TO PHILIP DUNNE

H OLLYWOOD IN 1950 was a town in the white heat of organizational and social transformation. The signposts were many. A Supreme Court ruling in 1948 forced the studios to divest themselves of the true source of their power, their theater chains. The House Un-American Activities Committee hearings and the Hollywood blacklist continued to haunt the industry. The "Hollywood Ten" started their prison terms for contempt of Congress in 1950, and film people moved with uncertainty and fear through a landscape littered with wrecked careers and ruined reputations. Television, still expanding, had made inroads into how people spent leisure time and leisure money. Worst of all, from the point of view of the studios, people were changing where, and how, they lived; the suburbs created a style of living antithetical to going "downtown" to the movies.

As film toppled from its privileged perch high atop public culture, the studios' profits diminished dramatically. The passing of Louis B. Mayer from power in 1951 was, in the epochs of Hollywood, as powerful a delineator of endings and openings as Thalberg's death had been fifteen years earlier. For, if Thalberg had represented the producer as a purveyor of quality, Mayer stood for other things: the authority of raw power and decisiveness. Such stances and figures no longer were tenable in the new Hollywood. They had been replaced by a complex constellation of alliances between talent agents and the creative personnel they represented. Business was conducted more on momentum than strategy, as old rituals continued to be evoked, often with ineffective results.[1]

"DOES IT PAY TO MAKE GOOD PICTURES?"

In February 1950, *Variety* conducted a half-century poll of the movie business. The results were illuminating: Garbo (retired) and Chaplin (soon to be driven out of the country) were accorded the best performer laurels; D. W. Griffith (who had died, largely forgotten, two years earlier) was voted best director. Irving Thalberg, dead for fourteen years, was judged best producer. Thus the Hollywood of 1950; balanced at the half century, with the bulk of its support resting on the glories of the past. If *Variety* spoke for show business and Hollywood, it clearly viewed the future with great anxiety and uncertainty. The June 12, 1950, issue of *Time* magazine, however, seemed to suggest that Irving Thalberg had a living rival who might dominate the second half of the century in the way that the boy wonder of MGM, dead fourteen years, had so characterized the first. Staring out from its cover, his head coroneted by a crown of celluloid, his face composed in an uncharacteristically serious gaze, Darryl F. Zanuck was judged by the magazine to be the country's greatest living producer. Under his image ran the magazine's hook question, "Does it pay to make good pictures?" The answer was a resounding yes. Praising him as "an idea man . . . probably unsurpassed in Hollywood," *Time* noted: "Since the war, Zanuck's 20th Century-Fox has consistently led the field in the quality of its films. . . . As in the past, each of them, from story conferences to cutting room, will be shaped in large measure—for better or for worse—by the taste and imagination of Cinemogul Zanuck."[2] So dependent was the Fox corporation on Zanuck, that it insured his life for the highest premium available—$900,000. He had made Fox the number-one studio in town, for which the studio offered him an unprecedented contract guaranteeing that he would be with the company for another twenty years.[3] His salary would remain $260,000 annually (where it had been since 1935). Despite the sense of security that should have accompanied this vote of confidence, Zanuck knew that both his kingdom and his hold on the kind of power he desired were tenuous.

Nineteen-fifty would be Zanuck's high-water mark in a career already gilded with praise. That year he would bring out a series of innovative and stunning films, including *All About Eve, The Gunfighter,* and *No Way Out.* The 1950 Academy Awards Ceremony was thoroughly dominated by Zanuck. He won a record third Best Picture Oscar (for *Eve;* the first two had been for *How Green Was My Valley* and *Gentleman's Agreement*). More impressive—because it requires that a two-thirds majority of your peers agree—he was also awarded a third Thalberg Award. (In 1962, no doubt because a fourth award was very likely for Zanuck after *The Longest Day,* the rules were changed so that no one could be the recipient more than once.) In 1950 Zanuck was the most valuable producer in Hollywood, a power astride a kingdom of some 284 acres. The question was, in this changed environment, could Zanuck continue to make the kind of pictures he liked, the way he was used to making them? In addition to the creative burnout that would plague anyone who had worked thirty years without respite, the decade forced Zanuck to deal with two new and powerful adversaries: TV and orchestrated governmental political censorship and blackmail. Both directly impinged upon his ability to run the system as he knew it. Each one profoundly altered the culture of Hollywood.

THE UNKNOWN ZANUCK: THE BLACKLIST ERA

Zanuck had never flinched from making a film that was critical of his country if there was something that needed to be said and it could be told as a good story. But even fearless Zanuck had been both intimidated and affected by the strange spectacle of HUAC. Zanuck was not, like Jack Warner or Louis B. Mayer, one of the moguls who went to Washington and testified before HUAC. He was not, like virtually every other major power broker, one of those who consented to the 1947 Waldorf Agreement that initiated the blacklist. (Of those present, only Sam Goldwyn, Walter Wanger, and Dore Schary spoke out against such a practice.) Zanuck *knew* that even if some of the accused writers and directors were Communists, because of the way things worked at Fox they did not represent a threat to the studio system or to the national welfare.

A number of personnel—including blacklisted directors Jules Dassin and Abraham Polonsky, blacklisted writer Ring Lardner, and liberal-activist Philip Dunne—tell of Zanuck trying to protect those under HUAC's assault. Jules Dassin liked Zanuck. "We were," he recently told an interviewer, "strange friends."[4] Dassin suspected that if any producer was *really* opposed to the blacklist, it was Zanuck. To test his suspicions, he went to him and asked: "I know you don't like the blacklist—do you want to break it?" Zanuck answered, "Yes, I do." Dassin then told him of a property he wanted to acquire, a novel called *The Journey of Simon McKeever*. The only problem was that it was by one of the Hollywood Ten's most vociferous spokesmen, screenwriter Albert Maltz. (Maltz, though blacklisted, would work—for reduced wages—with writer Philip Dunne on Fox's *The Robe.*) When Dassin told him that his good friend John Huston would do the screenplay and that Walter Huston would star, Zanuck agreed to do it but warned Dassin that he must "tell nobody." Zanuck would make sure that things were secure at Fox. It was Dassin's job to "take care of Maltz."[5]

Zanuck was doing what he could to help. He was also lining up a good project. The clandestine preparations and the surrounding intrigue no doubt appealed to his sense of adventure. Zanuck's idea was to take a skeleton crew to San Francisco, and by the time they had worked their way down to Hollywood, "it would be too late to stop the film."[6] Unfortunately, opening the next day's *Hollywood Reporter*, Zanuck saw the headline, "Albert Maltz Declares the Blacklist Is Broken." Maltz had talked. Since the only way the project could have succeeded was on the quiet, it was canceled. Fox Board Chairman Skouras was now fully involved. He threatened Dassin, telling him, "I'm going to step on your neck."[7] When questioned, Zanuck told Skouras he knew nothing of the project.

Zanuck may have caved when confronted by Skouras and the full weight of the Fox Board, but he still wanted to do the right thing. The same day Dassin had been threatened by Skouras, he had a surprise nighttime visitor at his home: Darryl Zanuck. Telling Dassin to "Get out fast," Zanuck gave him a book he thought would make a good film. Since this was a time when Fox was shooting quite a bit on location, Zanuck advised Dassin to go to London. There, after he had written a screenplay, he should quickly proceed to shoot "the most expensive scenes." After this, even with the blacklist, it was just possible that "then they might let you finish it." It was in this way that Dassin came to make *Night and the City*.[8]

During the filming, Zanuck approached Dassin and asked him for a favor: could he write in a part for Gene Tierney? Zanuck explained in his proudly acquired French that Tierney had just had "*une grande chagrin d'amour.*" He knew her, and felt that only work would prevent her from a suicide attempt. Dassin wrote in the part. Shortly after, he received a one-word telegram from Zanuck: "Thanks!" "That," recalled Dassin, "was the unknown Zanuck."[9]

When screenwriter Ring Lardner, Jr., one of the Hollywood Ten, had refused to name names before HUAC, the Fox Board called for Zanuck to use the seldom-employed morals clause in his contract to dismiss him. Lardner recalls that Zanuck told him he "would still respect my contract until commanded otherwise by his board of directors."[10] When the Board did just this, Zanuck dismissed Lardner through a functionary. Zanuck's relations with Abraham Polonsky tell a similar tale. Polonsky was brought to Fox after the success of his screenplay for Robert Rossen's *Body and Soul* (1947), for which he received an Academy Award nomination for Best Original Screen-play. John Garfield, the film's star, and also a victim of the blacklist, encouraged Polonsky to direct and not just write his next project. The resulting film, *Force of Evil,* was considered by critic Andrew Sarris to be "one of the great films of the modern American cinema."

Zanuck signed Polonsky on as a writer-director. Observing what HUAC was up to, Polonsky, a man of many interests, went off to Europe to lay low while working on a novel. But when he was subpoenaed before HUAC in 1951, he refused to say whether, as the odious phrase asked, he was or had ever been a Communist. Zanuck suggested to Polonsky that "he work at home until the whole thing blew over." He liked him, and "wanted no harm to come to him."[11] When pressure was applied by the New York office, particularly by virulently anti-Communist Skouras, as he had done with Lardner "Zanuck reluctantly fired him."

Zanuck considered himself a patriot. But unlike many of his fellow conservatives, he was opposed to the blacklist. In the climate of economic uncertainty and political harassment, he needed to be nudged. Philip Dunne, with whom he had worked closely since the mid-1930s, was most often the one doing the pushing. Along with two other men Zanuck respected, William Wyler and John Huston, Dunne was a founding member of the anti-blacklist "Committee for the First Amendment." Dunne always tried to appeal to what he saw as Zanuck's essential fairness. Once, when Dunne suggested he hire a writer accused of being a Communist, Zanuck told him this was a problem: the man "had joined the wrong clubs." Dunne told him, "We all joined clubs . . . but this was bad dope you've got on him."[12] Zanuck relented.

Dunne knew that whatever his own beliefs, Zanuck would listen to opposing points of view. In May 1949, at the height of HUAC's power, Dunne urged Zanuck to consider making a film that would re-spond—directly—to what was happening. The May 21, 1949, issue of *The New Yorker* had a piece by Daniel Lang about the unjust persecution of William W. Remington, a Department of Commerce economist accused of being a Communist. Here was the chance for Zanuck to do a 1950s version of *I Am a Fugitive from a Chain Gang.*

Dunne told Zanuck such a film "which fearlessly examined this situation would be applauded and supported in ever-widening circles. It would help create its own support, much in the fashion of *Gentleman's Agreement* and *The Snake Pit.*" If Zanuck had the guts to make this film, he "could strike a really telling blow against all kinds of totalitarianism, including Communism." "If I am wasting your time as a producer," Dunne noted, "I am certainly not wasting it as a citizen."[13]

Zanuck replied the next day. He told Dunne that the story was *already* under consideration. Zanuck was willing to make the picture, but he was worried that Communists and their friends "will immediately adopt the picture as their own and try to make it appear that all investigations and loyalty checks are phony." "Personally," he noted, "I believe in loyalty checks."[14] Dunne tried to point out that it was a short jump from loyalty oaths to investigating anybody who held unorthodox views. This was one appeal that failed. Zanuck did not make the film.

Dunne next tried to interest Zanuck in a criticism of HUAC in the form of parable. Pitching George Orwell's *1984,* Dunne made a claim that Orwell no doubt would have found astonishing: that with slight modification "we could make another *The Robe,* set in the future instead of the past."[15] Zanuck would neither be snowed by nor cajoled through Dunne's flattery. The problem was not just the material; it was the times in which they now lived:

> No matter how you treat it, this is a "message" picture. Can you name me one message picture in the last three years [1950–1953] that has not lost its shirt? Surely you have read all the notes I have written you and all of the box office facts I have given you and what happens to pictures that try to preach and "uplift."
>
> For good or bad, this is the age of entertainment. Audiences are sick of lectures even though they are good ones.[16]

By this time Dunne was familiar with Zanuck's contradictory nature. Zanuck's "own conscience," he observed "permitted him to accept the blacklist, but he recognized and respected the fact that mine did not."[17]

Though hardly courageous as he had been on a number of controversial issues in the past, his behavior in regard to blacklisting was better than almost all the other power brokers. Which Hollywood producer *had* stood up to HUAC and the list? Compare Zanuck's pattern of making films that, in parable form, opposed the reactionary politics of the blacklist, the cold war, and HUAC, or of keeping accused personnel on until ordered to fire them, of hiring blacklisted writers through or, of "fronts," or even his numerous attempts to try and protect them, to keep them quietly on the payroll, with L. B. Mayer's behavior.

Mayer tried to convince one of the Hollywood Ten, writer Lester Cole, to sign a loyalty oath and "make the break" with the Communists. His eyes welling with the tears he controlled with the same precision and ease with which he manipulated the studio personnel, Mayer implored Cole to "Be with *us*, be smart." He tried every trick he knew, including some astonishing perspectives not found even in mogul's manuals. He pointed out how quickly "that Communist Roosevelt," that "man of the people" had been forgotten by his leftist supports once he was dead: why, within a few minutes they had "pissed" on his grave! Is this what Cole wanted? Sacrifice with no purpose? If Cole would not do it for the sake of his career, or the good of the studio, Mayer reminded him: "You got kids, think of them." When Cole politely declined, the mask of concern dropped away. Shrieking that he was a "Goddam crazy Commie!" Mayer ordered Cole out of his office, and, as it happened, out of his career as a writer as well.[18]

If Hollywood screenwriters were being forced to take loyalty oaths, or lose their jobs, other Americans also pledged "reaffirmations" of who we were, and how we differed from "them." The delicate issues separating church and state guaranteed in the First Amendment of the U.S. Constitution were given a not-so-gentle nudge aside by the normally cautious Eisenhower, who held that "our government makes no sense unless it is founded in a deeply felt religious faith—and I don't care what it is."[19] On Flag Day 1954, President Eisenhower signed a bill that modified the Pledge of Allegiance, adding the phrase "one nation *under God*" to the litany repeated daily by millions of schoolchildren. Suddenly, our nation's faith in some God was what, in addition to democracy, separated us from the enemy. If all this was, indeed, part of the complex "age of entertainment" in which Zanuck felt we lived, what kind of material would he create to show us ourselves and to illuminate the values of our age?

STORY, STORY, STORY: ZANUCK AND TV

As if the specter of HUAC and (through the Supreme Court ruling) the loss of their theaters was not enough, there was the problem of television. There has been a general, almost folkloric, truth that television "killed" the movies. But the rapid growth and penetration of TV in the 1950s was in fact one of a host of factors explaining the shrinking movie audience. The markers of TV's power were present very early. In 1948, less than half of 1 percent of all American households owned a set. Yet a Gallup poll revealed a disconcerting fact: households with TV sets decreased their movie attendance by 10 percent.[20] Mythology suggested that just as the 1920s industry power brokers had been caught off guard and unprepared by sound, the moguls' tunnel vision had left them unprepared to deal with the postwar advent of TV. Appealing as this might be in offering up an explanation for the decline of the studio system, it simply is not true. As historian Tino Balio points out, the studios "monitored developments [in TV] closely and maneuvered to get in on the ground floor of the new medium."[21] But though the movies were outside their jurisdiction, the FCC had been following the *Paramount* case closely and refused to grant a TV license to the film corporations. The situation became so grim that even movie stars were not inured to the lure of TV. Lana Turner confessed that she had given up going to the movies to stay home and watch television!

Blocked by the FCC from owning stations, Fox became an innovator in the concept of theatrical TV. It was not a hit. Though Zanuck was involved in all of the studio's maneuvers to "go TV," publicly he talked his usual combative, promovie language. In 1952, he declared that "the picture business is in a much better position today than television."[22]

> Those TV guys have a tiger by the tail and they don't know what to do with it. I've heard some of the top television guys talking around here and I tell you they're worried silly. . . . The public won't be satisfied much longer just to watch those tired comedians come into their parlors and mug hour after hour.[23]

But by the mid decade, Berle and his successors had gotten to Zanuck.

Following the adage that "if you can't beat 'em, join 'em," Zanuck agreed to develop two TV series in 1955. Both flopped.

Despite all this, he claimed that he viewed the competition represented by TV as a good thing for the industry. Hollywood had grown complacent over the years, he thought, and TV just might shake people out of this rut. Zanuck even insisted that there was a benefit to TV. Though he did not hold the medium entirely responsible, he felt that "at last" the threat posed by TV would wean both studio and audiences away from the old star system, which, he claimed, had "turned into a monster that might have wrecked us." Exhibitors told him today's audiences responded only to "interesting subject[s]. They don't," he swore, "care who's in it."[24] Could it be possible that TV had driven audiences back to the Zanuck trinity: story, story, story?

Zanuck knew that while finding good stories in any era was not easy, he now faced new competition: the rise of the actor, talent agent, director, or producer who acted as an independent producer, without the enormous studio overhead. For the first time since he had broken into movies thirty years before, Zanuck's faith in his own sense of creativity seemed to waver.

The system in which Zanuck had always placed his belief was starting to fail. Surveying the terrain, he observed that "for the time being we should avoid the type of material that puts an accent on violence."[25] His good friend John Huston's *The Asphalt Jungle* was a "magnificent" picture, Zanuck said, but its film noir, gangster tones seemed out of sync with tastes, and it had flopped—badly. He also thought the postwar interest in Westerns, like his own *My Darling Clementine* (1946), was over. Zanuck saw Hollywood 1950 as a place bereft of these two genres. Their absence, or fall from grace, showed how difficult things were:

> There is no such thing as a 'safe' field. Theatregoers are more selective than ever before. Anything that is routine or formula can be expected to do that type of business. This does not mean that every picture we make must be a freak attraction completely off the beaten path but it does mean that it must have at least an *idea* that will lift it out of the commonplace.[26]

Audiences were tired of the stars who had brought Fox part of its fame. A puzzled Zanuck noted: "Apparently if we cannot give them new plots, they at least want us to use new people to make the plots *look* new." Projects could no longer be developed just because he—or someone else highly placed—was enthusiastic about them; they had to have real box office potential.

After thirty years of running at the highest pitch, both Zanuck and his Hollywood were starting to tire. At times, when he mourned the fact that "motion pictures have generally lost motion," that they "depend almost entirely on the spoken word," he sounded like Talleyrand bemoaning the vanished sweetness of life before the revolution. In puzzling out what would grab moviegoers' attention in the 1950s, he decided:

> Audiences want to *believe*. Whether it be comedy or drama they want to go into theaters and *believe* what you are showing them. If you can make an audience accept the story and go along with it half the battle is won. . . . The science fiction field offers great possibilities. Audiences are eager for pictures made in strange or foreign locales providing they are adventure stories.[27]

Zanuck was reaching back to his earliest roots in the silent cinema and his distaste for dialogue pictures. "An adventure story," he noted, "should be an adventure story and it should be resolved in terms of action, suspense and excitement." He wanted his writers and directors to come up with a film "that is not ashamed of what it is . . . not afraid of physical action and excitement even though it may be deemed hokey."[28]

A series of memos to a few people whose judgment he trusted—Bobbie McLean, Henry King, Lamar Trotti, Philip Dunne, Elia Kazan, and Nunnally Johnson—show increasingly that Zanuck was developing a hard edge: "This is a tough business today and we have had entirely too many casualties. We must have the guts to examine each story and each project with a cold and realistic eye."[29]

—

In addition to these political considerations, economic issues were never far from Zanuck's mind. Zanuck's cost-cutting measures included asking directors to work on one picture a year for no pay (not implemented); sticking with safer material, like the classics (*The Snows of Kilimanjaro, The Robe*); and urging directors to keep unused footage to a minimum. He knew that saving money was essential, but economizing would not draw people into the theaters. The question was, What would? The answer arrived from France in 1952.

CINEMASCOPE

Zanuck claimed the idea for CinemaScope came to him in a moment of inspiration: "I was playing croquet one Sunday at Palm Springs. On my croquet court we have a goldfish fountain. Looking down at the goldfish, I noticed the sense of depth. Here truly was three dimensions. It gave me an idea."[30] But in fact, though Zanuck would provide the enthusiasm needed to sell CinemaScope to moviegoers, the guiding spirit behind this innovation was not goldfish but Spyros Skouras, president of the Fox Corporation. Skouras had started in the sales and exhibition branch of the business, and he never lost the exhibitor's point of view. He was all in favor of a technique that drew people to the movies without the huge cost of revamping theaters, hiring new staff, or purchasing expensive equipment. Although not without its startup costs, CinemaScope required far less than other innovations, only new lenses and minor modifications to accommodate the larger screens.

Sound, then color, had reinvigorated film in earlier times of crisis or stagnation. CinemaScope, developed in the age of small-screen TV, was designed to remind Americans how puny their small black-and-white sets were. It made the big screen appear more formidable than ever. Before the 1950s, the average movie screen was 20 by 16 feet. Its dimensions were designed to accommodate the image created by the 35-millimeter film frame, which projected a picture with a standard aspect ratio of 1.33:1—meaning the ratio of the width to the height is 1.33 to 1. New technologies like Cinerama, CinemaScope (Fox), WarnerSuperScope (Warner Brothers), SuperScope (RKO), 3-D, VistaVision (Paramount), Panvision, and Technirama drew attention to the screen by either increasing the range of what the viewer could see or providing the illusion of a third dimension. Films utilizing these technologies accounted for fewer than 10 percent of films made in 1953; by 1959 that figure had risen to 40 percent.[31] Stereo sound provided another means by which these technologies gave viewers what television could not offer: the sense that they were participants, not just spectators, in the action on the screen. As it had been in the earliest days when a diverse array of showman were drawn to a "cinema of attractions," once again the very processes of display and looking were as important as good stories.

While the vogue for 3-D would be short-lived, wide-screen technologies have left a lasting impact. Cinerama achieved its effect by using three interlocking cameras to record and an equal number of projectors to screen. A special curved screen 25 by 51 feet increased the aspect ratio from the former 1.33:1 to as high as 2.77:1. Its main attraction was pure motion—the opening shot of *This Is Cinerama* was a point of view of a wild roller coaster. The secret of CinemaScope, invented by Henri Chrétien in 1928, was an anamorphic lens that compressed and distorted images during filming but spread them out during projection. Nunnally Johnson joked that with this new shape—roughly that of a business envelope—he "would have to put the paper in the typewriter sideways."[32]

As he had with sound and Technicolor, Zanuck wholeheartedly threw himself behind CinemaScope:

> We have a large screen that gives a semi-circle around the theatre. And you have the feeling that you are in the picture. The picture is around you. You have an opportunity to participate in the drama. To me, that is really and truly a new dimension because it's a new form of entertainment. It isn't just depth, it puts you into the drama.[33]

Zanuck insisted that CinemaScope was not just a desperate gimmick, a quick fix to lure people into the theaters with mere novelty. His shrewd, on-target assessment of the imperative behind Cinema-Scope shows he was as good a businessman as he was a creative producer or a showman:

> Producing companies no longer could depend on the movie-going *habit.* More powerful attractions were necessary to lure a public whose leisure time and inflation-shrunken dollar were being savagely competed for by television, pocket books, magazines, sports, hobby industries and a variety of other spare time and money distractions.[34]

The film that would test CinemaScope's viability was *The Robe.*

THE BIBLE FOR $20 MILLION

The Robe, based on Lutheran clergyman Lloyd Douglas's 1942 best-seller, chronicles the rise of Christianity through the lives of a number of fictional and real characters as they come into contact with the robe Christ handed down from the cross. In 1952 "B.C." (before CinemaScope), a year after Douglas's death, Zanuck began preproduction on the film, choosing Philip Dunne to write the screenplay. Earlier, Dunne had been Zanuck's surprising choice to write the biblical blockbuster *David and Bathsheba.* When Zanuck asked Dunne whether he could do a David and Bathsheba story with showmanship values like those DeMille had used in *Samson and Delilah,* Dunne—who despised DeMille, both the man and his films—said he could not: the two stories were too dissimilar.

While Zanuck continued to insist that Dunne was the man for the job, Dunne worked on convincing Zanuck that rather than emulating DeMille he should let him try a more cerebral approach, one that focused on the psychological dilemmas and moral ambiguities David faced. Resistant at first, Zanuck was encouraged when he read Dunne's draft material. In fact, "the only thing that disturbs me is . . . the 'sex' story of David and Bathsheba has been lost."[35] Dunne found it. When he suggested Laurence Olivier and Vivien Leigh to play the doomed lovers his boss demurred. Zanuck felt the roles should go to Gregory Peck and Susan Hayward.

Zanuck, inspired by some unknown, higher source, felt Peck had "a biblical face" and tried to convince him to take the part.[36] As Peck recalls: "I thought, well, DeMille has done that, and the idea of Americans with American accents playing biblical roles, and me playing King David seemed a little bit ridiculous." But he remembers that "Darryl was interested in a leader who was both good and bad, who had two entirely different sides to his character."[37] Zanuck's description of David as "a leader who was ambivalent in his personality, in his morality" as a man who "betrays his first wife"[38] suggests that, in part, the film appealed to Zanuck because David was so much like him.

Peck agreed to do the part. Zanuck told director Henry King that he had never heard Peck "as completely enthusiastic about any story as he is about this one. . . . He said it was the first time that he had read any Biblical story that gave him a sense of reading about human beings and not just mythical or legendary characters."[39] Dunne succeeded in his desire to make the film "as *unlike* a DeMille picture as I could."[40] When it came to assigning the source for the story, Zanuck told Dunne "Why don't you do it like DeMille does and say, 'From the Holy Bible?'" Dunne told him he preferred another attribution, "Based on an anonymous chronicle in the Old Testament." Zanuck was puzzled why Dunne wanted to use those precise words. But he knew he could convince Zanuck to do things his way by explaining that his way was better simply because it was different from DeMille's. Because Zanuck "had no respect for DeMille at all," Dunne got to do it his way.[41]

In March 1953 Zanuck and Skouras decided to gamble virtually

the entire studio production budget—$25 million for eleven films—
on CinemaScope. In a memo marked "Private and Confidential,"
Zanuck informed producers that upon completion of all films currently in production, they were to abandon any property "that does
not take full advantage of the new dimensions of CinemaScope."[42]

Though CinemaScope opened up a new vista of showmanship,
for the moment it also signaled an end to the small-scale films on
which Zanuck had cut part of his critical reputation. But the new invention spoke deeply—and directly—to Zanuck's first principle: action. He insisted that producer Frank Ross could learn a lesson from
The Snows of Kilimanjaro and apply it to *The Robe.* Zanuck was certain it had scored at the box office not because it faithfully repro-
duced Hemingway's terse dialogue but "because there actually is
very little dialogue in the picture and many things that might have
been *told* are left to the imagination of the audience."[43] (Zanuck never
knew that Hemingway hated the film, and considered it to be the
worst adaptation of all his work. When Hemingway referred to it at
all, he did so by the disparaging title "The Snows of Darryl
Zanuck.")[44]

Because of the vast amount of money poured into developing and
publicizing the new venture, Zanuck knew that like *The Jazz Singer,*
The Robe had to be "safe entertainment." It did not aspire to be anything but mainstream in its overall construction. As Zanuck told
Story Editor David Brown: "I do not want stories that will be helped
by CinemaScope. I want stories that will *help* CinemaScope."[45]

Zanuck must have relished beating Warner Brothers in this race—
Fox had tendered its offer to the inventor, Chrétien, literally one
day before Jack submitted his. Warner's tried to best Zanuck by presenting its own, inferior version, called WarnerScope. The choice
of name was a way to capitalize on Fox's publicity for its new process. Zanuck tried to persuade Jack to change the name, perhaps to
WarnerDimension. "We have spent a lot of money and effort in publicizing CinemaScope," he wrote to Jack; "it means as much to us as
Vitaphone once meant to you."[46] Jack refused to budge.

As they prepared for CinemaScope's debut, anticipation of a triumph pervaded the gloomy Fox lot. The film boasted a young Welsh

actor, Richard Burton, in his second American film, playing a role originally slated for Tyrone Power. The cast also included patrician Jean Simmons and beefcake star Victor Mature (replacing Burt Lancaster). Less than three weeks before its world premiere, Zanuck screened the final print of *The Robe* and told Dunne it was "one of the great pictures of all time."[47] Even the normally taciturn Skouras had been infected by the heady atmosphere. He cabled Dunne that "your creative contribution for ROBE and CinemaScope will go down in immortality."[48] Shortly after the film opened, Zanuck wrote Fox's greatest composer, Alfred Newman, a note of appreciation for his score to *The Robe*. Newman's work on *David and Bathsheba* proved to Zanuck that Newman could write "Jewish music." But he told the composer he had been stunned by his contribution on *The Robe:* "this is the best goy music I've ever heard."[49] A playful Newman responded that "I thought I made Our Boy a 'Lantzman.' [That is, he had made Jesus what he was: a Jew.] Did I miss?"[50]

Zanuck's gamble paid off. In the year that *From Here to Eternity* dominated the Academy Awards, *The Robe* did something even better. It cleaned up at the box office. (The gross for the film was certainly helped by the fact that Fox's recently divested theater chain, now called the National, was run by Spyros's brother Charles who was delighted to take all CinemaScope films.) Produced for a little over $4 million, it was the year's runaway top-grossing film, with earnings *Variety* estimated between $20 million and $30 million. After the success of *The Robe*, all the major studios except Paramount (which clung to its rival VistaVision) were forced to license the process from Fox for a fee of $25,000 per film.

Once the venture was launched, along with the obvious eye-filling spectacles and lavishly mounted, richly dressed musicals, Zanuck would eventually use CinemaScope for smaller pictures like *A Man Called Peter* and *Good Morning Miss Dove*, exercises in old-time religion and rural nostalgia like those that had put Fox on the map in the 1930s. While innovating CinemaScope had been motivated primarily by a depressed box office, there were other benefits that could be gained from the technology. In the current political climate, it is likely that master strategist Zanuck saw that the bigger dimensions of the wide screen would enable him to hide behind the Bible and the safe entertainment of musical spectacle the same way the rural films of musical nostalgia had in earlier decades shielded his studio from accusations of un-Americanism.

OTHER SPECTACLES: MARILYN MONROE

After *The Robe, How to Marry a Millionaire,* another CinemaScope effort, offered a different spectacle: Betty Grable, Lauren Bacall, and an actress Zanuck never had great faith in, Marilyn Monroe. Though Howard Hughes was curious about her, it was Zanuck who in 1946 signed Monroe to the standard beginner contract of $150 a week. Like a raft of other studio starlets, Monroe mainly had to look decorative—at events like a studio golf outing—while the studio figured out whether she had any talent. Zanuck, unimpressed, let her contract lapse.

Monroe drifted to Columbia. After a year, they dropped her, too. She had had small parts in forgotten films, and her options seemed to be running out. In May 1949, still trying to make something happen, Marilyn posed for a nudie calendar. She was paid $50. (The distributors of the calendar would make a profit of $750,000.) By this time she had found a powerful protector—and love—in Johnny Hyde, one of the top figures at the William Morris Agency. While Monroe had slept with a number of men who promised to advance her career, Hyde was different in that he actually believed she had talent.[51] He got Harry Cohn to sign her at Columbia, and he got her a small but coveted part in a "serious" film, that of Angela Phinlay in John Huston's *The Asphalt Jungle.*

When Hyde read the script for *All About Eve,* he decided the part of Claudia Casswell belonged to Marilyn. In director Joseph Mankiewicz's words, Hyde "haunted my office" until he assented to hire Monroe. Mankiewicz (an agency client) broke down Zanuck's resistance to taking Monroe back, and she was cast in the role.[52] After the film opened, Hyde managed to get her tested for the lead in a Fox project, *The Cold Shoulder*. Though the project was canceled, this time Monroe was offered $500 a week under the standard studio seven-year option contract.

In a decade not known for its clever financial moves, the second coming of Monroe to Fox was probably the greatest bargain the studio ever had. (At the time of her death, she was still locked into its limitations.) Hyde would never know how far his client would go; he died in 1951, at age fifty-five.

Whatever other claims have accreted to the Monroe myth, it must be pointed out that, considering her enormous cultural impact, her career in feature films was short, lasting barely ten years—1953 to 1962. She made only eleven films. Yet by 1953, with the scantest of resumes, she stood at the number-six position in the Quigley Publications poll of exhibitors, ahead of James Stewart, Susan Hayward, and Bob Hope. From 1955, her on again, off again feud with Fox and Zanuck meant that in the period of her greatest stardom, she was relatively inactive. But in 1953 she seemed to be everywhere. Her performance as the beautiful blonde with the bad eyesight in the CinemaScope follow up to *The Robe*, *How to Marry a Millionaire*, helped make the film the fourth highest box office draw in 1953.

Earlier that year, she had scored in another "dumb blonde" role, Lorelei Lee in *Gentlemen Prefer Blondes*. Director Howard Hawks claims he suggested Monroe for the part but that Zanuck balked, telling Hawks, "She can't sing." Hawks convinced him she could, and also claims to have given Zanuck a valuable bit of advice. He told him, "Darryl, you're making realism with a very unreal girl. She's a complete storybook character. And you're trying to make real movies."[53] (No one would accuse Monroe's Lorelei of being anything but delectably unreal.)

Once Zanuck had a "hook" for her character, he set about recrafting her golddigger role in *How to Marry a Millionaire*, updating it for the 1950s and conforming it to Monroe's gifts and CinemaScope's advantages. Zanuck immediately dropped all but three of the original show's songs. Though Hawks felt he deserved credit for setting

Zanuck right about how best to deploy Monroe, the producer very clearly had his own ideas. He told his writers, "This is not a satire. It is a solid and honest comedy in the same terms as I WAS A MALE WAR BRIDE, for instance. In WAR BRIDE the audience knew that our people had a very real problem, and they never lost sight of that no matter how ludicrous the comedy seemed at times."[54]

Because musical numbers (including the now famous Monroe version of "Diamonds Are a Girl's Best Friend") take up storytelling time, Zanuck urged the writers to get down to business quickly. His recommendation for what became the opening five minutes of the film show that late in his career, Zanuck was still the best in the business at illustrating how to efficiently execute the basic mechanics of story construction—and that his silent film training was still with him:

> *Opening:* After the [Fox] insignia but *before* any Titles come on we should see the following scene:
> We are on the deck of the boat, shooting down to the deck. We see passengers milling around, etc. Camera comes down to the Olympic team standing in line, being checked in. One guy, staring off as though hypnotized, nudges the man next to him; he turns, looks off, gets that hypnotized look, nudges the man next to him. This routine continues to the end of the line, so that we have a line of guys all staring off in the same direction. When the last man turns and looks off we cut to what they are looking at: Lorelei and Dorothy coming down the dock, heading for the passport officials. One Olympic says to another: "Suppose the ship hit an iceberg and sank, which one would you save from drowning?" The other Olympic replies, "Those girls wouldn't drown. Something about them tells me they can't sink."[55]

Zanuck never appreciated Monroe's talent, but he understood her economic value to the company. Zanuck found some of her demands—like the request that her dramatic coach be present while someone else was directing—"completely impractical and impossible."[56] Zanuck had faith that in *Don't Bother to Knock* (in which Monroe played a psychotic babysitter) "you are capable of playing this role without the help of anyone but the director and yourself."

Zanuck then delivered a well-intentioned, but blunt, assessment of how the studio system saw her:

> You have built up a Svengali and if you are going to progress with your career and become as important talent-wise as you have publicity-wise then you must destroy this Svengali before it destroys you. When I cast you for the role I cast you as an individual.[57]

But the two had different images of how each fit within the Hollywood culture. Looking about her, Monroe saw "independents," if not independence, everywhere: she wanted to be part of this. To Zanuck, she was another talent who, like Edward G. Robinson twenty years earlier, should put herself in his wise hands. Zanuck wanted to showcase Monroe in Technicolor, CinemaScope extravaganzas, while she saw herself doing Grushenka and Ibsen. When she bolted from the studio demanding better parts, Zanuck reluctantly lured her back with *Bus Stop*. Though Monroe received the best reviews of her career, her most productive days were behind her. Her suicide in 1962 virtually coincided with Zanuck's triumphant homecoming. This odd symmetry was a fitting end for this pair, who were neither in sync nor in sympathy with each other throughout the sixteen years they worked together.

MAKING THE EARTH STAND STILL AND LEARNING ALL ABOUT JOSEPH MANKIEWICZ

The Day the Earth Stood Still (1950) is a landmark in science fiction. Based on Harry Bates's short story "Farewell to the Master," the film tells the tale of Klaatu, a peace-loving emissary from more technologically advanced galaxy. He has come to Earth to warn its inhabitants to abandon their warlike ways. Even when dressed in futuristic trappings, this was not a popular position in 1950, amid the strident cries of the cold war.

Zanuck felt that science fiction was one of the few new genres that might prove promising. The first thing he changed was the title,

"Farewell to the Master," telling the producer "we must have an exciting, provocative title that will tell an audience what to *expect*."[58] Of course, standing still was something Zanuck knew little about. Making *others* do so *was* something he understood. Even in a genre whose main characteristic is the creation of a world that defies the realities we know on Earth, Zanuck felt the film must still engender belief. He did not like the original opening aboard an alien spaceship because it was not believable: "When you open a picture on something that does not 'exist,'" he noted, "you have great trouble in capturing your audience."[59] Why not open the film "as realistically as you possibly can," perhaps through radio broadcasts whose dramatic announcements bring listeners the startling news of the spaceship's arrival as if it were a real bulletin?[60] This was what director Robert Wise did.

The film also showed that Zanuck still had his uncanny knack for casting. Robert Wise wanted to cast Claude Rains as Klaatu, even though the gifted actor was rumored to be very difficult to work with. But the actor was not available. Wise recalled Zanuck's idea: "Fellas, I've just come back from England, and I saw a young man on the stage there. He's never been in any films here, and I don't think any films in England. . . . I think you should look at him as a possibility for your picture." Wise agreed to look at test footage of the actor, Michael Rennie. Zanuck was playing one of his hunches. Rennie was new to the screen, and he had what Wise called a "certain ascetic quality."[61] This combination endowed Klaatu with the "alien" nature that might have eluded an actor with whom audiences were more familiar. It was also Zanuck who came up with the idea for the phrase "Klaatu Barada Nikto," the oft-quoted password that Klaatu uses to control his killer robot, Gort.[62] Shot for a little under $1 million, the film grossed twice that amount.

In *The Day the Earth Stood Still* Zanuck turned his gaze to other planets. In *All About Eve*, he looked at another world: that of the theater. Zanuck's relationship with *Eve*'s writer/director, Joseph L. Mankiewicz, was one of the most important and difficult professional associations of his life. Mankiewicz's father, an intellectual German-born teacher, instilled a love of literature in both his sons, Herman (the co-author of *Citizen Kane*) and Joseph. After graduating from Columbia University, Joe worked as a reporter in Berlin before gravitating back to New York. Herman's younger brother (as he was known at this point) first came to Hollywood to write titles for silent films. With sound, he moved to writing features. He had been at MGM since 1934, working more as a producer than as a screenwriter. Though Mankiewicz wanted to direct, he was blocked by Louis Mayer, who felt Mankiewicz's executive abilities were far greater than any contribution he might make behind the camera. As Mankiewicz became increasingly frustrated, the shrewd Mayer tried to entice him with the prospect of becoming the studio's next Thalberg. The supremely theatrical L. B. chose a bizarre moment to dangle this prize. At the funeral of MGM executive Bernie Hyman, Mayer gestured toward the coffin and told Mankiewicz, "He was weak. You are strong."[63]

When Mayer and Mankiewicz had their inevitable falling-out, it was over Judy Garland. Mankiewicz and Garland first met in 1942. He found her "the most remarkably bright, gay, happy, helpless, and engaging girl" he had ever met, and became both friends and lovers.[64] (Though their affair ended badly, Garland confessed that Mankiewicz was "probably the great love of my life.")[65] When Mayer accused him of meddling in Garland's life (which he considered *his* preserve), Mankiewicz quit. His agent, Bert Allenberg, set up a meeting with Joe Schenck. Of course, since Joe had leverage over Mayer through the latter's boss (Joe's brother), Mankiewicz was able to thwart Mayer's revenge, and instead of being assigned by Mayer to a studio he hated, he wound up going where he wanted, to Fox. With Zanuck's approval, Fox gave Mankiewicz what Mayer would not: the right to stipulate whether he would write and/or produce and/or *direct* each project. Mankiewicz was ecstatic. He wrote Zanuck a grateful note, saying he could not foresee "*any* situation . . . in which I would not rely upon you to the utmost for guidance, advice and cooperation."[66] When Zanuck showed Joe Schenck the letter, his worldly mentor underlined Mankiewicz's promise. Perhaps seeing into the future, Zanuck forwarded the note to Fox's lawyer with the laconic remark: "Put this in your files."[67]

Zanuck offered advice. When Mankiewicz was over-using the camera boom, he received a witty memo from Zanuck: "You've earned your wings. You can come down now."[68] After *Dragonwyck,*—on which Mankiewicz fought bitterly with the film's producer Zanuck's old crony Ernst Lubitsch—Mankiewicz scored a critical, though not a box office hit with *The Ghost and Mrs. Muir.* Zanuck imagined he could pull off a dramatic casting coup by assigning the part of the young widow whose seaside home is haunted by a virile, charming ghost with whom she falls in love to Irving Thalberg's widow (and his friend) Norma Shearer. (The former "First Lady of the Screen" had last appeared before the cameras in 1942.) Zanuck told writer, Philip Dunne that the film could prove what he and "many people . . . believe," namely, "that Norma Shearer has one great picture left in her yet." Shearer would astound Hollywood and "make the same comeback Joan Crawford made last year [in *Mildred Pierce*]."[69] But Zanuck's tantalizing fantasy of what the forty-six-year-old star might have made of Lucy Muir was never tested. Shearer's retirement was permanent. Rex Harrison was superb as the captain, but Mrs. Lucy Muir was played by an actress twenty years Shearer's junior, Gene Tierney.

After four films at Fox, Mankiewicz had only one modest financial success, with *Dragonwyck,* a gothic tale. Had Mayer been correct, and Zanuck wrong? Starting with *Letter to Three Wives,* he proved that Zanuck's judgment had been sound. Mankiewicz saw *Letter* as the first in a series of five consecutive films in which he was trying to make "a continuing comment on the manners-and-mores of our contemporary society in general, and the male-female interrelationships in particular."[70] But while *Letter to Three Wives* was a serious attempt at understanding how part of Americans lives had altered, another "sociological" dissection not directed by Mankiewicz, *Sitting Pretty* (1948), viewed the doings of suburbanites with malicious humor. Here, Clifton Webb originated the character of Mr. Lynn Belvedere, an acerbic jack-of-all-trades. Belvedere is researching the behavior and mores of the residents of "Hummingbird Hill" for a book that will expose the hidden social codes of suburbia. To get the facts right, he goes to live undercover in the suburb, answering a newspaper ad for a babysitter that a young mother of three (Maureen O'Hara) has placed when all attempts to control her brood have failed. Belvedere is the answer to her prayers. No problem or task is beyond his reach, or admission. He dances superbly; he "excels in fisticuffs," he is a world-class psychologist. He uses yoga to calm and charm the children. He sculpts like Rodin. When asked what he does for a living, Belvedere frostily answers, "I am a genius." The film was a surprise hit, earning Webb an Academy Award nomination. Against all odds, it established him, at the age of fifty-seven, as Hollywood's leading character star.

While Zanuck was so enthralled with both the character of Belvedere and his impersonator, Clifton Webb, that he approved two sequels to this initial triumph, he was less than thrilled with the success of another talent he had nurtured. Humble at first (or at least acting that way), Zanuck now found Mankiewicz to be "an arrogant bastard." Speaking of *A Letter to Three Wives,* a film about postwar suburban life that Mankiewicz was writing and directing, Zanuck said, "if he gets a hit with this, he'll be unlivable."[71] *Letter,* and not Zanuck's own *Twelve O'Clock High,* would win both Best Director and Best Screenplay Oscars in 1949. (Mankiewicz would repeat the same double feat the next year. While Leo McCarey, Billy Wilder, John Huston, Francis Ford Coppola, Woody Allen, James Brooks, and Bernardo Bertolucci also pulled off this "double," Mankiewicz is still the only person to do this twice—in consecutive years, no less.) When Spyros Skouras refused to give his next film, *House of Strangers,* the support it needed because he was certain the leading character (played by Edward G. Robinson) was unflatteringly modeled on him, this move like many other changes since the war gave Zanuck yet another illustration on how altered Hollywood and the culture of the producer was.[72]

NO WAY OUT

Mankiewicz's choice of his next film was dictated by his growing sense of competition with another young Fox director, Elia Kazan.

Kazan was preparing *Pinky,* and Zanuck was uncertain whether the studio needed to buy another story of racial tension, Lesser Samuels's *No Way Out.* Using normal studio procedure, he circulated a draft of the story to all the directors and producers under contract. Otto Preminger was very interested. He sent the vacationing Zanuck a telegram to Sun Valley, telling him "I am completely enthusiastic about this story and would like to do it." (When Mankiewicz learned of Preminger's timing, he wryly observed to Zanuck: "I believe Otto, with his usual facility for stepping over the other customers, has already sent you a wire about it.")[73] Other candidates chimed in. The charming Jean Negelescu put in his bid. From Zanuck's friend, the agent Charlie Feldman, came a pitch for his client Robert Rossen.

A film on America's race relations would be timely. The late 1940s saw the stirrings of the modern Civil Rights movement, with President Truman's Committee on Civil Rights issuing its historic call to end discrimination in 1947. That year, a study sponsored by the United Negro College Fund showed the systematic underrepresentation of African-Americans in every white-collar profession; in medicine, there were four times as many white doctors as black.[74] This was the climate in which Zanuck decided to film a story about a black doctor in a white world, *No Way Out.*

The plot of *No Way Out* concerns Luther Brooks, an African-American intern at a public urban hospital. He treats two white brothers, Ray and Johnnie Biddle, who have been shot while attempting a hold-up. In the course of his medical treatment, Johnnie dies. Ray (Richard Widmark), a psychopathic racist, is certain his brother's death resulted from an unnecessary surgical procedure Luther insisted upon, and he vows revenge. Throughout the film, he abuses and torments Luther, and, though incarcerated in a prison hospital, still manages to instigate a race riot, modern Hollywood's first. (The "Negroes" win.) Balancing Widmark's racist white monster are Dr. Daniel Wharton (Stephen McNally), Luther's mentor at the hospital, and Edie Johnson, Johnnie Biddle's widow, who in the course of the film is transformed from racist to enlightened figure.

Mankiewicz went to New York to direct the tests of the finalists for the part of the young medical intern, Luther Brooks. After audition-ing almost a dozen young actors, he offered the part to Sidney Poitier. (To get it, Poitier, then twenty-two, claimed he was twenty-six, the same age as the character.) Zanuck wanted Anne Baxter to play Edie, but Mankiewicz convinced him to go with Linda Darnell, who had done so well as the bride from the wrong side of the tracks in *A Letter to Three Wives*. In addition to Poitier, the film marked the debut of a number of important African-American actors, notably Ruby Dee and Ossie Davis.

Zanuck was after his usual style, reminding Mankiewicz that "while we are telling a story which deals with a most serious issue, we must consciously avoid propaganda."[75] They would avoid obvious messages, but "the final result of our efforts should be a picture which is actually powerful propaganda against intolerance."[76]

Zanuck was told by the studio's public relations counsel that "even in certain so-called white cities, such as Detroit, Omaha, St. Louis and Philadelphia, we are apt to have the picture banned totally by the Police Commission" because it depicted a race riot.[77] With this in mind, he suggested that the race riot be more of a contained "bar-room brawl or a corner street fight" than an all-out vicious affair.[78] But knowing how important the scene (which took three days to shoot) was to the film's vow to pull few punches in showing the ugliness of racism, Zanuck made sure the riot was filmed as originally conceived. Calls of protest were both strong and numerous. Fox was forced to do what Zanuck wished to avoid: to edit the scene after the film's release.

Zanuck also altered the ending. Originally, Ray lured Luther to a coal cellar, where he butchered him and hid his body amid a mound of coal. Zanuck felt that the "hideous slaughter" of "a wonderful character" did not make sense:

> If his death resulted in *something*, if something were accomplished either characterwise or otherwise, it would be different and I would accept it. Perhaps the reason I shrink from this is because it violates a cardinal principle which I have always adhered to, and that is, "Never kill the leading man unless something is gained by it."[79]

Zanuck had insisted that in *No Way Out* he wanted to "aim for realism and guts." Yet, he was clearly not comfortable with an ending whose bleak options demonstrated that when it came to changing many people's attitudes there *was* no way out. As he had in *The Jazz Singer,* he suggested some safer, more commercially pragmatic endings for the film. Even if we view these proposals as starting points meant to get the writers thinking, Zanuck's suggestions seem absurd, even unintentionally, comically entertaining. Ray and a third Biddle brother, George (a mute), lure Luther away with a phone call. When he arrives, they hit him over the head with a blackjack, tie him up, and dump him into their car. Then they proceed to a cemetery, where Ray tries to bury him alive. We are back to the best nickelodeon mind in Hollywood, to the Zanuck of "For Men Only."

George panics and flees. A crazed Ray "is trying to stuff dirt into Luther's mouth." Enter Edie. She has figured out where Ray might be, and tries to stop him. But he knocks her into the open grave, and as she stumbles onto the jagged edges of a broken headstone, she gets an idea. Picking up a rock, she hits Ray on the head. "He falls into an open grave; for a moment he looks up at her; then he dies."[80] Having disposed of Ray, the film ended the way Zanuck wanted: with Luther alive. And "as a camera pulls back . . . [it] reveals two white doctors in interns' garb" while Luther "wears the dark grey trousers and black shoes of the Resident." Virtue has triumphed.

Mankiewicz would not consider Zanuck's Mack Sennett–inspired solution. But its absurdities and exaggerations did what they were intended to do: they forced him to come up with something better. In the final version, Ray does try to kill Luther but instead gets shot himself. The film ends with Luther, assisted by Edie, once again trying to save this horrid man's life. Using Ray's gun to create the pressure for a tourniquet, Luther bitterly tells the whimpering racist, "Don't cry, white boy. You're gonna live." The chief visual metaphor of the uneasy relations between white and black was Poitier's dark skin against the gleaming whites of his intern's garb. Zanuck wisely tried to downplay too heavy a use of this, telling Mankiewicz to take out a line where Luther talks about "putting on his whites."[81] Zanuck also excised some of the more brutal lines of dialogue, such as Ray's reference to "nosy jigaboos just like you," and he cut a scene where a black patient asks for a white doctor in preference to Luther.[82]

Even with cuts, the language of *No Way Out* was unheard of for Hollywood. Terms like *nigger, dinge, coon,* and *boogey* pepper the script. But the film's depiction of "Negro home life" as warm, supportive, and just as lovingly unreal as Hollywood's white version may have been more subversive than the shock of corrosive hate speech, or the image of a moral black man triumphing in a slot where moviegoers always saw this as a white perogative. We owe this directly to Zanuck's intervention. Very early in the project he decided "we will go into Luther's home. We will see real Negroes and how they live, as human beings. He will have a real brother, a real sister, a real father— all human beings."[83] Zanuck also saw to it that Luther was strong-willed, and not a saint.

The African-American press of the era gave the film a lot of attention and gave Zanuck high marks for hiring a number of fine black actors. But by and large, *No Way Out* has been overlooked by the white cultural establishment. It has not been accorded the status of *Pinky, Lost Boundaries,* or *Home of the Brave,* other films of the era that deal with race in far more compromising ways. To this day, some feel that the film's language (which reflected Zanuck's demands on carrying home its message) keeps it off broadcast TV.[84]

ALL ABOUT EVE

After working very closely with Mankiewicz on *No Way Out,* Zanuck was thinking ahead to their next project together from his vacation perch at Cap d'Antibes. It would be *All About Eve,* based on the short story "The Wisdom of Eve" by a sometime actress and writer, Mary Orr.

NBC Radio City Playhouse had already broadcast a radio play version of the story. Mankiewicz was attracted to the piece because he had a lifelong fascination with the nature of creative folk, particularly actresses, and he thought it might be a superb vehicle for rising Fox star Susan Hayward.[85] He began the screenplay late in the summer of 1949, retitling it *Best Performance.*

In Orr's story, Margolo Cranston is well past forty-five and happily married. Mankiewicz changed her name to the more euphonious, starlike Margo Channing, altered her status from married to single, and lowered her age to forty. Mankiewicz also softened—considerably—the character of Eve. In the short story she not only steal's Karen Richard's playwright husband, Lloyd, she lands a lucrative contract and happily heads off to Hollywood, the bad woman unpunished for her sins. In the film, Eve triumphs professionally, but is a washout romantically. Mankiewicz altered the character of Margo's best friend, Karen. In the short story she too, is an actress. In the film, she is the well-bred spouse of the genius playwright, and her status as an outsider to the inner workings of the theater endows the film with at least one nontheatrical vantage point from which to judge these odd people.

The title claims the film is all about one figure, Eve. But as rewritten by Mankiewicz, it is a meditation on the nature of women, period. Those women who are in the theater merely make us all aware of how gender roles and intimate relationships of any and all permutations are all performances, on or off the stage. Celeste Holm, the film's memorable Karen Richards, felt that the film should perhaps have been renamed "All About Women."[86] In the same way each of Mankiewicz's three wives in *Letter to Three Wives* can be thought of as representing a problem in postwar male-female relations, in *Eve,* Margo, Karen, and Eve each hold one part of the composite picture of woman up for scrutiny. But we should not overlook the contribution of a fourth female, Margo's inimitable ex-vaudevillian dresser/companion, Birdie Coonan. Mankiewicz conceived and wrote the part exclusively for Thelma Ritter, Hollywood's greatest character comedian of the postwar period. While there is no debate that the role of Birdie was written for Ritter, numerous stories have persisted that Margo was modeled on any number of divas, including Tallulah Bankhead and Bette Davis. Mankiewicz swears that he had a number of actresses—ranging from the eighteenth-century Peg Woffington to

Bette Davis, Joan Crawford, and Bankhead—in mind when he created Margo.[87]

Zanuck's first choice to play Margo was slightly off center: the ageless Marlene Dietrich, who, if one were counting, was one year shy of fifty. But annotations on an early draft of the script show he was also considering Claudette Colbert (age forty-seven) and Barbara Stanwyck (forty-three); Mankiewicz strongly opposed Dietrich.[88] On the director's advice, Zanuck signed on Colbert in February 1950. Shortly before production began, she injured her back and had to withdraw. Since locations had been booked and actors and personnel had already set their schedules, the filming could not be postponed. Mankiewicz then offered the part to his second choice, Gertrude Lawrence. But Lawrence insisted on two changes. Mankiewicz would have to remove or rewrite the drunk scene at Bill's welcome-home party (the first time Margo publicly confronts Eve); and, rather than listen to the endless versions of *Liebestraum* the self-pitying (but always theatrical) Margo keeps asking her hired pianist to play, Lawrence insisted on singing a torch song. Mankiewicz refused. There was even talk that Ingrid Bergman, in exile since her scandal with Roberto Rossellini (a child out of wedlock) could be lured back to Hollywood to play the part. (The "apostle of degradation," as she was called on the floor of the United States Senate, stayed in Europe.)

After Lawrence took herself out of the running with her demands, Zanuck personally contacted Bette Davis and asked her if she were interested and available.

It could not have been an easy call to make. In 1941, Zanuck had sponsored her bid for president of the Motion Picture Academy of Arts and Sciences. (She became the first woman to hold the post.) But a combination of stress and the unpopularity of some of the innovations she wished to implement made her resign the office after only three months. Furious Zanuck is alleged to have responded to Davis's departure with the oft-used and seldom meant line, "You'll never work in Hollywood again."[89] When he caught up with her nine years later, she was filming *Payment on Demand* for RKO, and had hoped to take a break between projects. But one look at the script for *All About Eve* convinced her to change her plans.

Mankiewicz had been warned by writer/composer/director Edmund Goulding that Davis would "destroy" him, "grind you down to a fine powder and blow you away," but he found the actress well prepared and more than able to deliver the goods.[90] Allegedly, Mankiewicz gave Davis only one insight into how she might play the character of Margo: she was a woman who would "treat her mink coat like a poncho."[91]

The two men also disagreed over the key role of Eve Harrington, the worshipful would-be actress who turns out to be not quite the naive thing Margo presumed when they first met. Zanuck wanted Jeanne Crain for the role, but Mankiewicz had conceived of Eve as an ambitious young woman with a lesbian component, among other things, as part of her makeup.[92] Crain, a wholesome mother of seven, with limited dramatic range would have found it difficult to pull this off in 1950s Hollywood. When Crain became pregnant, Ann Baxter, Mankiewicz's choice, was asked to take over the part.

Mankiewicz completed his shooting script in March 1950. Zanuck exercised his usual editorial acumen. When Margo's loyal dresser, Birdie, is overtly hostile too early on, Zanuck cautioned him to "beware of Birdie's jealousy as it will tip off that Eve is a villain."[93] Zanuck wanted the audience to be uncertain whether Margo's increasing hostility toward Eve was a manifestation of her paranoia about her age or the real thing. To realize this, Mankiewicz wrote witty, sharply delineated dialogue. When Bill Sampson, Margo's love interest, accuses her of "paranoiac insecurity" toward Eve and her youth, Margo spits out—as only Bette Davis could—"Cut! Print it! What happens in the next reel? Do I get dragged off screaming to the snake pit?"

The last bit is, of course, a veiled reference to Zanuck's 1948 Olivia de Havilland vehicle. This was not the film's only self-reflexive line. Though concerned with theater folk, *All About Eve* could easily be read as a look at Hollywood. There are numerous references comparing the stage and New York to the movies and Hollywood. When Eve asks Bill why he would even consider going to Hollywood when he could work in the theater, his answer is both Zanuck's and Mankiewicz's:

The Theatuh, the Theatuh—what book of rules says the Theater exists only within some ugly buildings crowded into one square mile of New York City? Or London, Paris or Vienna? . . . Want to know what the Theater is? A flea circus. Also opera. Also rodeos, carnivals, ballets, Indian tribal dances, Punch and Judy, a one man band—all Theater. Wherever there's magic and make-believe and an audience—there's theater.

In a more direct—and funny—exchanges, Bill tells Margo: "The airlines have clocks, even if you haven't! I start shooting a week from Monday—Zanuck is impatient, he wants me, he needs me!" To which Margo replies: "Zanuck, Zanuck, Zanuck! What are you two—lovers?" "Only in some ways," Bill says. "You're prettier."

Zanuck wanted the lines cut. Not because of the implication of homosexuality but because he thought "the use of my name in a picture I am associated with will be considered self-aggrandizing."[94] This battle he lost.

Shooting was completed in six weeks. Mankiewicz delivered his first rough cut to Zanuck (and Bobbie McLean) to edit. Zanuck's most serious cut—one Mankiewicz fought bitterly—was his elimination of the Rashomon-type use of overlapping, contradictory narrators to show the party sequence from different vantage points. (He may have been more influenced in this by brother Herman's structure of multiple narrators in his screenplay for *Citizen Kane* than by Kurosawa's film *Rashomon,* which used a similar device.) Mankiewicz opens the sequence with one of Zanuck's favorite devices, "the Voice" narrating a flashback. The voice is supplied by Margo, who, in addition to Karen and Addison, is one of *Eve*'s three narrators. She recalls the night: "Bill's welcome-home birthday party . . . a night to go down in history. Like the Chicago fire and the Massacre of the Huguenots. Even before the party started, I could smell disaster in the air. . . . I knew it, I sensed it even as I finished dressing for that blasted party."

It is the moment in which Bette Davis delivers perhaps the film's most famous bit. When Karen realizes that Margo is about to make a scene, she inquires, "Is it over—or just beginning?" Wheeling about on the set with its long staircase Mankiewicz has used so well in staging the scene, eyes moving restlessly, Davis/Margo warns her friends: "Fasten your seatbelts. It's going to be a bumpy night." In addition to Margo's perspective, Mankiewicz covered one moment of this bumpy night—Eve's speech about the meaning of applause—from Addison's and Karen's vantage points as well. Zanuck cut the scene (although it was in the shooting script that he had approved) because he felt it altered the rhythm of what was already a rather long film.

The film, which ran two hours and ten minutes, opened at New York's Rivoli Theatre in early October 1950 to astonishing reviews. For their work, Mankiewicz and Zanuck each won his last major Oscar (Mankiewicz for Best Screenplay and Best Director, Zanuck for Best Picture). With this film's fourteen Oscar nominations, Zanuck finally broke *Gone with the Wind*'s record of thirteen. Davis lost the Oscar when voters, torn between her performance and that of Gloria Swanson as Norma Desmond in *Sunset Boulevard,* opted to go with Judy Holliday in *Born Yesterday.*

Zanuck and Mankiewicz worked together twice more in the 1950s, on *People Will Talk* (a parable about McCarthyism) and *Five Fingers* (an espionage story starring James Mason). When, over the director's strong objection, Zanuck cut out precious parts at the conclusion of *Five Fingers,* both men knew it was time to call it quits. (Mankiewicz—ever the author of great dialogue—would later say Zanuck had edited the last part of the film "with his polo mallet.")[95] Zanuck continued to produce many successful films without Mankiewicz but, until his comeback with *Sleuth* in 1972, Mankiewicz without Zanuck had a poor track record. The breakup of the powerful duo of Zanuck-Mankiewicz happened because each man, so certain that his, and not the other's, was the right vision, was unwilling to change. Each had gone as far as he could together.

WAIT TILL THE SUN SHINES, NELLIE

With *Wait Till the Sun Shines, Nellie* (1952), Zanuck was consciously marking the end of an era and a way of mediating America on film. *Nellie* is the bookend for *Rebecca of Sunnybrook Farm.* It shows how much had changed in America—and in Hollywood—in less than fifteen years since Shirley visited the farm and made the country love radio and vaudeville. Though the notes of the director, Henry King, show how carefully he set up the film's visual compositions, it was Zanuck who, in story conferences, dictated entire sequences off the top of his head. What might have afforded him the chance to make a *Rebecca*-like valentine to the country life becomes, in *Nellie,* a somber and at times bitter meditation on the transformation of rural America as he imagined it existed at the turn of the century. Although full of the barbershop music of the 1890s one would expect to find in a Fox film of musical nostalgia, unlike his earlier films in this genre, *Nellie*'s harsh and even shocking plot shows the stultifying, claustrophobic power of the small-town life once pictured as utopian. Zanuck would never have taken this position, particularly with the film of musical nostalgia, had the culture of Hollywood not undergone such unsettling changes in this decade, and had he not been prompted by similar feelings in his personal and professional life.

The film tells the story of Ben and Nellie Halper (David Wayne and Jean Peters), newlyweds en route, by train, to Chicago. Nellie is excited because this is her first real trip away from her hometown. Ben, a traveling salesman and itinerant barber, has "seen the world." When they stop off at a small town several hours from Chicago, Nellie presumes it is just to rest. But Ben reveals that he has a surprise: he has arranged to open a barber shop, and they will settle in the town of Sevillinois until they can save enough money to go to Chicago. This is but the first in a series of ruses by which Ben gets what he wants—a home, a business, children—presuming in all these moves that his desires define Nellie's as well. They don't. When Nellie realizes that Ben has refused to take her into his confidence and has lied about his vision of the future to placate her, she abandons him and their children and flees to Chicago with her husband's best friend, smooth-talking jobber Ed Jordan (*Eve*'s Hugh Marlowe). No one can be that transgressive in 1952 Hollywood and get away with it; Nellie is killed in a train wreck on her way to freedom in the city. (Along with *Psycho* and *L'Aventurra, Nellie* is the only major film in which the heroine is killed—or disappears—so early in the film.)

The time span of the film, revealed in a flashback by "the Voice," encompasses the fifty years from film's invention to the crucial year that World War II ended. Made four years before Zanuck left Hollywood, it remains one of the key texts in his final but reluctant acceptance of the studio's destruction and his deconstruction of his own past.

In *Nellie,* Zanuck was after the big questions a middle-aged man might ask of his life: Have I made the right decisions? Did I make a difference? Is there still time left to do what I want? The film asks bigger questions, still, about the nature of community and conformity. Zanuck went through an unusual number of drafts and writers to get this one right. Paul Trivers was hired in 1947 to adapt Ferdinand Reyher's novel, *I Heard Them Sing.* Three years later, another draft was written by Maxwell Shane. In his version, the town was called Bonne Terre rather than Sevillinois, and Nellie is Millie. Ben has his barber shop. Through its glass windows, we see the town change as paved streets replace dirt roads, electric lights replace gaslight, and telephone wires spring up amid cow pastures. While Ben has joined every male institution the town offers, Nellie, who has been experimenting with cosmetics using materials in Ben's shop, is smothered by his refusal to let her have a career. Stifled by Ben, and thwarted by the limited social avenues such small towns offered women, Millie runs away, but no train bars her path. She escapes and files for divorce through the mail. She resurfaces many years later as an Elizabeth Arden cosmetics queen, and offers to help her grown grandchild, who has no idea of her identity.

But, intriguing as some of these ideas were, Shane was replaced by a third writer, Allan Scott, who expanded the original ten-year time period to the fifty years the film would finally cover. In his script, a train crushes Nellie's carriage as she flees with Ed Jordan.[96] Perhaps drawing his inspiration from the lyrics of Harry Von Tilzer's 1905 song that supplied the film's title, Nellie's desperate flight is one of many examples Zanuck has placed within the narrative comparing the placidity of the small town and the action of the city, of staying put and moving on, remaining the same or changing. Contemporary postwar audiences confronted similar possibilities and changes brought about by their new mobility. As his female characters had done in the past, Nellie is putting forth Zanuck's own feelings of claustrophobia and containment.

Zanuck also saw an opportunity to preach a little on what he felt were America's virtues, values he saw slipping away. Zanuck singled out a line Ben delivers to his son—"This country owes you nothing— not even a wheelbarrow"—and wrote to the film's producer George Jessel, "It seems to me this is a pretty solid foundation for the theme of any story about America." Zanuck then gives Jessel the speech he swore he had no intention of delivering:

> Because they pay high taxes and fight wars, everybody believes the Government owes them a living. I believe we all owe America something and that the privilege of living in this sort of democracy is a rich reward. Now I am not looking for a big message or propaganda for this picture, but today when everybody is looking for security from the cradle to the grave and when everybody is expecting the Government to nurse them along, it seems to me that our barber, in his own quaint way, might reflect and remind people of what they owe America.[97]

Getting across this philosophy was "the POINT of the whole thing." But Zanuck made sure that when it was delivered, it was accomplished in such a way that it came across as an honest meditation and not as a politician's oration. Ben tells his commanding officer during the Spanish American War that traveling with the army has made him aware that Sevillinois has everything he wants: "It's got work, home, neighbors, children, hope. I guess there's no more than that to anywhere. When I get back I'm never going to leave the place." But even as Ben is peering into his future and finds that it contains all he wants, Nellie has made a discovery of her own: Ben has deceived her. He always told her he rented the barber shop, and that soon they would go to Chicago. Zanuck wrote the scene that occurs early in the film in which she finds out he owns the shop, a lot, and even a burial plot. The scene where she discovers Ben's betrayal is amazing compared to other films of this period and how they picture the inner thoughts held by women of Nellie's era. When pious Ed Jordan, who has been urging Nellie to run off with him to Chicago from the very first, is confronted with a truly rebellious woman, he drops his pose of dashing small-town roué and reveals the side of a bourgeois patriarch. Nellie can't break open the strongbox: it's Ben's! In a cry for identity, Nellie screams, "It belongs to me, too."

She finally gets the box open, only to discover she and Ben are homeowners, not renters. She vows to leave, and this is the last we see of her. Nellie's departure is more than a dramatic gesture against the confinement of patriarchs (even benign ones like Ben). Her honest outburst is Zanuck's own cry of suffocation. Zanuck is confessing that neither utopia—the celluloid small town or the real Hollywood—is any longer tenable. This is reaffirmed when Ben's son is gunned down in a mob hit. Even rural enclaves are not safe from the city culture and its pollutants. Like Nellie, Zanuck wants to get out from a culture in which he no longer recognizes the rules.

Zanuck dictated the film's ending in a story conference. It is one of the most poignant in his entire catalog:

> the street is deserted. In the distance, in a long shot, we see a lone figure. A dog barks sharply, then is silent. Far in the distance a train whistles; then again there is silence. We come to a close shot of the lone figure, and we see that it is Ben. He stands on the curb in front of the barber shop. We feel that perhaps he has been taking a walk around town by himself. He stands there on the curb for a moment, looking down the street. He turns, looks in the opposite direction. Then he turns around, looks at the barber shop. From his pensive expression we realize that he has been remembering, reliving the past. Under this we hear, through an echo chamber, the old quartet singing "WAIT 'TILL THE SUN SHINES, NELLIE." We come to a close shot of Ben, and of course we know the voices and music are in his mind. Suddenly, he smiles as he thinks of the past.[98]

Nellie's beautifully conceived, spare images are Zanuck's valedictory on what made America great, on film and in his heart. The curtain is being drawn on this figure and his era. Zanuck's musings about

Ben reveal his thoughts about his own impending farewell: "The town, the country, nobody owes him a cent. It has been a privilege to live there. He has known life and love and friends, and it hasn't been wasted."[99]

IRVING BERLIN

If *Nellie* allows us to peer into how Zanuck felt about his previous anchor, the small town, nothing shows how the entire culture of show business had changed like Zanuck's thirty-year professional relationship with Irving Berlin. From Jolson's serenading his mother with "Blue Skies" in *The Jazz Singer,* to Marilyn Monroe stunning Ethel Merman's vaudeville mama with "Heat Wave" in *There's No Business Like Show Business* (1954), Berlin would enjoy a long running relationship with Zanuck. Each of these two dominating, strong personalities derived a substantial benefit from their association. In Berlin's work for Fox, Zanuck emphasized one particular facet of Berlin's image that other studios had largely overlooked, what today might be called family values. It was a shrewd call. Berlin had an image no other living popular composer could claim. His steady presence (by 1938, he had published more than half of his life's oeuvre of 1,500 songs) made him seem like a folk figure whose songs came from the people's consciousness, rather than emerging as they did from the machinery of the music industry. To paraphrase Jerome Kern's famous assessment, Zanuck saw that for many Americans, Berlin's work did not represent the best of American popular song: the composer *was* American popular music.

Zanuck's formula for an Irving Berlin musical was simple. In each of the four films on which they collaborated, he made sure that Berlin's music was part of one or two plots. One had Zanuck build a movie around a historical cavalcade of family growth in which the composer's work is present at every phase of our popular culture. A variation plot showed the hard and contested battle to secure the correct standard that American entertainment should take: by movie's end, the two seemingly incompatible musical or performance modes of the leads have resolved their conflict by coming to dwell in the democratic (and stylistic) middle ground. To these, Zanuck added the value of Berlin's music, and each film trotted out a veritable trunk full of Berlin's old songs, luring customers into the theater with the additional promise of three or four eagerly anticipated original works Berlin would compose for each film. To Zanuck, it was very important that at the end of the film Berlin's music was sheltered within the wholesome and classy settings toward which the performers throughout have aspired: in *Alexander's* it is playing Carnegie Hall, while in *Show Business* it is the Palace.

But beyond their nostalgic, rural slant, a further distinction that musicals held at this studio was the yearning they expressed for respectability. If "There's no place like home" is the nineteenth-century homily all Hollywood lived by, home and its aura of respectability was, for Zanuck's vaudevillians, a lure as great as success would be for performers working at other studios. This search for respectability and official recognition in music is what Berlin at Fox is all about. Zanuck was shrewd enough to know that this is what American movies are about as well.

Zanuck and Berlin were linked early on. Berlin's first contact with movies had been the interpolation of his hit song, "Blue Skies," into *The Jazz Singer*. While it is likely that Berlin had some contact with Zanuck during the making of *The Jazz Singer*, it was through Joe Schenck that Berlin came to work with Zanuck on *Alexander's* and other films. Schenck and Berlin grew up in the same part of the Lower East Side; even after each had left the neighborhood and become established in their respective fields, they kept track of each other. Before he became Zanuck's partner in 1933, Schenck had been the head of United Artists, working at a time when sound was new and musicals were the rage. So it was out of loyalty and with good business sense that in 1929 Joe Schenck hired his childhood friend Irving to write the music for a startling proposal: one of the first science-fiction musicals, *Reaching for the Moon*. The composer obliged and, as was his working method, quickly wrote five songs.

But when the public's fascination with the novelty of musicals seemed to fade, United Artists decided to "demusicalize" *Reaching for the Moon*, and in its reincarnation—even with Bing Crosby and Bebe Daniels in the cast—only one of Berlin's tunes (the lovely title song) made it into the final release print. Berlin was profoundly embittered, and for the next four years concentrated on Tin Pan Alley and Broadway, steering clear of movies. When he did return, it was not with the mixed results of his work with Schenck but with an enormous triumph. This time, he signed with another studio, and his hit score for RKO's *Top Hat* is still one of his best ever composed for Hollywood.

The songwriter and Zanuck became reacquainted when Berlin sold the producer the aptly named "You're Laughing at Me," one of a large number of unpublished works he referred to as his "trunk songs." (Trunk songs were compositions Berlin judged to be of too low a quality to be published.)[100] So when Zanuck astounded Berlin by buying one of these discarded songs for a large sum of money, the songwriter may have felt that in putting one over on *this* mogul, he was drawing even with Hollywood.[101] In all likelihood, however, Zanuck used this transaction as an entree for what he truly wanted: a future working partnership with Irving Berlin. With typical Zanuck energy and determination, after the initial sale things moved quickly, and "the next thing Irving knew he was writing an entire score [*On the Avenue*] for Zanuck."[102]

In a decade that witnessed so many ends, this was to be the pair's final collaboration, and *There's No Business Like Show Business* was Berlin's farewell to Zanuck and to Hollywood. The cycle that he and Zanuck began when Jolson sang "Blue Skies" to his mother in *The Jazz Singer* is here ended.[103]

Zanuck tried to conjure up, one last time, a compendium of all his work with Berlin meant, and to pay tribute to the old culture that had spawned them both:

> Here is the story of family we are thinking about . . . They are not Barrymores, but they are people who, for two or three or even four generations, have been in the business—who know nothing else— who think, talk, eat and sleep nothing but theater. . . . They are Irish . . . They are fighting, sentimental, humorous, lovable and loving group of people . . . They have something in common with the

O'Learys in IN OLD CHICAGO, with the family in YOU CAN'T TAKE IT WITH YOU, with the family in MOTHER WORE TIGHTS.[104]

If *Nellie* updates *Rebecca of Sunnybrook Farm, Show Business* closes the argument he first made in *The Jazz Singer*. The young singer in *Show Business* (played by Johnnie Ray) is confronted with the same spiritual dilemma as his counterpart Jake Rabinowitz: Does he stay in show business, or does he cast his lot with religion? In fact, the two films are marvelous structural inversions of one another, showing just how topsy-turvy the rhetoric of entertainment and Hollywood culture had become in the years between their creations. *The Jazz Singer* has religious parents with a secular son: *Show Business* has secular parents with a religious son. In either case, the child is attempting to go against family and cultural tradition, and in both cases it is the father who opposes such a breach. Both films blur the metaphors of religion and show business, mixing wardrobe with uniform, congregation with audience, ritual with public performance. But Steve Donahue does what Jake could not do (or, more accurately, was not allowed to do): he gives up show biz for religious life. This being Fox (rather than Warner's), and the actor being the lachrymose Johnnie Ray (and not Jolson), in *Show Biz* the sacrifice takes the wardrobe change of the priest's collar rather than that of *tallis* and cantorial robes.

If lead Ethel Merman (seen in *Alexander's Ragtime Band,* an earlier Zanuck-Berlin collaboration) is musical theater, then showgirl Marilyn Monroe is now the cinema, including the movie's mediation of what the musical theater in the age of stereo and widescreen should look and sound like. (Even though Merman, as Molly, at one point dyes her hair blonde, no one would mistake her for Monroe.) How Monroe came to the project is a tale unto itself. Berlin saw her photo at the home of his childhood chum, Joe Schenck. He was seized with the inspiration that just as Merman had personified the thirties in *Alexander's Ragtime Band,* by singing "Heat Wave" Monroe could enliven this cavalcade and bring it into the spirit of the fifties. He insisted that Schenck call Monroe, even though it was two in the morning.[105] Despite Berlin's pleas, Monroe refused to take the bait until the wily Zanuck dangled the possibility of the lead in Billy Wilder's *The Seven Year Itch*. Suddenly, Marilyn was intrigued.

At first, Phoebe and Henry Ephron (the husband and wife writing team who had succeeded Lamar Trotti, who died midway through preproduction) were distinctly *not* thrilled to be assigned to this particular project. Phoebe remarked, "I won't go to see it, why should I write it?"[106] The participants in the film seem to know this. *Show Business* was made just at the moment when the mode of entertainment it extolled, the kind that had put both Berlin and Zanuck in power, was trembling. (At first, they had Monroe playing Merman's daughter; neither would-be mother nor child could bear the thought, and the script was rewritten with Monroe cast as a showgirl.) Deep into her short but troubled courtship with Joe DiMaggio, Monroe arrived late—as she had on the set of *All About Eve*—which enraged the veteran Merman. It thus came to pass in this film's plot that, as it was in real life, Monroe is offered material that was once the province of Merman. New Hollywood has triumphed over the old.

If *Alexander's* is about the eternal value of this kind of entertainment, *Show Business* is about its dissolution. If *Alexander's* makes the couple, the latter film shows the breakup of the vaudeville family. All the five Donohues (plus Monroe) unite for an overblown finale of "There's No Business Like Show Business," an ending that takes full advantage of the vertical composition of CinemaScope's frame.

But the center of a utopia once inspired by Berlin's music will no longer hold; the film's unity is illusory. The finale takes place at a benefit of the Hippodrome, the last gasp of that great house before it rings down the curtain on its own glorious past, and that of vaudeville as well. Still, *Show Business* is loaded with signifiers proclaiming the film's link to the old culture of Broadway. (Posters for Shirley Temple and Will Rogers plug Fox films; Sophie Tucker briefly passes through.) Hearkening back to the days when he ruled radio and allied himself with Zanuck, even Walter Winchell—his power minuscule compared to what it had been—is trotted out and does a voiceover promo of the Donohue's act. But try as he might to pretend that the film still is linked to these old truths and old performers, *Show Busi-*

ness is really a plug for CinemaScope and Monroe, not Berlin and Broadway. In this climate, the vaudeville entertainment that would have been at its center seems oddly out of kilter.

Jolson could resist the pull of his dying father, tradition, and the tears of his *yiddishe mumme* and, in the face of such an alignment of forces *still* opt for show biz. This demonstration of superhuman willpower that forges his career and enables him to resist such pressure is understandable: in *The Jazz Singer* he did so in a culture in which his brand of performance was, in fact, thriving. By 1954, this turf of popular music had been gerrymandred away from the tradition represented by Berlin. It migrated toward the younger market of rock and roll. Though both *The Jazz Singer* and *There's No Business Like Show Business* are united by a rationale that placed primacy on technology over performance (synchronized sound for one, CinemaScope for the other), they are bookends supporting different polarities and marking different eras of the larger entertainment culture.

"THEY'LL NEVER RUN MY BUSINESS"

Zanuck had been working sixteen-hour days since the mid-1920s. Though he enjoyed remarkably good physical health, it was apparent to many people with whom he worked—Gregory Peck, Story Editor David Brown, his son—that he needed a change. In the past, he had always found that one way to dispel tension was to take a long trip. Sometimes he would go to Africa or Alaska to hunt game. But most summers since the late 1920s, the Zanucks had been going to Europe. On a trip to France in 1951, they encountered an acquaintance of Virginia's, the character actor Alex D'Arcy. With him was a ravishing young woman named Bella Wegier. After joining them for a pleasant talk, both Zanucks dined with D'Arcy and Bella that night. Both were charmed by D'Arcy's companion.

Bella was a thirty-three-year-old Polish-born beauty. Jewish, she had known much hardship during the war, including incarceration in a concentration camp. She was currently separated from her industrialist husband. Like Zanuck, she had a passion for gambling. (Unlike

Zanuck, she usually lost.) Soon after this meeting, Zanuck and Bella became lovers—nothing unusual by Hollywood standards. (Virginia even supported the fact that Zanuck paid her gambling debts.) But then Zanuck and his wife invented a permutation novel even within the elastic norms of Hollywood's culture: they invited Bella to live with them in Santa Monica, in their Ocean Front Drive beach house annex. To announce their mutual obsession with (as well as their "joint custody" of) the young woman, they renamed her Bella Darvi—the last name a combination of Darryl's and Virginia's names. Zanuck set about making a star of his protégée. He succeeded, instead, in making a fool out of himself. Their subsequent escapades embroiled the trio in one of Hollywood's juiciest scandals in years.

The start of Zanuck's downfall took place in a nightclub. On January 18, 1954, Virginia and Darryl threw an enormous party at Ciro's to welcome back their daughter Susan who, along with starlets like Terri Moore, had been entertaining American soldiers in Korea. The interior of the club had been decorated in an Oriental motif, with unexplained circus overtones. At one point late in the evening, the fifty-one-year-old Zanuck stripped off his shirt and, grabbing a trapeze, attempted to do a one-handed chin-up in front of the amazed party-goers. When he failed, his humiliation was both total and public: *Time* covered the episode in its February 1 issue, and *Life* published a spread of photos. (What went almost unreported is that to help him save face, Virginia attempted the feat as well.)

Soon after this fiasco, Susan Zanuck told her mother that Darryl's relations with Bella were more than a sponsor to his protégée.[107] Virginia threw Bella out of the house, along with Darryl. But he came—or was taken—back. While Zanuck was pilloried in the press for his out-of-control behavior, his protégée encountered her own rough reception. Darvi received cruelly negative reviews for her "acting" in films like *Hell and High Water* and in the disaster-plagued *The Egyptian,* where she was cast opposite an appalled Marlon Brando, who sat through one or two script readings and promptly fled. Virginia presumed that with the dissolution of her acting career, and after Darvi returned to France in 1955, the affair was over. But Zanuck seemed to find more and more reasons to go abroad. Why was

Zanuck suddenly so out of control? In part, he was experiencing a mid-life crisis; in part he was simply burned out.

It was clear that as the old culture slipped away, Zanuck had been increasingly alienated from and even disturbed by the way movies were being made in the 1950s. The producer was no longer the all-powerful/creative force Zanuck had known in 1935. He had become, in his own words, "a negotiator, an executive, a peacemaker." He was no longer a cultural impresario. In a Hollywood where "everyone was becoming a corporation, with their own managers, their own agents, their own lawyers," a despairing Zanuck mourned the fact that "you can't deal with individuals any longer."[108] Finally, with his three children grown and out of the house, Zanuck made the break. He announced in 1956 that he was leaving Fox to set up shop in France as an independent producer. Virginia, his wife of thirty-two years, found out he was quitting Fox from the newspapers. She was not invited along to France.

In part, Zanuck's flight—or self-exile—was based on his awareness of the diminution of his power to make movies the way he wanted. Richard Zanuck felt that "he was starting to realize that his grip on the absolute power was not as strong as it was because the business was changing." His daughter, Darrylin, feels that the public face he lost with the entire Darvi affair made his diminished status hard to bear. When her parents separated, "it was like Hollywood went to war . . . everybody took sides." Because Virginia was "very, very popular," her father couldn't stand some of the social snubs he received or the snide remarks he heard, or imagined. "He just wanted to get away from the whole thing." David Brown said it simpler: "Darryl Zanuck had no use for Hollywood."[109]

Philip Dunne recalls the moment he knew that Zanuck had had enough. After the preview of Dunne's directorial debut, *The View from Pompey's Head* (1955), he and Zanuck sat down for a drink in the famous long, green office. It was after two in the morning. Letting his hair down, Zanuck made a prediction:

> In a very short time, the business will be completely dominated by the stars and their agents. Last week in this office, a goddam agent

started to tell me how a script should be rewritten. I kicked the bastard out, but next week he, or another like him, will be back. We made the stars, but they've forgotten that. Now they think that they're entitled to run the business. Faces, that's all they are, just faces, but in today's market it's only faces that count, not brains.

Zanuck ended the late-night monologue asserting, "I'll tell you one thing: they'll never run my business, because I won't be here."[110]

In March 1956, at the age of fifty-three, Zanuck left the town he had lived and worked in for forty-six years. He left behind the people he knew, the studio he had founded, his friends, and his family. He was going to France to make movies. With the farewell of the studio era's last giant, an epoch in the culture of Hollywood ended.

=Epilogue=

What a bore. Hollywood has changed.
There's no more excitement—we
haven't had a good rape or murder
since Errol [Flynn] died.

—HEDDA HOPPER TO DARRYL
ZANUCK, JULY 1961

AWAY FROM HOLLYWOOD, Zanuck lived a peripatetic existence. Throughout his adulthood he had spent a good deal of time in France, and even spoke the language after a fashion, but he had no real roots there. Under his new arrangement, Twentieth Century-Fox still paid him $150,000 annually with the obligation to distribute his independent films (DFZ Productions). Until his independent films started to clean up at the box office, his principal income would come from his enormous block of Fox stock: he was the largest, though by no means the controlling, shareholder in the company.

Like the well-heeled expatriates in *The Razor's Edge*, he could have rented or purchased a flashy home on the Riviera, or an elegant apartment or townhouse in some fashionable Paris arrondissement.

Instead, the little boy who was born in a hotel made his main Paris residence the George V or the Plaza Athenée. The liaison with Darvi, the ostensible reason for Zanuck's departure from Hollywood, was over by late 1956. Her gambling debts were too large for even Zanuck to cover. (Nunnally Johnson when asked to explain Zanuck's attraction to Bella Darvi said it was obvious: "Bella made Darryl take her to bed. Until then, Darryl thought it was something you did on a desk.")[1] Because of his separation agreement with Virginia, and his diminished salary as head of DFZ Productions ($110,000 less than he was earning when he quit as studio chief), Zanuck actually had to borrow money to set himself up in business. At one point, things were so desperate that Zanuck borrowed $50,000 from his old companion Howard Hughes. In typical Hughesian style, the money was flown over by a courier, who carried it as if transporting state secrets, passing it to Zanuck in a dispatch bag. It is unclear whether Zanuck ever repaid Hughes. (Perhaps Zanuck viewed this as a delayed payment for his secret editing of Hughes's famous film *The Outlaw*.)[2]

Zanuck was an independent producer from 1956 to 1962. During that period, he produced six films. Five of them were not very good. His son's explanation for the low quality of his father's output is the string of affairs that took up more and more of Zanuck's time:

> He wasn't thinking as clearly as he did. I mean, he still had the same enthusiasm for the pictures. But his main thrust really was the belief in the girls, really. 'Cause behind every picture, you'll see, there's a girl that he was going with.[3]

Richard Zanuck, now working for his father as vice president of DFZ Productions, often had to run interference back at the studio. Fox's executives wondered what their former chief was up to, beyond his well-publicized sybaritic pursuits. This obsession with the girl was "not the way he operated at all" in the past, "but by now it became the main motivation."[4] Zanuck thought that as he had done with Rin Tin Tin, Tyrone Power, Alice Faye, Betty Grable and Sonja Henie, he could make a star out of any of his new female protégées. His son, with some pain, recalls the "new" DFZ:

He thought he could make anybody a star. And he thought that he could make any good subject into a successful picture. It didn't work out that way. So it was just a bad period. . . . Until *The Longest Day,* there wasn't anything that showed the real brilliance of the old DFZ. You know it was because the motivations were wrong for making the pictures.[5]

Zanuck lived in Europe, but he stayed in touch with the studio through his son, and through meetings with the new hand-picked production head, Buddy Adler.[6] Skouras and Zanuck also stayed in touch. The two men had a very complicated relationship. Utterly un-alike, with interests in different areas of the film business, they had a wary mutual respect for each other. Edward Leggewie, head of the Fox Paris office at this time, recalls that the two were like "deux com-pères froids," an oddly matched, closely linked pair who "gave the appearance of not liking each other and maybe it was true that they were at odds. But at the same time, they respected each other . . . at the same time they disguised it. It was a game they were playing."[7]

Back at the studio, the game was getting serious. Though Buddy Adler had an impossible act to follow after Zanuck, in 1957–58 he guided the studio through two profitable years. But in 1960, an above-average year for the industry as a whole, the studio suffered through the unexpected death of Adler, and a financial deficit of $2.9 million. The next year it lost more than seven times that amount. A desperate Skouras asked Zanuck to come back and save the studio. But to avoid others' finding out, he sent telexes in code to Paris substituting Ed-ward Leggewie's name for Zanuck's. As Leggewie recalls, "they didn't want to say 'you' [Zanuck] should come back," so "Skouras was using me, my name, to disguise this so if anyone found the telex and read it they would think they were attacking me!"[8]

Skouras was not alone. Back at the studio, a band of old pros like Philip Dunne, George Stevens, writer Charles Brackett, and direc-tors Walter Lang and Mark Robson decided that drastic steps had to be taken before the whole enterprise failed. As Dunne put it, "early in 1961 the peasants revolted."[9] They decided to go to Skouras and tell him that only Darryl Zanuck could turn things around. Interestingly, Dunne added a coda: if DFZ would not come back, then they "would accept Dick Zanuck, who, when his studies at Stanford permitted, had been included in production meetings and story conferences from the early years of the decade. It was clear that Zanuck's only son "had inherited much of his father's drive and enthusiasm, as production boss. It was a desperate measure," but, added Dunne, "these were desperate times."[10]

But was Zanuck up to the task? Reports filtering back from the set of his latest film, *Crack in the Mirror,* suggested that at age fifty-eight he seemed strangely detached from the proceedings. As an observer remarked, "It was as if DZ was attending his own funeral and knew it."[11] When his latest girlfriend, café singer and actress Juliet Greco, walked out on him, Zanuck holed himself up in his hotel suite. Soon the management asked him to move out of the Plaza Athénée because of damage his lover's dog (a going-away present from her) had visited upon the furnishings. Like his father, he began to drink heavily. He would be rescued by a book and the opportunity to restage D-Day.

In October 1960 Zanuck read *The Longest Day,* journalist Cornelius Ryan's chronicle of the Allied and German stories in D-Day. Richard, who had produced DFZ Productions' only real hit with his version of the Leopold and Loeb case, *Compulsion* (and was perhaps feeling his producer's oats), warned his father not to make the film. He thought nobody wanted to look at war movies. But Zanuck was firmly convinced that this was a story worth telling. With a project that riveted his imagination, he stopped the heavy drinking and returned to form. The old DFZ was back.

He somehow convinced the floundering studio to commit $8 million for a budget, a huge sum in those days. Using his lifetime of connections, he personally lobbied with Lord Mountbatten, several generals, and a head of state or two to get the complicated logistics of filming on location under way. He had "antique" military equipment built from scratch. When he found that key parts were no longer manufactured for the airplanes he needed, he had Rolls Royce build the engines.

It was evident that Zanuck had lost neither his executive brilliance nor his showman's instincts. He made a number of unprecedented decisions in marshaling forces for *The Longest Day.* Because there were essentially four strands to stories set in four different locations—France, England, the United States, and Germany—Zanuck came up with a bold, economically shrewd plan. He shot the film by simultaneously deploying a number of units that operated under his oversight, but which took their particular commands from each of the different directors working that unit. Zanuck organized an army as well as any general, telling Hopper "I had to shoot *The Longest Day* in this unique and unparalleled fashion because of several basic problems. In order to get a top international cast, and to get them when the armies, the military equipment were available, we had to double our activities." Zanuck himself? He confessed to Hedda that "I lived in a helicopter going back and forth between the studio and the location."[12]

Richard Zanuck recalls that he and his father talked about these problems "at length." Zanuck pointed out to his son that he saw two main decisions that had to be made, quickly. One was the issue of whether to shoot in black and white or in color; the other was, in a film with over forty identifiable, important characters, whether to use stars or less expensive (but also less familiar) actors. Richard Zanuck recalls that, with regard to their first dilemma, DFZ said "every instinct told him to shoot in black and white because it will give you a very authentic look." But he was worried that, in the age of Technicolor, everyone would look at the black and white images and think he had used stock footage. Richard recalls the shock that greeted DFZ's announcement. "You know, it's like at that time every picture with scope had . . . it's like saying 'We're going to make *Cleopatra* in black and white.' You've gotta be kidding."[13] Audiences were used to thinking of movies as colorful extravaganzas they couldn't see on TV, but Zanuck decided to shoot in black and white for authenticity. (Until Steven Spielberg's *Schindler's List,* thirty years later, *The Longest Day* would be the highest-grossing black and white film of all time.)

He also decided to populate his film with big stars—John Wayne, Henry Fonda, Red Buttons, Robert Mitchum, Peter Lawford, Richard Burton, Roddy McDowall, and others. He did this not solely for their marquee value but because this would make it easier for audiences to keep track of the many characters in this long film. (Zanuck's choice would become an industry practice.) In another bold move, because he wanted the German military to be seen as real people, and not as Nazi caricatures of Fox war films, he used extensive German dialogue with English subtitles.

Before shooting began, Skouras summoned Zanuck to New York. Fox's Board, looking for a scapegoat to explain its terrible box office, turned to DFZ Productions' poor performance and the huge cost of Zanuck's new venture. Somehow the growing debacle of *Cleopatra* and the uncertain drift the studio had taken since his departure, the more serendipitous explanation, was never raised. The situation with the ill-fated epic was emblematic of how differently things were done in the post-Zanuck, new culture of Hollywood. It had grown from a normal feature to the studio's most problem-plagued project to date. Director Rouben Mamoulian was fired and replaced with Joseph Mankiewicz. Writers came and went. Elizabeth Taylor nearly died, then left her fourth husband for co-star Richard Burton. Mankiewicz rewrote; costs escalated. There seemed to be no end in sight. Zanuck talked his way out of his situation—barely—but was warned that (unlike the wildly profligate *Cleopatra* company) if he went a cent over budget, "they would take my cameras away."[14]

Zanuck started to shoot in the summer of 1961, and finished the principal photography in six months. The biggest risk, as it had been for Eisenhower, was timing the staging of the Normandy landing to avoid weather-induced delays. By the time he had staved off the insurrection on the Fox Board and had worked out the logistics of the key invasion sequences, it was winter. The overwhelming opinion was to wait until spring or summer, but Zanuck, after checking the local meteorological history, decided he would shoot the landing on Omaha Beach in the dead of winter.

As he proudly recalled, "we were never held up, except for a day, in six months of exteriors."[15] And what about the cast? "Mitchum, Albert, Lawford, Fonda went into the icy waters of the Atlantic in November, and they did it time and time again without complaint."[16]

Zanuck was only half kidding when he told Lord Louis Mounbatten that "I believe I had a tougher job than Ike had on D-Day—at least he had the equipment."[17] To get the realism he insisted upon, Zanuck claimed "we had to manufacture ammunition—some 500,000 rounds of blanks—and this is one of the big cost items of the film." They found and rebuilt Spitfires and Messerschmidts, but they had to construct their own gliders: "everything else we obtained, including sixty World War II landing craft were in mothballs." He was particularly proud that to his knowledge, *The Longest Day* was "the first film to give the German side of D-Day, which, with all its errors—human and technical—is really fascinating."[18]

Zanuck exposed 360,000 feet of film—enough for a picture sixty-six hours long. The final film would run just over three hours.

For the first time with this film, Zanuck became a director. Though he had directed individual scenes (most notably in *The Grapes of Wrath*), these were usually retakes or sections changed after a preview screening. Richard Zanuck recalls that because he had preplanned and supervised nearly every aspect of every film with minimum impact from most of his directors, with rare exceptions, his father thought directors were really for the most part technicians and traffic cops.[19] But here, his directorial duties were substantial, and by his own estimate, he directed more than half of *The Longest Day*.[20] "This is a cinch," he said of the experience. "All my life I've been baffled by this. It's the easiest thing in the world!"[21] Perhaps it is if, like Zanuck, you've been in the business for over forty years and have supervised nearly a thousand films. *The Longest Day* joined a handful of Zanuck signature films—*The Public Enemy, I Am a Fugitive from a Chain Gang, The Grapes of Wrath, How Green Was My Valley*—into which he put everything he knew and believed about the American cinema. The story of D-Day offered the part of him that was drawn to a "cinema of attractions" the most spectacular opportunity of his life. The sheer scale of both the film itself and the preparations for it were astounding. The helicopter shots of the landing on Omaha Beach look so real that one would swear he had used stock footage. *The Longest Day* presented him with an enormous stage on which he could mount a tale told almost exclusively through action, rather than dialogue. Last, like the part played by one of his favorite plot devices, a trial, the ordeal of war gave his Victorian sense of right and wrong its most powerful, unambiguous staging ground.

Even though he brought the film in slightly under budget, Zanuck was in for a very rude surprise. A desperate Twentieth Century-Fox decided that Zanuck's film could give the floundering corporation the quick cash fix it needed. Rather than opening *The Longest Day* like the road-show attraction it clearly was, they decided to open it quickly, in as many theaters as possible, to get the money flowing in. Zanuck told Skouras that if Fox tried to do that, "he was going to come in and take" the company back.[22]

During production of *The Longest Day,* stories of disasters on *Cleopatra* found their way to Paris, and when he heard them Zanuck was "disgusted . . . with the way the studio was being run."[23] Reinvigorated by what he was sure was going to be a major triumph, and in love once again, he decided that the only way to protect his film and his investment in Fox stock was to get back the studio he had abandoned six years before.

Skouras had been forced to resign the chairmanship in late June, and Judge Samuel Rosenman, a fabled jurist and ally of Franklin Roosevelt, was put in temporary control. With the wily Louis Nizer acting as his attorney, Zanuck made his pitch to the Board in July 1962. They wanted to see the film, but Zanuck refused. He was using himself as the lure. Richard Zanuck recalls the dramatic scene before the Board of Directors:

> He had them absolutely mesmerized for four hours. I was there. I was sitting in a corner. And I've never seen a performance like it. He kept circling the table, and he sat down. At the end of this long, long thing, [he] looked at them all, and said: "And then the picture starts." He had 'em, and they were absolutely blown away.[24]

After executing his coup d'etat, Zanuck intended to go back to Paris the next day. He told Richard:

> Look, you know the studio. I haven't been there for years. I don't know anybody. And I don't know the town anymore. . . . You go back to your room, and we'll meet here in a couple of hours and go to dinner. [Bring] a list of people who you think would be good to run the studio.[25]

When they met for dinner, Richard handed his father a list with one name on it—his own. Zanuck reacted with a mixture of pride and hesitation. He mulled it over, and by the end of the evening he had made his son the head of the studio.

In his unfinished Hollywood novel *The Last Tycoon*, F. Scott Fitzgerald wrote that, "There are no second acts in American lives." Darryl Zanuck's resurrection with *The Longest Day* proved that there can be second acts. But they might be short ones. And the last act, which closes the story, might be a part of the script so tragic that no one wants to see it enacted. This, in fact, is what happened to Darryl F. Zanuck. He came back. But the movie business was so changed that there was little room for the absolute maneuverings of the DFZ of the studio age. Probably, this is part of the reason he appointed his son to run the studio, leaving himself in the novel role as chairman of the corporation. Richard had become Darryl, and Darryl had become "the home office" he was used to struggling with.

At the outset I noted that this book was about Hollywood culture as much as it was a study of Zanuck's place and presence in this world—how, out of a particular organization of material and personnel, the studio executives like Zanuck produced movies that created a unique American culture made not only in Hollywood but by Hollywood. Zanuck had been able to gauge this state of affairs when he entered movies in the decade of the 1920s. The rapid and enormous success he had was due in large part to his abilities both to follow and finesse his place in the system. As each decade offered up a new permutation or threat that altered some part of the equation of studio-era filmmaking, he rose to the challenge; he improvised, he moved one step ahead of everyone else. But when Zanuck returned in 1962, many parts of this classical world as he knew it had not existed for several years.[26] In the end, there reached a moment when he could not adapt to a system so altered that it bore few scant traces of Scott Fitzgerald's fabled formulation of "pictures in his head" that he, and Thalberg and Selznick before him, had carried about. Zanuck simply had outlived the culture that gave his skills a value, validated his norms, offered him a frame of reference for his professional and social selves.

Late one morning in 1951 (all these stories are set "late one morning") Ben Hecht and Selznick were walking the empty streets of Hollywood. Selznick was talking. "The movies, said David, were over and done with. Hollywood was already a ghost town making foolish efforts to seem alive." Selznick warmed to his subject, even though it was a maudlin one. Characteristically, even when speaking of decline, Selznick could only imagine in grandiose terms: "Hollywood's like Egypt," said David. "Full of crumbled pyramids. It'll never come back. It'll just keep on crumbling until finally the wind blows the last studio prop across the sands."[27]

Two days after his dramatic return as Chairman of the Board, Zanuck was interviewed by Hedda Hopper. Hopper, like Selznick and Zanuck, a relic seemingly from the age of the pyramids, proclaimed of Zanuck's return that "bells are ringing all over town." Zanuck cut her short. "I have no illusions about what I'm facing . . . and this is between us—the company's in worse shape than you can imagine, than I imagined until yesterday. It's now a struggle." In a way, it was 1935 all over, when he had first come to Fox. With a contempt he did little to hide, he told Hopper of his predecessors, "The only policy they've had to date is to economize and make good pictures. That's not a policy—that's a dream—that's fantasy." With the cadences of *The Longest Day* still ringing in his ears, he proclaimed, "We know there's a war. We've got to find out what tactics we're using. Then we'll decide how many generals, how many colonels and how many privates we need." Though he was as feisty as ever, Zanuck revealed the real cause of his anxiety: "This has changed my private and personal life. I am not getting any more money than I was as a part-time consultant. It's a great sacrifice. I like my life. But that's gone. Now I'm mad and determined and nobody's gonna stop me." He concluded his interview sounding like one of his besieged Warner Brothers figures, or the last honest man on trial addressing a jury, or even the subject of one of his great man biopics: "I'm in clean as a whistle. I have no commitments to anybody—and that includes my own son. And I ain't running for re-election. I don't owe any goddamned politician anything."[28]

The Longest Day opened in Paris on the anniversary of D-Day. Somehow, the Chevalier of the Legion of Honor managed to convince the French government and the City of Paris to treat the event as if it were a national holiday. The film was ushered in with a military parade and the illumination of the Trocadero Gardens. The highlight of the evening was the image of a frail Edith Piaf (who would be dead within a year) singing "La Marseillese" from atop an Eiffel Tower emblazoned with electric lights that spelled out the French title of the movie, *Le Jour le Plus Long.* Short of De Gaulle popping out of a cake, Zanuck could not have done better.

The American opening was almost as spectacular. The film was a critical and box office smash. Like the hero in the last reel of a silent scenario, Darryl Zanuck had ridden to the rescue, saved his studio, and done the seemingly impossible: he had come back more powerful than before.

But the studio continued to be in dire trouble, and the catastrophic cost of *Cleopatra* and its disaster at the box office broke Fox's back.

Darryl and Richard Zanuck virtually shut down the studio, laying off 2,000 employees, including well-known directors and writers. Perhaps nothing better illustrated the changed conditions Zanuck faced in the new Hollywood culture more than the following irony: the only source of revenue was coming in from lucrative TV shows like "Dobie Gillis" and the nearly $18 million gross of *The Longest Day.* Some of his fellow survivors from the *ancienne regime* were not happy with the *realpolitik* decisions Zanuck had to make to move forward in the new culture. An enraged Billy Wilder seething over Zanuck's "firing" (and then "rehiring") of *Cleopatra's* director, Joseph L. Mankiewicz, sent Zanuck a telegram responding to an invitation to direct a film for Fox: "No self-respecting picture-maker would ever want to work for your company. The sooner the bulldozers raze your studio, the better it will be for the industry."[29] Many people doubted whether the studio would ever re-open.

The fiscal crunch, however, made them look at what they had on the shelf already. One of the properties was *The Sound of Music.* No one would have guessed at the time that it would become the largest-grossing film in Hollywood's history up to then, but the move, mostly Richard's, was a temporary palliative. From 1963 to 1968, with Dick Zanuck running the studio, it was often the second most profitable lot in town (after United Artists). But innovative, inexpensive hits like *M*A*S*H* (1970), *Butch Cassidy and the Sundance Kid* (1969), and *Planet of the Apes* (1967) could not compensate for a disastrous string of costly failures: *Star!* (-$10,000,000), *Doctor Doolittle* (-$11,000,000), and—what looked like a sure thing but was anything but—*Hello Dolly* (-$10,000,000). Zanuck tried to rescue the situation with a replay of D-Day, this time with Pearl Harbor: *Tora! Tora! Tora!* Despite his father's enthusiasm, Richard had his own premonitions: "always lurking in the back of my mind was *The Longest Day* . . . a re-creation of a successful operation, whereas the other was the destruction of our fleet." The film's Japanese director, the revered Kurosawa, had a nervous breakdown, and Richard was dispatched to Japan with the unpleasant task of replacing him ("one of the worst things I ever had to do").[30]

The movie failed miserably. But sixty-two-year-old Darryl Zanuck was in love again, this time with a nineteen-year-old model named Genevieve Gillaizeau. Of all his girlfriends, she lasted the longest and, in the opinion of his family, was the most destructive. She was an aspiring actress, and Zanuck convinced his son that the studio should sign her. Her "star" vehicle, *Hello-Goodbye*, was savaged by the critics.

The financial picture for Fox continued to deteriorate, and at the end of 1970, the Board of Directors asked Richard to resign; Darryl had agreed to the decision. Searching for a description, Richard summed up the whole disastrous affair: "It was like an execution."[31] He couldn't get his car out of his reserved parking space because there was a painter beneath the wheels painting out his name. He had virtually grown up at the studio. Now, "the guard was watching me as if I was about to steal an ashtray."

The family firings didn't stop there. When a group of disaffected stockholders who called themselves the Twentieth Century-Fox Stockholders Protective Committee decided to oust the management team, of which Darryl was titular head (though at this point hardly in control), Virginia Zanuck and her 100,000-plus shares joined them. Making a rare dramatic public appearance, she said that her husband was "destroying" the dynasty he had built up. She was publicly siding with her son against her husband because she had her grandchildren's future to think of.[32] (One wonders, in addition, whether after a lifetime of living by the dictates of *his* whims, Virginia might finally be allowing herself to get some measure of revenge against her husband.)

And so, on April 19, 1971, almost thirty-six years after he founded the studio, Darryl F. Zanuck was ousted from power. The Board merely redefined the duties of his CEO position so that they were largely ceremonial: to convene Board meetings. The next month he resigned from even this position. He was given the title of Chairman Emeritus and a two-picture deal as a way of salving the consciences of the people who had thrown out the founder of the company. His contract would expire in May 1973, after which he would receive a $50,000 annual salary as a consultant.

Without work and the tumult and attention and action it generated, his health deteriorated rapidly. In 1972, he underwent surgery for cancer of the jaw. (He had listed Genevieve as next of kin.) Though the surgery was a success, the recovery was long and painful. About this time Zanuck started to suffer memory lapses. On a couple of occasions, he went walking in New York's Central Park near his rooms at the Plaza Hotel, and forgot where he lived. Upon a thorough neurological examination it was determined that Zanuck had "an organic brain syndrome—which now would be called Alzheimer's disease."[33] He could be fairly lucid about general topics, but his behavior at times became irrational, paranoid, and depressive. During some periods he could not properly take care of himself. This was not the glamorous life Genevieve had dreamed of, and finding myriad reasons to be anywhere but New York, she was absent more and more often. During one of her absences, Zanuck had to be hospitalized. When she returned, she found all three of Zanuck's children at the hospital preparing to take him to his house in Palm Springs, for what Genevieve thought would be a short visit.

On April 7, 1973, Zanuck flew back to California. His wife, whom he had not seen in seventeen years, greeted him at the airport. Enfeebled during the flight, he literally ran to Virginia, took her hand, and walked off into a waiting limousine. After an unpleasant scene, Genevieve was sent off. She never saw Zanuck again. Back at the house, it became apparent that Zanuck was happy to be in the domain where he always had been the center of attention. He virtually disappeared from public life, seemingly content to putter around the house, watch TV, and dote on his two Yorkshire terriers. As his mental condition deteriorated, he needed constant attention, but Virginia seemed not to resent the role of caring for a senile, sometimes incontinent spouse. When Philip Dunne called in 1978 Virginia said she had read her husband portions of Dunne's memoir in progress. DFZ thought Dunne "had been much too kind to [his] old boss." Today, she told Dunne, was a good day. Darryl was excited about going with his nurse to the Hamburger Hamlet for a malted. Hearing this, Dunne sadly thought of the words he had included in one of his triumphs with DFZ, *David and Bathsheba:* "The Beauty of Israel is slain upon thy high places: How are the mighty fallen."[34]

Some people still remembered him around his birthday. In 1975 old friend Irving Berlin sent him a card with a gift of an Irving Hoffman caricature of the songwriter. But the world of Berlin and Hollywood was now a hazy memory. His hair turned snow white, like his mother's, and as he aged, Zanuck seemed to shrink into himself. In October 1979, he was hospitalized for pneumonia. Soon he was placed on a respirator, and his wife and children gathered around for the death vigil.

Like a government preparing for the funeral of an ex–head of state, the studio readied itself for Zanuck's death. Jet Fore, the Publicity Manager, alerted Fox's employees that Zanuck was close to death. Then, like the more impersonal corporation it, like all the studios, had become, he got to the issues at hand: "realizing the deadlines that most of you are on because of the time factor therein," Fore thoughtfully provided "a fact sheet relevant to Mr. Zanuck's death." He concluded by saying "When/if it happens, someone from Twentieth Century-Fox's publicity department will call you and fill in all the blanks."[35] Even with death, this was a different culture of Hollywood.

Zanuck died on December 22, 1979. A private funeral was held in

Los Angeles, with Orson Welles delivering the eulogy. After praising Zanuck's gifts ("Of all the big boss producers, Darryl was unquestionably the man with the greatest gifts") Welles paid him a special personal tribute. He knew, he said, that:

> if I did something really outrageous, that if I committed some abominable crime, which I believe is in most of us to do under the right circumstances, that if I were guilty of something unspeakable, and if all the police in the world were after me, there was one man and only one man I would come to and that was Darryl. He would not have made me a speech about the good of the industry or the good of the studio. . . . He would have hid me under the bed.[36]

The eulogies and assessments continue to come in. Elia Kazan, winner of two Best Director Oscars and the greatest director of the postwar theater, said of Zanuck that "everyone who worked for him respected him. So did I." He called Zanuck "the best executive I've ever known."[37] Yet in 1993, when *Weekly Variety* assessed his career, it presented its readership with a rather different verdict. While admitting that "no detail was too large or small" for the man who "ran Fox remarkably free of interference from its New York owners," nevertheless "Zanuck was less visionary than editor." In that publication's estimation, "his colleagues in skirt-chasing and gambling, Selznick—not to mention Samuel Goldwyn and the angelic Irving Thalberg—[are] the more admired today."[38] Many of the creative personnel who worked with and for Zanuck—such as Philip Dunne, Robert Wise, and Gregory Peck—would be puzzled by such an appraisal. Shortly before he died, Dunne summed up his bewilderment at how history had treated Darryl Zanuck: "no Hollywood personality has been so maligned, in history and fiction, as has Darryl Zanuck since his death in 1979. He is usually described or portrayed as an arrogant and tasteless boor, a sadistic bully who, in one worthless 'biography,' enjoyed torturing various nameless 'writers of the day' in an imagined hot seat. Nothing could be further from the truth."[39] In Dunne's estimation, Darryl F. Zanuck was "the most talented producer in the history of the movies."[40]

Perhaps the problem people had in seeing Zanuck as the equal of his rivals was uncovered by a *New York Times* reviewer who found that "he lived too long to be sentimentalized . . . his flaws were well known."[41] Thalberg was canonized because he died at thirty-seven. Selznick, as determined to write his own obituary as he was to meddle in others' scripts, predicted that his tragedy would be that when he died, people would know he had reached his peak at thirty-seven with *Gone With the Wind*. But, if they cared to try (and they didn't seem so inclined), writers could not come up with a sad, noble label to attach to Zanuck. And without such a label, they had trouble according him stature.

Further, few people really understand what producers—or this producer—did to shape a film. In *Hollywood: The Movie Colony, The Movie Makers* Leo Rosten suggested the question "What is a producer?" is best answered with the Talmudic rejoinder of "What kind of producer?" In fiction, a producer is presented as a lucky, vulgar, shrewd buffoon who, with little insight into what makes a story work, is canny enough to know, if not art, then the way to exploit human nature and frailty to capitalize on the creative work of others. Zanuck? Where did Zanuck fit into this equation? In a word, he was an anomaly. He was a native-born Protestant from the Midwest in an industry and culture defined by immigrants or first-generation Jews. Where Zanuck learned about what it means to be American from a grandfather who had fought Indians, other moguls found in the different mix of East Coast, urban centers. Previous histories of Hollywood have misread both Zanuck's character and, with less justification, his ability. Often they have conflated aspects of his unique creative gifts with selected facets of his public character: the tabloid later years of his private life; the mistresses; the entourage; the aging mogul who couldn't quite pull himself up in the awful photograph, shirtless, chinning himself on a trapeze at Ciro's. Instead of the creative achievements most of his co-workers knew were his legacy, following Joyce Carol Oates's observation that a modern life's history is more "pathography" than "biography," they have written of Zanuck's pathological aspects: of his alleged sexual appetites, his cruel practical jokes, or his sometimes oblique approach to English that led Eddie Cantor to refer to him as "Sam Goldwyn without the accent."

No single theory or model exists that can explain anyone's life, certainly not one as complex as Darryl Francis Zanuck's. While Thornton Wilder could, in *The Eighth Day,* note that "Nothing is more interesting than the inquiry as to how creativity operates in anyone, in everyone," few seem to have applied this to the life of Zanuck. I take comfort, however, from an observation made not by the very American Wilder, but by a citizen of Zanuck's other adopted country, Jean-Paul Sartre. In *Search for a Method,* seeking to understand how a prosaic background still manages to "produce" an astonishingly original figure like Paul Valéry, Sartre observed the following: "[Paul] Valéry is a petit bourgeois intellectual, no doubt about it. But not every petit bourgeois intellectual is Valéry."[42]

If Sartre used this *aperçu* to point out the heuristic shortcomings of Marxist theory, I bring it up to raise a similar methodological issue. After employing a number of models and theories about history, biography, authorship, cultural work, after all the data I could muster—the corporate memos, interviews, films, newspapers, and legal files—have been culled and searched again, I have insisted in this book that the overall context for evaluating Zanuck's professional worth was the possibilities of the organizational culture out of which he operated. However, one must also factor in the hunch, the guesswork, the nonempirical instinct that any writer starts with and that can be returned to in a conclusion only after marshaling and reconsidering all of these possibilities. In Zanuck's case, I return to what first drew him to movies, his trinity of story, story, story. Whatever power he accrued and then lost, whatever awards and honors were accorded him in his fifty-year career, behind his relentless energy and the force of his authority was a simple fact: he had a story to tell, and he knew how to tell it. From the first, the young man from Wahoo, Nebraska, was a teller of tales. Nothing in his background, environment, or training suggested he could do what he came to do, or aspire to even a small portion of what he eventually accomplished. To Zanuck, it was always the stories that counted.

At times, though history books have suggested otherwise, the very concept of major films could be traced directly to him. Directors like John Ford, perhaps chafing under the authority of a man like Zanuck, went out of their way to deny all but the smallest creative power to most producers. Ford made an exception in Zanuck's case for the simple reason that he felt that "Zanuck was a genius." Zanuck was reported to be furious that in *Prisoner of Shark Island,* many of the touches lauded by one critic as evidence of Ford's genius were in fact the result of Zanuck's direct editorial intervention. As Nunnally Johnson recalls:

> This woman [film critic] chose four points which I happened to know all about. One was a big cut which to her was an example of Ford's elliptical directing, which I knew was a cut that Zanuck had made with Ford screaming like a banshee against it.[43]

Though the public would never know this, the major architect of the destiny of every single Fox film was Zanuck. In *How Green Was My Valley,* Huw says that there is no fence around time, that we can go back if we can remember. We should keep this in mind when trying to gauge Zanuck's abilities and his impact on American culture. Zanuck's movies allow us to look past the sad last years of his life, beyond his human frailties and his professional shortcomings, and see a distinctly American type: the natural. Zanuck had a lot in common with another natural, his good friend Irving Berlin. Both were rumored to be fronts for someone else's work: such poorly educated people couldn't possibly produce such wonderful music or make such brilliant films. Like another poorly educated American original, Ernest Hemingway, Zanuck was "less freighted with cultural baggage" than more conventionally educated figures, so he could "fashion with little resistance or waste the new . . . tools the modern experience demanded."[44]

Even if his work appeared to be unadorned, spontaneous, even raw, it was carefully thought out and meticulously crafted. Good movies don't get made any other way. But this same liberating unorthodoxy that freed Zanuck to create with little concern for previous standards had its downside. Zanuck's ideas could be rather naive, the result of an absence of a certain kind of critical thinking that often arises out of formal education. Lacking a larger historical perspective about what he was creating, Zanuck was capable of stubbornly understating what his work owed to past standards.

Fittingly, the last project he was working on—and had been working on since the early 1960s, before his mental deterioration made this impossible—was a script for what would be the greatest Zanuck film ever: *The Day Christ Died.* In a 1960 interview he pitched the film:

> This picture would be different from any biblical picture that has ever been made. . . . The whole story takes place in 24 hours . . . it's a thriller, a Hitchcock suspense story. The plot is just a bunch of men who tried to kill a guy who happened to be Jesus. . . . And some of it's very funny—they're not sure when they capture him—maybe he *is* the son of God. . . . You see the real star is Judas, he's the real star in my version.

"All you hear in the end," he says, "is the distant nails being driven into the cross. . . . I wanted Hitch [Alfred Hitchcock] to direct it, but he's got two projects that he's signed for. . . . I'm talking also to Jacques Clouzot. . . ."[45]

The voice trails off. We see him pacing about his green office, gesturing emphatically, acting out all the parts. Darryl F. Zanuck. If John Ford was right that when he got to heaven, he would find a sign that read "Produced by Darryl F. Zanuck," then maybe Zanuck can get his story of Christ made, yet.

I jump, one last time, to 1972. Gregory Peck and his wife, Veronique, are dining out in the Oak Room at New York's Plaza Hotel. Scanning the room, Peck spies his old sponsor and friend Darryl Zanuck dining with his companion Genevieve. Peck recalls, "I think his strength had declined, and he didn't look quite the same. And by that time the system had completely changed [and] he was pretty much out of the picture." Touched by his old friend's vulnerability, Peck told his wife, "I'm going over to him and say to this man that I'm grateful that he gave me such a wonderful start in my career, that he gave me so many opportunities, and that I have great pride and satisfaction in the work that we did."

Returning to his table after thanking Zanuck, Peck told his wife that Zanuck had tears in his eyes. For the moment, Zanuck was once again Zanuck, and Genevieve had to acknowledge this: "He looked over at her, and she paid close attention." He told Veronique, "I'm so glad I did that. I think it meant something to him." Thinking back on Zanuck's life, the images that pass before our eyes are not of an old, ill, and confused man sitting with a surly, self-involved companion. Rather, they are from his films—over a thousand of them.

That was the last time Gregory Peck saw Darryl Zanuck. Thinking of the encounter, the actor mused: "if he burned out, he certainly burned brightly for a long time."[46]

Notes

THE FOLLOWING COLLECTIONS were consulted in the preparation of this book. At the University of California at Los Angeles: Twentieth Century-Fox Script and Legal; Kenneth Macgowan; RKO. At the University of Southern California, The Doheny Library: Warner Bros.; Philip Dunne; Edward G. Robinson. At the Margaret Herrick Library of the Academy of Motion Picture Arts and Sciences: William Wyler, Hedda Hopper, George Schlaifer, Sol Dolgin, George Cukor. At the Louis B. Mayer Library of the American Film Institute: the Darryl F. Zanuck Collection.

ABBREVIATIONS

AFI	American Film Institute, LB Mayer Library
AMPAS	Academy of Motion Picture Arts and Sciences, The Margaret Herrick Library
DFZ	Darryl F. Zanuck
EGR	Edward G. Robinson Collection, Doheny Library, USC
EK	Elia Kazan
EP	Ernst Pascal
FN	Frank Nugent
GC	George Cukor Collection, AMPAS

HH	Hedda Hopper, AMPAS
HK	Henry King, AMPAS
JF	John Ford
KM	Kenneth Macgowan Collection, UCLA
LT	Lamar Trotti
NJ	Nunnally Johnson
OP	Otto Preminger
PCA	Production Code Administration, AMPAS
PD	Philip Dunne Collection, Doheny Library, USC
RK	Ray Klune
RM	Rouben Mamoulian
TCF	Twentieth Century-Fox Collection, UCLA
WSM	W. Somerset Maugham
WW	William Wyler Collection, AMPAS

INTRODUCTION. THE MARK OF ZANUCK

1. Vincent Canby, "Zanuck, the Boy from Wahoo," Los Angeles *Herald Examiner*, 8 January 1980, p. E5.

2. Allen Rivkin, quoted in James R. Silke, *Here's Looking at You Kid: Fifty Years of Fighting, Working and Dreaming at Warner Brothers* (Boston: Little, Brown, 1976), p. 64.

3. "One-Man Studio," *Time*, 12 June 1950, p. 64.

4. Hortense Powdermaker, *Hollywood the Dream Factory: An Anthropologist Looks at the Movie-Makers* (Boston: Little, Brown, 1950), p. 39 (emphasis mine).

5. In Powdermaker, *Hollywood,* p. 3.

6. Kevin Starr, *Material Dreams: Southern California Through the 1920s* (New York: Oxford University Press, 1990), p. 176.

7. Bill Desowitz, "Darryl F. Zanuck: The Twentieth Century Fox," *The Hollywood Reporter*, 13 November 1984, p. 2.

8. Orson Welles, "Zanuck Eulogy," *Los Angeles Times,* 28 December, 1979.

9. Richard Zanuck, interview with author, February 1994, Beverly Hills, California.

10. William Wellman, *A Short Time for Insanity: An Autobiography* (New York: Hawthorn Books, 1974), p. 28.

11. Edward Leggewie, interview with the author, 3 January 1995, Nice, France.

12. Ibid.

13. Celeste Holm, interview with the author, January 1995, New York, NY.

14. In *Backstory: Interviews with Screenwriters of Hollywood's Golden Age,* ed. Pat McGilligan (Berkeley: University of California Press, 1986), p. 76.

15. Gregory Peck, interview with the author, 11 March 1994, Los Angeles, California.

16. Nunnally Johnson, *Oral History*, vol. 1. AMPAS, pp. 37–38.

17. Dorris Johnson and Ellen Leventhal, eds., *The Letters of Nunnally Johnson* (New York: Knopf, 1981), p. 38.

18. In Marlys J. Harris, *The Zanucks of Hollywood: The Dark Legacy of an American Dynasty* (New York: Crown, 1989), p. 70.

19. "One-Man Studio," p. 65.

20. Daniel Selznick, "Growing Up in Hollywood," *M. Inc.*, February 1991, p. 93.

21. In Harris, *The Zanucks of Hollywood,* p. 62.

22. DFZ to Jessell and McCall, memo, 7 May 1946, *Dancing in the Dark* (a.k.a. *The Bandwagon*), box FX-PRS–1183, TCF Collection, UCLA, p. 1.

23. Ibid., shooting final, dated 29 November 1948.

24. For an analysis of how the biopic shaped a particular version of public history, see George Custen, *Bio/Pics: How Hollywood Constructed Public History* (New Brunswick, N.J.: Rutgers University Press, 1992).

25. In John Kobal, *People Will Talk* (New York: Knopf, 1985), p. 544.

26. Jean Negelescu, quoted in Stephen M. Silverman, *The Fox That Got Away: The Last Days of the Zanuck Dynasty at Twentieth Century-Fox* (Secaucus, N.J.: Lyle Stuart, 1988), p. 71.

27. Bobbie McLean, interviewed by Tom Stemple, *Oral History*, p. 37. AFI Library.

28. Philip Dunne, "Darryl from A to Z," *American Film* 9, no. 19 (July-August, 1984): 47.

29. KM to DFZ, 3 September 1938, Macgowan Collection, UCLA, box 29, folder 11.

30. In Otto Friedrich, *City of Nets: A Portrait of Hollywood in the 1940s* (New York: Harper & Row, 1987), p. 179.

31. Leo C. Rosten, *Hollywood: The Movie Colony, the Movie Makers* (New York: Harcourt, Brace and Company, 1941), p. 244.

CHAPTER 1. EXCAVATING ZANUCK

1. In Cass Warner Sperling and Cork Millner, *Hollywood Be Thy Name: The Warner Brothers Story* (Rocklin, Calif.: Prima, 1995), p. 167.

2. Little Darryl Zanuck as Indian maid is cited in Alva Johnston's *New Yorker* profile, "The Wahoo Boy," 10 November 1934, p. 27. It is also cited in the 1954 issue of *Current Biography*, p. 674.

3. Mel Gussow, *Don't Say Yes Until I Finish Talking: A Biography of Darryl F. Zanuck* (New York: Doubleday, 1971), p. 10.

4. We frequently see this young-man-meets-his-future-destiny motif in Zanuck's films: as when the future Lord Nelson stares out to sea in *Lloyds of London*; or, on American soil, in *Young Mr. Lincoln*, in which, as director John Ford describes him, "a jack legged young lawyer" displays in his judgment and action the qualities that would enshrine him in the American pantheon.

5. See Norman Zierold, *The Moguls: Hollywood's Merchants of Myth* (Los Angeles: Silman-James Press, 1991 [orig. 1969]), p. 258.

6. Stephen M. Silverman, *The Fox That Got Away: The Last Days of the Zanuck Dynasty at Twentieth Century-Fox* (Secaucus, N.J.: Lyle Stuart, 1988), p. 34.

7. In Gussow, *Don't Say Yes*, p. 8.

8. Silverman, *The Fox That Got Away*, p. 35.

9. Zanuck had a difficult relationship with his mother. He must have resented her refusal—or inability—to defend him against the attacks of his abusive stepfather. Though Louise Zanuck Norton lived the rest of her life in Los Angeles, her grandson Richard remembers meeting her only a handful of times. (Interview with the author, 22 May 1996, Beverly Hills, California.)

10. See Gussow, *Don't Say Yes*, p. 12.

11. Ibid. A family scrapbook in the Howard Hanson House, in Wahoo, suggests 1890 as the date Torpin settled in Oakdale.

12. Darryl Zanuck, "Los Angeles to Oakdale, Observations of Darryl Zanuck, Age 11, on His Trip from Los Angeles, Calif.," *Oakdale Sentinel*, 17 July 1914. Cited in Marlys J. Harris, *The Zanucks of Hollywood: The Dark Legacy of an American Dynasty* (New York: Crown, 1989), p. 17.

13. In Harris, *The Zanucks of Hollywood*, p. 17.

14. Richard Zanuck, interview with the author, 2 February 1994, Berverly Hills, California.

15. In Gussow, *Don't Say Yes*, p. 11.

16. In Leonard Mosley, *Zanuck: The Rise and Fall of Hollywood's Last Tycoon* (Boston: Little, Brown, 1984), p. 14.

17. In Silverman, *The Fox That Got Away*, p. 35.

18. In Gussow, *Don't Say Yes*, p. 8.

19. Howard Hanson House, Wahoo, Nebraska. Zanuck family scrapbook.

20. Interestingly, as he would do with so many other proven hits, he would remake this tale, as a 1927 Warner Brothers film with hard-working Monte Blue in the lead. In Mosley, *Zanuck*, p. 14. For the background of Wahoo during Zanuck's youth, see *The History of Saunders County*; and for the background of Oakdale, see Eugene Budde, "A Penny a Head at Torpin's Loft," in *The History of Antelope County, Nebraska 1868–1985* (Dallas, Tex.: Curtis Media, 1986).

21. Like many of the early dates in Zanuck's life, there is disagreement about his age at the time of enlistment. Zanuck apparently told Gussow he enlisted in 1916 (*Don't Say Yes*, p. 13), but most other sources date this at 1917. Quotations from pp. 15, 16.

22. Army C.O. # 36, 5 March 1918. At the Howard Hanson House, Wahoo, Nebraska.

23. In Gussow, *Don't Say Yes*, p. 16.

24. Ibid., p. 17.

25. "Oakdale Boy Sees Real Fighting," letter from Darryl Zanuck, 136 Amb. Co., 109 Sanitary Train, A.E.F., Le Mans, France, 28 November 1918, in *Oakdale Sentinel*, 18 December 1918.

26. In Gussow, *Don't Say Yes*, p. 18.

27. In Mosley, *Zanuck*, p. 25.

28. According to Mosley (ibid., pp. 25–26), Torpin's illness at the time of Zanuck's homecoming robbed him of the presence, and support, of the one figure who might have convinced Darryl to stay put.

29. In Gussow, *Don't Say Yes*, p. 18.

30. Frank S. Nugent, "Meet Mr. Darryl Zanuck," *New York Times*, 21 April 1935. See Gussow, *Don't Say Yes*, p. 18, on Zanuck's short stay in New York.

31. In Harris, *The Zanucks of Hollywood*, p. 18.

32. Ibid. Director Frank Capra and noted Los Angeles District Attorney Burton Fitts were also alumni. Some of Zanuck's classmates would go on to

be a world-famous operatic baritone, a governor of California, and an air force general. More than thirty years after they first met, they would all come together at a gala tribute to Zanuck. See Jimmy Starr, "Who's Who of Hollywood in Gala Tribute to Zanuck," *Los Angeles Herald and Express*, 23 November 1953, p. B1.

33. Both Gregory Peck (11 March 1994, Los Angeles, California) and Art Director George Davis (12 August 1995, Santa Monica, California), in separate interviews with me, recall the almost atavistic quality of Zanuck's energy.

CHAPTER 2. ZANUCK THE WRITER

1. "Closeups," *Photoplay*, August 1915, p. 121.

2. The term *feature* was coined by *The Motion Picture News* in 1913, and was inherited from vaudeville's cosmology. It had initially referred to any film (or act) accorded special publicity value: that is, an act that was featured above the others on the mixed bill of fare. But it was also used to contrast the new multireel films with their shorter predecessors. In 1909, some "features" ran twenty minutes (two reels). From 1909 on, the length of the "typical" film increased each year.

3. See Douglas Gomery's *Shared Pleasures: A History of Movie Presentation in the United States* (Madison: University of Wisconsin Press, 1992) on Balaban and Katz's revolutionary approach to theater construction. See William Leach's *Land of Desire: Merchants, Power, and the Rise of a New American Culture* (New York: Pantheon, 1993) for histories of film adapting industrial techniques. I do not mean to imply here that the increased demands for features were the monolithic cause of the expansion of what was a small industry into an organized, larger one. See Eileen Bowser, *The Transformation of Cinema: 1907–1915* (New York: Scribner's, 1990) for some of the multivalent factors that could explain the emergence of American film into a new phase.

4. For the most part, until D. W. Griffith and Thomas Ince emerged, American writers wishing to believe film could be the equal of theater or the novel had only to look at the work of certain of their European counterparts to see the possibilities opened up by the feature. Pastrone's sophisticated and lengthy history of the Carthaginian epoch, *Cabiria* (1914), with its impressive sets, sprawling narrative, and historical value pointed out one direction in which the cinema might head. See Charles Affron and Mirella Jona Affron, *Sets in Motion: Art Direction and Film Narrative* (New Brunswick, N.J.: Rutgers University Press, 1995), pp. 96–100.

5. In *Before the Nickelodeon: Edwin S. Porter and the Edison Manufac-turing Company* (Berkeley: University of California Press, 1991), Charles Musser suggests that early filmmakers filmed their subject matter presum-ing that audiences were already familiar with it. Thus, when films started to tell more complex stories, or presented actions outside the knowledge of many spectators, this strategy of "prior familiarity" gave rise to a kind of cri-sis in comprehension. Some of this was solved by agreeing on continuity conventions, but other ways of coping—like hiring a live lecturer to inter-pret the film after it had been projected—were also used. As *Billboard* mag-azine noted in early 1908, "the explanation of the pictures by an efficient talker adds much to their realism" (in Musser, p. 395).

6. Cited in Lizzie Francke, *Script Girls: Women Screenwriters in Holly-wood* (London: British Film Institute, 1994), pp. 6, 8.

7. In Richard Koszarski, *An Evening's Entertainment: The Age of the Silent Feature, 1915–1928* (New York: Scribner's, 1990), p. 104. Or tenable only for the rare director like D. W. Griffith or Erich von Stroheim who preferred to work this way, and had the clout to do it.

8. Ibid., p. 105.

9. The first feature film's frequent unauthorized adaptation of hit novels (notably a 1907 version of *Ben Hur*) caused both the film industry and the American legal system to reconsider the status of the film story and the per-son who crafted it. In 1912, partly as a result of Hollywood's tendency to produce bowdlerized versions of literary properties without paying either royalties or acknowledging credit, American copyright laws were amended so that films were recognized to be "products of authors rather than stories that just happened to be made up by actors on the screen." In Francke, *Script Girls*, p. 5.

10. Sumiko Higashi, *Cecil B. De Mille and American Culture: The Silent Era* (Berkeley: University of California Press, 1995), p. 29.

11. Jesse L. Lasky, "Production Problems," in *The Story of Film: As Told by Leaders of the Industry to the Students of the Graduate School of Business Administration, George F. Baker Foundation, Harvard University*, ed. Joseph P. Kennedy (Chicago: A. W. Shaw, 1927), p. 101.

12. In Patrick McGilligan, *Backstory: Interviews with Screenwriters of Hollywood's Golden Age* (Berkeley: University of California Press, 1986), pp. 1–2.

13. As Douglas Gomery has noted: "It was through the theatrical end of the industry, constituting some 90 percent of all their assets, that the Big Five [Warner's, Fox, MGM, Paramount, and RKO] operated as a collusive unit, protecting each other, shutting out all potential competitors, and

guaranteeing profits for even the worst performer, usually RKO" (*The Hollywood Studio System* [New York: St. Martin's Press, 1986], p. 14).

14. In Koszarski, *An Evening's Entertainment*, p. 9.

15. Darryl F. Zanuck, *Beyond the Valley of Reason*, n.d., AFI, LB Mayer Library, DFZ Collection, box 14, "forward," p. 1.

16. Ibid., p. 2.

17. Darryl F. Zanuck, "Say It with Dreams," *Habit and Other Short Stories* (Los Angeles: Times-Mirror Press, 1923), pp. 134–35. In fact, since Zanuck's grandparents eventually relocated to Southern California, he returned to Nebraska only for premieres (like the one for *Wilson*), when he could act the part of small-town boy who made good.

18. Alva Johnston, "Zanuck Crashes the Movies," *Film Weekly*, 9 July 1938, p. 2. Another self-taught writer of this era who used O. Henry as a guide was Ayn Rand. See *The New Yorker*, 24 July 1995, p. 73.

19. Hollywood's own gossip columnists—though not its fan magazines—surfaced only after Winchell's clout had made this an acceptable part of journalism. Louella Parsons, enjoying the powerful patronage of William Randolph Hearst, arrived first on the scene, in 1925. Initially squired by Hearst's mistress, actress Marion Davies, she had the field virtually to herself until Hedda Hopper, in 1938, began her syndicated column for Hearst's rival, the *Los Angeles Times*. Physically contrastive, and loathing each other, Parsons and Hopper (and their less powerful colleagues) wielded enormous influence; they were forces with whom all the studios had to reckon.

20. In Neal Gabler, *Winchell: Gossip, Power, and the Culture of Celebrity* (New York: Knopf, 1994), p. 65.

21. Ibid., p. 71.

22. Alva Johnston, "The Wahoo Boy–II," *The New Yorker*, 17 November 1934, p. 24.

23. R. P. White, "The Miracle Man of Hollywood," *Los Angeles Times Magazine*, 4 November 1934, p. 2.

24. Alva Johnston, who did a two-part profile of Zanuck for *The New Yorker*, claimed elsewhere in a 1938 article in *Film Weekly* that it was in the army, "on the advice of a major, an admirer of Zanuck's correspondence in *Stars and Stripes*, that the boy decided to become an author."

25. Darryl Zanuck, "Does Love Last?" unpublished short story (late 1920), p. 1, AFI, LB Mayer Library, Darryl Zanuck Collection, box 14.

26. Although a number of sources name this as his first professional fiction, I have been unable to turn up the full citation of this work. A copy

does not appear with any of the Zanuck papers at the AFI, or at the Zanuck Museum in Wahoo, Nebraska.

27. See "For Men Only (A Comedy-Drama of Adventure)," unpublished story (1921) by Darryl Francis Zanuck and Ralph Dietrich, AFI, LB Mayer Library, Darryl Zanuck Collection.

28. Intriguingly, it was the eccentric Macfadden who, in addition to giving Zanuck an important boost to his career, also gave another icon of the era, Walter Winchell, his major career lift by hiring him for his groundbreaking tabloid, *The Graphic*. Over a thirty-year period, Zanuck's and Winchell's lives, and world views, would cross at many key junctures.

29. In Mel Gussow, *Don't Say Yes Until I Finish Talking: A Biography of Darryl F. Zanuck* (New York: Doubleday, 1971), pp. 19–20. Lloyd's film (with Jackie Coogan as Oliver and Lon Chaney as Fagin) was released in 1922.

30. In ibid., p. 19.

31. In ibid., p. 39. Zanuck contended that one of the reasons he worked so fast at Warner Brothers was that if you didn't, "they would take the camera away."

32. Nunnally Johnson, *Oral History*, AMPAS, vol. 1, p. 45.

33. In Lawrence Levine, *Highbrow/Lowbrow: The Emergence of Cultural Hierarchy in America* (Cambridge: Harvard University Press, 1988), p. 46.

34. One source claims that at least half of the 25,000 American film scenarios registered for copyright between 1912 and 1929 were written by women (Ann Martin and Virginia Clark, *What Women Wrote: Scenarios, 1912–1919* [University Publications of America, Cinema History Microfilm Series, 1987], cited in Francke, *Script Girls*, p. 27).

35. This was Irving Thalberg's innovation, and he felt that through this method (one that, from most writers' perspectives, created competition rather than teamwork) one could increase productivity as well as enhance the chance of coming up with a well-crafted scenario.

36. In McGilligan, *Backstory*, p. 1.

37. The data from Leo Rosten's 1938 survey of Hollywood (published in 1941), drawn largely from the salaries of prestige writers working at four studios (Fox, Warner's, MGM, and Paramount), suggest that as a group, while these writers were well paid (the median salary was $25,000 per year), their scale was far below that of comparably placed actors, directors, or producers. (Today, this is no longer true.) The junior writer could receive as little as $50 a week.

38. Hortense Powdermaker, *Hollywood the Dream Factory: An Anthropologist Looks at the Movie-Makers* (Boston: Little, Brown, 1950), p. 151.

39. Darryl F. Zanuck biography, AMPAS biography file, microfiche, c. 1935.

40. Because of his social pretensions and the disdainful way he treated writers, Chaplin was one of the few creative figures Zanuck detested. As Zanuck recalled, "He would love to use words he looked up in the dictionary—to crush us. Words like *outré.* . . . Very superior, you know." In Gussow, *Don't Say Yes*, p. 28.

41. Johnston, "Wahoo Boy–II," p. 27. Zanuck's serial output in Gussow, *Don't Say Yes*, p. 29.

42. Ibid., p. 24.

43. In Ian Hamilton, *Writers in Hollywood: 1915–1951* (New York: Carroll and Graf, 1990), p. 20.

44. See Darryl Francis Zanuck, "First Draft Continuity *Money to Burns*," 7 July 1923, RKO Collection (003), scripts box RKO-S-7, UCLA Film and Television Library.

45. Darryl F. Zanuck, "Working Synopsis for *When Knighthood Was in Tower*," p. 2, 17 December 1923, RKO Collection, ibid.

46. In H. C. Witwer, "Sherlock's Home," *Cosmopolitan,* April 1923, p. 80.

47. *The Telephone Girl Series,* chap. 7, "For the Love of Mike," continuity by Darryl Zanuck, 21 February 1924, RKO Collection, UCLA.

48. "Darryl F. Zanuck," *Examiner*, 6 May 1951, p. 2.

49. In Marlys J. Harris, *The Zanucks of Hollywood: The Dark Legacy of an American Dynasty* (New York: Crown, 1989), p. 92.

50. In Gussow, *Don't Say Yes*, p. 21.

51. In ibid., p. 22. The script was probably based on Zanuck's story "The Scarlet Ladder." (See Leonard Mosley, *Zanuck: The Rise and Fall of Hollywood's Last Tycoon* [Boston: Little, Brown, 1984], p. 36.) Many saw Wurtzel as an unpleasant, tyrannical figure. He was, however, a competent administrator, and would remain with Zanuck at Fox, assuming responsibility for all "B" production.

52. Richard Zanuck, interview with the author, 2 February 1994, Beverly Hills, California.

53. In Cass Warner Sperling and Cork Millner, *Hollywood Be Thy Name: The Warner Brothers Story* (Rocklin, Calif.: Prima, 1994), p. 167.

54. "One-Man Studio," *Time*, 12 June 1950, p. 66.

55. In Gussow, *Don't Say Yes*, p. 21.

56. "Habit" was, in part, a reworking of one of Zanuck's earliest efforts, the unpublished "The Mute of Chinatown—Without Words," which Zanuck registered in March 1922. At the AFI, LB Mayer Library, DFZ Collection, box 14.

57. Zanuck, *Habit and Other Short Stories*, p. 11.

58. Ibid., p. 18.

59. *New York Times*, 15 April 1923.

60. Though he was definitive in his opinions about director's work, according to Philip Dunne, the reason Zanuck didn't become a director was that he "possibly feare[d] that he couldn't bring [it] off." In Philip Dunne, *Take Two: A Life in Movies and Politics* (New York: Limelight Editions, 1992), p. 14. All his life he attached a kind of mystical quality to what the director did. When, uncredited, he finally directed a substantial portion of his production of *The Longest Day*, his son, Richard, recalls his surprise: "And I remember after the first day, because I was there for the beginning of the film, he was almost boyish, he said, 'This is ridiculous, this is so easy. All my life I've been baffled by this. It's the easiest thing in the world. This is a joke.'" Interview with the author, 2 February 1994, Beverly Hills, California.

61. In Harris, *The Zanucks of Hollywood*, p. 27.

62. In Clive Hirschorn, *The Warner Bros. Story* (New York: Crown, 1979), p. 20.

63. It was for the very reason that the dog's "meaning" as a film figure was determined not by his personality but by the context of the stories in which he appeared and the editing structures supporting them (and was thus loosely in accord with certain theories of film montage) that some Soviet directors named the dog as their favorite film actor.

64. Jack L. Warner (with Dean Jennings), *My First Hundred Years in Hollywood: An Autobiography* (New York: Random House, 1964), p. 129.

65. Ibid., p. 132.

CHAPTER 3. "THE HARDEST-WORKING LITTLE GUY":
ZANUCK AT WARNER BROTHERS

1. Jack L. Warner (with Dean Jennings), *My First Hundred Years in Hollywood: An Autobiography* (New York: Random House, 1964), p. 27.

2. Neal Gabler, *An Empire of Their Own: How the Jews Invented Hollywood* (New York: Crown, 1988), p. 143.

3. In ibid., p. 120.

4. In ibid., p. 239.

5. Warner, *My First Hundred Years*, pp. 129–30.

6. Darryl Francis Zanuck, "My Buddy," p. 4, AFI, LB Mayer Library, DFZ Collection, box 5.

7. Ibid., p. 54.

8. This ending would not be used here, but would be recycled in next year's Rin Tin Tin film *Clash of the Wolves*. Though Charles Logue is credited with this scenario, the Zanuck ending discarded from "My Buddy" is used here. This suggests the possibility that as early as 1925, Zanuck was supervising others' scripts.

9. Warner, *My First Hundred Years*, p. 130.

10. See Clive Hirschorn, *The Warner Bros. Story* (New York: Crown, 1979), p. 36.

11. In ibid., p. 22.

12. In ibid., p. 26.

13. AFI, LB Mayer Library, DFZ Collection, box 14, *Beyond the Valley of Reason*, p. 2.

14. In Mel Gussow, *Don't Say Yes Until I Finish Talking: A Biography of Darryl F. Zanuck* (New York: Doubleday, 1971), p. 40.

15. In ibid., p. 38.

16. William Reynolds, interview with the author, 23 May 1994, Santa Monica, California.

17. In Gussow, *Don't Say Yes*, p. 91.

18. Marlys J. Harris, *The Zanucks of Hollywood: The Dark Legacy of an American Dynasty* (New York: Crown, 1989), p. 30.

19. Gussow is imprecise, merely noting that Zanuck told him: "One day . . . Jack Warner called him in and said, 'You know [Raymond] Shrock is out,' and then added, 'Well, you're in as head of production.'" (*Don't Say Yes*, p. 42.) Rudy Behlmer (*Memo from Darryl F. Zanuck: The Golden Years at Twentieth Century-Fox* [New York: Grove Press, 1993], p. 263) has this occurring in 1928, while Schatz (*The Genius of the System: Hollywood Filmmaking in the Studio Era* [New York: Pantheon, 1988]) dates it at 1927. Additionally, when Zanuck became supervisor of both Warner's and First National, Schatz actually gives this occurrence two different dates, stating (on p. 66) that he became "full-blown production chief in 1929"; but later he contradicts himself and states that "Zanuck assumed command of all production in November, 1930" (p. 136). Behlmer has this latter promotion occurring in 1931 (p. 264).

20. Harris, *The Zanucks of Hollywood*, p. 30.

21. In Gussow, *Don't Say Yes*, p. 42.

22. In ibid., p. 30.

23. *Moving Picture World*, 22 October 1927, p. 475.

24. In Scott Eyman, *Ernst Lubitsch: Laughter in Paradise* (New York: Simon and Schuster, 1993), p. 13.

25. Cass Warner Sperling and Cork Millner, *Hollywood Be Thy Name: The Warner Brothers Story* (Rocklin, Calif.: Prima, 1994), p. 82.

26. Samson Raphaelson, *"Freundschaft," The New Yorker*, 11 May 1981, p. 42.

27. In Sperling and Millner, *Hollywood Be Thy Name*, p. 83.

28. In Raphaelson, *"Freundschaft,"* p. 42.

29. Ephraim Katz, "Ernst Lubitsch," *The Encyclopedia of Film* (New York: Harper Perennial, 1994), p. 849.

30. Pickford quoted in Walter Kerr, *The Silent Clowns* (New York: Alfred A. Knopf, 1975), pp. 2–3.

31. Harris, *The Zanucks of Hollywood*, p. 52.

32. Celeste Holm, interview with the author, January 1995, New York, NY.

33. Gussow, *Don't Say Yes*, p. 31.

34. In Harris, *The Zanucks of Hollywood*, p. 55.

35. In Gussow, *Don't Say Yes*, p. 34.

CHAPTER 4. "THE TALKING THING":
THE SAFE ENTERTAINMENT OF *THE JAZZ SINGER*

1. Carolyn Marvin, *When Old Technologies Were New: Thinking About Electric Communication in the Late Nineteenth Century* (New York: Oxford University Press, 1988), p. 4. It is no coincidence that a censorship with teeth arrived simultaneously with sound. The rise of the PCA was a recognition that words allied to images embodied ideas more succinctly—and more powerfully—than the silent cinema ever could.

2. According to the *Film Daily Yearbook of Motion Pictures* (1951, p. 90), by the mid-1920s, there were about 25,000 movie theaters in the United States. In 1926, yearly movie attendance was 50,000,000, rising to 57,000,000 the year of *The Jazz Singer*. By the time sound was almost fully innovated, in 1929, attendance stood at 95,000,000, nearly double its 1926 mark.

3. Samson Raphaelson, "How I Came to Write *The Jazz Singer*," in *Souvenir Programs of Twelve Classic Movies, 1927–1941*, ed. Miles Kreuger

(New York: Dover Publications, 1977 [orig 1927]). See also Scott Eyman, *The Speed of Sound: Hollywood and the Talkie Revolution, 1926–1930* (New York: Simon and Schuster, 1997).

4. In Neal Gabler, *An Empire of Their Own: How the Jews Invented Hollywood* (New York: Crown, 1988), p. 139.

5. Neal Gabler (ibid.) suggests $50,000 as the sum the Warners laid out for *The Jazz Singer*, while Clive Hirschorn (*The Warner Bros. Story* [New York: Crown, 1979], p. 34) claims the figure was $30,000.

6. According to Richard Zanuck, one person this gambit was wasted on was Warren Beatty. When Jack tried his usual "water tower" trick with the producer/actor/director, Beatty's response was that the "WB" in the studio logo stood for Warren Beatty. For once, Jack had no comeback. Richard Zanuck, interview with the author, 28 May 1996, Beverly Hills, California.

7. See *The Jazz Singer*, ed Robert Carringer (Madison: University of Wisconsin Press, 1979), p. 16.

8. *The Jazz Singer* script, title 28, AFI, LB Mayer Library, DFZ Collection, box 50.

9. In Joseph P. Kennedy, ed., *The Story of Films* (Chicago and New York: A. W. Shaw, 1927), p. 327.

10. Jessel would always insist he refused to do the film because Zanuck's change in the plot line was degrading to Jews. As he claimed in the second version of his autobiography, *The World I Lived In,* the "betrayal of the material" meant that "money or no money . . . I would not do this version." Another story suggests that when the decision was made to add musical numbers, Jessel doubled his asking price and the Warners balked. See Carringer, *The Jazz Singer*, pp. 14, 17.

11. In Eyman, *The Speed of Sound*, p. 132.

12. In ibid., p. 133.

13. In Mel Gussow, *Don't Say Yes Until I Finish Talking: A Biography of Darryl F. Zanuck* (New York: Doubleday, 1971), p. 44.

14. *Moving Picture World,* 28 May 1927, p. 253.

15. See *The Jazz Singer* file in the Warners Collection, USC, Doheny Library, "Cutting Notes on *The Jazz Singer*," 18 August 1927.

16. AFI, LB Mayer Library, *The Jazz Singer* script, DFZ Collection.

17. USC, Warner's Archives, *Jazz Singer* file, "Final Script," n.d. Edwin Schallert's article, "Vitaphone Activity in Hollywood," in *Motion Picture News*, 8 July 1927, p. 35, had referred to this prayer as "the culminating episode . . . there was a deep appeal to this denouement on the stage. It is hoped to preserve this on the screen through the Vitaphone."

18. Michael Freedland, *Jolson* (New York: Warner Books, 1971), p. 125.

19. "My Mammy" was shot with the other sound segments, in August, and could have been released as a separate Vitaphone short if *The Jazz Singer* had fizzled out at the box office. See Eyman, *Speed of Sound*, p. 13.

20. As Maltby explains "harmless entertainment":

The moguls made themselves the men who gave the public what it wanted. What the public wanted was in large part revealed by what they went to see, but the studio heads secured for themselves the vital position of determining what it was about any successful film that had appealed to audiences. ... Their attitudes permeated everything Hollywood produced, and those attitudes were chiefly influenced by a commitment to short-term profitability which geared production to the repetition of successful ingredients via generic formulae and the star system and by an equal commitment to the ideal of "harmless entertainment" which structured the expression of ideology in the American cinema. [Richard Maltby, *Harmless Entertainment: Hollywood and the Ideology of Consensus* (Metuchen, N.J.: Scarecrow Press, 1983), pp. 52–53]

21. In Tino Balio, ed., *Grand Design: Hollywood as a Modern Business Enterprise, 1930–1939* (New York: Scribner's, 1993), p. 45.

22. As Lawrence Levine has noted, the duality "progress/nostalgia" has long been a significant dynamic in American culture but "seldom has it been more central than during the decade after the First World War." See "Progress and Nostalgia: The Self-Image of the Nineteen-Twenties," in Lawrence Levine, *The Unpredictable Past: Explorations in American Cultural History* (New York: Oxford University Press, 1993), p. 191.

23. Richard Maltby, "The Production Code and the Hays Office," in Balio, ed., *Grand Design*, p. 45.

24. No author, "The Story of *The Jazz Singer*," in Kreuger, ed., *Souvenir Programs of Twelve Classic Movies, 1927–1941* (New York: Dover, 1977), p. 5.

25. "Jack's Speech on Fourth Curtain," USC, *The Jazz Singer* file, Warner Brothers Collection.

26. Cohn contract, USC, Warner Brothers Collection, *The Jazz Singer* file, letter from Darryl Zanuck to Alfred A. Cohn, 14 March 1927. As Carringer suggests, Cohn had written the scenarios for *His People* (1925), *The Cohens and the Kellys* (1926), and *Frisco Sally Levy* (1927) before drifting out of the insecurity of film employment for a civil service job with the City of Los Angeles.

27. Carringer, "Introduction," pp. 20–21.

28. Edmund Wilson, *The American Earthquake: A Documentary of the Twenties amd Thirties* (Garden City, N.Y.: Doubleday, 1958), p. 114.

29. The Warners, imitating Loews and Paramount, bought music publishers, starting with M. Witmark and Sons (owners of the works of Cohan, Romberg, and Victor Herbert). Soon after, in 1929, Warners added the Harms Music Publishing Company and a half interest in Remick Music Corporation. All this new ownership resulted in the Warners forming the Musical Publishers Corporation, a holding company composed of all their musical interests.

30. Krin Gabbard, *Jammin' at the Margins: Jazz and the American Cinema* (Chicago: University of Chicago Press, 1996), p. 17.

31. In Levine, *Unpredictable Past*, p. 184.

32. For the shifting status of Jews as ethnically and racially ambiguous, see Edward W. Said, *Orientalism* (New York: Vintage, 1978); Ella Shohat, *Israeli Cinema: East/West and the Politics of Representation* (Austin: University of Texas Press, 1989); Ella Shohat and Robert Stam, *Unthinking Eurocentrism: Multiculturalism and the Media* (New York: Routledge, 1995); and, most recently, Michael Rogin, *Blackface, White Noise: Jewish Immigrants in the Hollywood Melting Pot* (Berkeley: University of California Press, 1996), p. 12, who notes: "During the period of mass European immigration . . . the racial status of Irish, Italians, Jews and Slavs was in dispute. As anti-Semitism racialized Jews in Europe . . . immigrants to the United States were coming under the banner of a new racial invention: whiteness." This thesis is central to David Nasaw's *Going Out: The Rise and Fall of Public Amusements* (New York: Basic Books, 1993).

33. See the TCF Collection at UCLA, the *There's No Business Like Show Business* file, memo, DFZ to Irving Berlin, 17 December 1952, box FX-PRS-581.

34. "The Jazz Singer," Adaptation and Continuity by Alfred A. Cohn, in AFI, LB Mayer Library, DFZ Collection.

35. In Alfred A. Cohn, *The Jazz Singer*, in Carringer, *The Jazz Singer*, p. 83.

36. Michael Rogin also cites this anecdote in *Blackface, White Noise*, p. 286.

37. The film was remade, at Warner Brothers in 1953, with veteran Michael Curtiz directing Peggy Lee and Danny Thomas (!) in the McAvoy and Jolson roles. In 1980, Richard Fleisher directed Neil Diamond in love, this time, with *shiksa* Lucie Arnaz. This time Jake is a rock star whose cantor father, played by Laurence Olivier, is stunned at his son's career. So

were the critics, who panned the film. In an intriguing bit of analysis, Krin Gabbard suggests that since "the first *Jazz Singer* occupies a special role in American cinema, in effect establishing a set of conventions for narratives about race and Oedipal conflict in which the white hero transcends his ethnic background" by blacking up, a large number of films (seven) follow its tropes closely enough to be deemed remakes. See *Jammin' at the Margins*, pp. 37–39.

38. Michael Rogin makes the point in *Blackface, White Noise* that "by painting himself black, he washes himself white" and is thus freed from his father's world (p. 102).

39. Ibid., p. 100.

40. Richard Zanuck told me his family, nominally Methodists, never went to church. Interview with the author, 28 May 1996, Beverly Hills, California.

41. USC, Warners Collection, *The Jazz Singer* file, "Notes of Samson Raphaelson for *The Jazz Singer*," n.d.

42. "Sid.", "Review of *The Jazz Singer*," *Variety*, 12 October 1927.

CHAPTER 5. DREAMING OF THE ACTUAL WORLD: TRANSFORMING WARNER BROTHERS' STYLE

1. In Samuel Marx, *Mayer and Thalberg: The Make-Believe Saints* (Los Angeles: Samuel French, 1975), p. 100.

2. Robert C. Allen and Douglas Gomery, *Film History Theory and Practice* (New York: Knopf, 1985), p. 123.

3. Ibid. Fox's Movietone was a sound-on-film method. The Vitaphone used ten-minute records linked to the projector, and unlike Movietone it eliminated the possibility of shooting outdoors or editing *within* the sequence. Hollywood (including the Warners) switched to a sound-on-film method by 1930.

4. In addition to two silent films, *Beware of Bachelors* and *Pay As You Enter*, Zanuck's Vitaphone efforts were: as Gregory Rogers, he wrote the original story for *The Midnight Taxi*, as Melville Crossman, he wrote the proto-gangster story for *Tenderloin* and the story for *State Street Sadie*, and as Mark Canfield he provided the story for *My Man*.

5. In Mel Gussow, *Don't Say Yes Until I Finish Talking: A Biography of Darryl F. Zanuck* (New York: Doubleday, 1971), p. 45.

6. In ibid., p. 45.

7. Ibid.

8. Ibid.

9. In Gene Brown, *Movie Time: A Chronology of Hollywood and the Movie Industry from Its Beginnings to the Present* (New York: Macmillan, 1995), p. 91.

10. In Clive Hirschorn, *The Warner Bros. Story* (New York: Crown, 1979), p. 59.

11. Curtiz to Harry Warner, 22 July 1927. Personal collection of the author.

12. Darryl Zanuck, "Notes on 'Noah's Ark,'" 19 July 1927, collection of the author, p. 1. Zanuck's suggestion for the dissolve is "borrowed" from his own first Rin Tin Tin film, *Find Your Man*.

13. In Alva Johnston, "The Wahoo Boy–II," *The New Yorker*, 17 November 1934, p. 27.

14. Hirschorn, *The Warner Bros. Story*, p. 73.

15. Johnston, "Wahoo Boy–II," p. 27.

16. In Marlys J. Harris, *The Zanucks of Hollywood: The Dark Legacy of An American Dynasty* (New York: Crown, 1989), p. 31.

17. Ann Douglas, *Terrible Honesty: Mongrel Manhattan in the 1920s* (New York: Farrar, Straus & Giroux, 1994), p. 192.

18. In ibid., p. 216.

19. Thomas Schatz, *The Genius of the System: Hollywood Filmmaking in the Studio Era* (New York: Pantheon, 1988), p. 136.

20. Alva Johnston, "The Wahoo Boy," *The New Yorker*, 10 November 1934, p. 24.

21. Richard Zanuck, in *Darryl F. Zanuck: Twentieth Century Filmmaker*, a 1996 film by Kevin Burns.

22. Johnston, "Wahoo Boy," p. 25.

CHAPTER 6. A CRIMINAL TALENT

1. From *Examiner*, 1935 (Darryl F. Zanuck, biography file microfiche), AMPAS.

2. In Alva Johnston, "The Wahoo Boy," *The New Yorker*, 10 November 1934, p. 25.

3. Warner Brothers publicity encouraged viewers to become involved in this world of slang. The "Warner Bros. Press Sheet" for *Doorway to Hell* distributed to exhibitors suggested that theater managers "offer free tickets to those sending in correct definitions of the following gang terms: Hot shot = The Electric Chair, Cracked Ice = Diamonds." Warner Bros. Collection, USC, *Doorway to Hell* file.

4. The original script for *The Public Enemy* contained even grittier language. Zanuck had an exasperated Cagney tell Mae Clarke, "Shut your mouth and open your legs, for God's sake." In Leonard Mosley, *Zanuck: The Rise and Fall of Hollywood's Last Tycoon* (Boston: Little, Brown, 1984), p. 116.

5. In Marlys J. Harris, *The Zanucks of Hollywood: The Dark Legacy of an American Dynasty* (New York: Crown, 1989), p. 32.

6. Ibid.

7. Johnston, "Wahoo Boy," p. 25.

8. Ibid. Reckless or not, all these gangster films—save *Doorway*—hid the true source of the gangster's power: that, except for the individual murder here and there, they were operating within virtually the same structures and rules as the American corporation. It wasn't called "organized crime" for nothing. In fact, as Richard Maltby has suggested, much of the gangland killing stemmed from crime's *imperfect* organization. (See Richard Maltby, "A Short and Dangerous Life: The Gangster Film, 1930–1932," in *Prima Dei Codici 2 Alle porte di Hays* [Venice: Edizioni Biennale, 1991].)

9. Johnston, "Wahoo Boy," p. 25.

10. Letter from DFZ to Jason Joy, PCA Collection, AMPAS, *Doorway to Hell* file.

11. For comparisons between production numbers and story in pornography and similar big moments in nonadult films, see Linda Williams, *Hard Core: Power, Pleasure, and the "Frenzy of the Visible"* (Berkeley: University of California Press, 1989). In musical films, both Richard Dyer ("Entertainment and Utopia," in Richard Dyer, ed., *Only Entertainment* [New York: Routledge, 1992]) and Rick Altman (*The American Film Musical* [Bloomington, Ind.: University of Indiana Press, 1989) draw parallels similar to Williams's between film structures that integrate these numbers within the predominant flow of the narrative and those that foreground the disjunction between the two.

12. A. P. Waxman, ed., Publicity Sheet for *Doorway to Hell*, Warner Bros. Collection, USC.

13. Edwin Schallert, "Reality Rules Gangland," *Los Angeles Times*, USC, Warner Bros. Collection, Doheny Library, *Doorway to Hell* file.

14. In *That Yankee Doodle Dandy*, Gideon Productions, 1981. Written and directed by Richard Schickel.

15. In Mel Gussow, *Don't Say Yes Until I Finish Talking: A Biography of Darryl F. Zanuck* (New York: Doubleday, 1971), p. 49.

16. James Cagney, interviewed in *That Yankee Doodle Dandy*.

17. In Richard Schickel, *That Yankee Doodle Dandy*.

18. In Gussow, *Don't Say Yes*, p. 49.

19. Ibid.

20. Letter from DFZ to Jason Joy, PCA Collection, AMPAS, *The Public Enemy* file.

21. In Mosley, *Zanuck*, p. 115.

22. In Gregory D. Black, *Hollywood Censored: Morality Codes, Catholics, and the Movies* (Cambridge, U.K.: University of Cambridge Press, 1994), p. 116.

23. In Mosley, *Zanuck*, p. 115.

24. In Gussow, *Don't Say Yes*, p. 81.

25. In Johnston, "Wahoo Boy," pp. 25–26.

26. *Variety*, 29 April 1931, p. 12.

27. In Gene Brown, *Movie Time: A Chronology of Hollywood and the Movie Industry from Its Beginnings to the Present* (New York: Macmillan, 1995), p. 104.

28. In Black, *Hollywood Censored*, p. 109.

29. In Gussow, *Don't Say Yes*, p. 49.

30. In Axel Madsen, *Stanwyck: A Biography* (New York: Harper Paperbacks, 1994), p. 105.

31. Letter, DFZ to Wingate, 29 March 1933. The ending Zanuck talks about must be a different one than the final one, for as late as May 13, the PCA was still making suggestions for an ending in which Lil has demonstrated sufficient compensatory behavior for her life of sin.

32. Wingate to Zanuck, 3 January 1933, in *Prima Dei Codici 2*, p. 321.

33. Breen to Wallis, *Baby Face* file, PCA Collection, 12 May 1933.

34. Joseph W. Alsop, Jr., "Screen Moving Toward Opera, Zanuck Holds," *New York Herald Tribune*, 8 June 1934.

35. Even if small-town newspapers did not reflect the tabloids' values, their readers would have been somewhat conditioned to this world by Winchell's first radio broadcasts, "Before Dinner—Walter Winchell," in May 1930 over William Paley's CBS network. See Neal Gabler, *Winchell: Gossip, Power, and the Culture of Celebrity* (New York: Knopf, 1994).

36. The Ventura *Free Press*, 10 November 1931.

37. Joy to Breen, 12 November 1931, PCA Collection, *Five Star Final* file, AMPAS.

38. In Johnston, "Wahoo Boy–II," p. 27.

39. Esme Ward to DFZ, 19 February 1932, Warner Bros. Collection, USC, Doheny Library, *I Am a Fugitive from a Chain Gang* file.

40. Del Ruth to Wallis, n.d., Warner Bros. Collection, USC, Doheny Library, *I Am a Fugitive from a Chain Gang* file.

41. Will Hays, "Papers Relating to the AMPP Reaffirmation, March 7, 1933," in *Prima Dei Codici,* p. 379.

42. In Black, *Hollywood Censored,* p. 135.

43. Letter from Joy to DFZ and Thalberg, 26 February 1932, AMPAS, PCA Collection, *I Am a Fugitive from a Chain Gang* file.

44. In Thomas Schatz, *The Genius of the System: Hollywood Filmmaking in the Studio Era* (New York: Pantheon, 1988), p. 145.

45. In ibid., pp. 147, 150.

46. Ethan Mordden claims the scene's famous blackout was the result of an inadvertent failure of the stage lights. But, as he perceptively notes, rather than retaking the scene, Zanuck kept it in, for "it was very Warners . . . to keep the cameras rolling, not only because the studio liked one-take shooting but because the social implications of the picture of a man erased into a non-person suited the Warner's approach." Ethan Mordden, *The Hollywood Studios: House Style in the Golden Age of the Movies* (New York: Knopf, 1988), p. 230.

47. In Mosley, *Zanuck,* p. 112.

48. The Bonus Law of 1924 had granted every World War I veteran a stipend, payable in 1945. In June 1932, a group of unemployed veterans and their families marched on the nation's capital hoping to pressure the government into making the payment ahead of schedule. President Hoover called out federal troops under General Douglas MacArthur's command with orders to disperse the "army." MacArthur's attack thus provided the nation with shocking newsreel images of American soldiers using force against American veterans, women, and children.

49. In Black, *Hollywood Censored,* p. 136.

50. Telegram, DFZ, 12 November 1932, *I Am a Fugitive from a Chain Gang* file, Warner Brothers Collection, USC.

51. See Schatz, *The Genius of the System* (p. 136) for the Warners' frugality and its impact on their style. Aubrey Solomon (*Twentieth Century-Fox: A Corporate and Financial History* [Metuchen, N.J.: Scarecrow Press, 1988], p. 28) notes that at Warner Brothers by this time Zanuck was given a budget of $225,000 per "A" picture. The Warner Brothers art directors, in particular, had to be creative for they were told to economize by designing not entire sets, but only those portions the camera would photograph. Few anticipated that such parsimony resulted in giving the art director greater control. These limitations meant that his designs and not the director's commands could determine camera angles and lighting schemes. (See Tino Balio, ed., *Grand Design: Hollywood as a Modern Business Enterprise, 1930–1939* [New York: Scribner's, 1993], p. 91.) At Fox in 1935,

Zanuck's budgets ($500,000 per "A" picture) were twice what he was allocated at Warner Brothers, making Fox's films (with MGM's) the most "deluxe" in town.

52. In J. P. McEvoy, "He's Got Something," *Saturday Evening Post*, 1 July 1939, p. 67.

53. Zanuck, in Rudy Behlmer, ed., *Inside Warner Bros.: (1935–1951)* (New York: Simon and Schuster, 1985), pp. 9–10.

54. See J. Hoberman, *42nd Street* (London: British Film Institute, 1993).

55. McEvoy, "He's Got Something," p. 16.

56. Of the 23,000 movie theaters operating in 1930, only 8,860 were wired for sound, most of these in urban areas. By 1939, this number was down to 17,329. See Gene Brown, *Movie Time: A Chronology of Hollywood and the Movie Industry from Its Beginnings to the Present* (New York: Macmillan, 1995), p. 99. In many instances, movie theaters took over former vaudeville and theatrical sites.

CHAPTER 7. 1933: STRUGGLES, ARTISTIC AND FISCAL

1. See microfiche #1, biography file, AMPAS, Darryl Zanuck.

2. See Barbara Leaming, *Bette Davis: A Biography* (New York: Simon and Schuster, 1992), p. 134. Zanuck had given Davis her big break by acceding to George Arliss's request to cast her as the ingenue lead in the 1932 film *The Man Who Played God*. Though Zanuck and the actress got on well enough during her Warner tenure (her resistance started only after Zanuck left the studio), they would later have a serious falling out.

3. Memo, DFZ to EGR, 14 March 1932, Robinson Collection, USC.

4. Letter, DFZ to EGR, 26 October 1932, Robinson Collection, USC, p. 3.

5. EGR to Hal Wallis, 11 November 1933, Robinson Collection, USC.

6. Letter, DFZ to EGR, 26 October 1932, Robinson Collection, USC, p. 2.

7. Letter, DFZ to EGR, 21 November 1932, Robinson Collection, USC.

8. Ibid.

9. Letter, DFZ to EGR, 26 October 1932, Robinson Collection, USC, p. 3.

10. Ibid.

11. Peter Viertel, interview with the author, 11 November 1994.

12. Telegram, DFZ to EGR, 30 November 1932, Robinson Collection, USC.

13. EGR to DFZ, 30 November 1932, Robinson Collection, USC.

14. From 1931 to 1935, the studio lost money. See Joel L. Finler, *The Hollywood Story* (New York: Crown, 1988), p. 238.

15. In Tino Balio, ed., *Grand Design: Hollywood as a Modern Business Enterprise, 1930–1939* (New York: Scribner's, 1993), p. 99.

16. Samuel Marx, *Mayer and Thalberg: The Make-Believe Saints* (Los Angeles: Samuel French, 1975), p. 206.

17. Ibid., p. 207.

18. *Fortune*, December 1937, reprinted in *Inside Warner Bros.: (1935–1951),* ed. Rudy Behlmer (New York: Simon and Schuster, 1985), p. 61.

19. Telegram, Jack Warner to EGR, 8 February 1933, Robinson Collection, USC, Doheny Library.

20. Telegram, Jack Warner to EGR, 10 March 1933, Robinson Collection, USC, Doheny Library.

21. In Cass Warner Sperling and Cork Millner, *Hollywood Be Thy Name: The Warner Brothers Story* (Rocklin, Calif.: Prima, 1995), p. 182.

22. In Thomas Schatz, *The Genius of the System: Hollywood Filmmaking in the Studio Era* (New York: Pantheon, 1988), p. 153.

23. Sperling and Millner, *Hollywood Be Thy Name*, p. 177.

24. In Schatz, *The Genius of the System*, p. 154.

25. In Mel Gussow, *Don't Say Yes Until I Finish Talking: A Biography of Darryl F. Zanuck* (New York: Doubleday, 1971), p. 57.

26. In Behlmer, *Inside Warner Bros.*, pp. 12–13.

27. Schatz, *The Genius of the System*, p. 155.

28. Ethan Mordden, *The Hollywood Studios: House Style in the Golden Age of the Movies* (New York: Knopf, 1988), p. 234.

29. Roland Flamini, *On Borrowed Time: Irving Thalberg and the World of MGM* (New York: Crown, 1994), p. 274.

30. Leonard Mosley, *Zanuck: The Rise and Fall of Hollywood's Last Tycoon* (Boston: Little, Brown, 1984), p. 74.

31. In Sperling and Millner, *Hollywood Be Thy Name*, pp. 182–83. Ironically, the Warners restored the pay cuts on April 12, 1933. In Gene Brown, *Movie Time: A Chronology of Hollywood and the Movie Industry from Its Beginnings to the Present* (New York: Macmillan, 1995), p. 112.

CHAPTER 8. TWENTIETH CENTURY—AND AFTER

1. Laemmle had offered Zanuck a niche as a kind of in-house independent producer who was expected to turn out a few pictures each year.

Zanuck's goal was far grander, and after his success at Warner Brothers, working for Universal, a company with a shabby house style and a poor profit record, would be a step backward. In Marlys J. Harris, *The Zanucks of Hollywood: The Dark Legacy of an American Dynasty* (New York: Crown, 1989), p. 40.

2. In Neal Gabler, *An Empire of Their Own: How the Jews Invented Hollywood* (New York: Crown, 1988), p. 113.

3. In Scott Eyman, *Ernst Lubitsch: Laughter in Paradise* (New York: Simon and Schuster, 1993), pp. 306, 307.

4. In Samuel Marx, *Mayer and Thalberg: The Make-Believe Saints* (Los Angeles: Samuel French, 1975), p. 205.

5. In Mel Gussow, *Don't Say Yes Until I Finish Talking: A Biography of Darryl F. Zanuck* (New York: Doubleday, 1971), p. 59.

6. In *Current Biography 1954*, Microfiche, Biography file, AMPAS, p. 674.

7. In Leonard Mosley, *Zanuck: The Rise and Fall of Hollywood's Last Tycoon* (Boston: Little, Brown, 1984), p. 131.

8. In David Thomson, *Showman: The Life of David O. Selznick* (New York: Knopf, 1992), p. 159. Aubrey Solomon (*Twentieth Century-Fox: A Corporate and Financial History* [Metuchen, N.J.: Scarecrow Press, 1988], p. 20) claims Mayer's contribution was $1.2 million.

9. In Stephen M. Silverman, *The Fox That Got Away: The Last Days of the Zanuck Dynasty at Twentieth Century-Fox* (Secaucus, N.J.: Lyle Stuart, 1988), p. 49.

10. In Elia Kazan, *Elia Kazan: A Life* (New York: Doubleday, 1988), p. 490.

11. In Solomon, *Twentieth Century-Fox*, p. 20.

12. In Gussow, *Don't Say Yes*, p. 59.

13. In Douglas Gomery, *The Hollywood Studio System* (New York: St. Martin's Press, 1986), pp. 176–79.

14. In Richard Fine, *West of Eden: Writers in Hollywood 1928–1940* (Washington, D.C.: Smithsonian Press, 1979), p. 136.

15. Matthew Bernstein, *Walter Wanger: Hollywood Independent* (Berkeley: University of California Press, 1994), p. xv. See also David Bordwell, Kristin Thompson, and Janet Staiger, *The Classical Hollywood Cinema: Film Style and Mode of Production to 1960* (New York: Columbia University Press, 1985), and Thomas Schatz, *The Genius of the System: Hollywood Filmmaking in the Studio Era* (New York: Pantheon, 1988), for analyses of the role of independents operating within the studio mode.

16. In Tony Thomas and Aubrey Solomon, *The Films of Twentieth Century-Fox* (Secaucus, N.J.: Citadel Press, 1985), p. 16.

17. Barbara McLean, *Oral History*, AFI, LB Mayer Library, p. 8.

18. In Gussow, *Don't Say Yes*, p. 60.

19. As Philip Dunne put it, "At Twentieth, the script was the star. . . . Zanuck wisely decided to build up from the script, rather than down from the star." In Philip Dunne, *Take Two: A Life in Film and Politics* (New York: Limelight Editions, 1992 [orig. 1980]), p. 54.

20. The four films Zanuck produced that were based on material previously published in another form were *Les Misérables*, *Call of the Wild*, *The Affairs of Cellini* (based on a play by Edwin Justus Mayer), and *The House of Rothschild*.

21. In Rudy Behlmer, ed., *Inside Warner Bros.: (1935–1951)* (New York: Simon and Schuster, 1985), pp. 12, 13.

22. In Neal Gabler, *Winchell: Gossip, Power, and the Culture of Celebrity* (New York: Knopf, 1995), photo insert.

23. Ben Hecht, "Enter the Movies," in *Film: An Anthology*, ed. Daniel Talbot (Berkeley: University of California Press, 1967), p. 271.

24. In Gabler, *Winchell* (New York: Knopf, 1994), p. 175.

25. Neal Gabler's excellent biography of Winchell contains a detailed report of the Keeler-Jolson-Costello affair.

26. In Gabler, *Winchell*, p. 179.

27. In Alva Johnston, "The Wahoo Boy–II," *The New Yorker*, 17 November 1934, p. 28.

28. In Nunnally Johnson, *The Letters of Nunnally Johnson*, selected and edited by Dorris Johnson and Ellen Leventhal (New York: Knopf, 1981), p. 9.

29. In Solomon, *Twentieth Century-Fox*, pp. 20–21.

30. Frank S. Nugent, "Meet Mr. Darryl Zanuck," *New York Times*, 21 April 1935.

31. In Greg Mitchell, *The Campaign of the Century: Upton Sinclair's Race for the Governor of California* (New York: Random House, 1992), p. xi.

32. R. P. White, "The Miracle Man of Hollywood," *LAT Magazine*, 4 November 1934 (emphasis in original).

33. In Johnston, "The Wahoo Boy–II," p. 26.

34. White, "The Miracle Man."

35. J. P. McEvoy, "He's Got Something," *Saturday Evening Post*, 1 July 1939, p. 66. Ian Watt has observed that one of the great breakthroughs of

the novel was that every major character, rather than advancing the omniscient author's agenda, in fact now had a point of view. This illusion of the sanctity of the single soul did much to foster the myth of individualism. See Ian Watt's *The Rise of the Novel.*

36. DFZ conference notes, 16 November 1934, TCF Collection, *Les Misérables* file, UCLA.

37. Ibid.

38. DFZ to Trotti and Levien, 20 December 1938, UCLA, Twentieth Century-Fox Collection, *Drums Along the Mohawk* file, box FX-PRS-754.

39. DFZ, comments on "First Continuity of Drums Along the Mohawk," ibid.

40. DFZ, conference notes, *Les Misérables* file, TCF Collection, UCLA, 16 November 1934, p. 1.

41. DFZ, conference notes, *Les Misérables* file, 31 October 1934.

42. In Nugent, "Meet Mr. Darryl Zanuck."

43. In Dan Thomas, "Hollywood Day by Day," *Post Record,* 5 September 1934.

44. In Tony Thomas and Aubrey Solomon, *The Films of Twentieth Century-Fox* (Secaucus, N.J.: Citadel Press, 1985), p. 491.

45. In Gussow, *Don't Say Yes,* p. 61. In *Beyond the Valley of Reason,* a thinly disguised autobiographical sketch Zanuck wrote in 1921, one character is described as a man who "had more blood and thunder and romance in his little toe than a dozen average mortals, and that mathematical figures meant nothing to him. . . . I confess those failings are my personal detriments." DFZ, *Beyond the Valley of Reason,* AFI, LB Mayer Library, DFZ Collection.

46. In 1933, the low water mark of the Depression, Fox had the second-largest profit ($1.7 million) in the industry (after MGM). In 1934, while Fox's profits dropped to $1.3 million, MGM had rebounded with a $8.6 million profit. But profit is not the entire story. In 1930 Fox's assets were valued at $102 million, in 1933 at $24.3 million, a decrease of almost 75 percent.

47. Eleanor Barnes, "Zanuck to Head Production of New Group," *Illustrated Daily News,* 18 July 1935.

48. In Solomon, *Twentieth Century-Fox,* p. 22.

49. Barnes, "Zanuck to Head Production."

50. "Zanuck's Start," *Time,* 25 November 1935, p. 48.

51. *Variety,* 18 July 1935.

52. DFZ to Wyler, 6 December 1940, William Wyler Collection, AMPAS.

53. In *Examiner*, 18 July 1935.

CHAPTER 9. "THE SMILING FACE OF A BABY":
SHIRLEY TEMPLE, MOVIES, AND MEMORY

1. For example, during the 1940s, 22 percent of Fox films (81 of 371) were set in the era between the wars, or earlier. A third of these (26 of 81) were musicals, with the majority made after World War II. If you compare this total to Warner Brothers', where 12 percent of the studio's films were set in the past (33 of 274), with the musical accounting for less than 15 percent (5 of 33), you can see how much nostalgia—and musical nostalgia, in particular—characterized Zanuck's world view at Fox.

2. Joel Finler, *The Hollywood Story* (New York: Crown, 1989), p. 281. The first two-strip Technicolor film, *The Gulf Between*, was produced in 1917. But the system's cost, and its limitations, meant it was used more for selected sequences than for entire films. When the three-color process was perfected in 1932, it was largely innovated with shorts—or, as Zanuck's *The House of Rothschild* shows, with selected sequences, rather than with the whole feature. Three years later, the first feature shot entirely in Technicolor, Rouben Mamoulian's *Becky Sharpe* (1935), opened the door for a wider industry use of this technology. As he had been at Warner's, Zanuck was in the forefront of using it to enhance certain showmanship aspects of his films.

3. See Rick Altman, *The American Film Musical* (Bloomington: Indiana University Press, 1989), p. 277, on the significance of the sets for the film musicals' sense of home and community.

4. In Rudy Behlmer, *Memo from Darryl F. Zanuck: The Golden Years at Twentieth Century-Fox* (New York: Grove Press, 1993), p. 74.

5. In Eric H. Monkkonen, *America Becomes Urban* (Berkeley: University of California Press, 1988), p. 1.

6. Zanuck actually testified under oath that it was Berlin and Gershwin and other white figures (like Paul Whiteman) who "invented" ragtime and jazz. In "Brief for Twentieth Century-Fox Film Corporation, Defendant-Appellant," U.S. Circuit Court of Appeals, 8th Circuit, Civil Action No. 13,121, *Twentieth Century-Fox Film Corporation*, Defendant-Appellant vs. Marie Cooper Oehler Dieckhaus, Plaintiff-Appellee, Fox's attorneys as-

serted: "Both Irving Berlin and Darryl Zanuck testified that the basic purpose of the motion picture 'Alexander's Ragtime Band' was to reveal this same historical development of jazz as shown in the lives of Whiteman, Berlin and Gershwin" (tr. pp. 432–34). The film neither mentions, nor contains, a single African-American figure.

7. See, e.g., letters in the Philip Dunne Collection at USC concerning *Pinky* (1949), and Zanuck's correspondence with Wyler on *How Green Was My Valley* in the Wyler Collection at the Margaret Herrick Library, AMPAS.

8. James R. Parish, interviewed in *Shirley Temple: The Biggest Little Star* (dir. Jeff Scheftel and Andy Thomas, Prod. Van Ness Films, 1996).

9. Ann Edwards, interviewed in *Shirley Temple*.

10. In Shirley Temple Black, *Child Star: An Autobiography* (New York: McGraw Hill, 1988), p. 108.

11. Ibid., p. 33.

12. Ibid., p. 45.

13. Ibid., p. 59.

14. In Tino Balio, "Selling Stars," in *Grand Design: Hollywood as a Modern Business Enterprise, 1930–1939*, ed. Tino Balio (New York: Scribner's, 1993), p. 147.

15. In Black, *Child Star,* p. 144.

16. Ibid., p. 221.

17. Ibid.

18. Franken to DFZ, box FX-PRS–1193, *Poor Little Rich Girl*, TCF Collection, UCLA.

19. DFZ to DaSylva, 6 August 1935, TCF Collection, UCLA.

20. Leonard Mosley, *Zanuck: The Rise and Fall of Hollywood's Last Tycoon* (Boston: Little, Brown, 1984), p. 163.

21. In Black, *Child Star*, photo insert.

22. Ibid., p. 107.

23. In Behlmer, *Memo*, p. 17.

24. Black, *Child Star*, p. 92.

25. Ibid., p. 98.

26. Ibid., p. 164.

27. Ibid., pp. 184–85, 23–24.

28. Ibid., p. 186.

29. Ibid., p. 165.

30. DFZ to John Ford, 30 July 1936. In Behlmer, *Memo*, pp. 6–7.

31. See James Naremore, *The Films of Vincente Minnelli* (New York: Cambridge University Press, 1993), pp. 72–73.

32. Letter to TCF talent scout Ivan Kahn, in *Stardust* file, Kenneth Macgowan Collection, UCLA.

33. In Black, *Child Star*, p. 200.

34. *Rebecca of Sunnybrook Farm* treatment by Conselman and Markson, 28 July 1937, TCF Collection, UCLA, p. 1.

35. In Black, *Child Star*, p. 208.

36. Ibid., pp. 116, 211.

37. Ibid., p. 210.

38. In Behlmer, *Memo*, p. 36.

39. DFZ, "Outline" for *The Comeback* (later *Show People*), in Behlmer, *Memo*, p. 37.

40. Black, *Child Star*, p. 313.

41. Edward Leggewie, interview with the author, January 1995, Nice, France.

42. Robert Snyder, *The Voice of the City: Vaudeville and Popular Culture in New York* (New York: Oxford University Press, 1989), p. 132.

43. See Robert M. Fogelson, *The Fragmented Metropolis: Los Angeles, 1850–1930* (Berkeley: University of California Press, 1967), p. 81 (footnote) on these data, or Kevin Starr, *Material Dreams: Southern California Through the 1920s* (New York: Oxford University Press, 1990), p. 132.

44. Starr, *Material Dreams*, p. 133.

CHAPTER 10. "THE ONLY WAY I KNOW HOW TO PRODUCE"

1. Edward Countryman, "John Ford's *Drums Along the Mohawk*: The Making of an American Myth," in *Presenting the Past: Essays on History and the Public*, ed. Susan Porter Benson, Stephen Brier, and Roy Rosenzweig (Philadelphia: Temple University Press, 1986), p. 102.

2. In Mel Gussow, *Don't Say Yes Until I Finish Talking: A Biography of Darryl F. Zanuck* (New York: Doubleday, 1971), p. 162.

3. In Rudy Behlmer, *Memo from Darryl F. Zanuck: The Golden Years at Twentieth Century-Fox* (New York: Grove Press, 1993), p. 35.

4. In ibid., p. 35.

5. In A. Scott Berg, *Goldwyn: A Biography* (New York: Ballantine Books, 1989), p. 316.

6. In J. P. McEvoy, "He's Got Something," *Saturday Evening Post*, 1 July 1939.

7. In Behlmer, *Memo*, p. 35.

8. Ibid., p. 35.

9. In Gussow, *Don't Say Yes*, p. 90.

10. Ibid., p. 91.

11. In Behlmer, *Memo*, p. 36.

12. In Russell Campbell, "Trampling Out the Vintage: Sour Grapes," in *The Modern American Novel and the Movies*, ed. Gerald Peary and Roger Shatzkin (New York: Frederick Ungar, 1978), p. 116.

13. In Gussow, *Don't Say Yes*, p. 90.

14. DFZ to NJ, 19 July 1939, in Behlmer, *Memo*, p. 33.

15. Ibid., comments on continuity of 13 July 1939, pp. 7, 12.

16. DFZ to NJ, 19 July 1939, story conference notes, *The Grapes of Wrath* file, UCLA.

17. DFZ to NJ, 19 July 1939, comments on continuity of 13 July 1939, p. 5.

18. In Gussow, *Don't Say Yes*, p. 92.

19. Ibid.

20. Frank Nugent, review of *The Grapes of Wrath*, *New York Times*, 25 January 1940.

21. Thomas Schatz, *The Genius of the System: Hollywood Filmmaking in the Studio Era* (New York: Pantheon, 1988), p. 223.

22. Philip Dunne, "No Fence Around Time," *How Green Was My Valley: The Screenplay for the Darryl F. Zanuck Film Production Directed by John Ford* (Santa Barbara, Calif.: Santa Teresa Press, 1990), p. 22.

23. Schatz, *The Genius of the System*, p. 222.

24. In Berg, *Goldwyn*, p. 327.

25. See Dunne, "No Fence Around Time," p. 20. Elsewhere, Dunne was more explicit, noting "*How Green Was My Valley* would be 20th Century-Fox's answer to *Gone with the Wind*." In Philip Dunne, *Take Two: A Life in Movie and Politics*, updated ed. (New York: Limelight Editions, 1992), p. 94.

26. Wyler's cast preferences, William Wyler Collection, *How Green Was My Valley* file, AMPAS, n.d.

27. Nancy Lynn Schwartz, *The Hollywood Writers' Wars* (New York: Knopf, 1982), p. 8.

28. Before shooting began on *Valley*, at a May 1941 meeting convened between studio executives and screenwriters to negotiate the conditions under which a screenwriters' union might be founded, Harry Warner referred to those who wanted to unionize as "dirty communist sons of bitches." To the shock of those gathered, he then let loose such a tirade of obscenities against the writers that Paramount's Y. Frank Freeman and

MGM's Eddie Mannix were forced to steer him out of the room physically. In Schwartz, *The Hollywood Writers' Wars,* p. 172.

29. DFZ to EP, 22 May 1940, TCF Collection, UCLA.

30. Ibid., story conference notes.

31. Dunne, "No Fence Around Time," p. 18.

32. Letter, Mrs. Herbert S. Denitz to DFZ, 27 September 1940, Wyler Collection, Margaret Herrick Library, AMPAS.

33. DFZ to WW, 28 September 1940, Wyler Collection, Margaret Herrick Library, AMPAS.

34. Berg, *Goldwyn,* p. 271.

35. In Dunne, *Take Two,* pp. 55, 56.

36. Ibid., p. 23.

37. DFZ to WW, 30 September 1940, Wyler Collection, Margaret Herrick Library, AMPAS.

38. DFZ to WW, 11 November 1940, Wyler Collection, Margaret Herrick Library, AMPAS.

39. DFZ, 22 May 1940, story conference notes on continuity of 18 May 1940.

40. In Dunne, *Take Two,* p. 97.

41. DFZ to WW, 13 November 1940, Wyler Collection, Margaret Herrick Library, AMPAS.

42. DFZ to WW, 15 November 1940, Wyler Collection, Margaret Herrick Library, AMPAS, p. 3.

43. Dunne, "No Fence Around Time," p. 33.

44. DFZ to WW, 15 November 1940.

45. Dunne, *Take Two,* p. 54.

46. DFZ to WW and PD, 6 December 1940, Wyler Collection, Margaret Herrick Library, AMPAS.

47. WW to DFZ, n.d. (c. December 1940), handwritten draft of confidential letter, Wyler Collection, Margaret Herrick Library, AMPAS.

48. Philip Dunne, *Take Two,* p. 97.

49. DFZ to JF, memo on *How Green Was My Valley,* 10 July 1941, in Behlmer, *Memo,* p. 44.

CHAPTER 11. "THE GLITTERING ROBES OF ENTERTAINMENT"

1. Cass Warner Sperling and Cork Millner, *Hollywood Be Thy Name: The Warner Brothers Story* (Rocklin, Calif.: Prima, 1994), p. 243.

2. Darryl F. Zanuck, *Tunis Expedition* (New York: Random House, 1943), pp. 40–42.

3. Ibid., p. 48.

4. In Mel Gussow, *Don't Say Yes Until I Finish Talking: A Biography of Darryl F. Zanuck* (New York: Doubleday, 1971), pp. 107, 111.

5. In Zanuck, *Tunis Expedition*, p. 64.

6. David Robb, "Zanuck Caught in D.C. Gunsights," *Variety*, 31 October 1989, pp. 144, 145.

7. Zanuck, *Tunis Expedition*, p. 54.

8. Fred Stanley, "Colonel Zanuck Back at the Helm," *New York Times*, 25 July 1943.

9. Robb, "Zanuck Caught in D.C. Gunsights," p. 145.

10. Ibid.

11. In Gussow, *Don't Say Yes*, p. 113.

12. In Robb, "Zanuck Caught in D.C. Gunsights," p. 146.

13. Ibid.

14. Ibid., p. 148.

15. Ibid.

16. Ibid., p. 147.

17. In Philip Dunne, *Oral History*, interview by Douglas Bell, 1991, Margaret Herrick Library, AMPAS, p. 189.

18. William Perlberg to Joe Schenck, October 1943, in Rudy Behlmer, *Memo from Darryl F. Zanuck: The Golden Years at Twentieth Century-Fox* (New York: Grove Press, 1993), pp. 63–64.

19. Stephen M. Silverman, *The Fox That Got Away: The Last Days of the Zanuck Dynasty at Twentieth Century-Fox* (Secaucus, N.J.: Lyle Stuart, 1988), p. 75.

20. Marlys J. Harris, *The Zanucks of Hollywood: The Dark Legacy of an American Dynasty* (New York: Crown, 1989), p. 70.

21. Leonard Mosley, *Zanuck: The Rise and Fall of Hollywood's Last Tycoon* (Boston: Little, Brown, 1984), p. 210.

22. "Col. Zanuck Put on Inactive List at Own Request," *Los Angeles Times*, 11 June 1943.

23. Harris, *The Zanucks of Hollywood*, p. 69.

24. In Robb, "Zanuck Caught in D.C. Gunsights," p. 148.

25. James MacGregor Burns, *Roosevelt: The Lion and the Fox, 1882–1940* (New York: Harcourt, Brace, Jovanovich, 1956), p. 433.

26. In ibid., p. 433.

27. Ibid., p. 447.

28. DFZ, story conference notes, 4 April 1941, *Remember the Day* file, box FX-PRS–961, TCF Collection, UCLA, p. 1.

29. Ibid., pp. 4–5.

30. Ibid., p. 283.

31. LT to DFZ, 25 October 1944, *One World* file, box FX-PRS–961, TCF Collection, UCLA.

32. In Gussow, *Don't Say Yes*, p. 121. John B. Wiseman, "Darryl F. Zanuck and the Failure of *One World*," *Historical Journal of Film, Radio and Television* 7, no. 3 (1987): 284. Wiseman suggests that the film Zanuck and Ford started working on within weeks of this memo, *My Darling Clementine*, was really a substitute for *One World*, "destined to become a metaphor for American action against the newest 'disturber of the peace,'" the Soviet Union. However, Winston Miller, who wrote the screenplay for *Clementine*, scoffs at such proposals: "I have read things about *My Darling Clementine* where people read things into it that weren't there. I knew because I wrote it. What you saw was what you got. There was no tertiary motivations." In Robert Lyons, "Interview with Winston Miller," in *My Darling Clementine*, ed. Robert Lyons (New Brunswick, N.J.: Rutgers University Press, 1984), p. 142.

33. Trotti to DFZ, *One World* legal files, 29 March 1944.

34. Aubrey Solomon, *Twentieth Century-Fox: A Corporate and Financial History* (Metuchen, N.J.: Scarecrow Press, 1988), p. 62.

35. In Mosley, *Zanuck*, pp. 210–11.

36. Ibid., p. 211.

37. "Produce Films of Purpose, Zanuck Tells Writers," *Motion Picture Herald*, 9 October 1943, p. 17.

38. The UCLA address was printed in the 30 October 1943, issue of *Saturday Review*.

39. William Wellman, *A Short Time for Insanity: An Autobiography* (New York: Hawthorn Books, 1974), p. 28.

40. DFZ to Julian Johnson, 5 May 1942, comments on Lamar Trotti's first draft continuity, *The Ox-Bow Incident*, FX-PRS–192.

41. FN to DFZ, 7 May 1942, *The Ox-Bow Incident* file, box FX-PRS–192.

42. Wellman, *A Short Time for Insanity*, p. 29.

43. Darryl F. Zanuck, "The Responsibility of the Industry," in *Proceedings of the Writers' Congress* (Berkeley: University of California Press, 1944), pp. 34–35.

44. Ibid., pp. 32–33.

45. Robb, "Zanuck Caught in D.C. Gunsights," p. 148.

46. In Gussow, *Don't Say Yes*, p. 118.

47. DFZ to LT, 20 September 1943, story conference on *Wilson*, box FX-PRS-445, TCF Collection, UCLA.

48. DFZ, story conference notes, 27 December 1943, TCF Collection, UCLA.

49. "Index" to "Research Notes for *Wilson*," Twentieth Century-Fox Research Library, pp. 1–2.

50. Bobbie McLean, *Oral History*, AFI, LB Mayer Library, p. 31.

51. On the *Wilson* study Freud collaborated with the American journalist and diplomat William Bullit.

52. In Peter Gay, *Freud: A Life for Our Time* (New York: Doubleday, 1988), p. 556.

53. DFZ to Trotti, 23 March 1944, story conference notes, *Wilson*, UCLA, emphasis in original.

54. Ibid., p. 143.

55. In Gussow, *Don't Say Yes,* pp. 119–20.

56. Ibid., p. 119.

57. Behlmer, *Memo*, p. 78.

58. Ibid.

59. "Letter of Agreement," 29 June 1944, box FX-LR–1221, TCF Collection, UCLA, p. 3.

60. In *On Cukor*, ed. Gavin Lambert (New York: Capricorn Books, 1973), p. 228.

61. GC to WSM, 29 March 1961, folder 835, George Cukor Collection, Margaret Herrick Library, AMPAS.

62. Ibid.

63. In Dunne, "Foreword," in Behlmer, *Memo*, p. xv.

64. WSM to GC, 20 November 1944, George Cukor Collection, Margaret Herrick Library, AMPAS.

65. WSM to GC, 10 December 1944, Margaret Herrick Library, AMPAS.

66. Fox's attorneys advised Zanuck that they interpreted this clause in Maugham's contract to apply to *continuous shooting* of the main part of the film, not second unit material. Should they not start principal photography before the February 1946 date, it was his advice that "we should make the additional $100,000 payment or we should secure a waiver of this requirement from Mr. Maugham." *The Razor's Edge* file, box FX-LR–1221, TCF Collection, UCLA.

67. GC to WSM, 18 March 1945, George Cukor Collection, Margaret Herrick Library, AMPAS.

68. In Dunne, "Foreword," in Behlmer, *Memo*, p. xv.

69. In Lambert, *On Cukor*, p. 229.

70. WSM to GC, 21 December 1944, George Cukor Collection, Margaret Herrick Library, AMPAS.

71. GC to WSM, 3 November 1945, George Cukor Collection, Margaret Herrick Library, AMPAS.

72. WSM to GC, 10 December 1944, George Cukor Collection, Margaret Herrick Library, AMPAS.

73. GC to WSM, 21 November 1945, George Cukor Collection, Margaret Herrick Library, AMPAS.

74. Though Maugham bemoaned to Cukor the fact that "not one of those beautiful scenes we wrote has remained," this is not, strictly speaking, true (WSM to GC, 7 February 1947, George Cukor Collection, Margaret Herrick Library, AMPAS). Though Goulding contributed small bits to the final script, Trotti swore in an affidavit that his screenplay was based, in part, on the Maugham-Cukor screenplay, specifically, on "dialogue by W. Somerset Maugham" (see Trotti Affadavit in "Letter of Agreement," 29 June 1944, *The Razor's Edge* file, box FX-LR–1221, TCF Collection, UCLA).

75. GC to WSM, 29 March 1961, George Cukor Collection, Margaret Herrick Library, AMPAS.

76. In Ted Morgan, *Maugham: A Biography* (New York: Simon and Schuster, 1980), p. 491.

77. "Clever Fellow," GC to WSM, 29 March 1961, George Cukor Collection, Margaret Herrick Library, AMPAS.

78. WSM to GC, 10 November 1945, George Cukor Collection, Margaret Herrick Library, AMPAS.

79. In Morgan, *Maugham*, p. 491.

80. Ibid.

81. In Otto Friedrich, *City of Nets: A Portrait of Hollywood in the 1940s* (New York: Harper Perennial, 1987), p. 182.

82. Ibid., p. 183.

83. DFZ to OP and RM, 21 March 1944, *Laura* file, TCF Collection, UCLA, p. 1.

84. Ibid., p. 10.

85. DFZ, story conference notes on continuity of 1 November 1943, *Laura* file, TCF Collection, UCLA, p. 3.

86. Ibid., p. 1.

87. DFZ, story conference notes, 21 March 1944, TCF Collection, UCLA, p. 9.

88. DFZ to OP and RM, story conference notes, 21 March 1944, TCF Collection, UCLA.

89. Jay Dratler and Ring Lardner, continuity script, 22 December 1943, *Laura* file, TCF Collection, UCLA, p. 134.

90. In Gussow, *Don't Say Yes*, p. 147.

91. In Friedrich, *City of Nets*, p. 184.

92. In Gussow, *Don't Say Yes*, p. 147.

93. Ibid.

94. In Friedrich, *City of Nets*, p. 299.

95. See Dalton Trumbo, *The Time of the Toad: A Study of Inquisition in America* (New York: Harper & Row, 1972 [orig. 1949]), p. 11. Winchell quote in Friedrich, *City of Nets*, p. 299.

96. In Friedrich, *City of Nets*, p. 361.

97. Ibid., p. 362.

98. Gregory Peck, interview with the author, 11 March 1994, Los Angeles, California.

99. In Friedrich, *City of Nets*, p. 356.

100. In Neal Gabler, *An Empire of Their Own: How the Jews Invented Hollywood* (New York: Crown, 1988), p. 349.

101. In A. Scott Berg, *Goldwyn: A Biography* (New York: Ballantine Books, 1989), p. 394.

102. Interview with the author, 11 March 1994, Los Angeles, California.

103. In Elia Kazan, *A Life* (New York: Doubleday, 1988), p. 331.

104. DFZ to RK, 27 March 1947, *Gentleman's Agreement* file, box FX-PRS–1260, TCF Collection, UCLA.

105. DFZ to EK, 18 June 1947, box FX-PRS–1260, TCF Collection, UCLA.

106. Interview with the author, 11 March 1994, Los Angeles, California.

107. Philip Dunne, interviewed by Douglas Bell, *Oral History* (Los Angeles: Academy Foundation, AMPAS, 1991), p. 125.

108. Harry Brand, "Vital Statistics Concerning Darryl F. Zanuck's Production of *Gentleman's Agreement*," 1947, p. 1, Fox Research Library.

109. Telegram, DFZ to Elia Kazan, 10 October 1947, Charles Schlaifer Collection, Margaret Herrick Library, AMPAS.

110. *Gentleman's Agreement* folder, Charles Schlaifer Collection, Margaret Herrick Library, AMPAS.

111. Friedrich, *City of Nets*, p. 366.

112. Ibid., p. 356.

113. PD to DFZ, 19 April 1948, box 2, folder 4, Philip Dunne Collection, Doheny Library, USC.

114. PD to DFZ, 2 February 1949, Philip Dunne Collection, Doheny Library, USC.

115. DFZ to Charles Einfeld, 10 February 1949, Doheny Library, USC.

116. DFZ to Kazan, Dunne, and Nichols, 25 May 1948, *Pinky* file, Doheny Library, USC.

117. Hedda Hopper, "Zanuck Has the Answers," *Chicago Tribune*, 5 October 1947.

118. Edwin Schallert, "Zanuck Sound Call for Better Pictures," *Los Angeles Times*, 13 May 1945.

119. Letter, Hedda Hopper to DFZ, 21 April 1947, Hedda Hopper Collection, AMPAS.

120. DFZ to HH, 21 April 1947, Hedda Hopper Collection, AMPAS.

121. Ibid.

122. DFZ to Sol Siegel, Martin Berkeley, Gen. Munson, Col. Joy, Anthony Muto (Washington), 9 April 1947, *The Iron Curtain* file, box FX-PRS–835, TCF Collection, UCLA.

123. Ibid., pp. 1, 2.

124. DFZ to Sol Siegel, 9 April 1947, confidential memo, *The Iron Curtain* file, box FX-PRS–835, TCF Collection, UCLA.

125. DFZ to Milton Krims, 24 October 1947, box FX-PRS–835, TCF Collection, UCLA, p. 3.

126. DFZ, 26 January 1948, notes on revised continuity, box FX-PRS–835, TCF Collection, UCLA.

127. DFZ, "Cutting Notes and New Scenes," 2 February 1948, box FX-PRS–835, TCF Collection, UCLA.

128. Ibid., p. 6.

129. In Charles Schlaifer Collection, AMPAS.

130. "Left Wing: The Movie That Hurts," *Time*, 1948.

131. DFZ to Sol Siegel, 20 March 1948, in Behlmer, *Memo*, p. 129.

132. DFZ to HK, 14 June 1950, Henry King Collection, AMPAS.

133. DFZ to HK, 12 October 1950, Henry King Collection, AMPAS, p. 5.

CHAPTER 12. SEEING RED AND GETTING RELIGION . . . IN CINEMASCOPE

1. See "Epilogue," in Thomas Schatz, *The Genius of the System: Hollywood Filmmaking in the Studio Era* (New York: Pantheon, 1988) for the

natural history of what might be called a representative case, the first major site of production, Universal Studios. The studio that started out as an oppositional force to the motion picture trust wound up owned by a talent agency (MCA) as part of a complicated entertainment multimedia empire, encompassing recordings, real estate, television, cable franchises, and a host of support industries. Today the studio itself is a quaint reminder, a kind of *memento mori* of the simple roots of the earliest studios compared to today's byzantine media and information environment.

2. "One-Man Studio," *Time*, 12 June 1950, pp. 64–72.

3. "New Pact Calls for Ten Years as Head of Production, Ten Years in Advisory Role," *Hollywood Reporter*, 10 October 1949, pp. 1, 2, 11. Under California law, contracts were limited to seven years. The agreement was thus drawn up in New York, which had a ten-year limit.

4. Dassin interviewed by Patrick McGilligan, "I'll Always be an AMERICAN," *Film Comment*, November 1996, p. 40.

5. Ibid.

6. Ibid.

7. Ibid.

8. Ibid.

9. In McGilligan, "I'll Always Be an AMERICAN," p. 40.

10. In Otto Friedrich, *City of Nets: A Portrait of Hollywood in the 1940s* (New York: Harper Perennial, 1987), p. 334.

11. Walter Bernstein, *Inside Out: A Memoir of the Blacklist* (New York: Knopf, 1996), p. 209.

12. Philip Dunne interviewed by Douglas Bell, *Oral History* (Los Angeles: Academy Foundation, AMPAS, 1991), p. 272.

13. PD to DFZ, 26 May 1949, Philip Dunne Collection, Doheny Library, USC.

14. DFZ to PD, 27 May 1949, Philip Dunne Collection, Doheny Library, USC.

15. PD to DFZ, 24 June 1953, Philip Dunne Collection, Doheny Library, USC.

16. DFZ to PD, 7 July 1953, Philip Dunne Collection, Doheny Library, USC.

17. Philip Dunne, *Take Two: A Life in Movies and Politics* (New York: Limelight Editions, 1992), p. 221.

18. In Friedrich, *City of Nets*, p. 315.

19. Alan Nadel, "God's Law and the Wide Screen: The Ten Commandments as Cold War 'Epic,'" *PMLA*, May 1993, p. 428.

20. TV set data in Christopher H. Sterling and John M. Kittross, *Stay*

Tuned: A Concise History of American Broadcasting (Belmont, Calif.: Wadsworth, 1990), p. 657. Gallup data in Gene Brown, *Movie Time: A Chronology of Hollywood and the Movie Industry from Its Beginnings to the Present* (New York: Macmillan, 1995), p. 193.

21. Tino Balio, "Introduction to Part I," in Tino Balio, ed., *Hollywood in the Age of Television* (Cambridge, Mass.: Unwin, Hyman, 1990), p. 20.

22. Florabel Muir, "Film's Position Far Better Than TV's, Zanuck Says," *Daily News* (New York), 19 February 1952, p. B8.

23. Ibid.

24. DFZ to HK, 14 June 1950, Henry King Collection, AMPAS.

25. Ibid.

26. Ibid.

27. DFZ to HK, 12 October 1950, confidential memo, Henry King Collection, AMPAS, p. 5.

28. Ibid.

29. Ibid.

30. In *Twentieth Century-Fox: The First Fifty Years,* a 1997 film produced by Shelley Lyons, directed by Kevin Burns.

31. Joel Finler, *The Hollywood Story* (New York: Crown, 1988), p. 282.

32. In John Belton, "Glorious Technicolor, Breathtaking Cinema-Scope, and Stereophonic Sound," in Balio, ed., *Hollywood in the Age of Television*, p. 185.

33. DFZ interviewed in *Twentieth Century-Fox: The First Fifty Years.*

34. Darryl F. Zanuck, "Stories with Depth as Well as Width," *Hollywood Reporter,* 12 November 1954.

35. DFZ to PD, 24 May 1951, Philip Dunne Collection, Doheny Library, USC.

36. In Dunne, *Take Two,* p. 252.

37. Gregory Peck, interview with the author, 11 March 1994, Los Angeles, California. Peck was "astounded, dumbfounded" when he received the Kennedy Center Lifetime Achievement Award and director Martin Scorsese toasted Peck and spoke glowingly of *David and Bathsheba.*

38. Gregory Peck, interview with the author, 11 March 1994, Los Angeles, California.

39. DFZ to HK, 1 August 1950, Henry King Collection, AMPAS.

40. Philip Dunne interviewed by Douglas Bell, *Oral History* (Los Angeles: Academy Foundation, AMPAS, 1991), p. 171.

41. Ibid.

42. DFZ to HK, PD, 12 March 1953, Philip Dunne Collection, Doheny Library, USC.

43. DFZ to Frank Ross, 29 December 1952, Philip Dunne Collection, Doheny Library, USC.

44. In Peter Viertel, *Dangerous Friends: Hemingway, Huston, and Others* (New York: Doubleday, 1992), p. 282.

45. Zanuck, "Stories with Depth."

46. DFZ to Jack Warner, 7 May 1953, in Rudy Behlmer, *Memo from Darryl F. Zanuck: The Golden Years at Twentieth Century-Fox* (New York: Grove Press, 1993), p. 237.

47. DFZ to PD, 25 August 1953, Philip Dunne Collection, Doheny Library, USC.

48. Skouras to Dunne, 25 August 1953, Philip Dunne Collection, Doheny Library, USC.

49. DFZ to Alfred Newman, 25 September 1953, Philip Dunne Collection, Doheny Library, USC.

50. Alfred Newman to DFZ, 29 September 1953, Philip Dunne Collection, Doheny Library, USC.

51. In Frank Rose, *The Agency: William Morris and the Hidden Story of Show Business* (New York: HarperCollins, 1995), p. 134.

52. In Gary Carey with Joseph L. Mankiewicz, *More About* All About Eve (New York: Random House, 1972), p. 77.

53. In John Kobal, *People Will Talk: Conversations with John Kobal* (New York: Knopf, 1985), p. 496.

54. DFZ to Sol Siegel, November 14, 1952, *Gentlemen Prefer Blondes* file, box FX-PRS-637, TCF Collection, UCLA.

55. DFZ, story conference notes, 27 September 1952, *Gentlemen Prefer Blondes* file, box FX-PRS-637, TCF Collection, UCLA.

56. DFZ to MM, in Behlmer, *Memo,* p. 205.

57. Ibid., p. 206.

58. DFZ to Julian Blaustein and Edmund North, 10 August 1950, *The Day the Earth Stood Still* file, FX-PRS-542, TCF Collection, UCLA.

59. Ibid.

60. Ibid.

61. Robert Wise, interview with the author, May 1994, Beverly Hills, California.

62. DFZ, story conference notes, 10 August 1950, *The Day the Earth Stood Still* file, TCF Collection, UCLA.

63. In Kenneth L. Geist, *Pictures Will Talk: The Life and Films of Joseph L. Mankiewicz* (New York: Scribner's, 1978), p. 110.

64. Ibid.

65. In Lloyd Shearer, "Judy Garland: The Child Who Never Grew Up," *Parade,* 13 April 1975, p. 6.

66. JLM to DFZ, 3 August 1943, TCF legal files, box 112, TCF Collection, UCLA.

67. DFZ to George Wasson, 5 August 1943, TCF legal files, box 112, TCF Collection, UCLA.

68. In Geist, *Pictures Will Talk*, p. 132.

69. In Behlmer, *Memo*, p. 111.

70. The films were *Letter to Three Wives, House of Strangers, People Will Talk, No Way Out,* and *Five Fingers* (Carey with Mankiewicz, *More About* All About Eve, p. 31).

71. In Geist, *Pictures Will Talk*, p. 138.

72. Ibid., p. 151.

73. Telegram, JLM to DFZ, 28 December 1948, *No Way Out* file, box FX-PRS–700, TCF Collection, UCLA.

74. Rita Lang Kleinfelder, *When We Were Young: A Baby-Boomer Yearbook* (New York: Prentice-Hall, 1993), p. 4.

75. DFZ to JM, 1 February 1949, *No Way Out* file, box FX-PRS–700, TCF Collection, UCLA.

76. Ibid.

77. Ibid., p. 5.

78. Ibid.

79. DFZ to Philip Yordan, 18 April 1949, *No Way Out* file, box FX-PRS–700, TCF Collection, UCLA.

80. Ibid.

81. DFZ to JM, 20 June 1949, *No Way Out* file, box FX-PRS–700, TCF Collection, UCLA.

82. Ibid.

83. DFZ to JM, 1 February 1949, *No Way Out* file, box FX-PRS–700, TCF Collection, UCLA.

84. Geist, *Pictures Will Talk*, p. 157.

85. In Behlmer, *Memo*, p. 165.

86. In Geist, *Pictures Will Talk*, p. 168.

87. Carey with Mankiewicz, *More About* All About Eve, pp. 72–73.

88. Ibid., p. 69.

89. In James Spada, *More Than a Woman: An Intimate Biography of Bette Davis* (New York: Bantam, 1993), p. 179; Barbara Leaming, *Bette Davis: A Biography* (New York: Simon and Schuster, 1992), p. 241.

90. In Spada, *More Than a Woman*, p. 272.

91. Ibid., p. 278.

92. Geist, *Pictures Will Talk*, p. 167n20.

93. In Behlmer, *Memo*, p. 166.

94. Ibid., p. 167.

95. In Geist, *Pictures Will Talk*, p. 217.

96. Allan Scott, "I Heard Them Sing," treatment of August 11 and 30, 1950, *Wait Till the Sun Shines, Nellie* file, box FX-PRS–745, TCF Collection, UCLA.

97. DFZ to GJ, 18 December 1950, conference notes, *Wait Till the Sun Shines, Nellie* file, box FX-PRS–746, TCF Collection, UCLA.

98. DFZ to GJ, 29 May 1951, *Wait Till the Sun Shines, Nellie* file, box FX-PRS–746, TCF Collection, UCLA, pp. 3–4.

99. Ibid.

100. Two of these discards, "God Bless America" and "Easter Parade" (originally called "Smile and Show Your Dimples"), were trunk songs.

101. In Lawrence Bergreen, *As Thousands Cheer* (New York: Viking, 1990), p. 358.

102. Ibid.

103. Ibid., p. 518. After *There's No Business Like Show Business* (1954), Berlin wrote no further film scores, and his last original work for Hollywood was the undistinguished title song he wrote for *Sayonara*. After the failure of his 1962 show *Mr. President*, except for the triumph he enjoyed with his new number, "Old-Fashioned Wedding" (written for a 1966 New York City Center revival of *Annie Get Your Gun*), he retired from composing. He died at 101 in 1989.

104. DFZ, story conference notes, 18 March 1952, *There's No Business Like Show Business* file, TCF Collection, UCLA, p. 2.

105. In Bergreen, *As Thousands Cheer*, p. 518.

106. Ibid.

107. In Marlys J. Harris, *The Zanucks of Hollywood: The Dark Legacy of an American Dynasty* (New York: Crown, 1989), p. 84.

108. In Kenneth Macgowan, *Behind the Screen: The History and Techniques of the Motion Picture* (New York: Delacorte Press, 1965), p. 315.

109. In *Darryl F. Zanuck: Twentieth Century Filmmaker*, directed by Kevin Burns, Van Ness Films, 1995.

110. In Dunne, *Take Two*, p. 277.

EPILOGUE

1. In Marlys J. Harris, *The Zanucks of Hollywood: The Dark Legacy of an American Dynasty* (New York: Crown, 1989), p. 82.

2. Zanuck edits *The Outlaw* from Edward Leggewie, interview with the author, January 1995, Nice, France.

3. Richard Zanuck, interview with the author, 20 April 1994, Beverly Hills, California.

4. Ibid.

5. Ibid.

6. Ibid.

7. Edward Leggewie, interview with the author, January 1995, Nice, France.

8. Ibid.

9. Philip Dunne, *Take Two: A Life in Movies and Politics* (New York: Limelight Editions, 1992), p. 301.

10. Ibid.

11. In Mel Gussow, *Don't Say Yes Until I Finish Talking: A Biography of Darryl F. Zanuck* (New York: Doubleday, 1970), p. 213.

12. DFZ to HH, 22 February 1962, Hedda Hopper Collection, AMPAS.

13. Richard Zanuck, interview with the author, Beverly Hills, California.

14. In Gussow, *Don't Say Yes*, p. 229.

15. DFZ interview with HH, 13 March 1962, Hedda Hopper Collection, AMPAS.

16. DFZ to HH, 22 February 1962, Hedda Hopper Collection, AMPAS, p. 7.

17. In Gussow, *Don't Say Yes*, p. 216.

18. DFZ to HH, 22 February 1962, Hedda Hopper Collection, AMPAS, pp. 6, 9.

19. Richard Zanuck, interview with the author, 2 February 1994, Beverly Hills, California.

20. In Gussow, *Don't Say Yes*, p. 234.

21. Richard Zanuck, interview with the author, 2 February 1994, Beverly Hills, California.

22. Ibid., 20 April 1994.

23. Ibid., 2 February 1994.

24. Ibid., 20 April 1994.

25. Ibid.

26. Though some of the conditions that defined the studio system expired before 1960, and some continued after (and still exist), "in the film industry it was widely believed that at the end of the decade Hollywood had reached the end of its mature existence." See David Bordwell, Janet Staiger, and Kristin Thompson, *The Classical Hollywood Cinema: Film Style and Mode of Production to 1960* (New York: Columbia University Press, 1985), p. 10.

27. Ben Hecht, "Enter the Movies," in *Film: An Anthology,* ed. Daniel Talbot (Berkeley: University of California Press, 1967 [orig. 1954]), p. 258.

28. DFZ interviewed by Hedda Hopper, 27 July 1962, Hedda Hopper Collection, AMPAS.

29. In Kenneth L. Geist, *Pictures Will Talk: The Life and Films of Joseph L. Mankiewicz* (New York: Scribner's, 1978), p. 331.

30. Richard Zanuck, interview with the author, 20 April 1994, Beverly Hills, California.

31. In Stephen M. Silverman, *The Fox That Got Away* (Secaucus, N.J.: Lyle Stuart, 1988), p. 276.

32. Ibid., p. 279.

33. Philip Dunne, "Darryl from A to Z," *American Film* (July–August 1984): 51.

34. In Harris, *The Zanucks of Hollywood,* p. 204.

35. Memo, Jet Fore to Fox employees, 28 November 1979, Fox Research Library.

36. Orson Welles's eulogy was printed in the *Los Angeles Times,* 28 December 1979.

37. Elia Kazan, *Elia Kazan: A Life* (New York: Doubleday, 1988), pp. 331, 250.

38. D. T. Maz, review of *Memo from Darryl F. Zanuck, Weekly Variety,* 3 May 1993.

39. Philip Dunne, "Foreword" to Rudy Behlmer, *Memo from Darryl F. Zanuck: The Golden Years at Twentieth Century-Fox* (New York: Grove Press, 1993), p. xiii.

40. Ibid.

41. Diane Jacobs's review of Harris, *The Zanucks of Hollywood, New York Times,* 23 July 1989.

42. In David Thomson, *Showman: The Life of David O. Selznick* (New York: Knopf, 1992).

43. Jean-Paul Sartre, *Search for a Method,* trans. Hazel Barnes (New York: Vintage, 1968), p. 63.

44. Nunnally Johnson, *Oral History,* vol. 1, AMPAS, p. 58.

45. Ann Douglas, *Terrible Honesty: Mongrel Manhattan in the 1920s* (New York: Farrar, Straus & Giroux, 1995), p. 199.

46. DFZ interviewed by HH, 12 November 1960, Hedda Hopper Collection, AMPAS.

47. Gregory Peck, interview with the author, 11 March 1994, Los Angeles, California.

Index